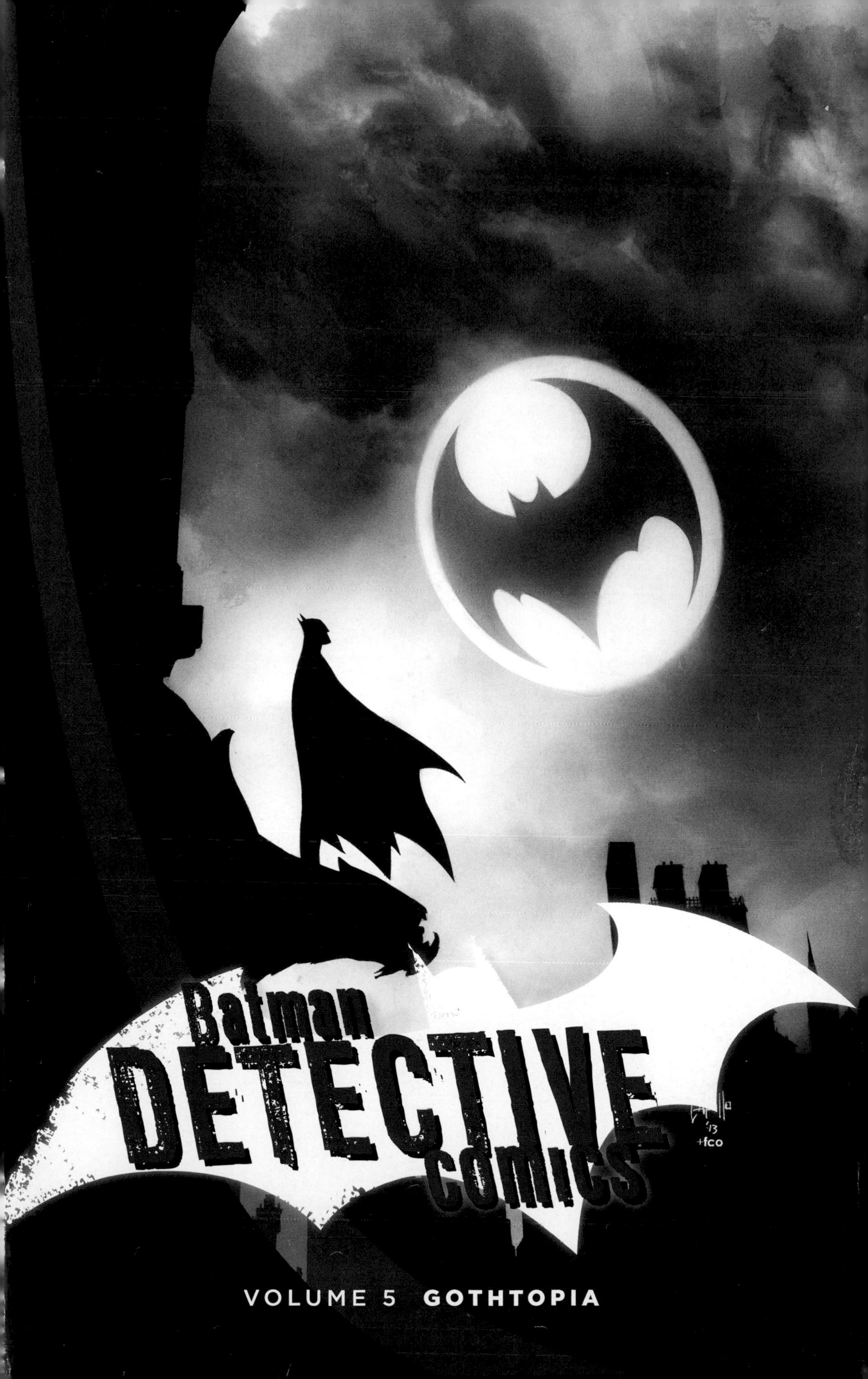
Batman
DETECTIVE
COMICS
'13
+fco
VOLUME 5 GOTHTOPIA

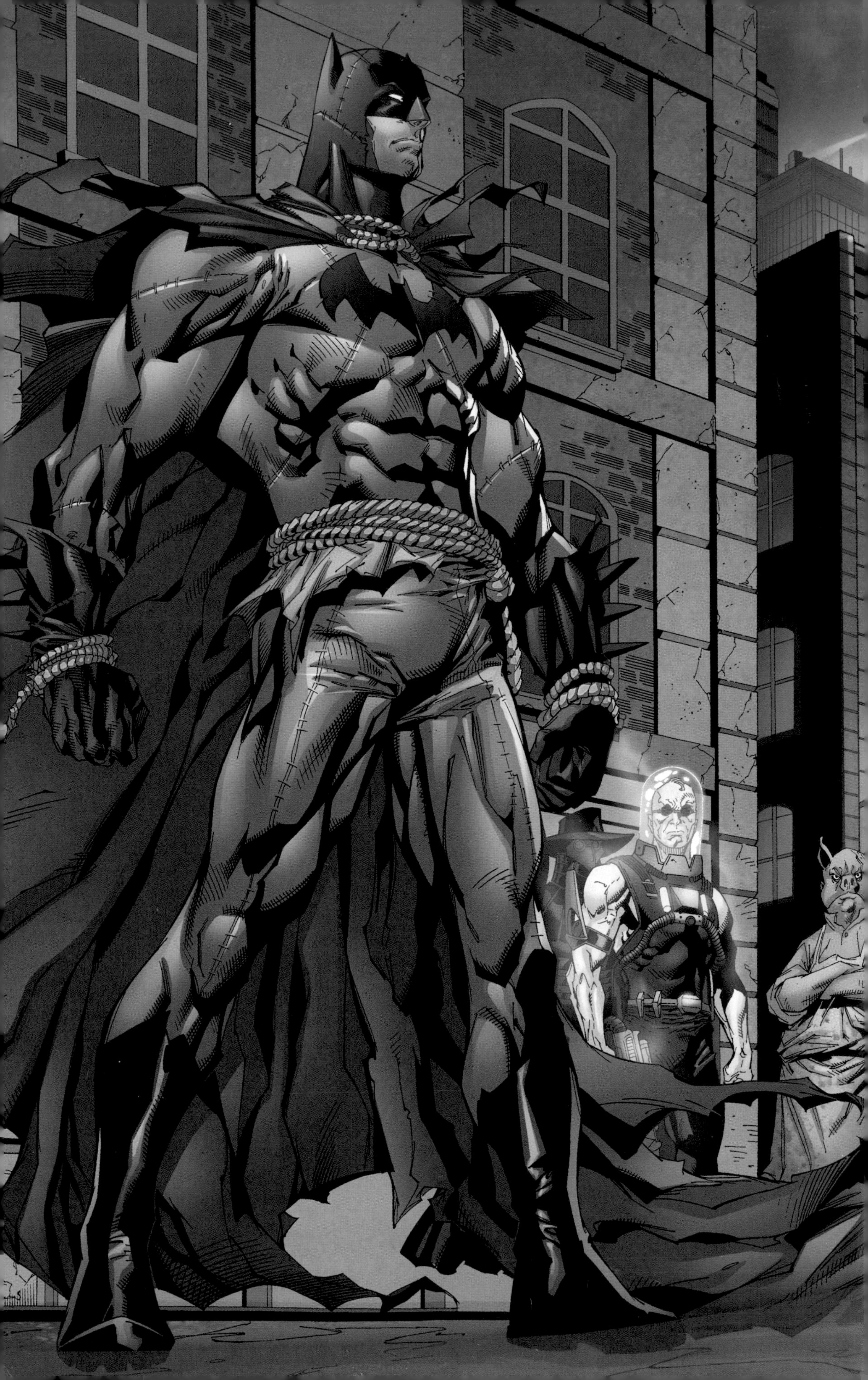

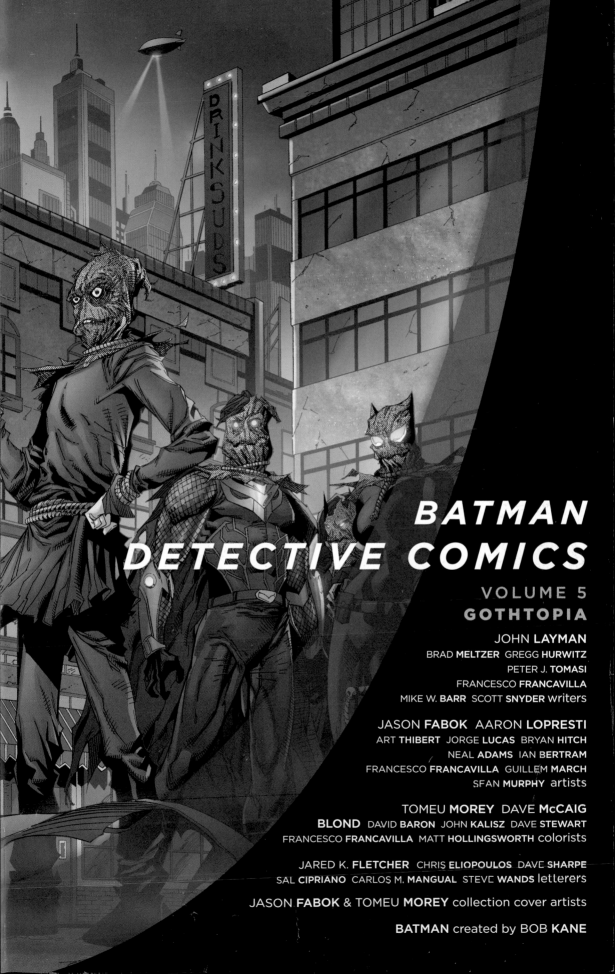

BATMAN
DETECTIVE COMICS

VOLUME 5
GOTHTOPIA

JOHN **LAYMAN**
BRAD **MELTZER** GREGG **HURWITZ**
PETER J. **TOMASI**
FRANCESCO **FRANCAVILLA**
MIKE W. **BARR** SCOTT **SNYDER** writers

JASON **FABOK** AARON **LOPRESTI**
ART **THIBERT** JORGE **LUCAS** BRYAN **HITCH**
NEAL **ADAMS** IAN **BERTRAM**
FRANCESCO **FRANCAVILLA** GUILLEM **MARCH**
SEAN **MURPHY** artists

TOMEU **MOREY** DAVE **McCAIG**
BLOND DAVID **BARON** JOHN **KALISZ** DAVE **STEWART**
FRANCESCO **FRANCAVILLA** MATT **HOLLINGSWORTH** colorists

JARED K. **FLETCHER** CHRIS **ELIOPOULOS** DAVE **SHARPE**
SAL **CIPRIANO** CARLOS M. **MANGUAL** STEVE **WANDS** letterers

JASON **FABOK** & TOMEU **MOREY** collection cover artists

BATMAN created by BOB **KANE**

MIKE MARTS Editor – Original Series KATIE KUBERT Associate Editor – Original Series RACHEL PINNELAS Editor
ROBBIN BROSTERMAN Design Director – Books ROBBIE BIEDERMAN Publication Design

BOB HARRAS Senior VP – Editor-in-Chief, DC Comics

DIANE NELSON President DAN DIDIO and JIM LEE Co-Publishers GEOFF JOHNS Chief Creative Officer
AMIT DESAI Senior VP – Marketing and Franchise Management
AMY GENKINS Senior VP – Business and Legal Affairs NAIRI GARDINER Senior VP – Finance
JEFF BOISON VP – Publishing Planning MARK CHIARELLO VP – Art Direction and Design
JOHN CUNNINGHAM VP – Marketing TERRI CUNNINGHAM VP – Editorial Administration
LARRY GANEM VP – Talent Relations and Services ALISON GILL Senior VP – Manufacturing and Operations
HANK KANALZ Senior VP – Vertigo and Integrated Publishing JAY KOGAN VP – Business and Legal Affairs, Publishing
JACK MAHAN VP – Business Affairs, Talent NICK NAPOLITANO VP – Manufacturing Administration SUE POHJA VP – Book Sales
FRED RUIZ VP – Manufacturing Operations COURTNEY SIMMONS Senior VP – Publicity BOB WAYNE Senior VP – Sales

BATMAN – DETECTIVE COMICS VOLUME 5: GOTHTOPIA

DC Comics, 1700 Broadway, New York, NY 10019
A Warner Bros. Entertainment Company.
Printed by RR Donnelley, Salem, VA, USA. 10/17/14. First Printing.

ISBN: 978-1-4012-4998-4

Certified Chain of Custody
20% Certified Forest Content,
80% Certified Sourcing
www.sfiprogram.org
SFI-01042
APPLIES TO TEXT STOCK ONLY

SUSTAINABLE
FORESTRY
INITIATIVE

Library of Congress Cataloging-in-Publication Data

Layman, John, 1967- author.
Batman/Detective Comics. Volume 5, Gothtopia / John Layman, writer ; Jason Fabok, artist.
ISBN 978-1-4012-4998-4 (hardback)
1. Graphic novels. I. Fabok, Jay, illustrator. II. Title. III. Title: Gothtopia.

PN6728.B36L394 2014
741.5'973—dc23

2014027351

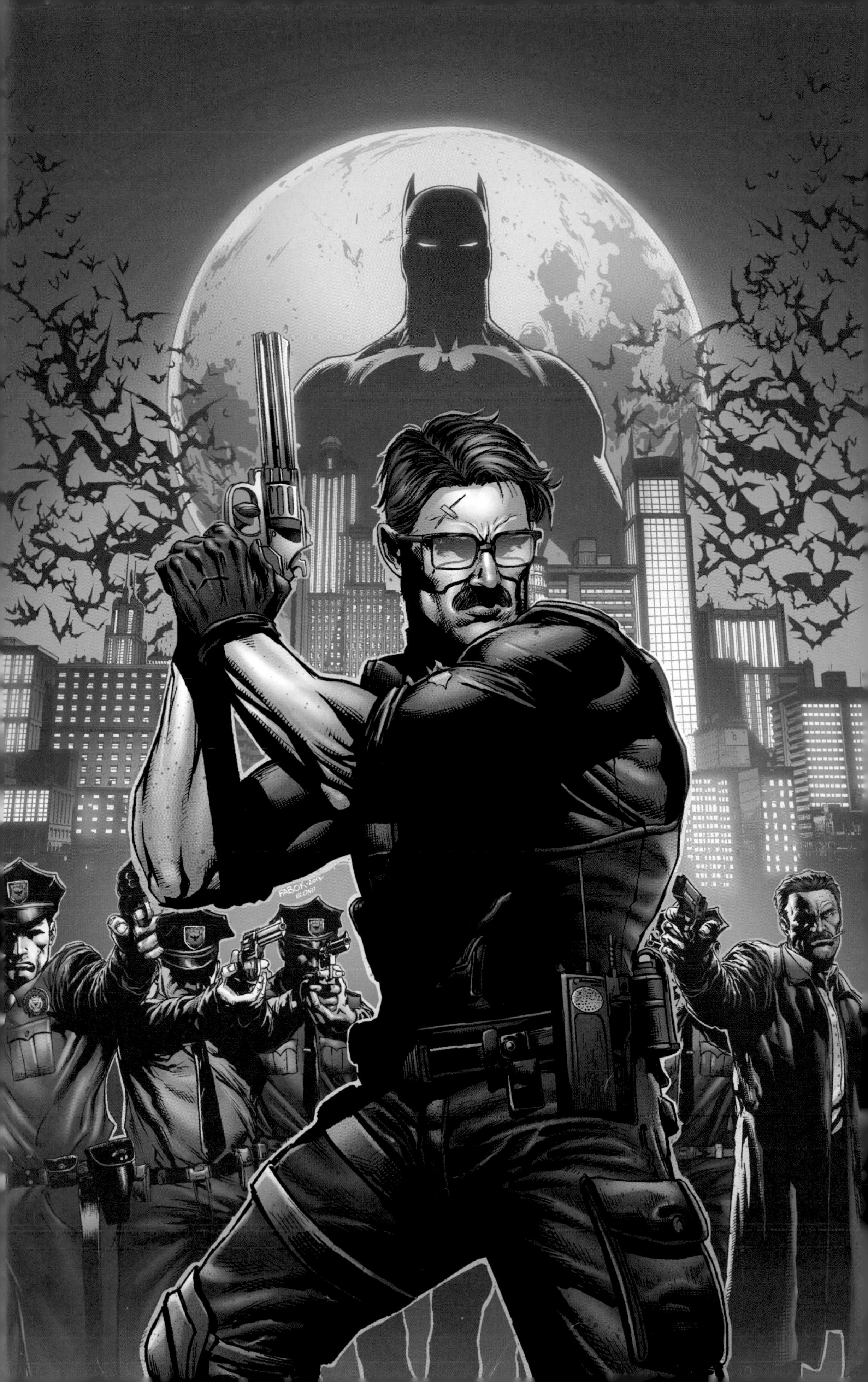
FABOK·2013·
BLOND

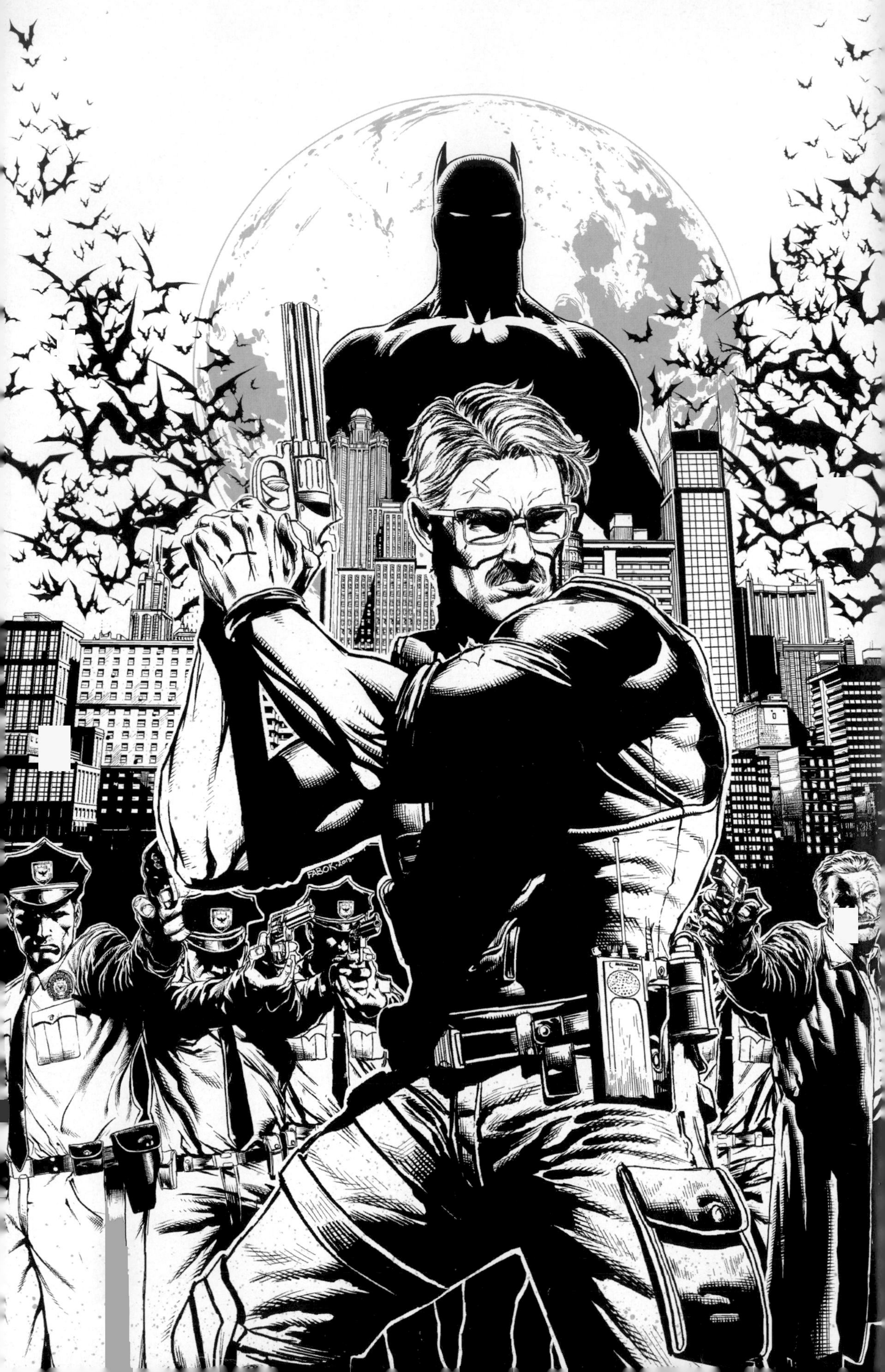

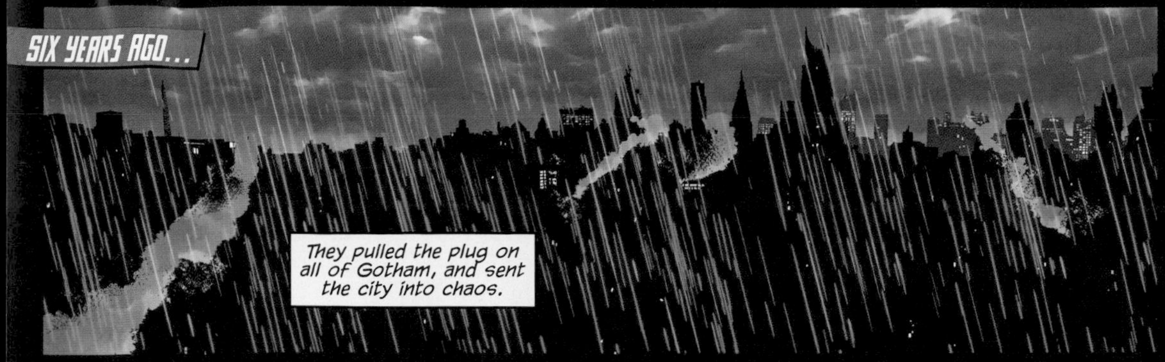
SIX YEARS AGO...
They pulled the plug on all of Gotham, and sent the city into chaos.

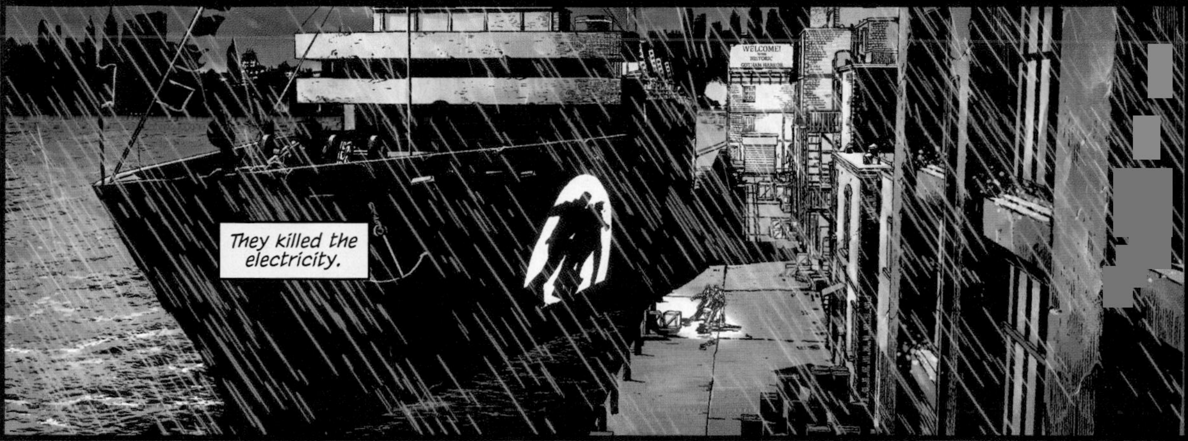
WELCOME!
HISTORIC
GOTHAM HARBOR
They killed the electricity.

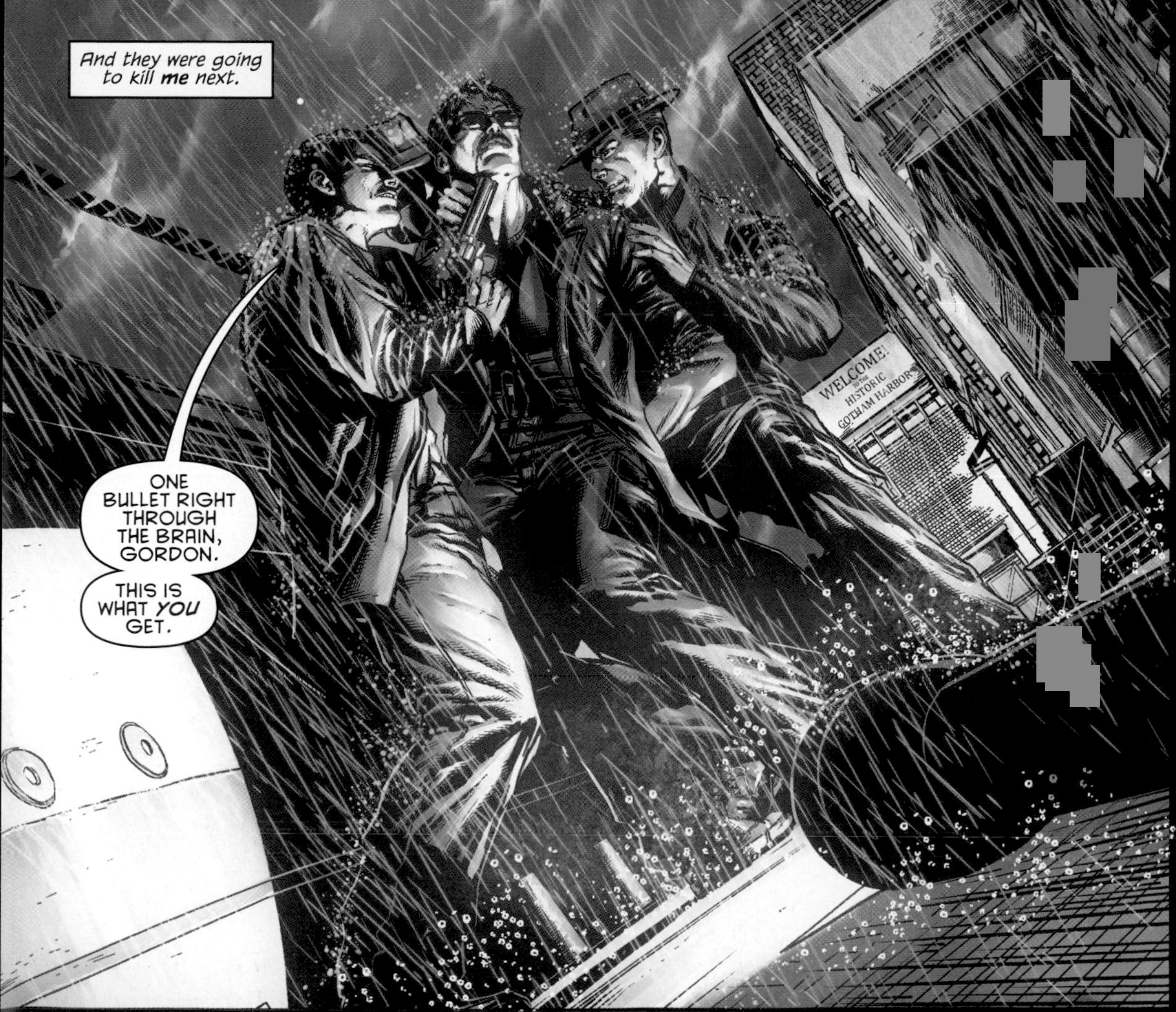
And they were going to kill **me** next.
WELCOME!
HISTORIC
GOTHAM HARBOR
ONE BULLET RIGHT THROUGH THE BRAIN, GORDON.
THIS IS WHAT *YOU* GET.

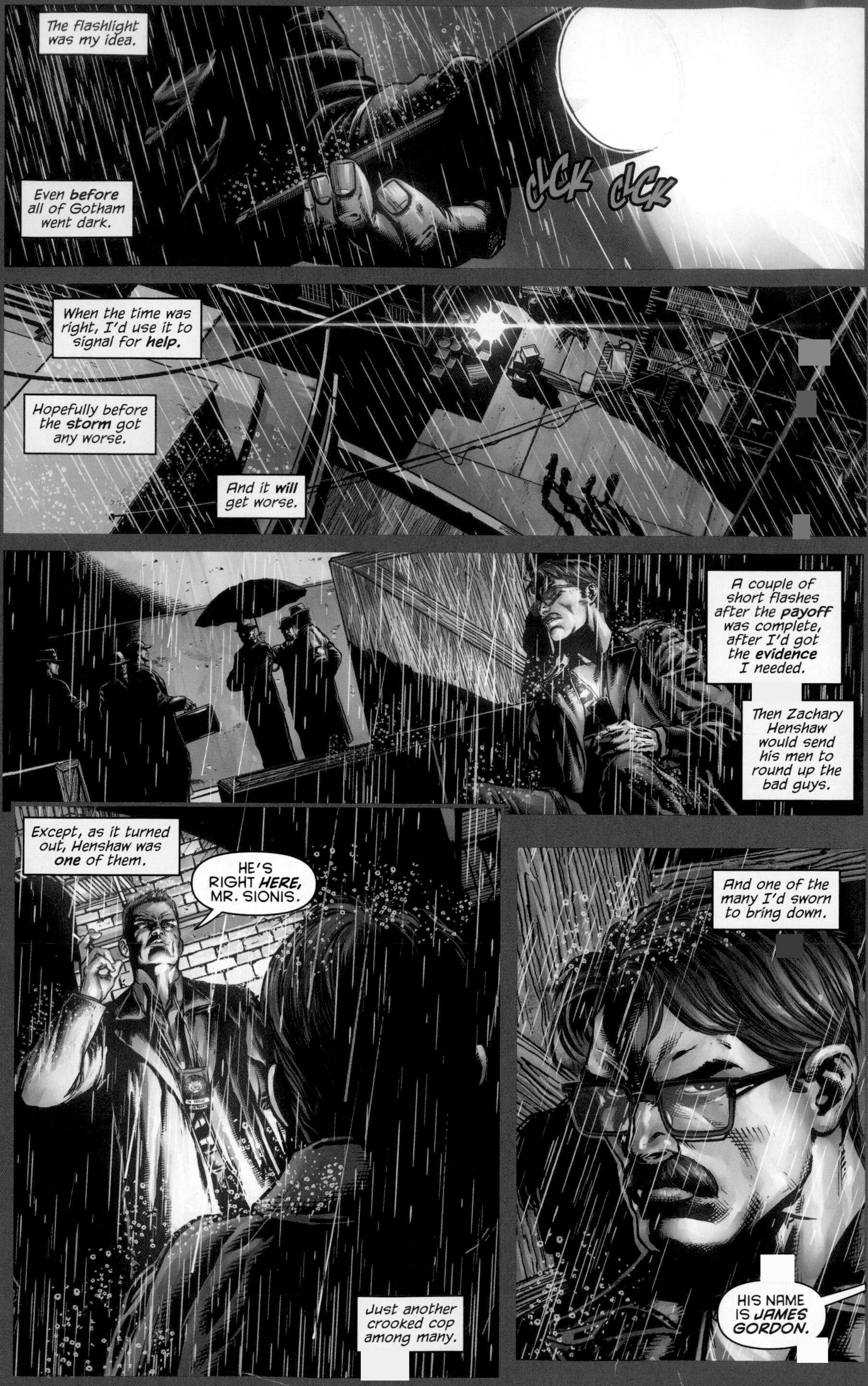
The flashlight was my idea.
CLICK CLICK
Even before all of Gotham went dark.
When the time was right, I'd use it to signal for help.
Hopefully before the storm got any worse.
And it will get worse.
A couple of short flashes after the payoff was complete, after I'd got the evidence I needed.
Then Zachary Henshaw would send his men to round up the bad guys.
Except, as it turned out, Henshaw was one of them.
HE'S RIGHT HERE, MR. SIONIS.
Just another crooked cop among many.
And one of the many I'd sworn to bring down.
HIS NAME IS JAMES GORDON.

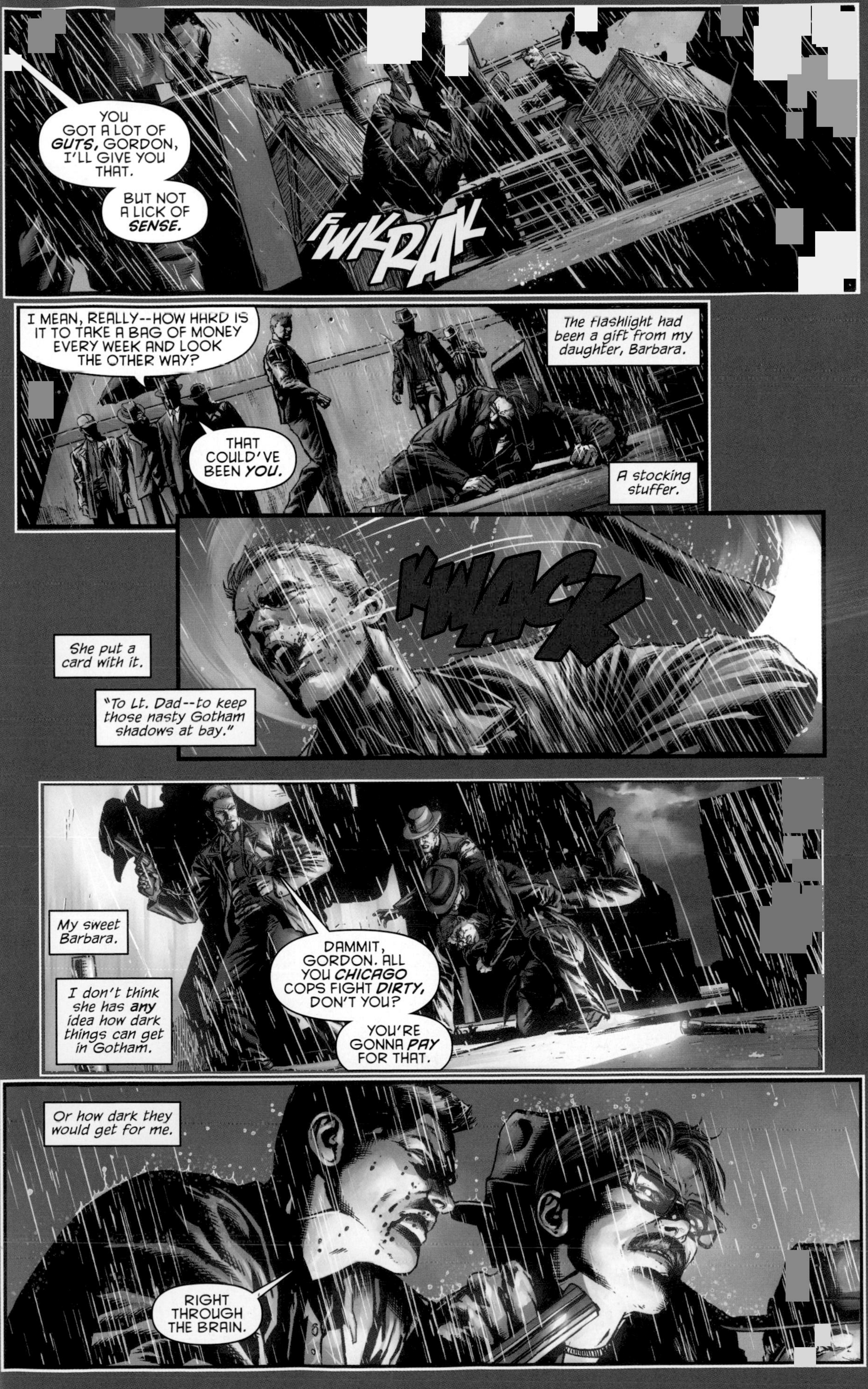
YOU GOT A LOT OF GUTS, GORDON, I'LL GIVE YOU THAT.
BUT NOT A LICK OF SENSE.
FWKRAK
I MEAN, REALLY--HOW HARD IS IT TO TAKE A BAG OF MONEY EVERY WEEK AND LOOK THE OTHER WAY?
THAT COULD'VE BEEN YOU.
The flashlight had been a gift from my daughter, Barbara.
A stocking stuffer.
She put a card with it.
"To Lt. Dad--to keep those nasty Gotham shadows at bay."
KWACK
My sweet Barbara.
I don't think she has any idea how dark things can get in Gotham.
DAMMIT, GORDON. ALL YOU CHICAGO COPS FIGHT DIRTY, DON'T YOU?
YOU'RE GONNA PAY FOR THAT.
Or how dark they would get for me.
RIGHT THROUGH THE BRAIN.

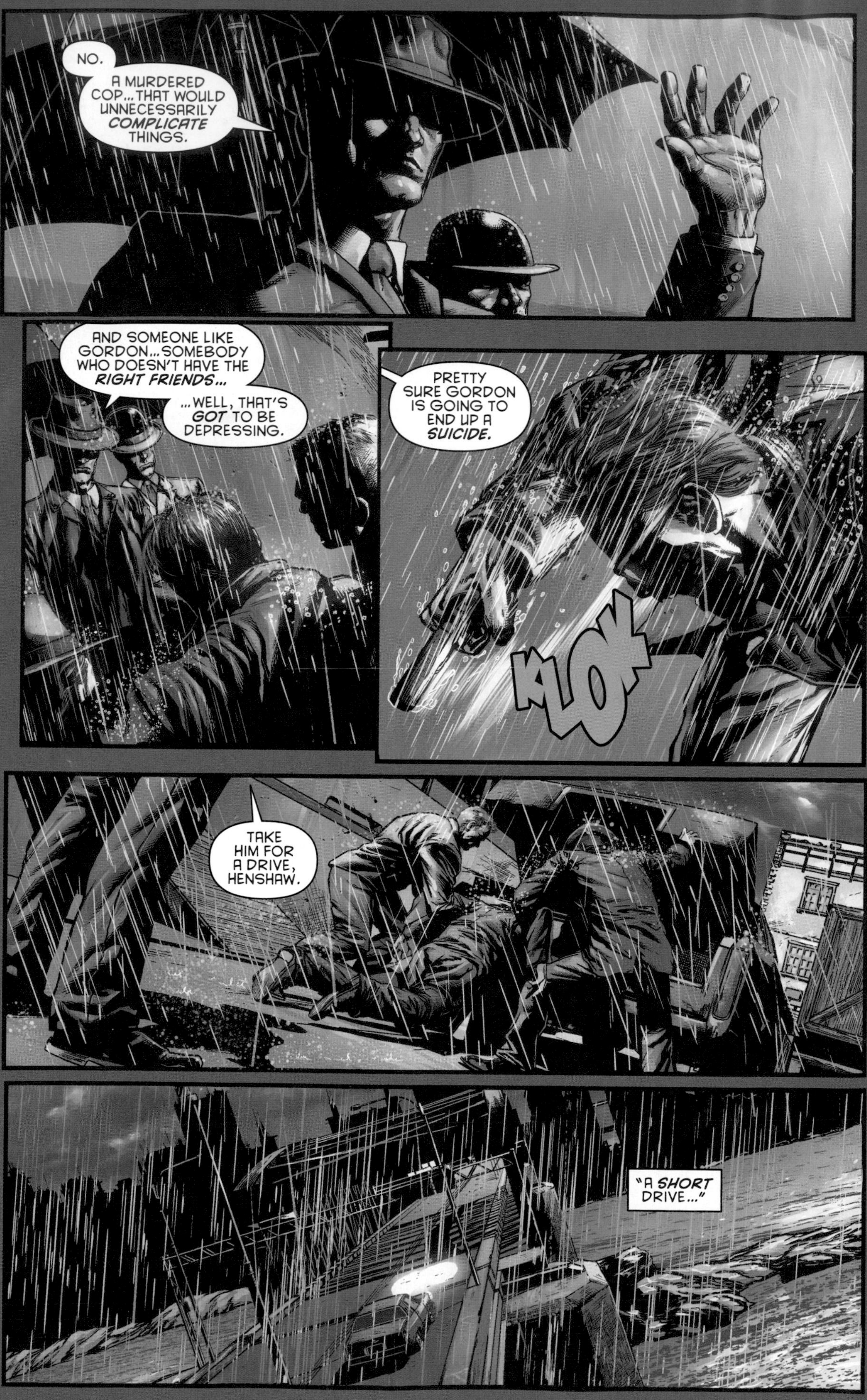
NO.
A MURDERED COP... THAT WOULD UNNECESSARILY *COMPLICATE* THINGS.
AND SOMEONE LIKE GORDON... SOMEBODY WHO DOESN'T HAVE THE *RIGHT FRIENDS*...
...WELL, THAT'S *GOT* TO BE DEPRESSING.
PRETTY SURE GORDON IS GOING TO END UP A *SUICIDE*.
KLOK
TAKE HIM FOR A DRIVE, HENSHAW.
"A *SHORT* DRIVE..."

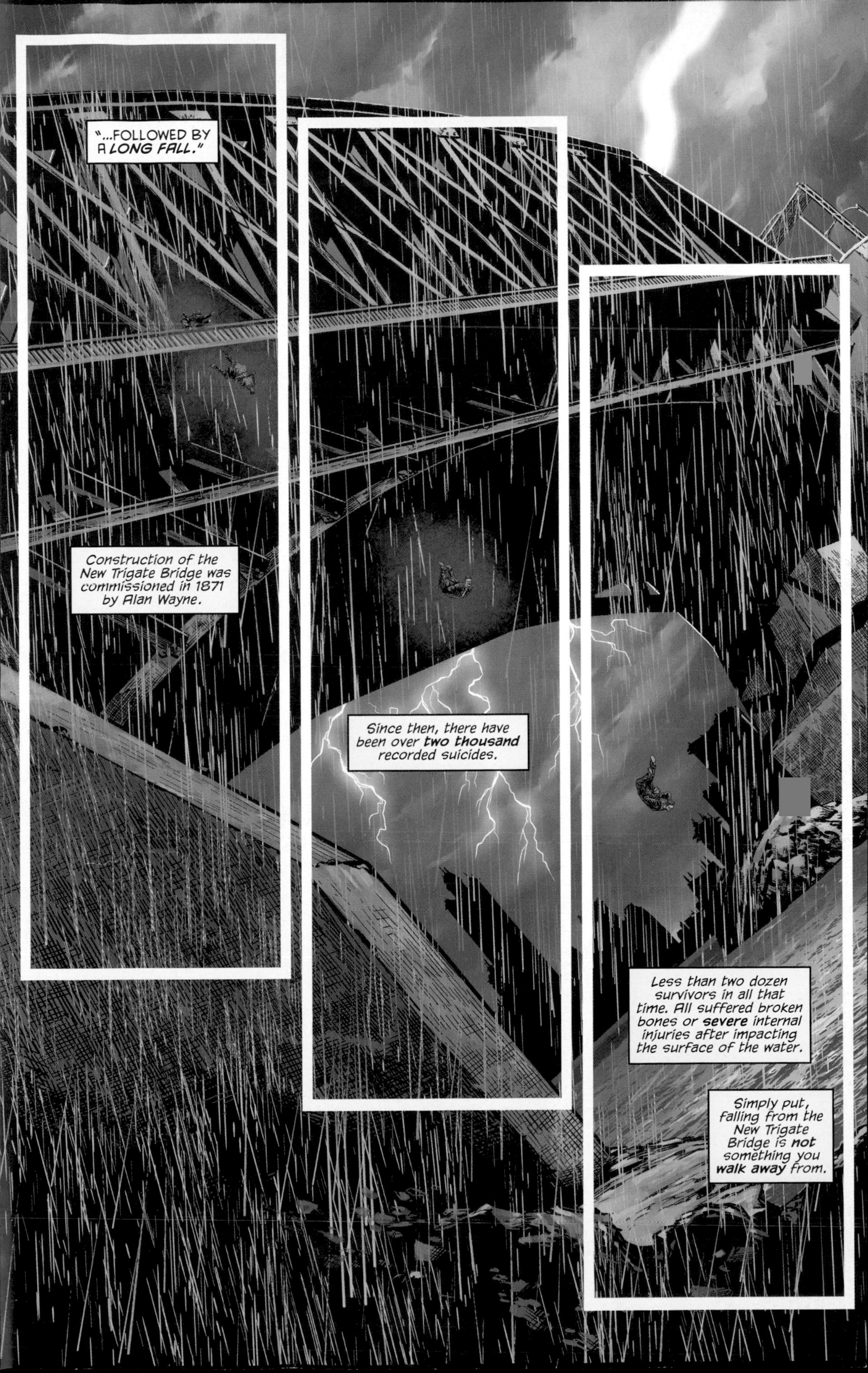
"...FOLLOWED BY A LONG FALL."
Construction of the New Trigate Bridge was commissioned in 1871 by Alan Wayne.
Since then, there have been over two thousand recorded suicides.
Less than two dozen survivors in all that time. All suffered broken bones or severe internal injuries after impacting the surface of the water.
Simply put, falling from the New Trigate Bridge is not something you walk away from.

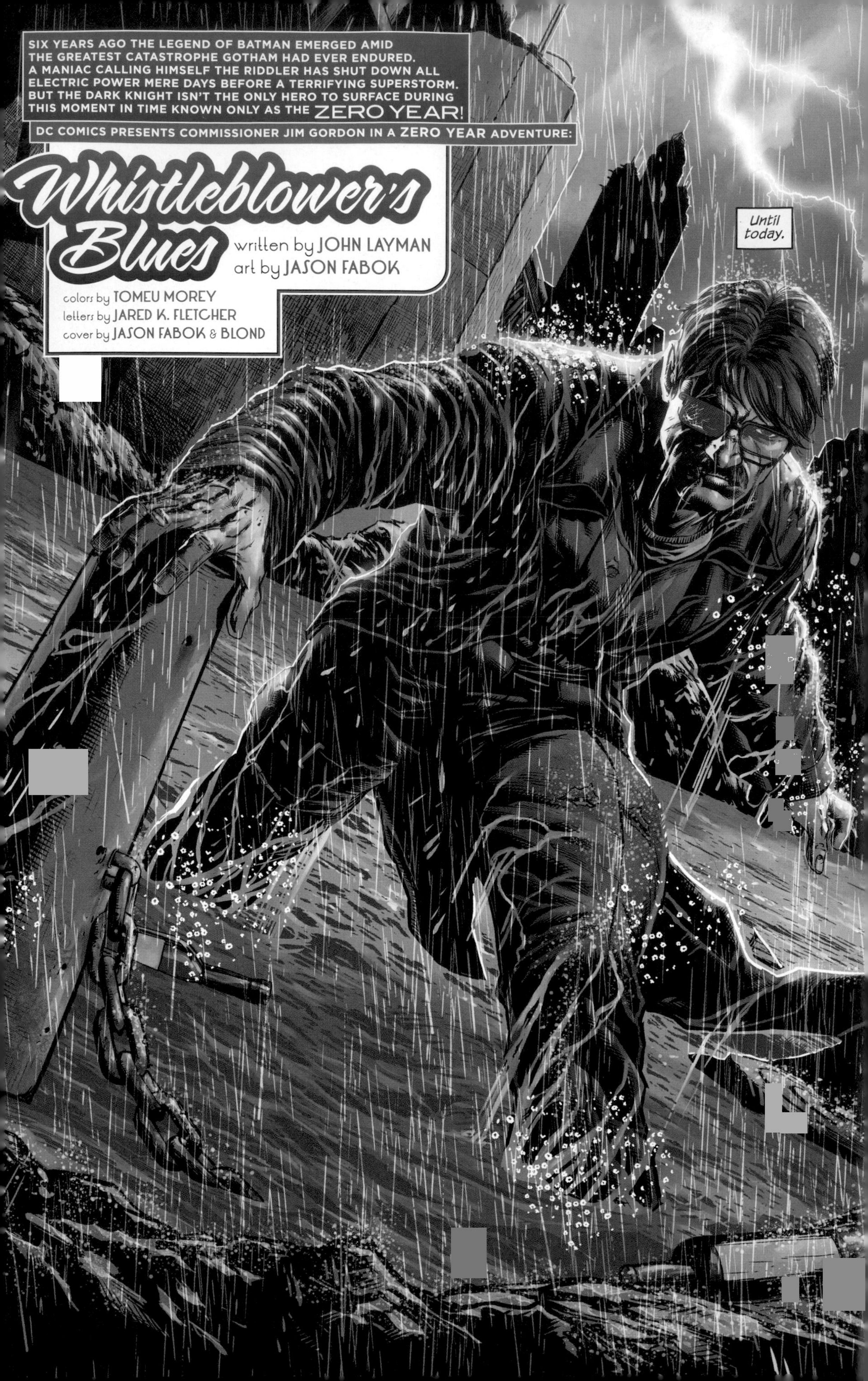
SIX YEARS AGO THE LEGEND OF BATMAN EMERGED AMID THE GREATEST CATASTROPHE GOTHAM HAD EVER ENDURED. A MANIAC CALLING HIMSELF THE RIDDLER HAS SHUT DOWN ALL ELECTRIC POWER MERE DAYS BEFORE A TERRIFYING SUPERSTORM. BUT THE DARK KNIGHT ISN'T THE ONLY HERO TO SURFACE DURING THIS MOMENT IN TIME KNOWN ONLY AS THE ZERO YEAR!
DC COMICS PRESENTS COMMISSIONER JIM GORDON IN A ZERO YEAR ADVENTURE:
Whistleblower's Blues
written by JOHN LAYMAN
art by JASON FABOK
colors by TOMEU MOREY
letters by JARED K. FLETCHER
cover by JASON FABOK & BLOND
Until today.

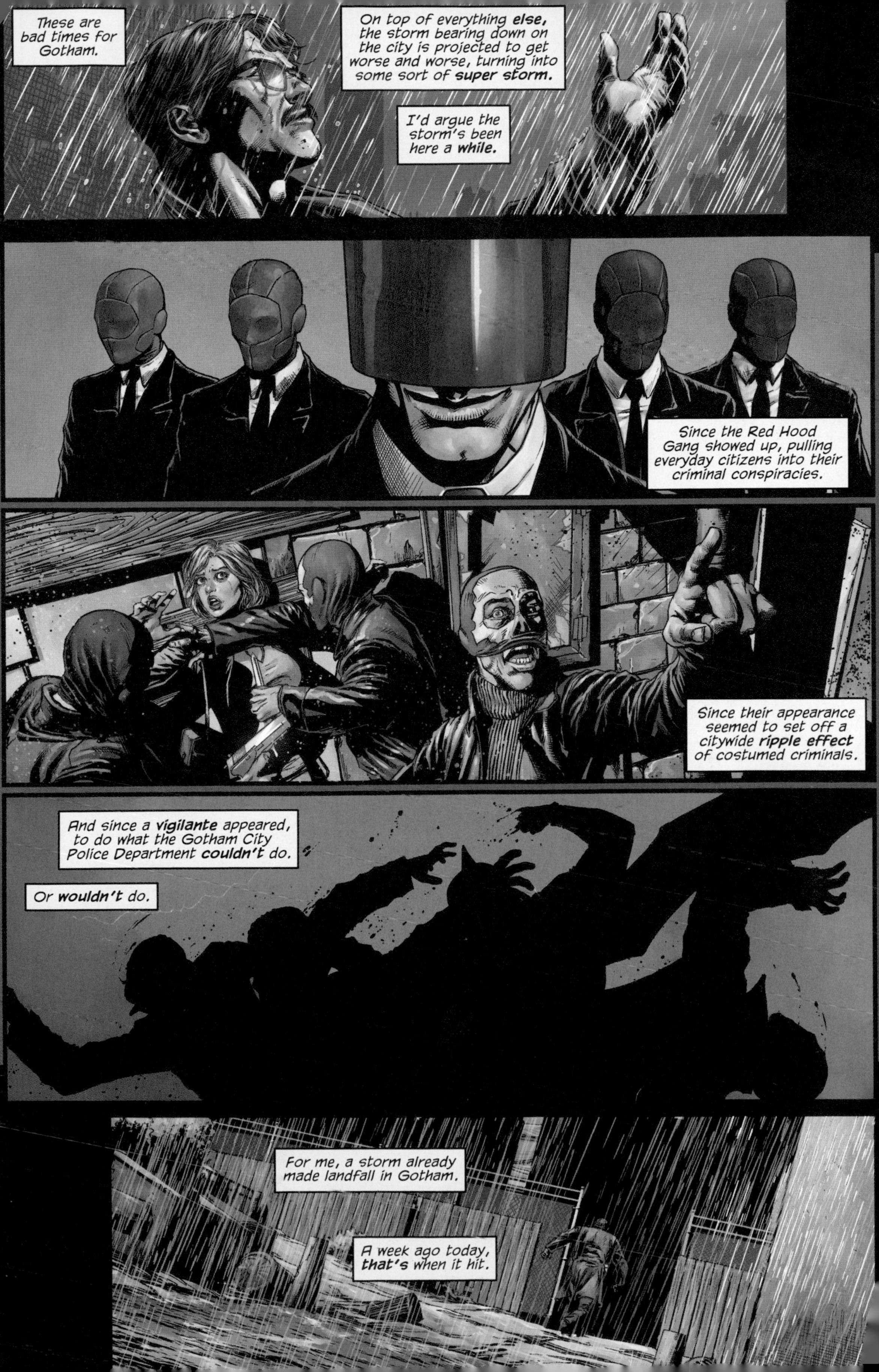
These are bad times for Gotham.
On top of everything else, the storm bearing down on the city is projected to get worse and worse, turning into some sort of super storm.
I'd argue the storm's been here a while.
Since the Red Hood Gang showed up, pulling everyday citizens into their criminal conspiracies.
Since their appearance seemed to set off a citywide ripple effect of costumed criminals.
And since a vigilante appeared, to do what the Gotham City Police Department couldn't do.
Or wouldn't do.
For me, a storm already made landfall in Gotham.
A week ago today, that's when it hit.

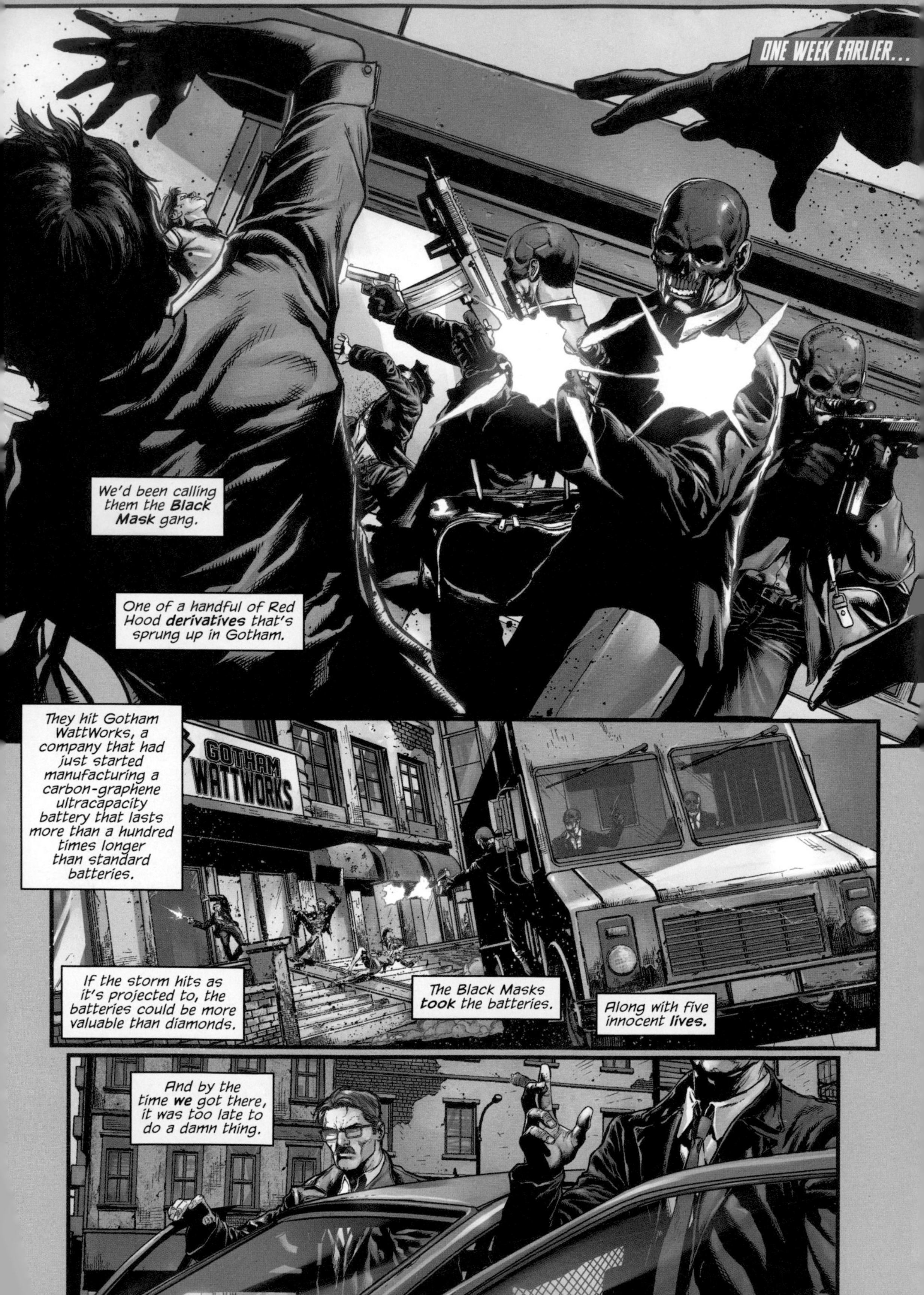
ONE WEEK EARLIER...
We'd been calling them the Black Mask gang.
One of a handful of Red Hood derivatives that's sprung up in Gotham.
They hit Gotham WattWorks, a company that had just started manufacturing a carbon-graphene ultracapacity battery that lasts more than a hundred times longer than standard batteries.
GOTHAM WATTWORKS
If the storm hits as it's projected to, the batteries could be more valuable than diamonds.
The Black Masks took the batteries.
Along with five innocent lives.
And by the time we got there, it was too late to do a damn thing.

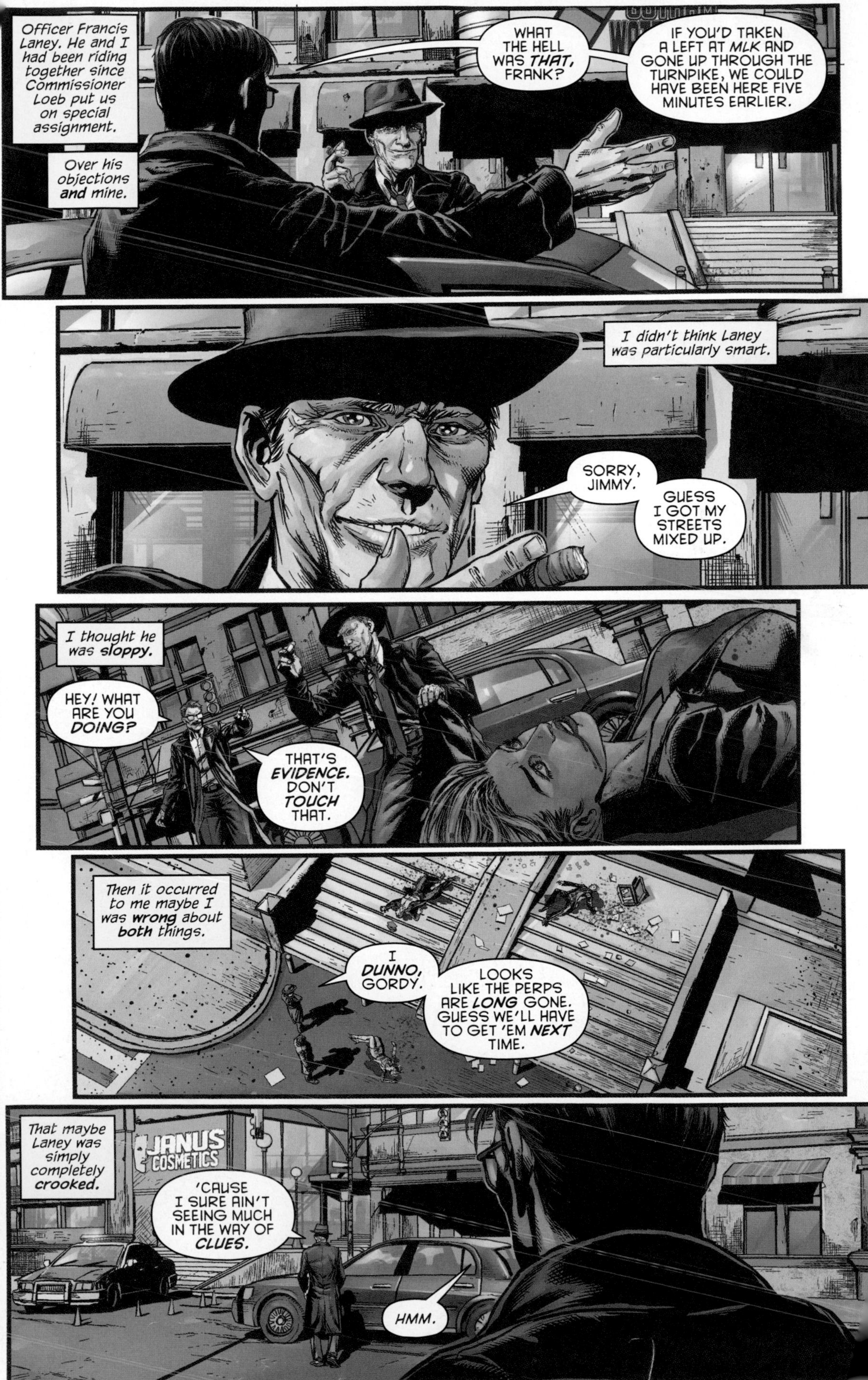
Officer Francis Laney. He and I had been riding together since Commissioner Loeb put us on special assignment.
Over his objections and mine.
WHAT THE HELL WAS THAT, FRANK?
IF YOU'D TAKEN A LEFT AT MLK AND GONE UP THROUGH THE TURNPIKE, WE COULD HAVE BEEN HERE FIVE MINUTES EARLIER.
I didn't think Laney was particularly smart.
SORRY, JIMMY.
GUESS I GOT MY STREETS MIXED UP.
I thought he was sloppy.
HEY! WHAT ARE YOU DOING?
THAT'S EVIDENCE. DON'T TOUCH THAT.
Then it occurred to me maybe I was wrong about both things.
I DUNNO, GORDY.
LOOKS LIKE THE PERPS ARE LONG GONE. GUESS WE'LL HAVE TO GET 'EM NEXT TIME.
That maybe Laney was simply completely crooked.
JANUS COSMETICS
'CAUSE I SURE AIN'T SEEING MUCH IN THE WAY OF CLUES.
HMM.

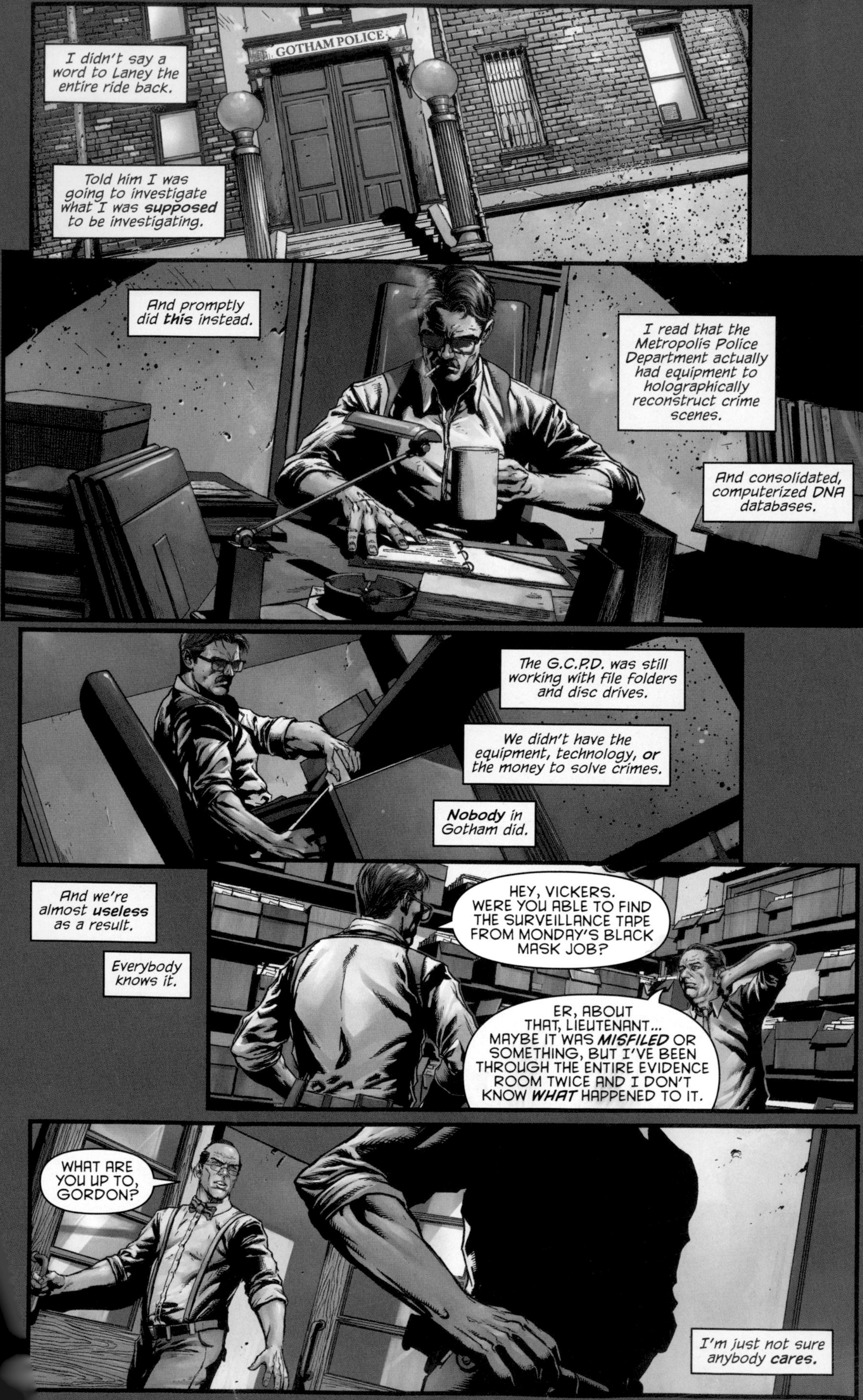
GOTHAM POLICE
I didn't say a word to Laney the entire ride back.
Told him I was going to investigate what I was **supposed** to be investigating.
And promptly did **this** instead.
I read that the Metropolis Police Department actually had equipment to holographically reconstruct crime scenes.
And consolidated, computerized DNA databases.
The G.C.P.D. was still working with file folders and disc drives.
We didn't have the equipment, technology, **or** the money to solve crimes.
Nobody in Gotham did.
And we're almost **useless** as a result.
Everybody knows it.
HEY, VICKERS. WERE YOU ABLE TO FIND THE SURVEILLANCE TAPE FROM MONDAY'S BLACK MASK JOB?
ER, ABOUT THAT, LIEUTENANT... MAYBE IT WAS ***MISFILED*** OR SOMETHING, BUT I'VE BEEN THROUGH THE ENTIRE EVIDENCE ROOM TWICE AND I DON'T KNOW ***WHAT*** HAPPENED TO IT.
WHAT ARE YOU UP TO, GORDON?
I'm just not sure anybody **cares.**

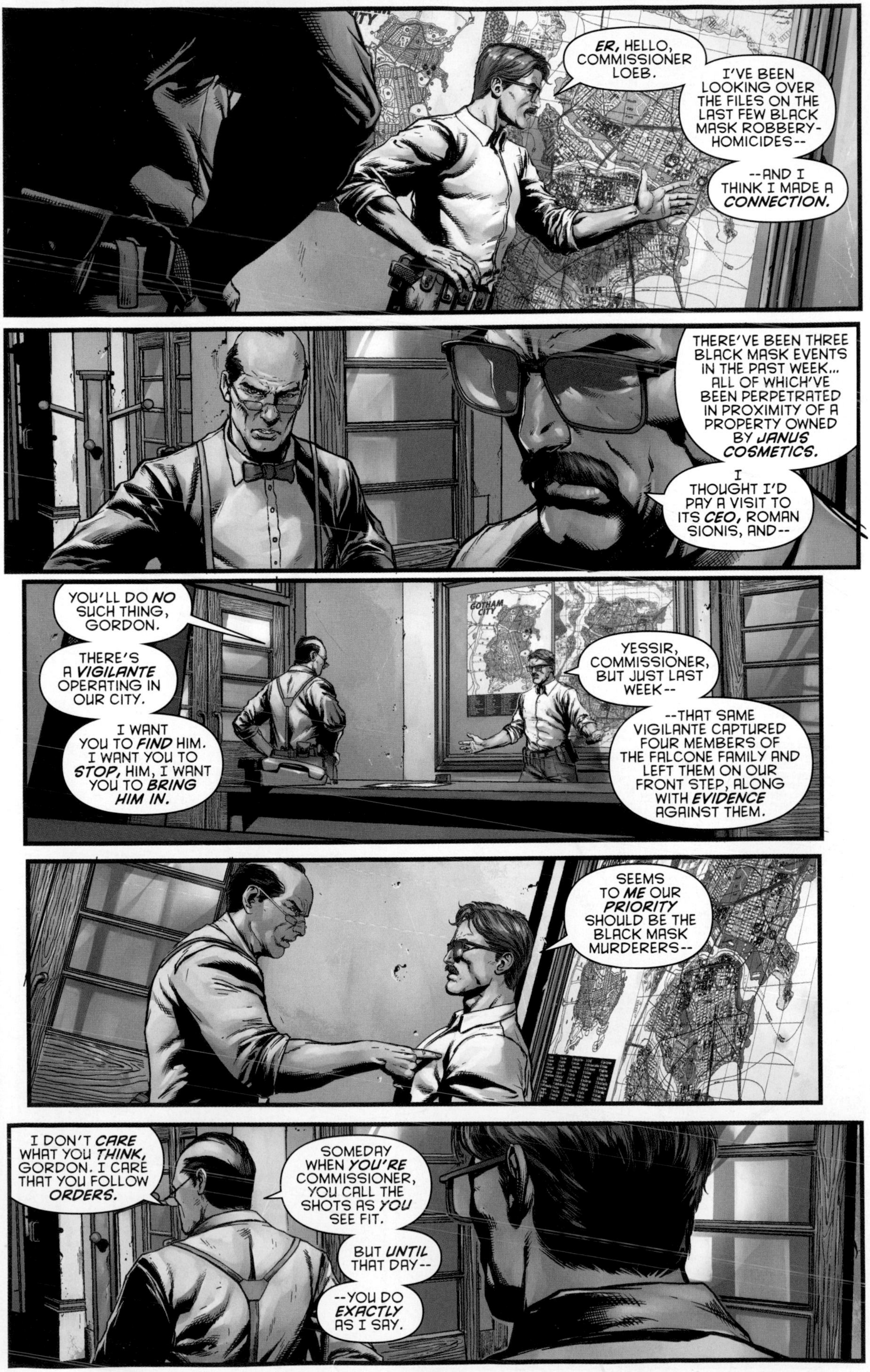
ER, HELLO, COMMISSIONER LOEB.
I'VE BEEN LOOKING OVER THE FILES ON THE LAST FEW BLACK MASK ROBBERY-HOMICIDES--
--AND I THINK I MADE A CONNECTION.
THERE'VE BEEN THREE BLACK MASK EVENTS IN THE PAST WEEK... ALL OF WHICH'VE BEEN PERPETRATED IN PROXIMITY OF A PROPERTY OWNED BY JANUS COSMETICS.
I THOUGHT I'D PAY A VISIT TO ITS CEO, ROMAN SIONIS, AND--
YOU'LL DO NO SUCH THING, GORDON.
THERE'S A VIGILANTE OPERATING IN OUR CITY.
I WANT YOU TO FIND HIM. I WANT YOU TO STOP, HIM, I WANT YOU TO BRING HIM IN.
GOTHAM CITY
YESSIR, COMMISSIONER, BUT JUST LAST WEEK--
--THAT SAME VIGILANTE CAPTURED FOUR MEMBERS OF THE FALCONE FAMILY AND LEFT THEM ON OUR FRONT STEP, ALONG WITH EVIDENCE AGAINST THEM.
SEEMS TO ME OUR PRIORITY SHOULD BE THE BLACK MASK MURDERERS--
I DON'T CARE WHAT YOU THINK, GORDON. I CARE THAT YOU FOLLOW ORDERS.
SOMEDAY WHEN YOU'RE COMMISSIONER, YOU CALL THE SHOTS AS YOU SEE FIT.
BUT UNTIL THAT DAY--
--YOU DO EXACTLY AS I SAY.

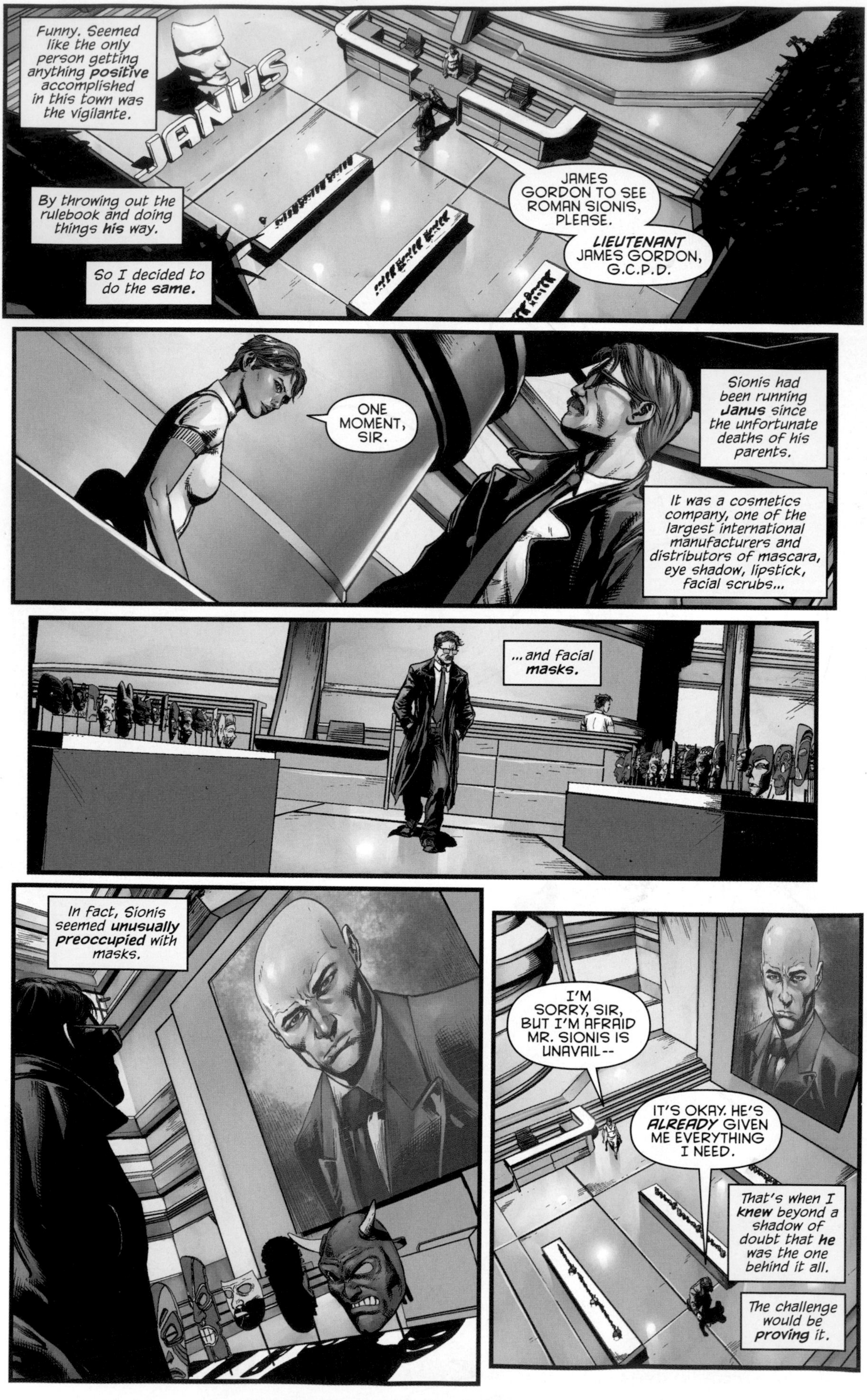
Funny. Seemed like the only person getting anything **positive** accomplished in this town was the vigilante.
JANUS
By throwing out the rulebook and doing things **his** way.
So I decided to do the **same.**
JAMES GORDON TO SEE ROMAN SIONIS, PLEASE.
LIEUTENANT JAMES GORDON, G.C.P.D.
ONE MOMENT, SIR.
Sionis had been running **Janus** since the unfortunate deaths of his parents.
It was a cosmetics company, one of the largest international manufacturers and distributors of mascara, eye shadow, lipstick, facial scrubs...
...and facial **masks.**
In fact, Sionis seemed **unusually preoccupied** with masks.
I'M SORRY, SIR, BUT I'M AFRAID MR. SIONIS IS UNAVAIL--
IT'S OKAY. HE'S ***ALREADY*** GIVEN ME EVERYTHING I NEED.
That's when I **knew** beyond a shadow of doubt that **he** was the one behind it all.
The challenge would be **proving** it.

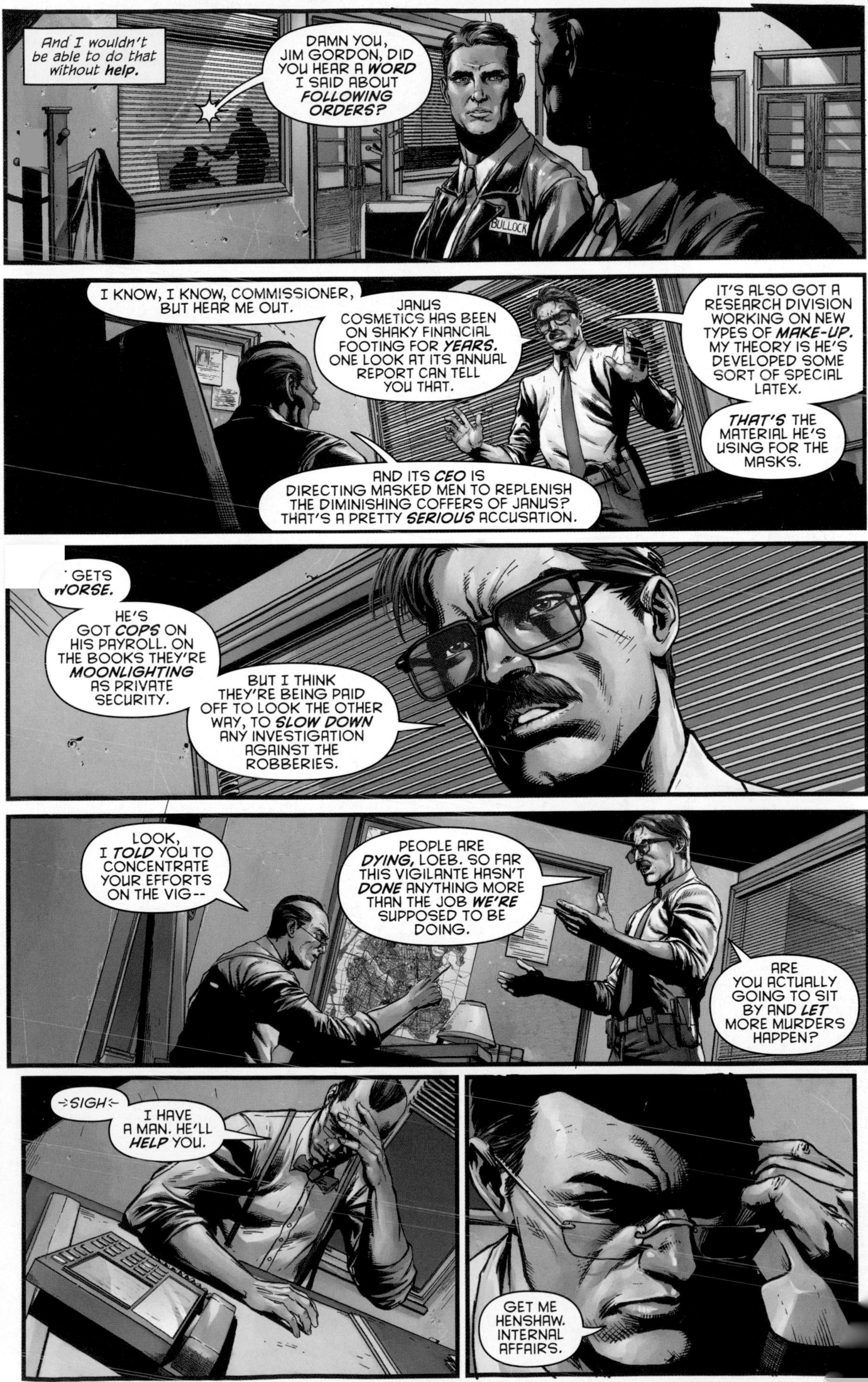
And I wouldn't be able to do that without **help.**
DAMN YOU, JIM GORDON, DID YOU HEAR A ***WORD*** I SAID ABOUT ***FOLLOWING ORDERS?***
BULLOCK
I KNOW, I KNOW, COMMISSIONER, BUT HEAR ME OUT.
JANUS COSMETICS HAS BEEN ON SHAKY FINANCIAL FOOTING FOR ***YEARS.*** ONE LOOK AT ITS ANNUAL REPORT CAN TELL YOU THAT.
IT'S ALSO GOT A RESEARCH DIVISION WORKING ON NEW TYPES OF ***MAKE-UP.*** MY THEORY IS HE'S DEVELOPED SOME SORT OF SPECIAL LATEX.
THAT'S THE MATERIAL HE'S USING FOR THE MASKS.
AND ITS ***CEO*** IS DIRECTING MASKED MEN TO REPLENISH THE DIMINISHING COFFERS OF JANUS? THAT'S A PRETTY ***SERIOUS*** ACCUSATION.
GETS ***WORSE.***
HE'S GOT ***COPS*** ON HIS PAYROLL. ON THE BOOKS THEY'RE ***MOONLIGHTING*** AS PRIVATE SECURITY.
BUT I THINK THEY'RE BEING PAID OFF TO LOOK THE OTHER WAY, TO ***SLOW DOWN*** ANY INVESTIGATION AGAINST THE ROBBERIES.
LOOK, I ***TOLD*** YOU TO CONCENTRATE YOUR EFFORTS ON THE VIG--
PEOPLE ARE ***DYING,*** LOEB. SO FAR THIS VIGILANTE HASN'T ***DONE*** ANYTHING MORE THAN THE JOB ***WE'RE*** SUPPOSED TO BE DOING.
ARE YOU ACTUALLY GOING TO SIT BY AND ***LET*** MORE MURDERS HAPPEN?
-SIGH-
I HAVE A MAN. HE'LL ***HELP*** YOU.
GET ME HENSHAW. INTERNAL AFFAIRS.

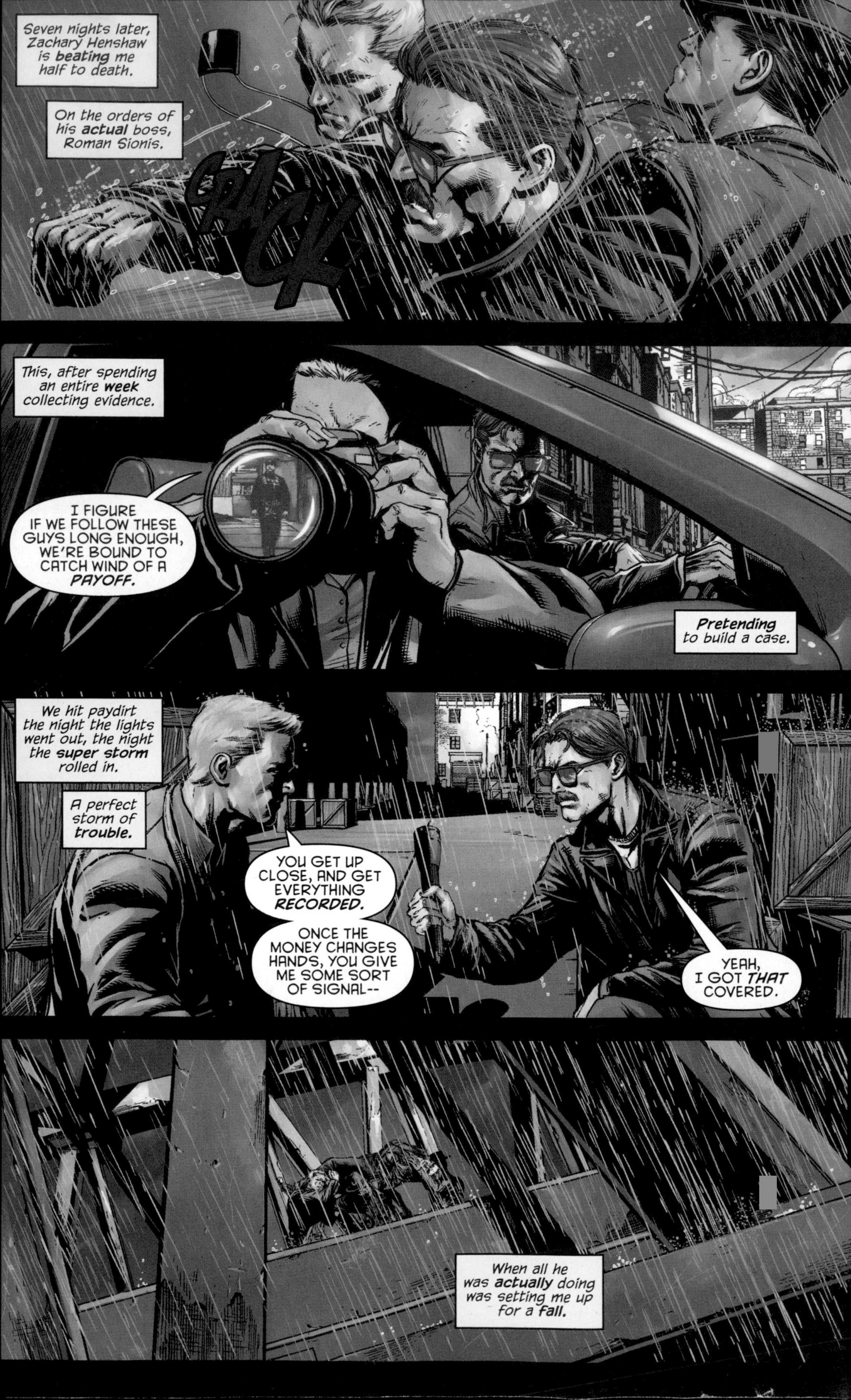
Seven nights later, Zachary Henshaw is **beating** me half to death.
On the orders of his **actual** boss, Roman Sionis.
CRACK
This, after spending an entire **week** collecting evidence.
I FIGURE IF WE FOLLOW THESE GUYS LONG ENOUGH, WE'RE BOUND TO CATCH WIND OF A ***PAYOFF.***
Pretending to build a case.
We hit paydirt the night the lights went out, the night the **super storm** rolled in.
A perfect storm of **trouble.**
YOU GET UP CLOSE, AND GET EVERYTHING ***RECORDED.***
ONCE THE MONEY CHANGES HANDS, YOU GIVE ME SOME SORT OF SIGNAL--
YEAH, I GOT ***THAT*** COVERED.
When all he was **actually** doing was setting me up for a **fall.**

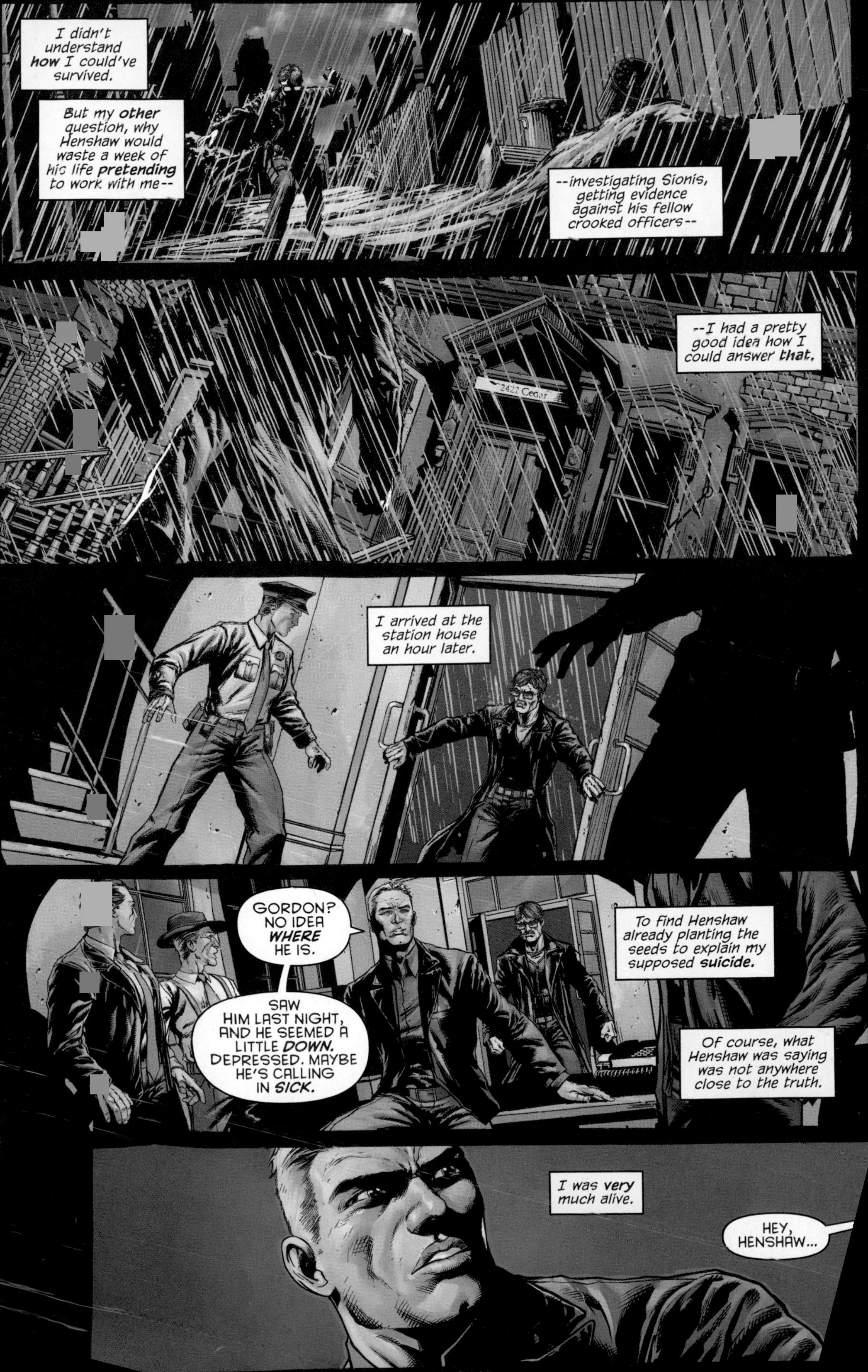
I didn't understand **how** I could've survived.
But my **other** question, why Henshaw would waste a week of his life **pretending** to work with me--
--investigating Sionis, getting evidence against his fellow crooked officers--
--I had a pretty good idea how I could answer **that.**
I arrived at the station house an hour later.
GORDON? NO IDEA ***WHERE*** HE IS.
SAW HIM LAST NIGHT, AND HE SEEMED A LITTLE ***DOWN.*** DEPRESSED. MAYBE HE'S CALLING IN ***SICK.***
To find Henshaw already planting the seeds to explain my supposed **suicide.**
Of course, what Henshaw was saying was not anywhere close to the truth.
I was **very** much alive.
HEY, HENSHAW...

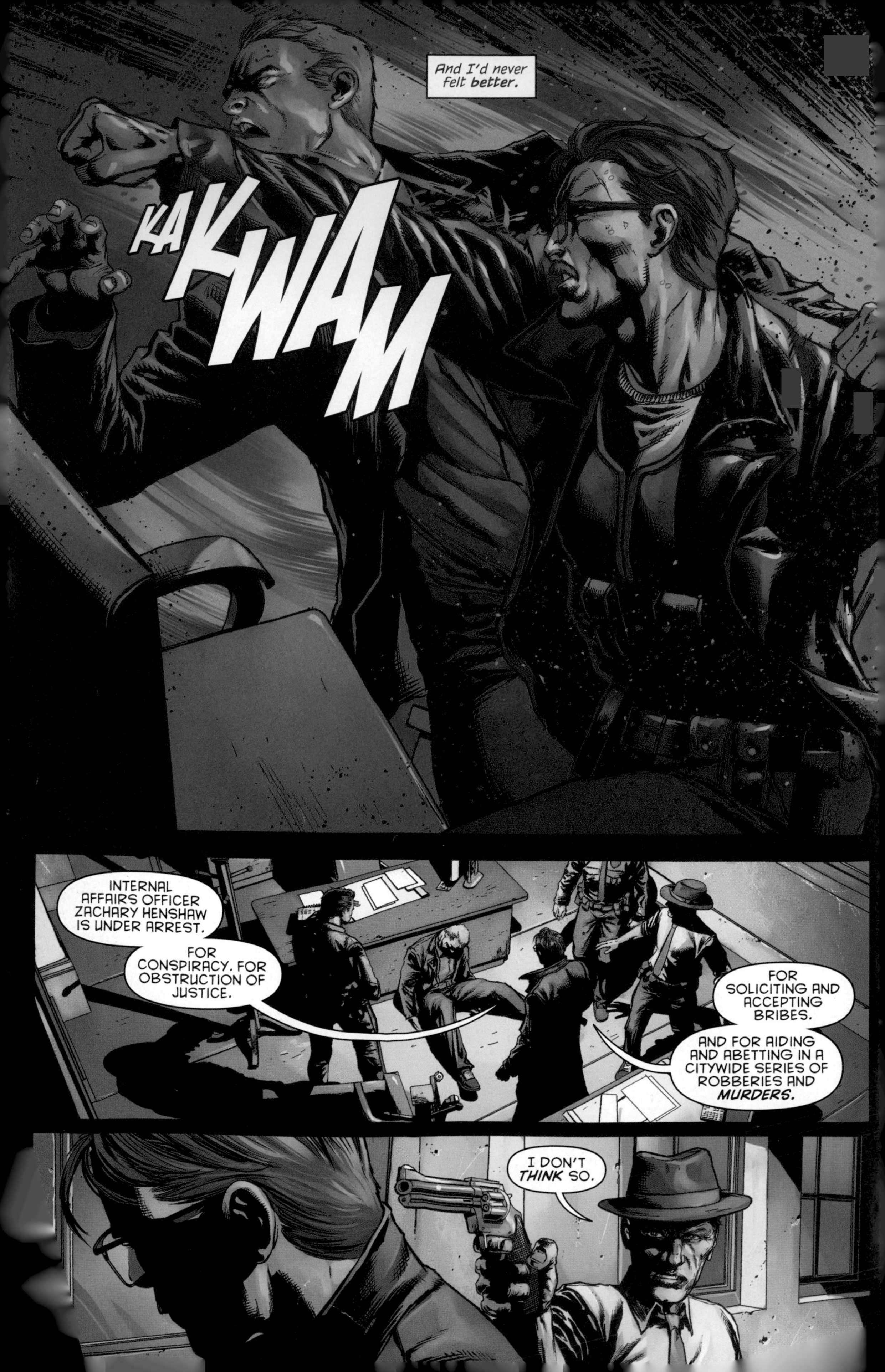
And I'd never felt better.
KAKWAM
INTERNAL AFFAIRS OFFICER ZACHARY HENSHAW IS UNDER ARREST.
FOR CONSPIRACY. FOR OBSTRUCTION OF JUSTICE.
FOR SOLICITING AND ACCEPTING BRIBES.
AND FOR AIDING AND ABETTING IN A CITYWIDE SERIES OF ROBBERIES AND MURDERS.
I DON'T THINK SO.

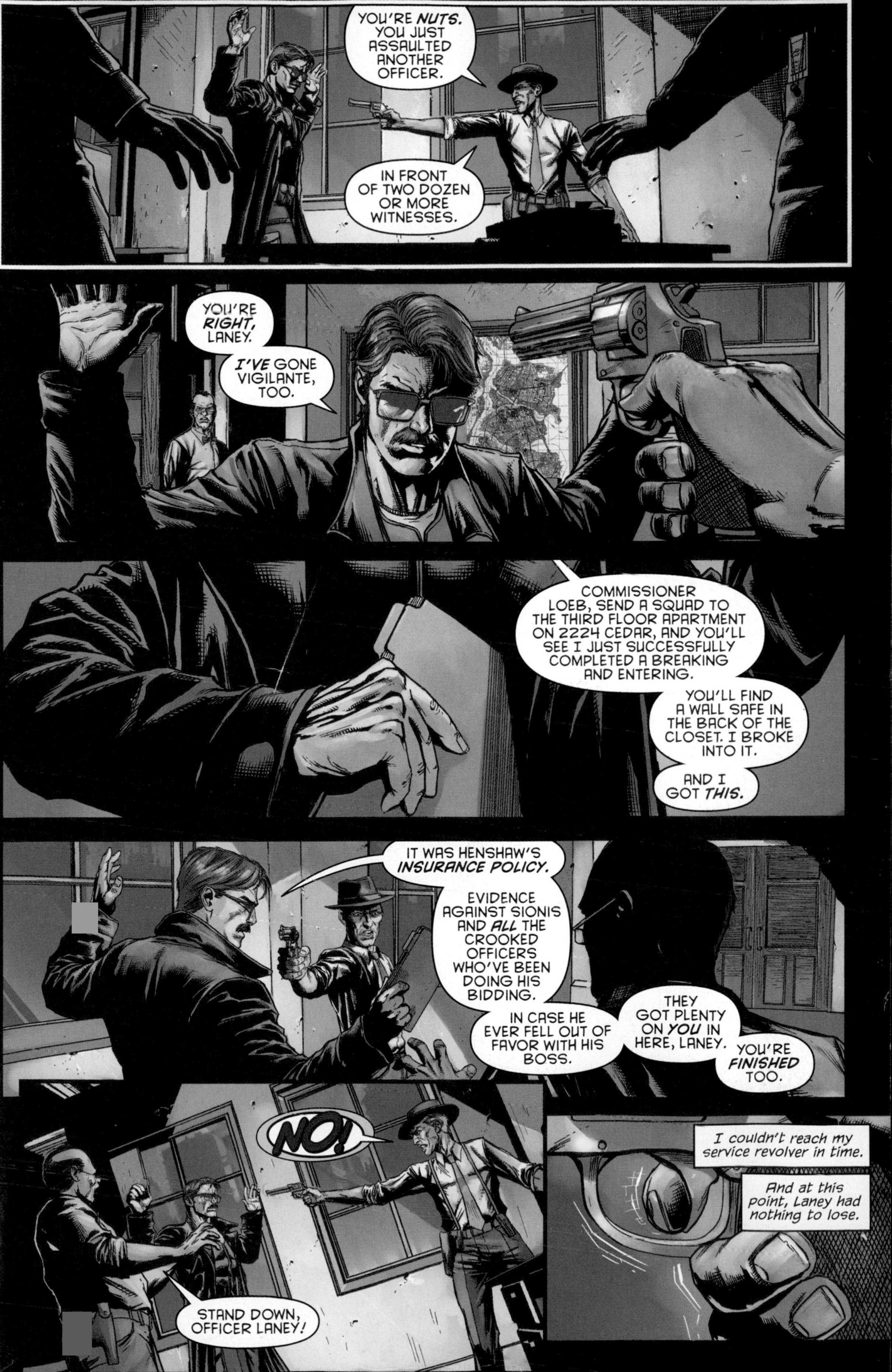
YOU'RE *NUTS.* YOU JUST ASSAULTED ANOTHER OFFICER.
IN FRONT OF TWO DOZEN OR MORE WITNESSES.
YOU'RE *RIGHT,* LANEY.
I'VE GONE VIGILANTE, TOO.
COMMISSIONER LOEB, SEND A SQUAD TO THE THIRD FLOOR APARTMENT ON 2224 CEDAR, AND YOU'LL SEE I JUST SUCCESSFULLY COMPLETED A BREAKING AND ENTERING.
YOU'LL FIND A WALL SAFE IN THE BACK OF THE CLOSET. I BROKE INTO IT.
AND I GOT *THIS.*
IT WAS HENSHAW'S *INSURANCE POLICY.*
EVIDENCE AGAINST SIONIS AND *ALL* THE CROOKED OFFICERS WHO'VE BEEN DOING HIS BIDDING.
IN CASE HE EVER FELL OUT OF FAVOR WITH HIS BOSS.
THEY GOT PLENTY ON *YOU* IN HERE, LANEY.
YOU'RE *FINISHED* TOO.
NO!
STAND DOWN, OFFICER LANEY!
I couldn't reach my service revolver in time.
And at this point, Laney had nothing to lose.

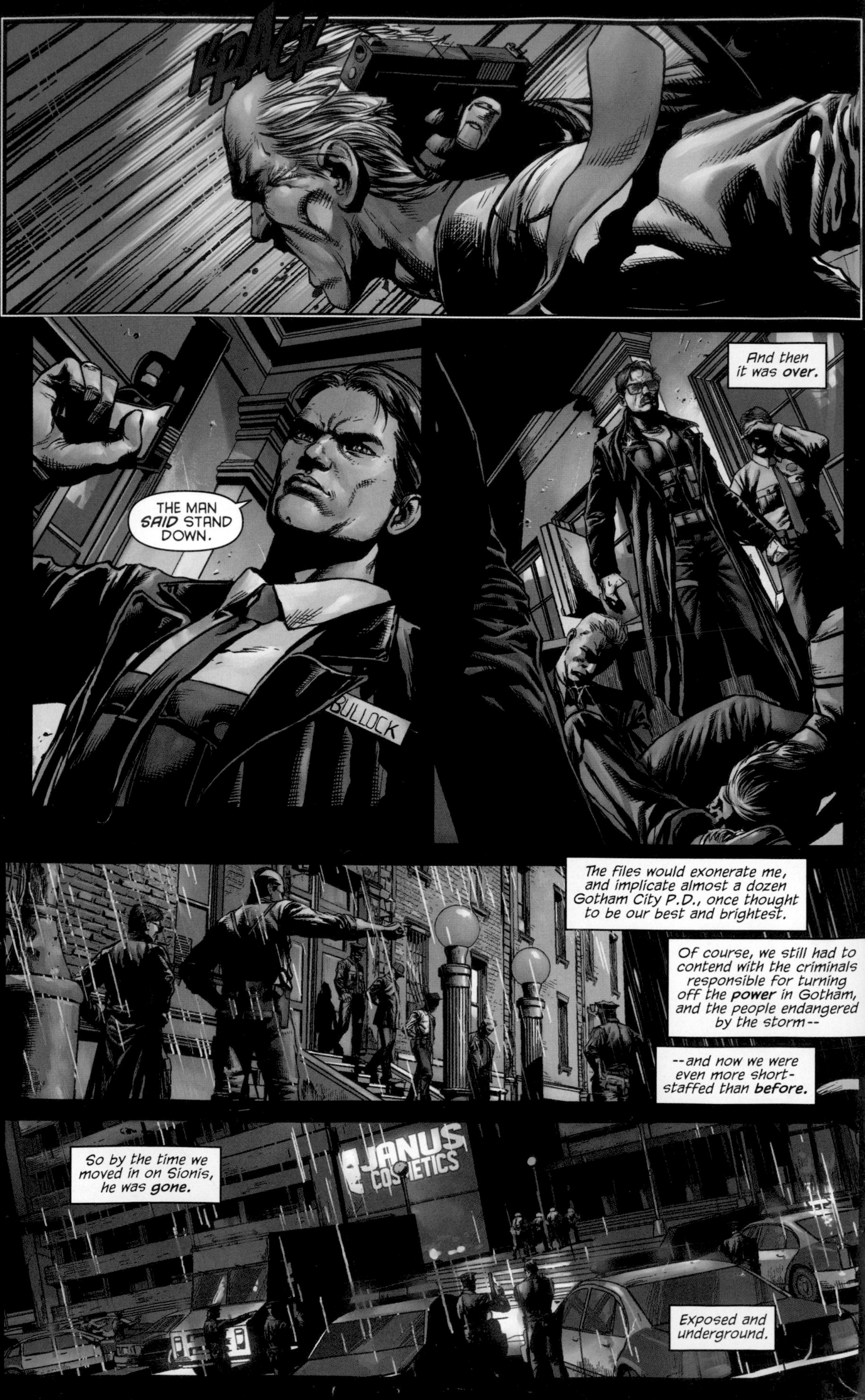
KRACK
THE MAN SAID STAND DOWN.
BULLOCK
And then it was over.
The files would exonerate me, and implicate almost a dozen Gotham City P.D., once thought to be our best and brightest.
Of course, we still had to contend with the criminals responsible for turning off the power in Gotham, and the people endangered by the storm--
--and now we were even more short-staffed than before.
JANUS COSMETICS
So by the time we moved in on Sionis, he was gone.
Exposed and underground.

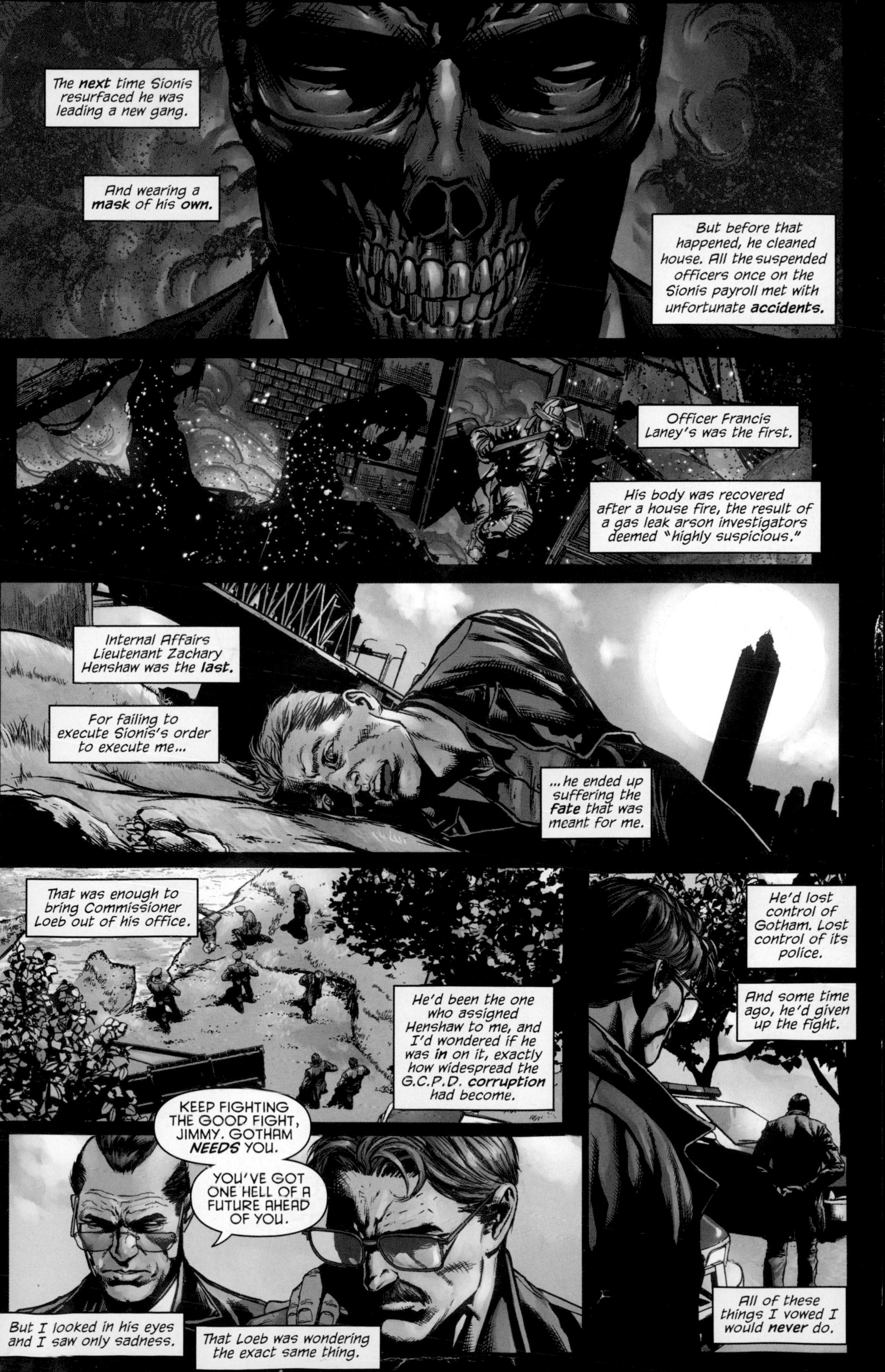
The next time Sionis resurfaced he was leading a new gang.
And wearing a mask of his own.
But before that happened, he cleaned house. All the suspended officers once on the Sionis payroll met with unfortunate accidents.
Officer Francis Laney's was the first.
His body was recovered after a house fire, the result of a gas leak arson investigators deemed "highly suspicious."
Internal Affairs Lieutenant Zachary Henshaw was the last.
For failing to execute Sionis's order to execute me...
...he ended up suffering the fate that was meant for me.
That was enough to bring Commissioner Loeb out of his office.
He'd been the one who assigned Henshaw to me, and I'd wondered if he was in on it, exactly how widespread the G.C.P.D. corruption had become.
KEEP FIGHTING THE GOOD FIGHT, JIMMY. GOTHAM NEEDS YOU.
YOU'VE GOT ONE HELL OF A FUTURE AHEAD OF YOU.
But I looked in his eyes and I saw only sadness.
That Loeb was wondering the exact same thing.
He'd lost control of Gotham. Lost control of its police.
And some time ago, he'd given up the fight.
All of these things I vowed I would never do.

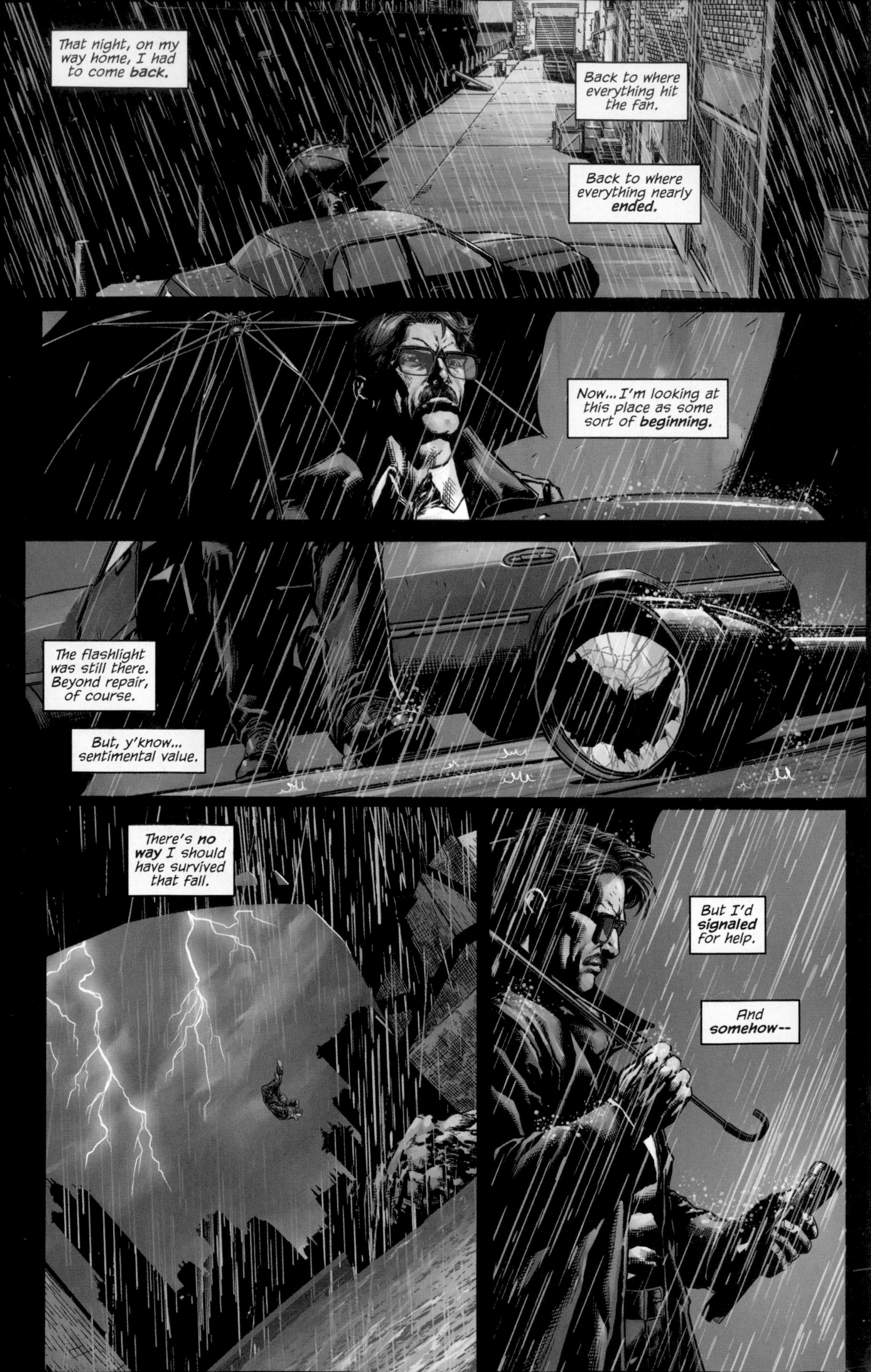
That night, on my way home, I had to come back.
Back to where everything hit the fan.
Back to where everything nearly ended.
Now... I'm looking at this place as some sort of beginning.
The flashlight was still there. Beyond repair, of course.
But, y'know... sentimental value.
There's no way I should have survived that fall.
But I'd signaled for help.
And somehow--

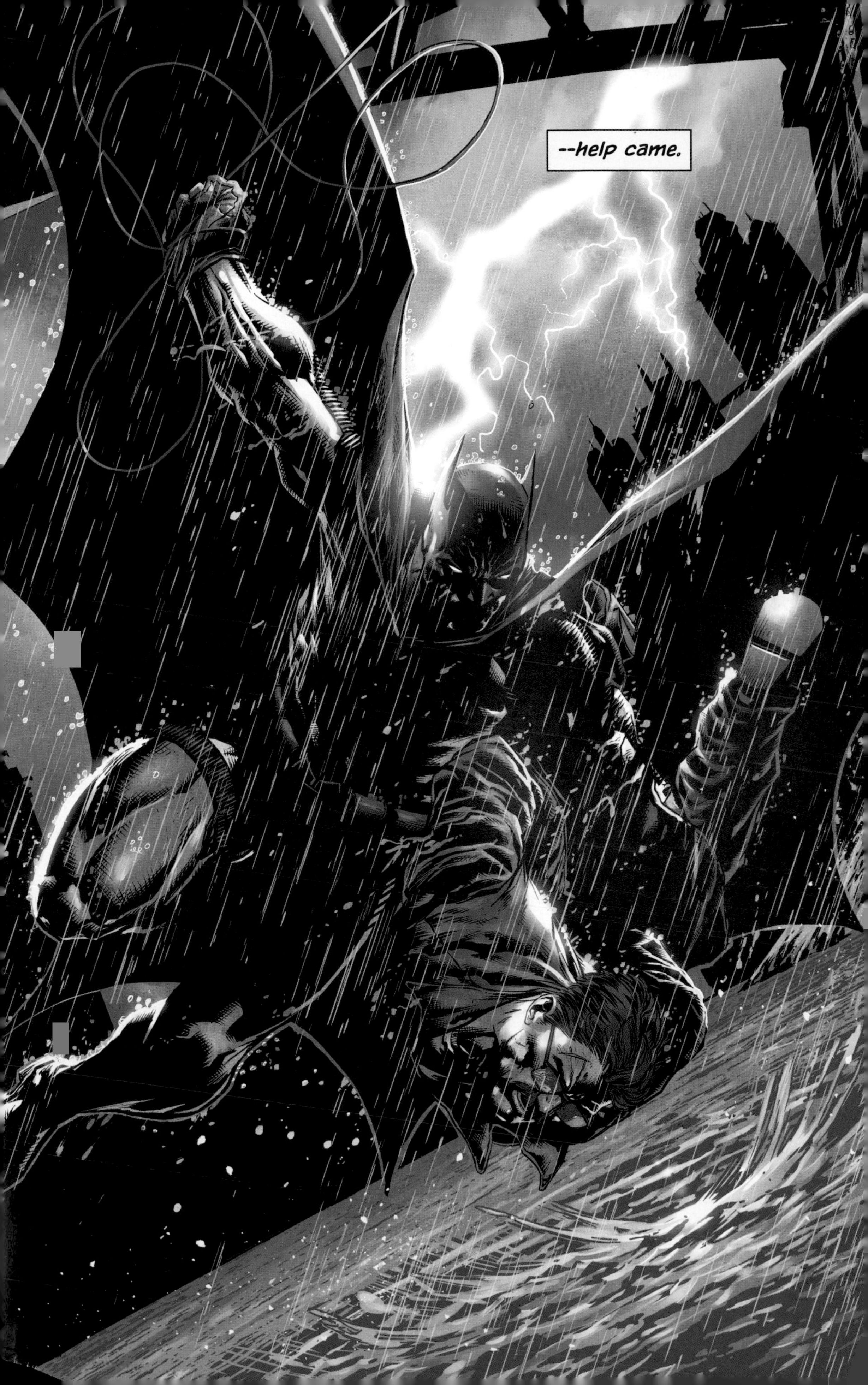
--help came.

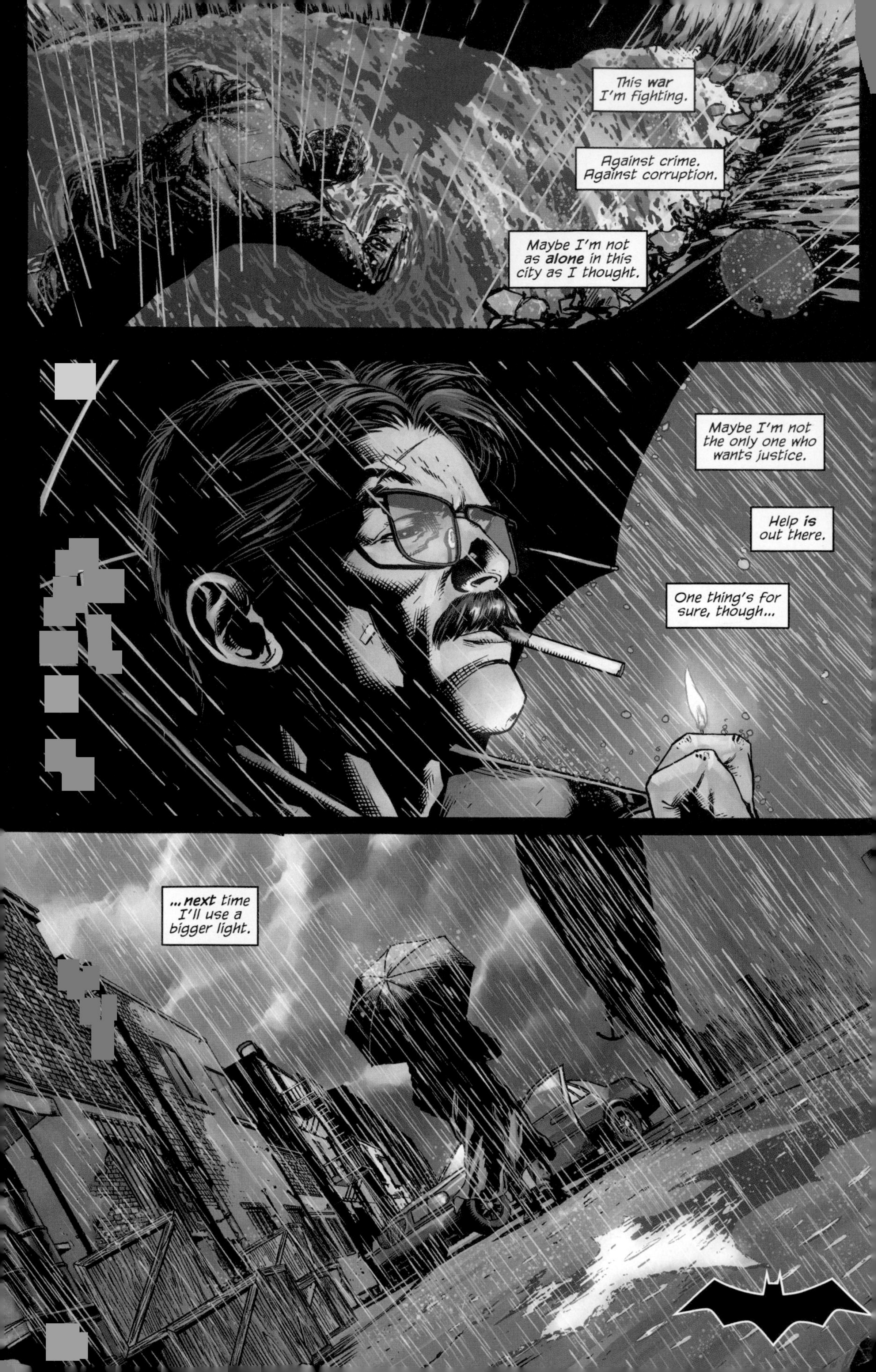
This war I'm fighting.
Against crime. Against corruption.
Maybe I'm not as alone in this city as I thought.
Maybe I'm not the only one who wants justice.
Help is out there.
One thing's for sure, though...
...next time I'll use a bigger light.

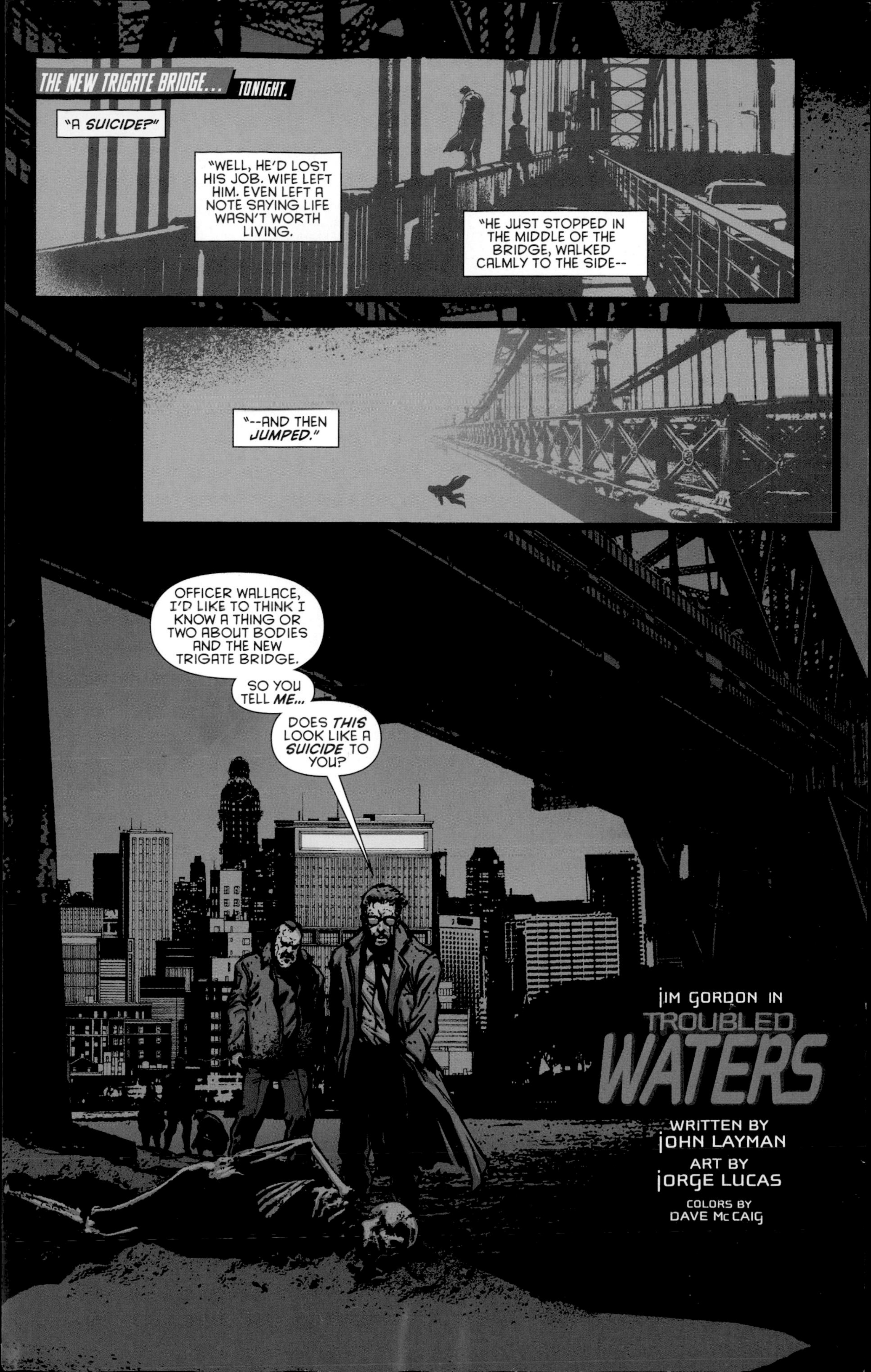
THE NEW TRIGATE BRIDGE... TONIGHT.
"A SUICIDE?"
"WELL, HE'D LOST HIS JOB. WIFE LEFT HIM. EVEN LEFT A NOTE SAYING LIFE WASN'T WORTH LIVING.
"HE JUST STOPPED IN THE MIDDLE OF THE BRIDGE, WALKED CALMLY TO THE SIDE--
"--AND THEN JUMPED."
OFFICER WALLACE, I'D LIKE TO THINK I KNOW A THING OR TWO ABOUT BODIES AND THE NEW TRIGATE BRIDGE.
SO YOU TELL ME...
DOES THIS LOOK LIKE A SUICIDE TO YOU?
JIM GORDON IN
TROUBLED WATERS
WRITTEN BY JOHN LAYMAN
ART BY JORGE LUCAS
COLORS BY DAVE McCAIG

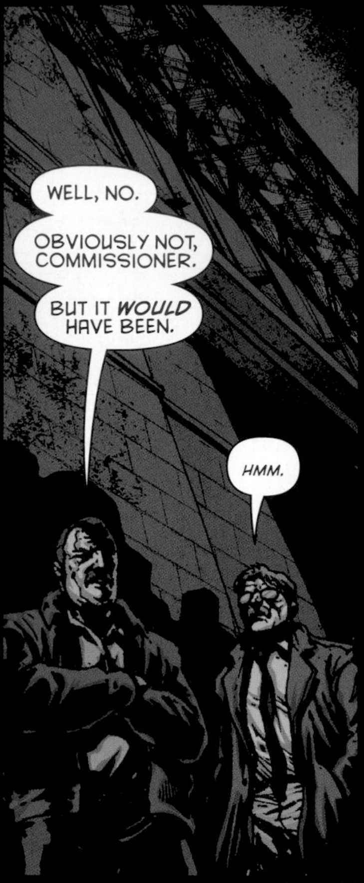
WELL, NO.
OBVIOUSLY NOT, COMMISSIONER.
BUT IT *WOULD* HAVE BEEN.
HMM.
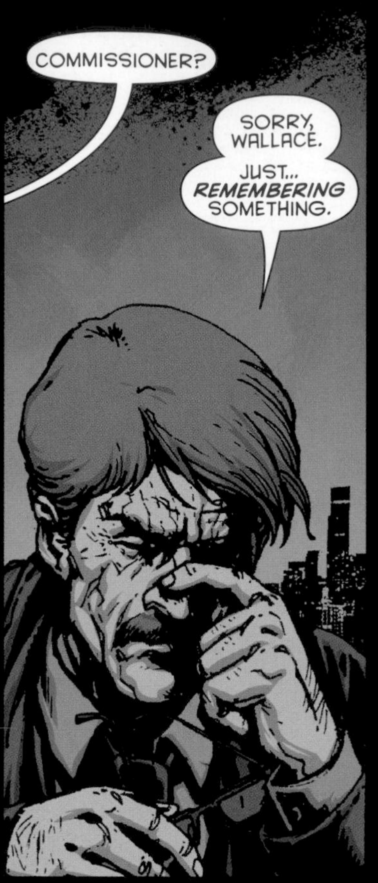
COMMISSIONER?
SORRY, WALLACE.
JUST... *REMEMBERING* SOMETHING.
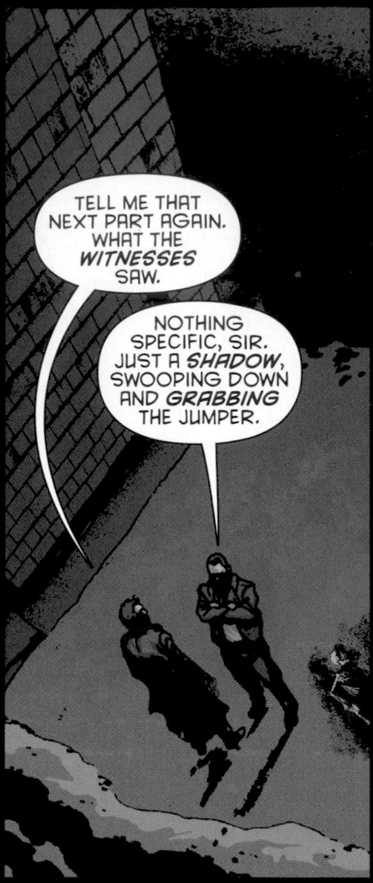
TELL ME THAT NEXT PART AGAIN. WHAT THE *WITNESSES* SAW.
NOTHING SPECIFIC, SIR. JUST A *SHADOW*, SWOOPING DOWN AND *GRABBING* THE JUMPER.
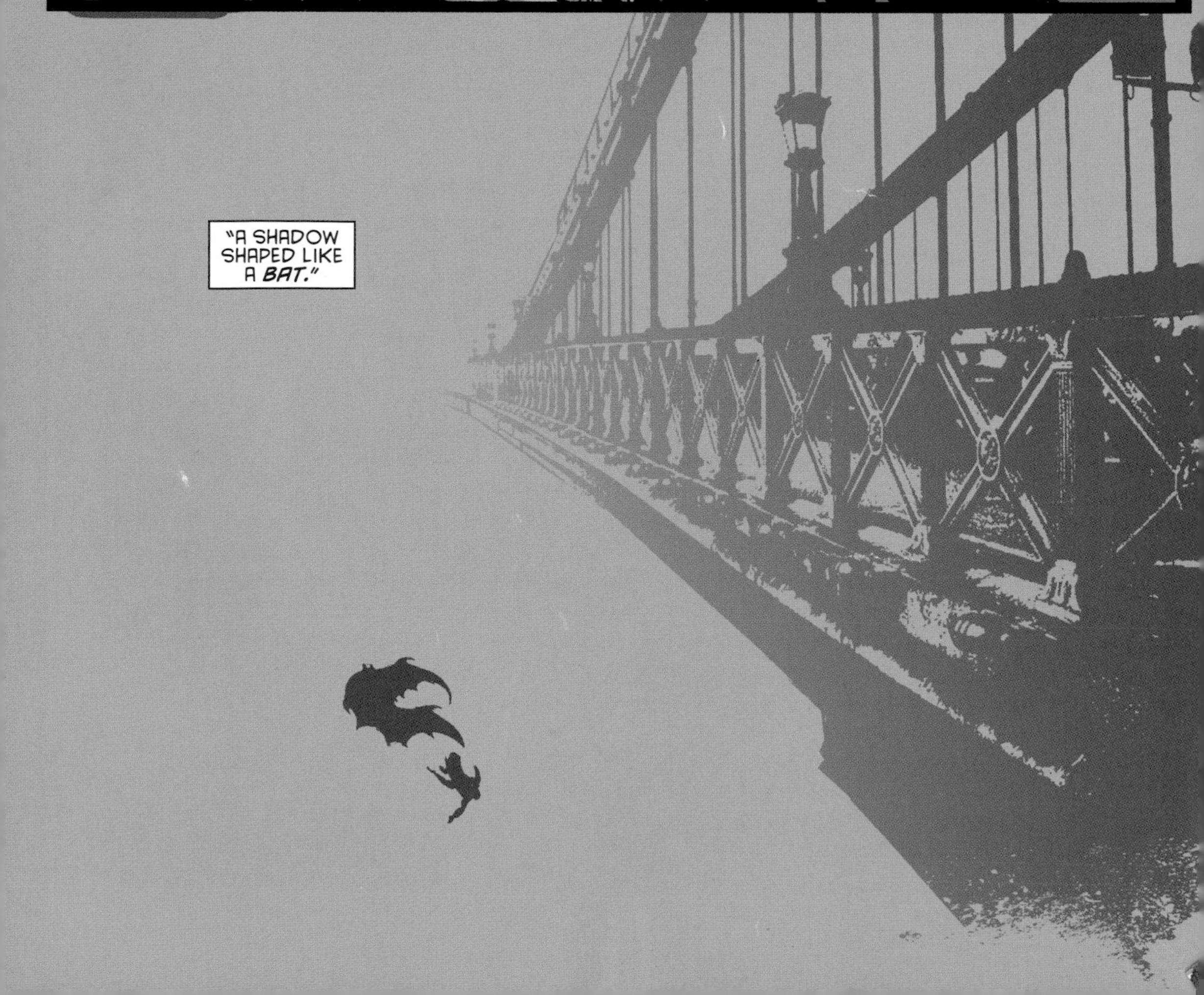
"A SHADOW SHAPED LIKE A *BAT*."

IF YOU ASK ME, IT WAS *BATMAN.*

OR ONE OF HIS CRAZY, CAPED PARTNERS OR *JUNIOR* BATMEN THAT RUN WITH HIM.

DID I USED TO SOUND AS DUMB AS YOU DO, CARDANTE?

IT *WASN'T* BATMAN, IDIOT.

OR ANYBODY *ASSOCIATED* WITH HIM.

THE WITNESS ON THE BRIDGE SAID THEY HEARD THE TEARING, RIPPING, SCREAMING--

"--AND THE FLAPPING OF *HUNDREDS* OF TINY *WINGS.*"

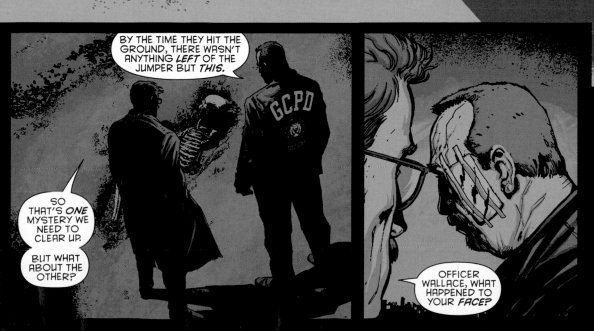

BY THE TIME THEY HIT THE GROUND, THERE WASN'T ANYTHING *LEFT* OF THE JUMPER BUT *THIS.*

SO THAT'S *ONE* MYSTERY WE NEED TO CLEAR UP.

BUT WHAT ABOUT THE OTHER?

OFFICER WALLACE, WHAT HAPPENED TO YOUR *FACE?*

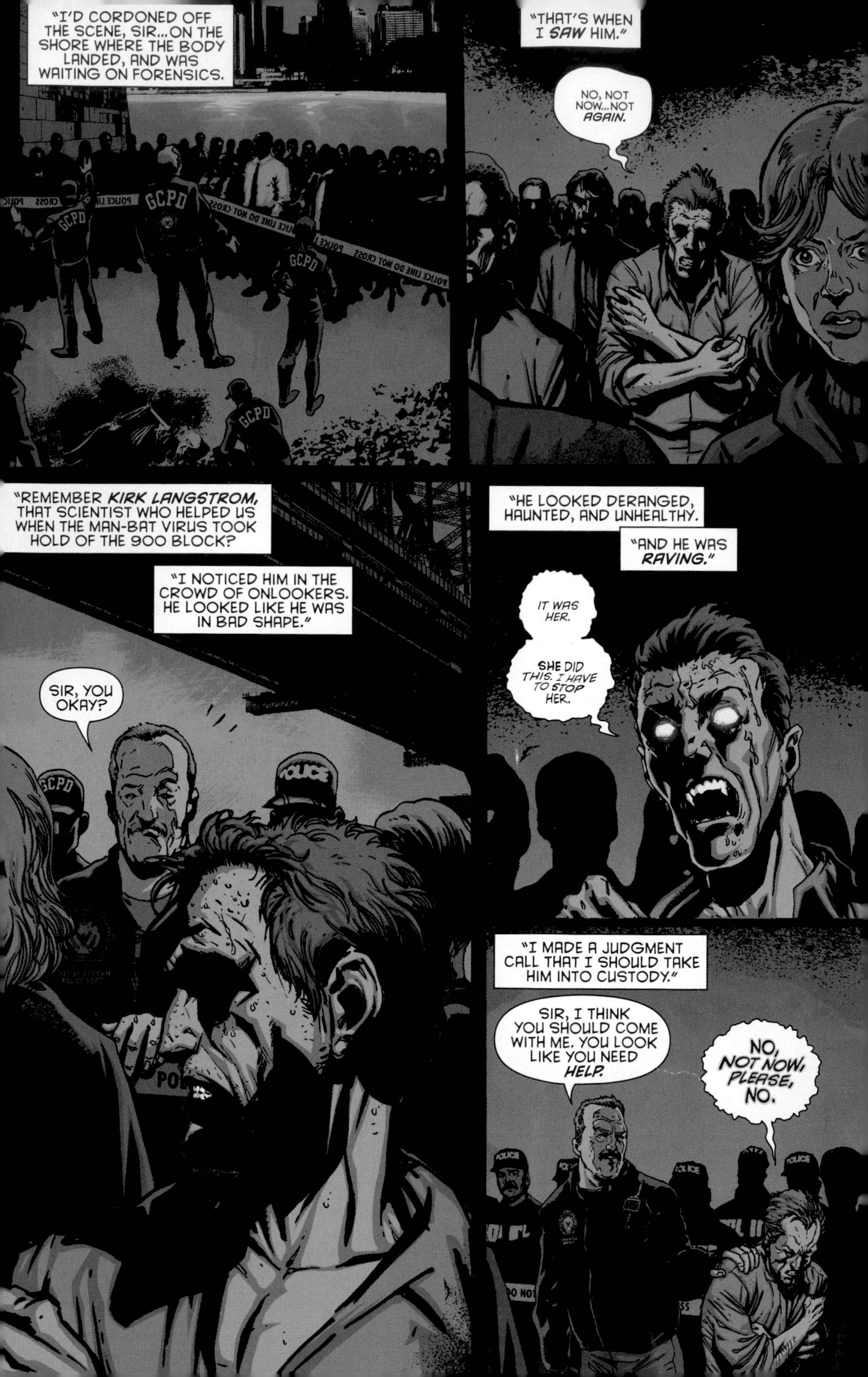
"I'D CORDONED OFF THE SCENE, SIR...ON THE SHORE WHERE THE BODY LANDED, AND WAS WAITING ON FORENSICS.
GCPD
POLICE LINE DO NOT CROSS
"THAT'S WHEN I SAW HIM."
NO, NOT NOW...NOT AGAIN.
"REMEMBER KIRK LANGSTROM, THAT SCIENTIST WHO HELPED US WHEN THE MAN-BAT VIRUS TOOK HOLD OF THE 900 BLOCK?
"I NOTICED HIM IN THE CROWD OF ONLOOKERS. HE LOOKED LIKE HE WAS IN BAD SHAPE."
SIR, YOU OKAY?
"HE LOOKED DERANGED, HAUNTED, AND UNHEALTHY.
"AND HE WAS RAVING."
IT WAS HER.
SHE DID THIS. I HAVE TO STOP HER.
"I MADE A JUDGMENT CALL THAT I SHOULD TAKE HIM INTO CUSTODY."
SIR, I THINK YOU SHOULD COME WITH ME. YOU LOOK LIKE YOU NEED HELP.
NO, NOT NOW, PLEASE, NO.

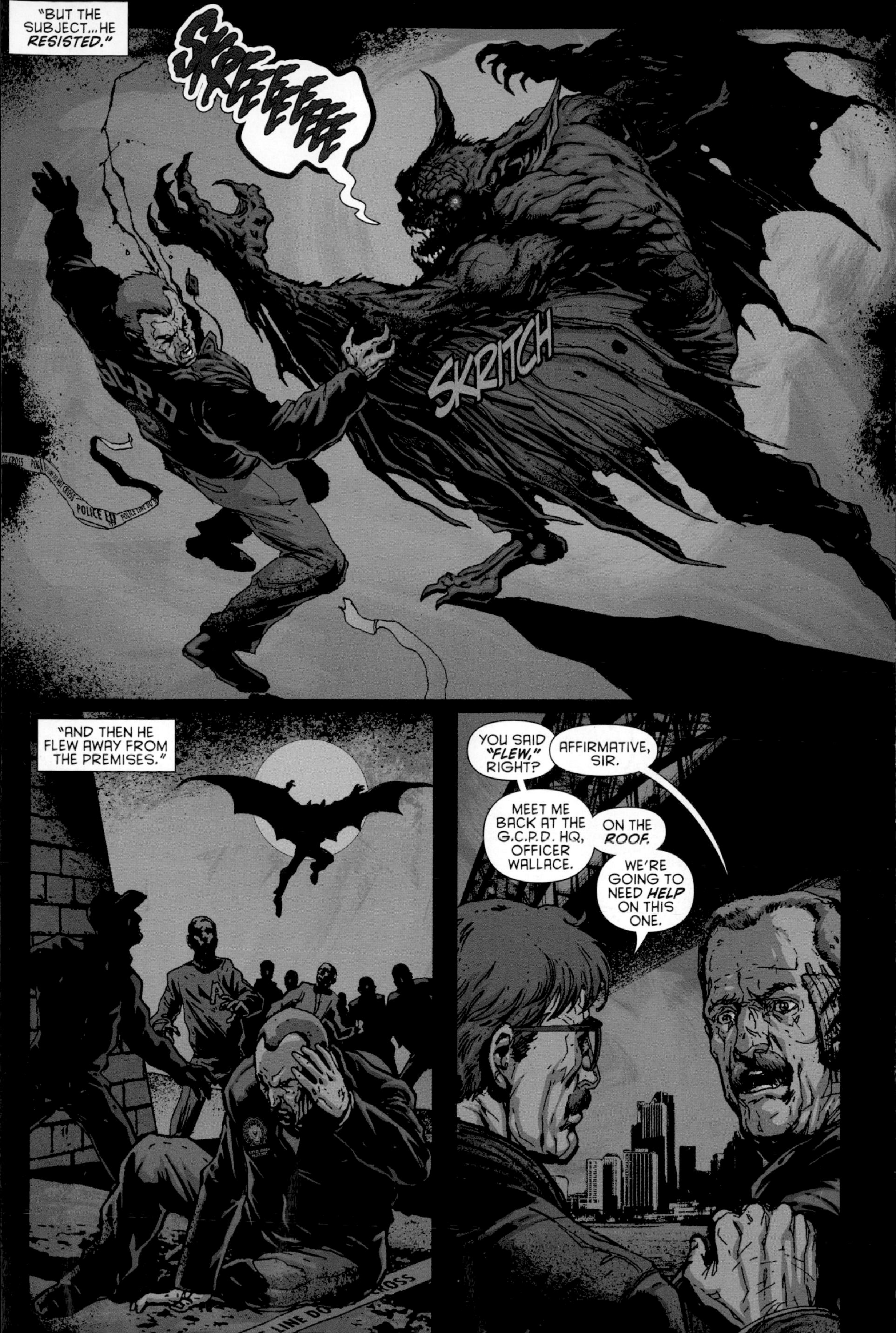
"BUT THE SUBJECT...HE *RESISTED.*"
SKREEEEEEEE
SKRITCH
"AND THEN HE FLEW AWAY FROM THE PREMISES."
YOU SAID *"FLEW,"* RIGHT?
AFFIRMATIVE, SIR.
MEET ME BACK AT THE G.C.P.D. HQ, OFFICER WALLACE.
ON THE *ROOF.*
WE'RE GOING TO NEED *HELP* ON THIS ONE.

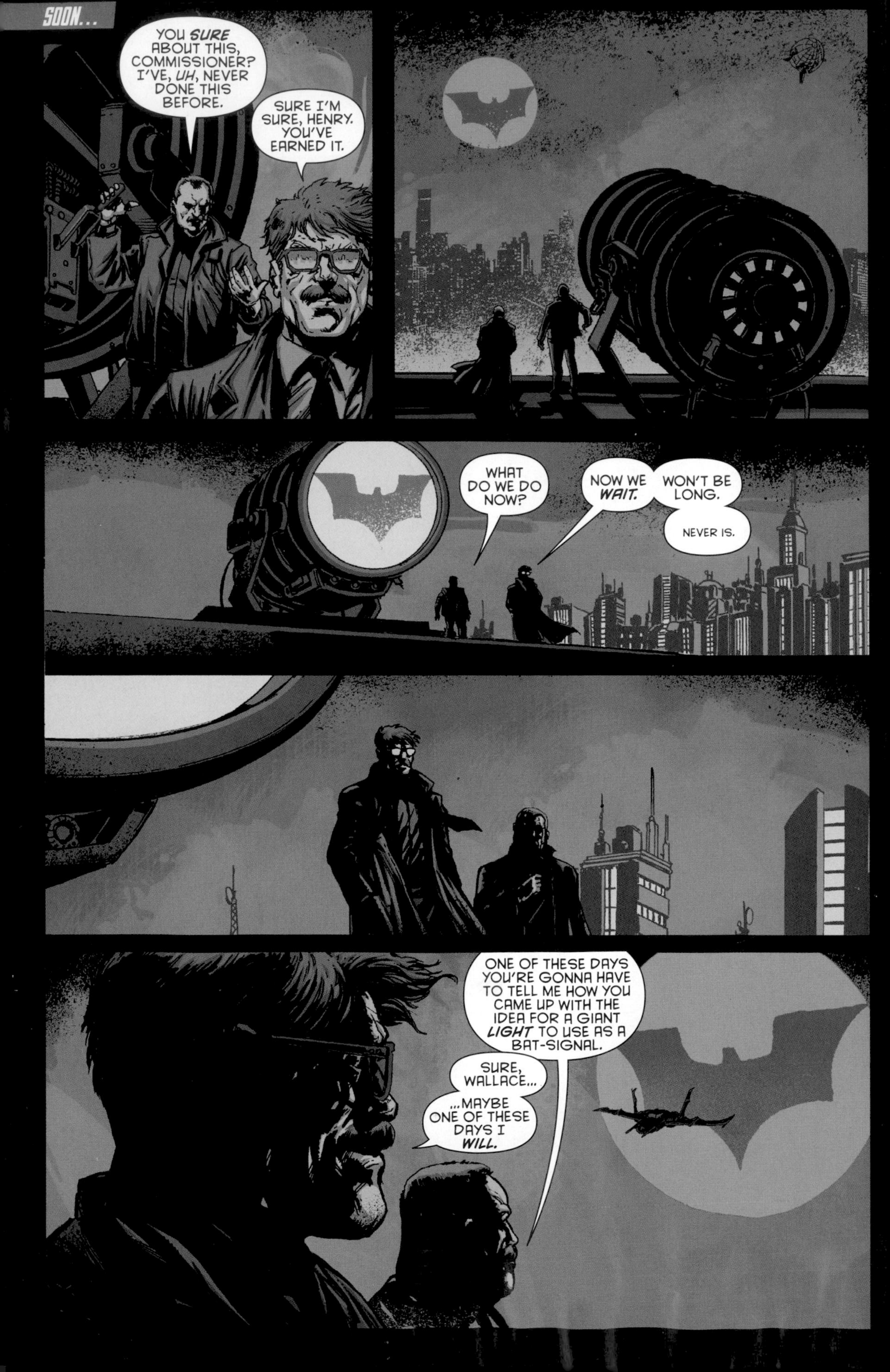
SOON...
YOU SURE ABOUT THIS, COMMISSIONER? I'VE, UH, NEVER DONE THIS BEFORE.
SURE I'M SURE, HENRY. YOU'VE EARNED IT.
WHAT DO WE DO NOW?
NOW WE WAIT.
WON'T BE LONG.
NEVER IS.
ONE OF THESE DAYS YOU'RE GONNA HAVE TO TELL ME HOW YOU CAME UP WITH THE IDEA FOR A GIANT LIGHT TO USE AS A BAT-SIGNAL.
SURE, WALLACE...
...MAYBE ONE OF THESE DAYS I WILL.

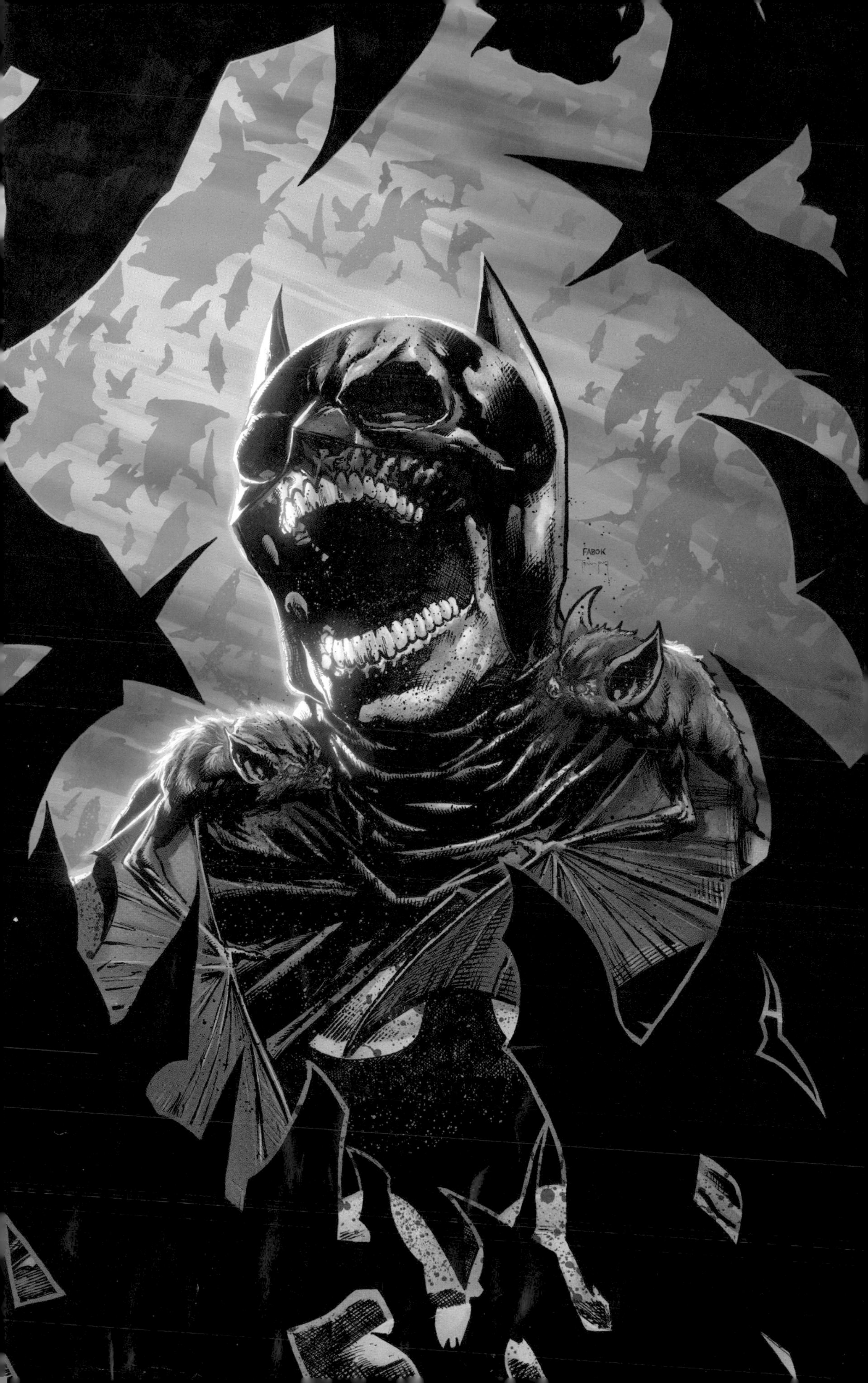

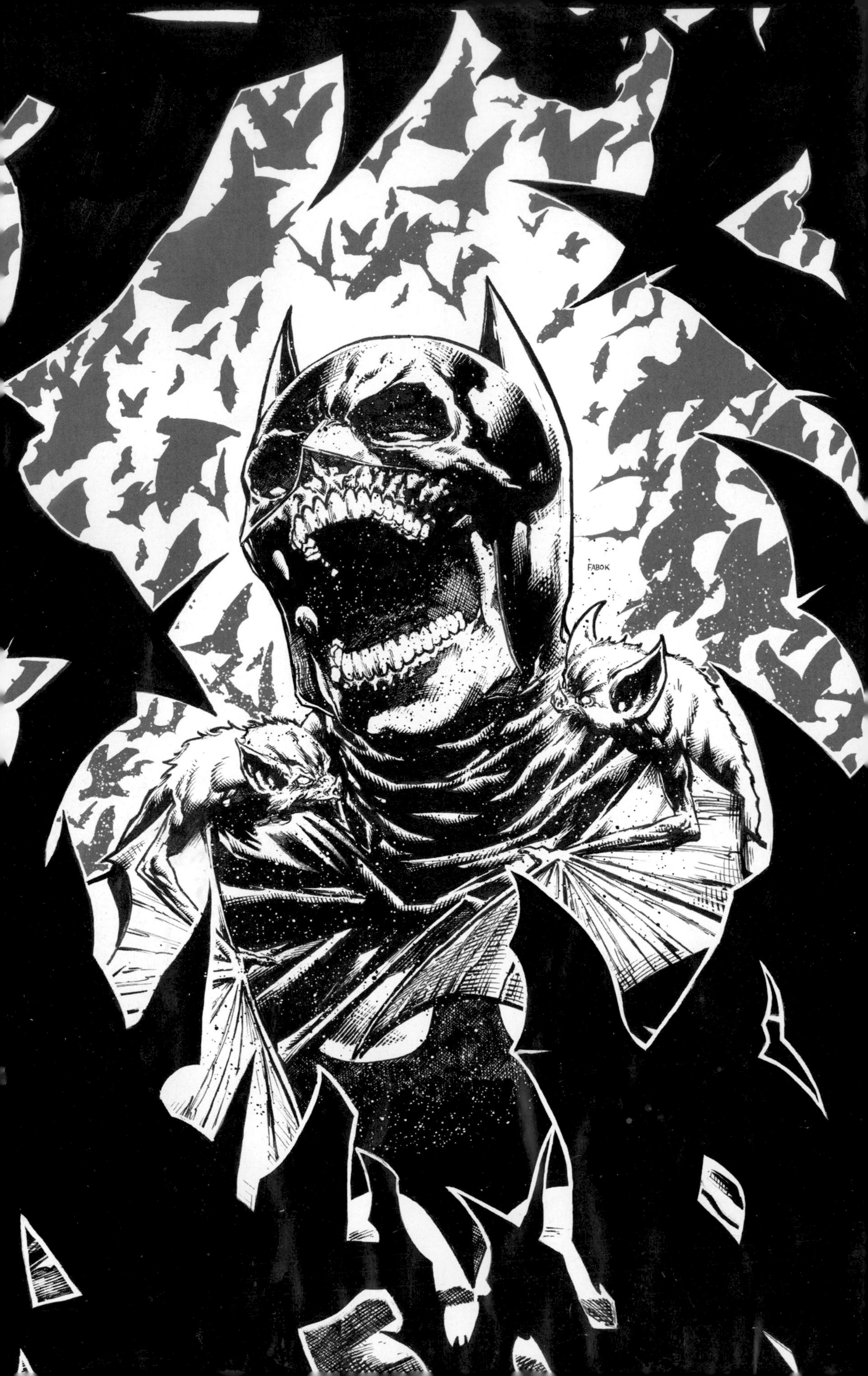
FABOK

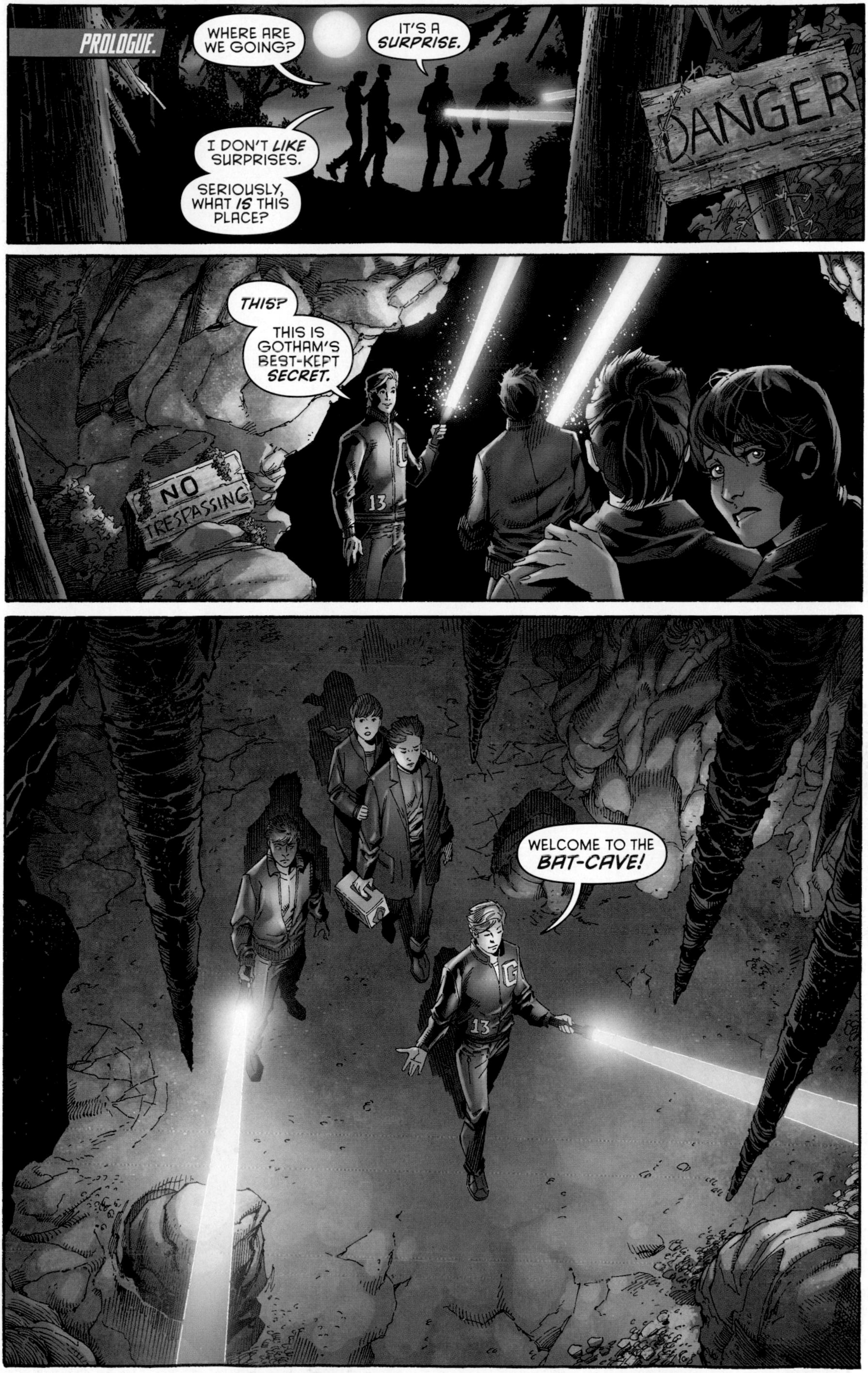
PROLOGUE.
WHERE ARE WE GOING?
IT'S A *SURPRISE.*
I DON'T *LIKE* SURPRISES.
SERIOUSLY, WHAT *IS* THIS PLACE?
DANGER
THIS?
THIS IS GOTHAM'S BEST-KEPT *SECRET.*
NO TRESPASSING
13
13
WELCOME TO THE *BAT-CAVE!*

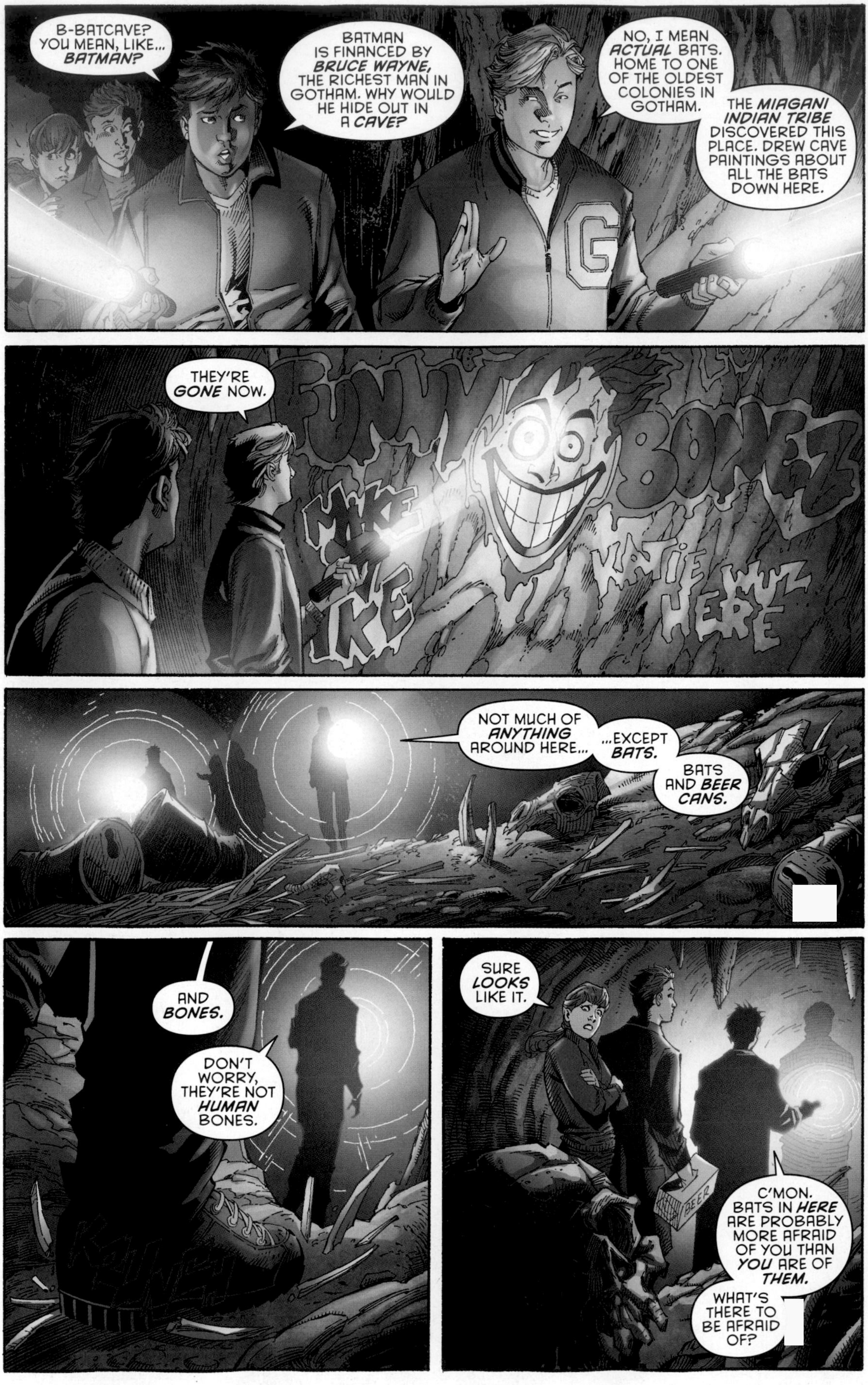
B-BATCAVE? YOU MEAN, LIKE... *BATMAN?*
BATMAN IS FINANCED BY *BRUCE WAYNE,* THE RICHEST MAN IN GOTHAM. WHY WOULD HE HIDE OUT IN A *CAVE?*
NO, I MEAN *ACTUAL* BATS. HOME TO ONE OF THE OLDEST COLONIES IN GOTHAM.
THE *MIAGANI INDIAN TRIBE* DISCOVERED THIS PLACE. DREW CAVE PAINTINGS ABOUT ALL THE BATS DOWN HERE.
THEY'RE *GONE* NOW.
BONEZ
WUZ HERE
NOT MUCH OF *ANYTHING* AROUND HERE...
...EXCEPT *BATS.*
BATS AND *BEER CANS.*
AND *BONES.*
DON'T WORRY, THEY'RE NOT *HUMAN* BONES.
SURE *LOOKS* LIKE IT.
BEER
C'MON. BATS IN *HERE* ARE PROBABLY MORE AFRAID OF YOU THAN *YOU* ARE OF *THEM.*
WHAT'S THERE TO BE AFRAID OF?

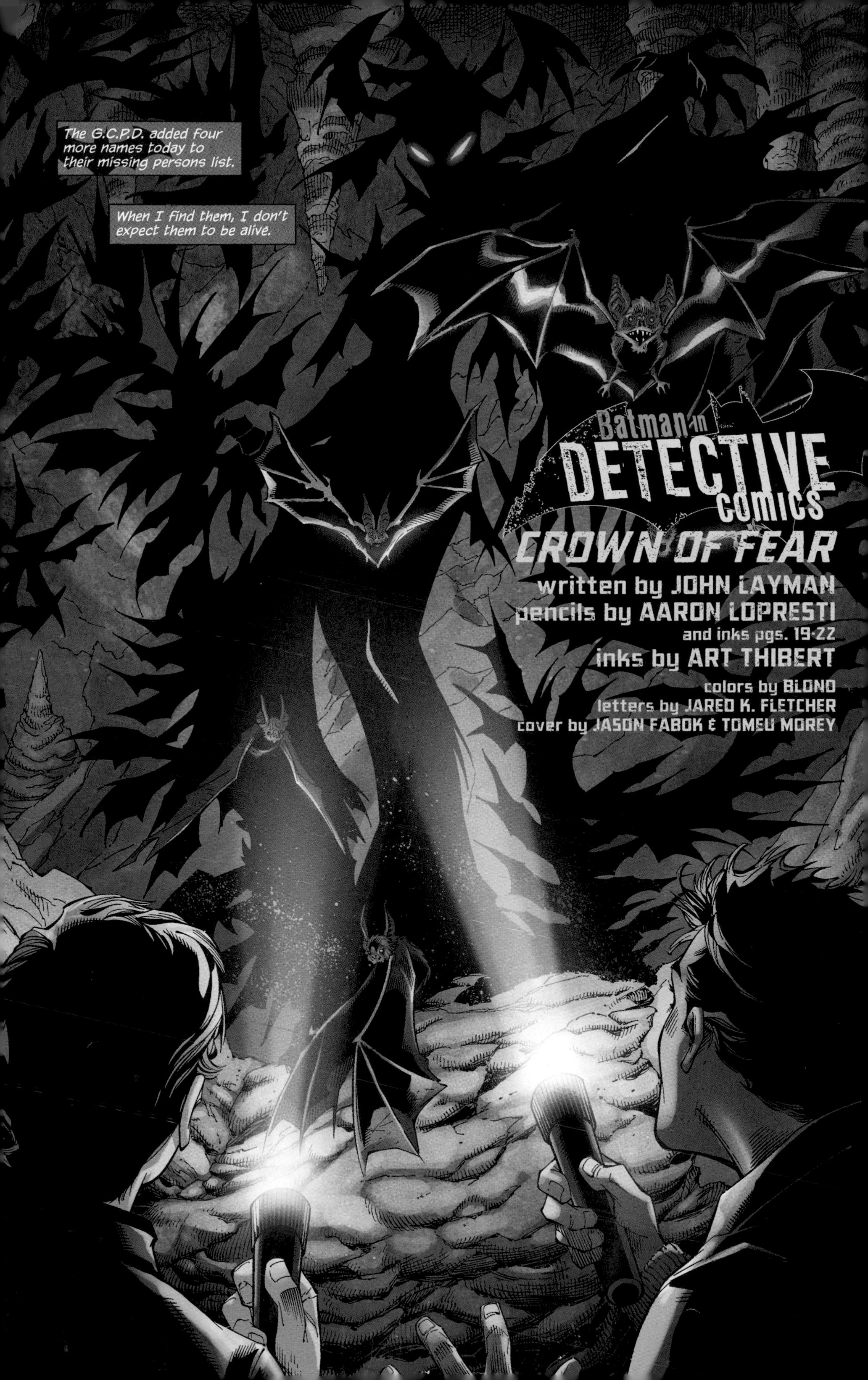
The G.C.P.D. added four more names today to their missing persons list.
When I find them, I don't expect them to be alive.
Batman in DETECTIVE COMICS
CROWN OF FEAR
written by JOHN LAYMAN
pencils by AARON LOPRESTI
and inks pgs. 19-22
inks by ART THIBERT
colors by BLOND
letters by JARED K. FLETCHER
cover by JASON FABOK & TOMEU MOREY

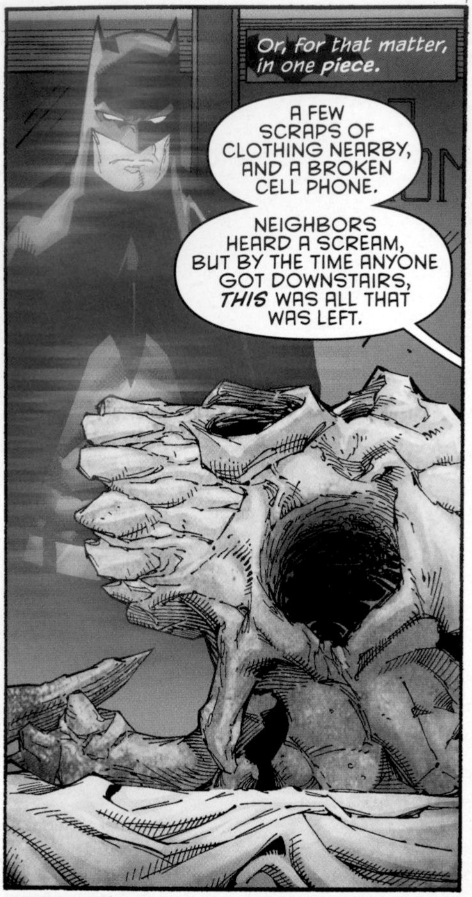
Or, for that matter, in one *piece.*
A FEW SCRAPS OF CLOTHING NEARBY, AND A BROKEN CELL PHONE.
NEIGHBORS HEARD A SCREAM, BUT BY THE TIME ANYONE GOT DOWNSTAIRS, *THIS* WAS ALL THAT WAS LEFT.

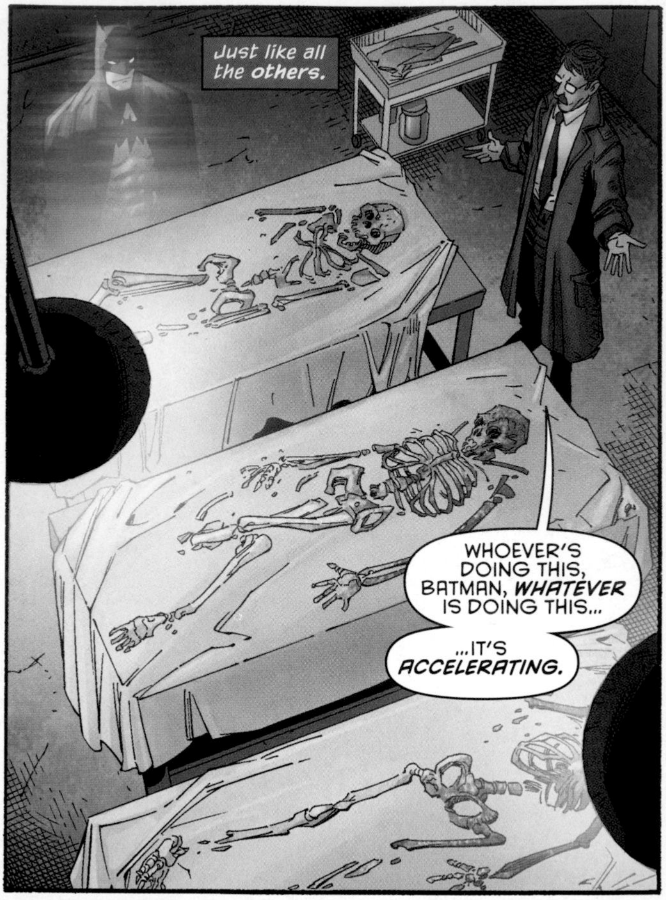
Just like all the *others.*
WHOEVER'S DOING THIS, BATMAN, *WHATEVER* IS DOING THIS...
...IT'S *ACCELERATING.*

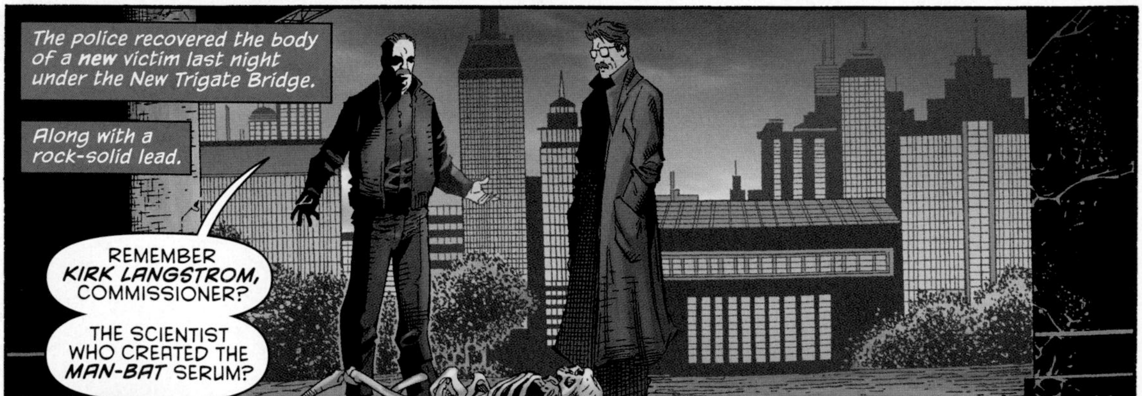
The police recovered the body of a *new* victim last night under the New Trigate Bridge.
Along with a rock-solid lead.
REMEMBER *KIRK LANGSTROM,* COMMISSIONER?
THE SCIENTIST WHO CREATED THE *MAN-BAT* SERUM?

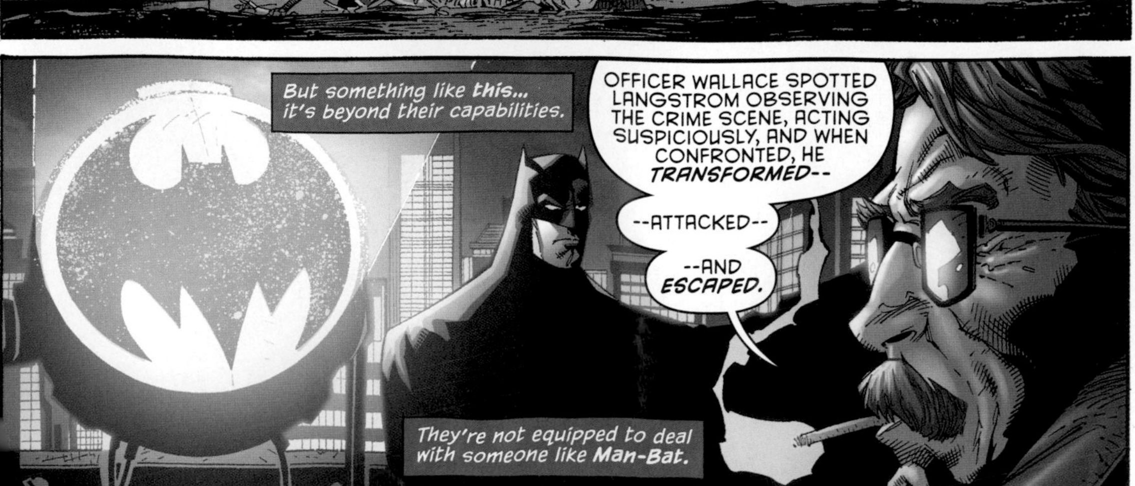
But something like *this...* it's beyond their capabilities.
OFFICER WALLACE SPOTTED LANGSTROM OBSERVING THE CRIME SCENE, ACTING SUSPICIOUSLY, AND WHEN CONFRONTED, HE *TRANSFORMED--*
--ATTACKED--
--AND *ESCAPED.*
They're not equipped to deal with someone like *Man-Bat.*

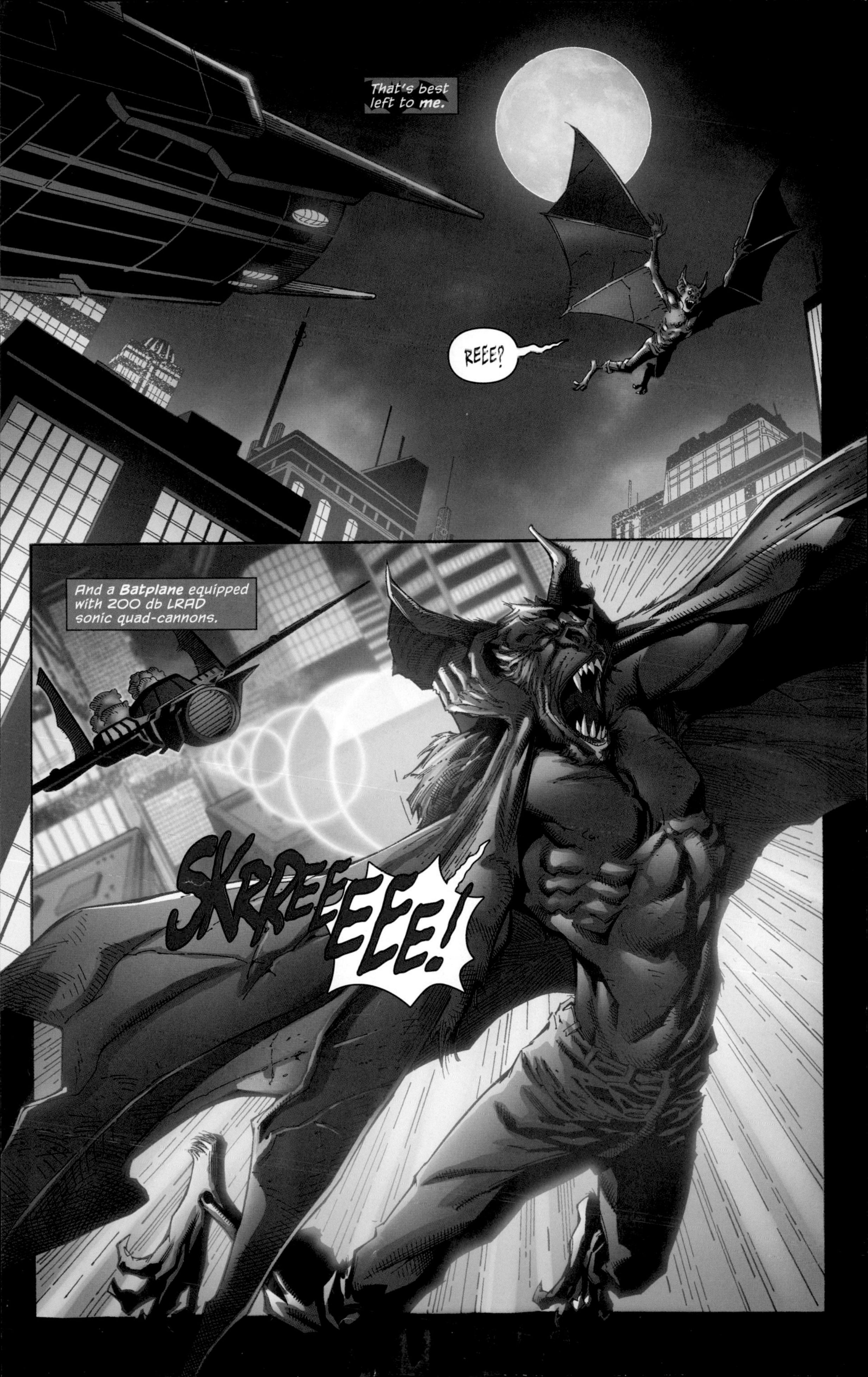
That's best left to me.
REEE?
And a Batplane equipped with 200 db LRAD sonic quad-cannons.
SKREEEEEE!

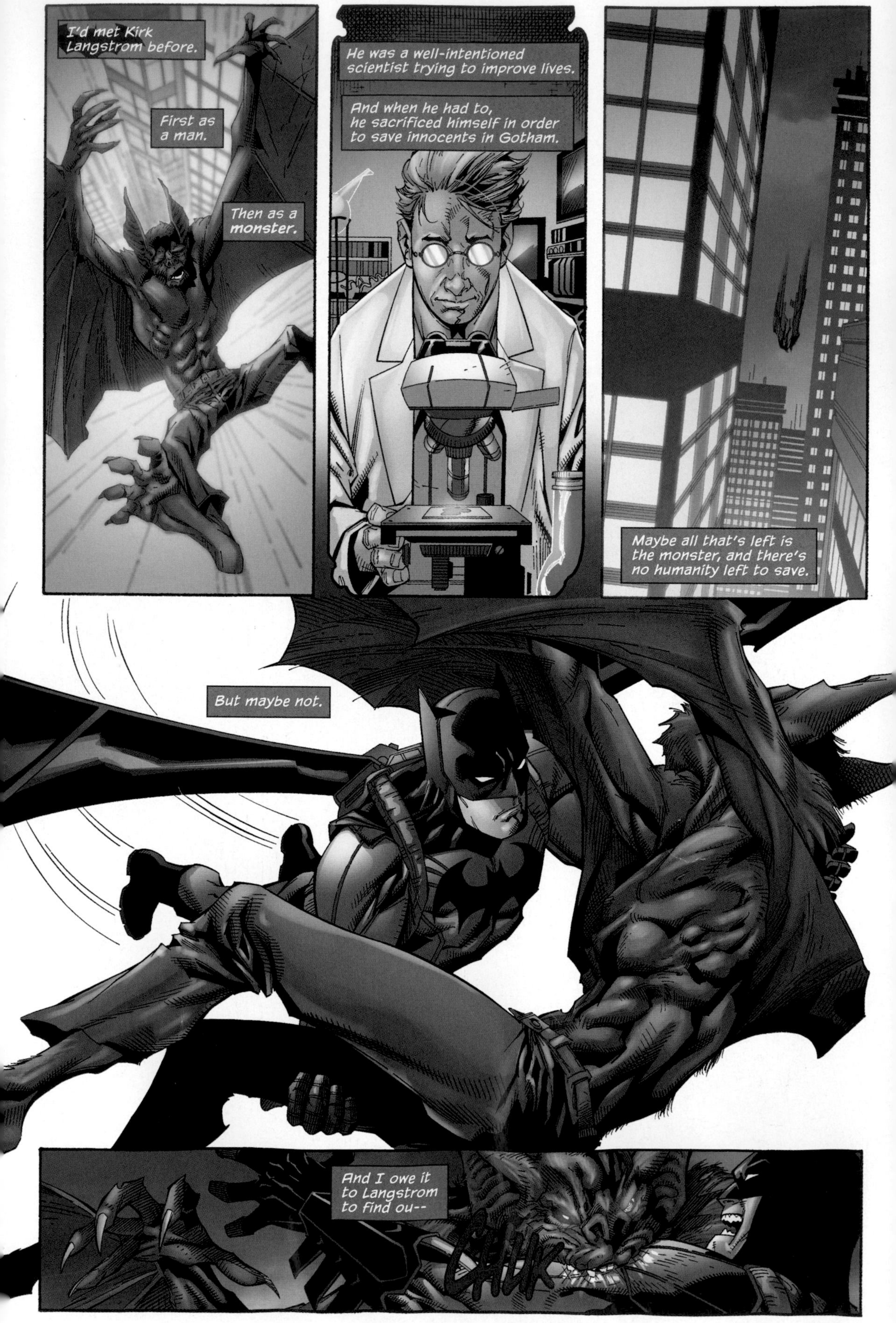
I'd met Kirk Langstrom before.
First as a man.
Then as a **monster**.
He was a well-intentioned scientist trying to improve lives.
And when he had to, he sacrificed himself in order to save innocents in Gotham.
Maybe all that's left is the monster, and there's no humanity left to save.
But maybe not.
And I owe it to Langstrom to find ou--
CHUK

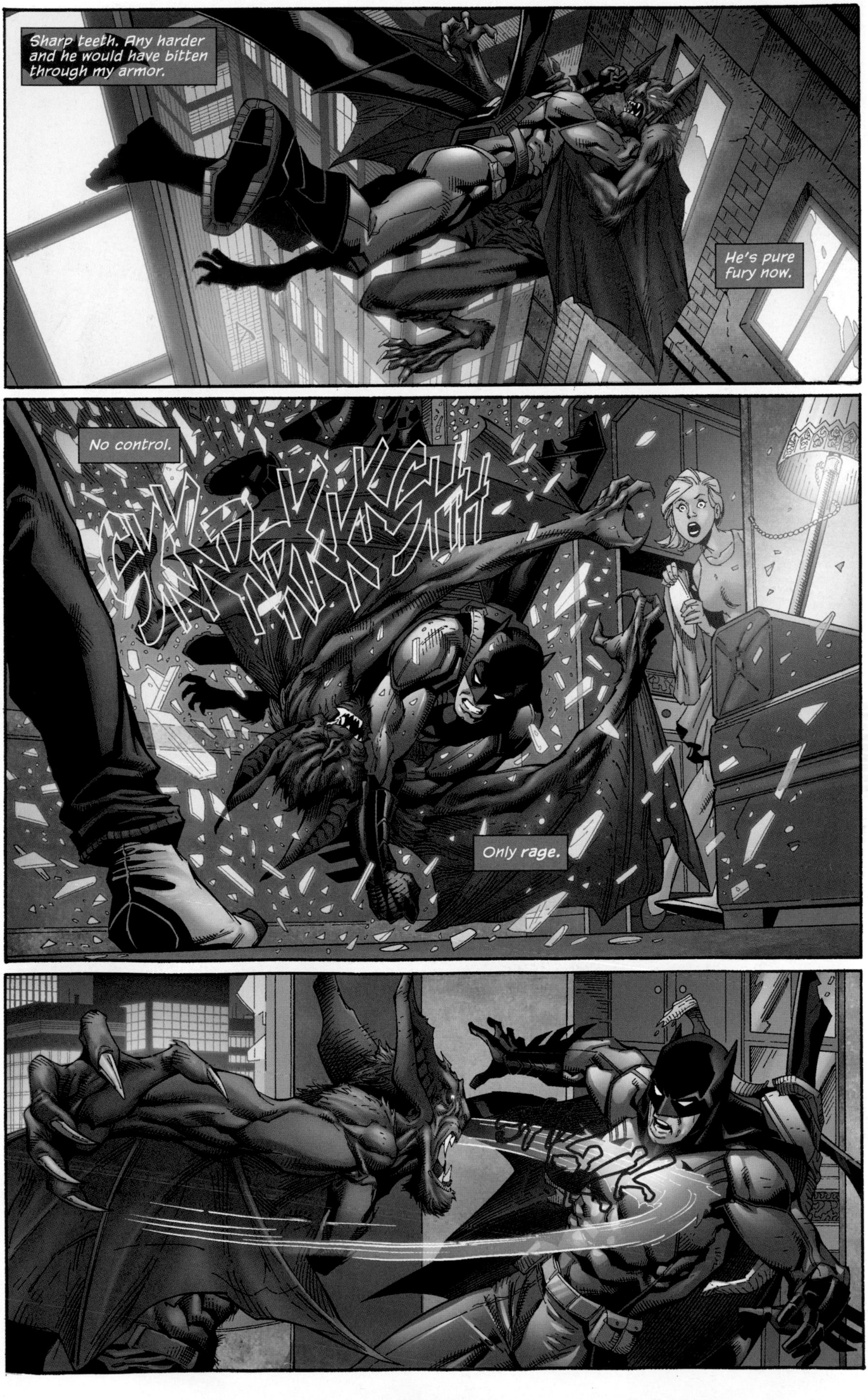
Sharp teeth. Any harder and he would have bitten through my armor.
He's pure fury now.
No control.
Only rage.

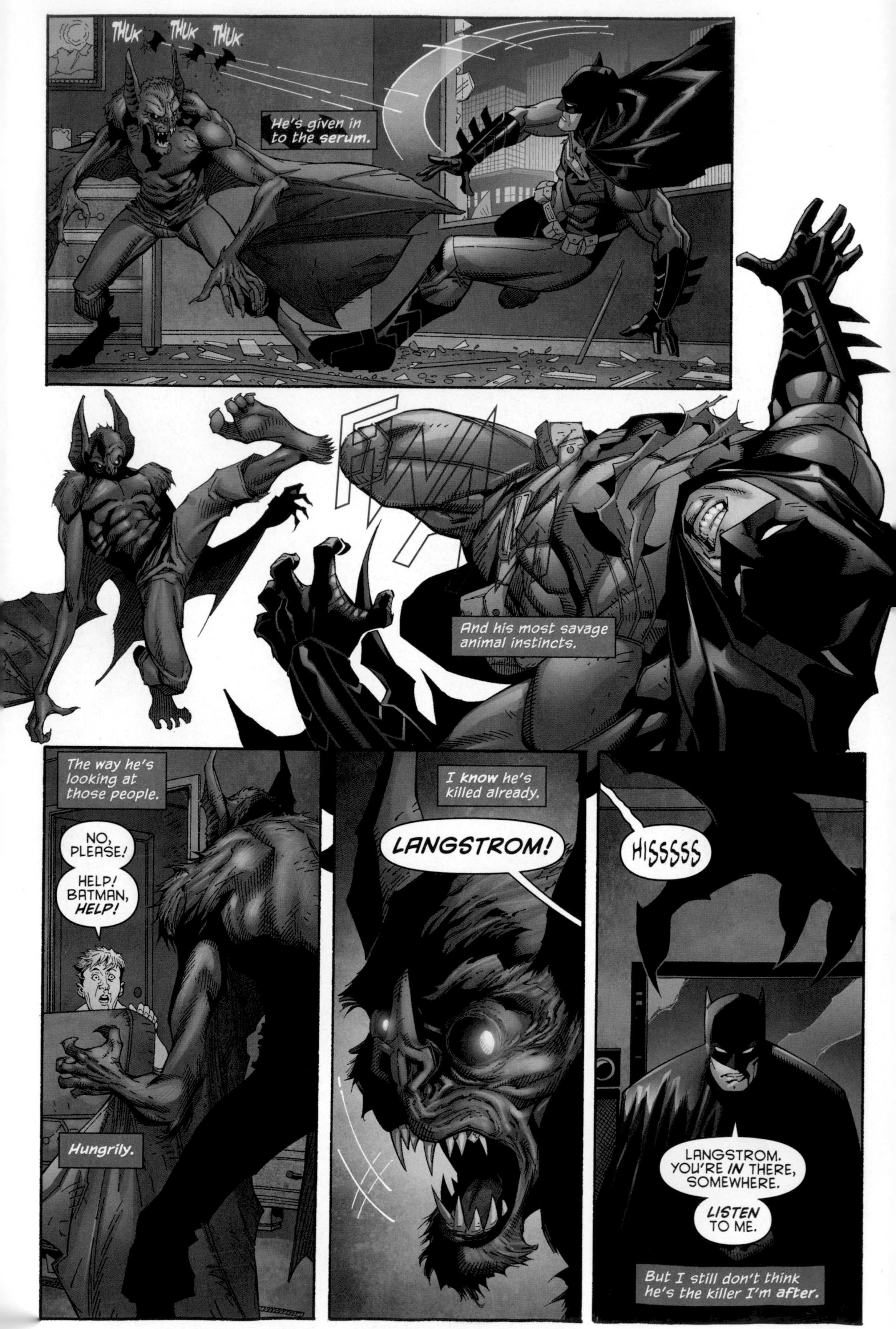
THUK THUK THUK
He's given in to the serum.
And his most savage animal instincts.
The way he's looking at those people.
NO, PLEASE!
HELP! BATMAN, HELP!
Hungrily.
I know he's killed already.
LANGSTROM!
HISSSSS
LANGSTROM. YOU'RE IN THERE, SOMEWHERE.
LISTEN TO ME.
But I still don't think he's the killer I'm after.

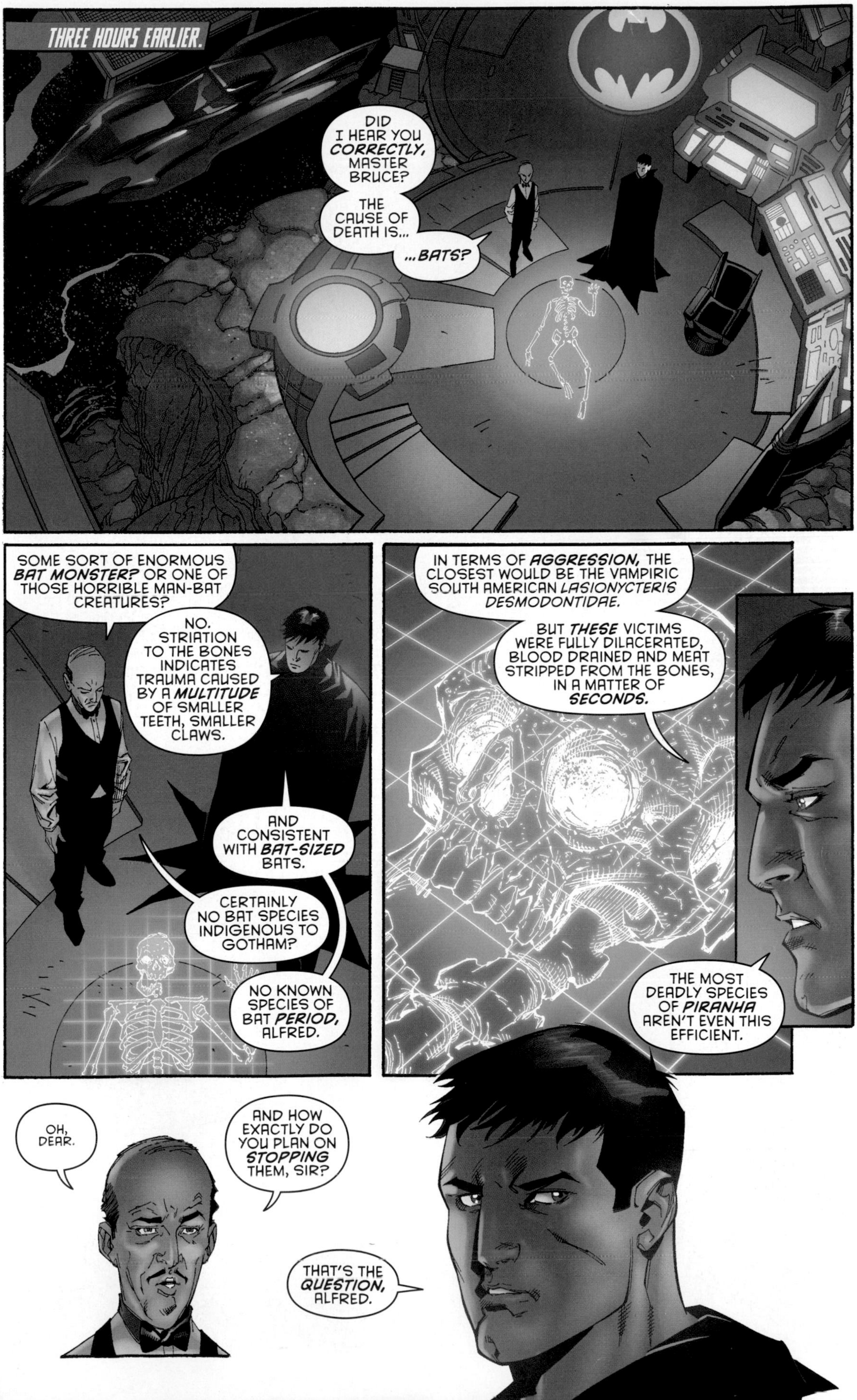
THREE HOURS EARLIER.
DID I HEAR YOU CORRECTLY, MASTER BRUCE?
THE CAUSE OF DEATH IS...
...BATS?
SOME SORT OF ENORMOUS BAT MONSTER? OR ONE OF THOSE HORRIBLE MAN-BAT CREATURES?
NO. STRIATION TO THE BONES INDICATES TRAUMA CAUSED BY A MULTITUDE OF SMALLER TEETH, SMALLER CLAWS.
AND CONSISTENT WITH BAT-SIZED BATS.
CERTAINLY NO BAT SPECIES INDIGENOUS TO GOTHAM?
NO KNOWN SPECIES OF BAT PERIOD, ALFRED.
IN TERMS OF AGGRESSION, THE CLOSEST WOULD BE THE VAMPIRIC SOUTH AMERICAN LASIONYCTERIS DESMODONTIDAE.
BUT THESE VICTIMS WERE FULLY DILACERATED, BLOOD DRAINED AND MEAT STRIPPED FROM THE BONES, IN A MATTER OF SECONDS.
THE MOST DEADLY SPECIES OF PIRANHA AREN'T EVEN THIS EFFICIENT.
OH, DEAR.
AND HOW EXACTLY DO YOU PLAN ON STOPPING THEM, SIR?
THAT'S THE QUESTION, ALFRED.

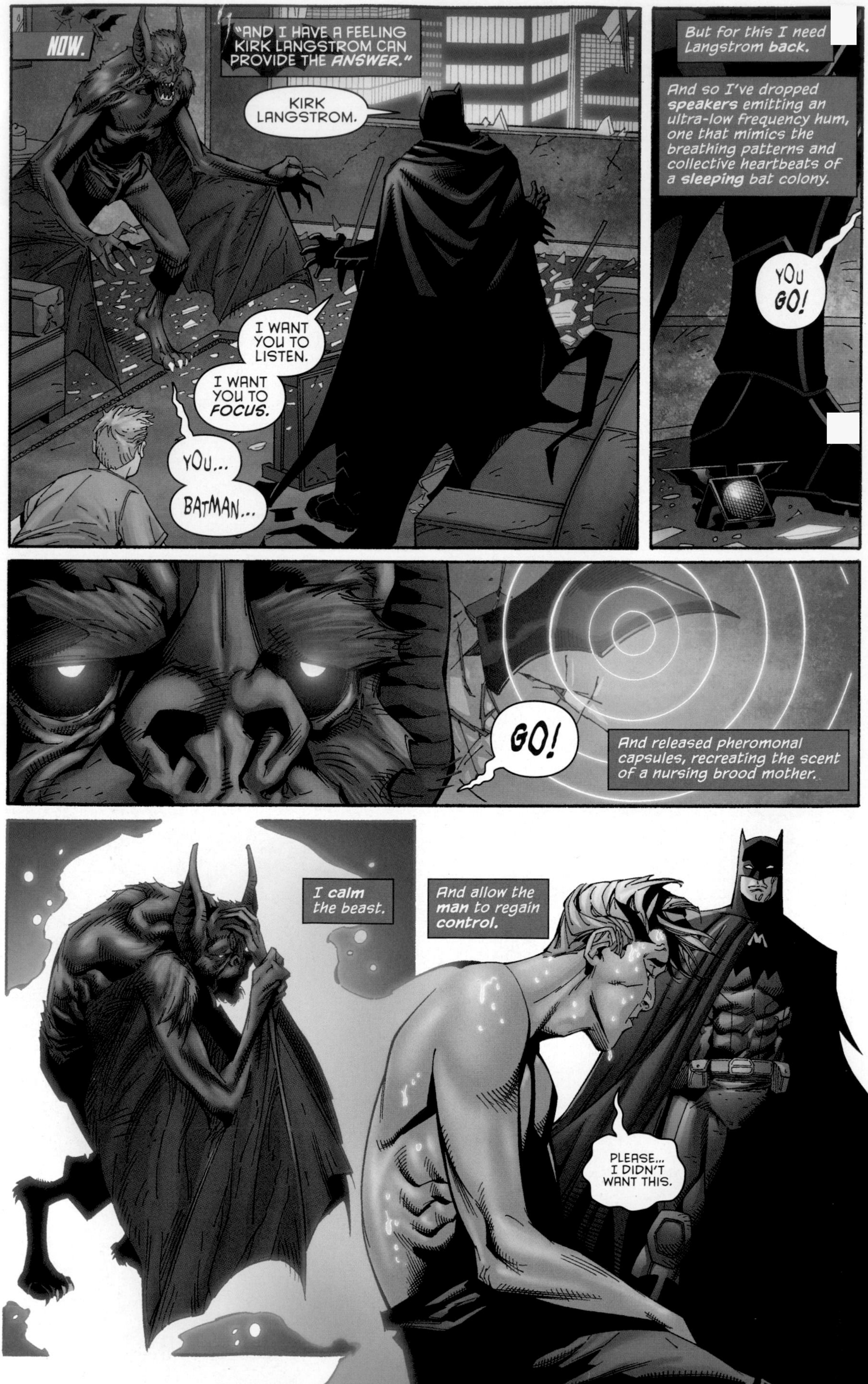
NOW.
"AND I HAVE A FEELING KIRK LANGSTROM CAN PROVIDE THE ANSWER."
KIRK LANGSTROM.
I WANT YOU TO LISTEN.
I WANT YOU TO FOCUS.
YOU...
BATMAN...
But for this I need Langstrom back.
And so I've dropped speakers emitting an ultra-low frequency hum, one that mimics the breathing patterns and collective heartbeats of a sleeping bat colony.
YOU GO!
GO!
And released pheromonal capsules, recreating the scent of a nursing brood mother.
I calm the beast.
And allow the man to regain control.
PLEASE... I DIDN'T WANT THIS.

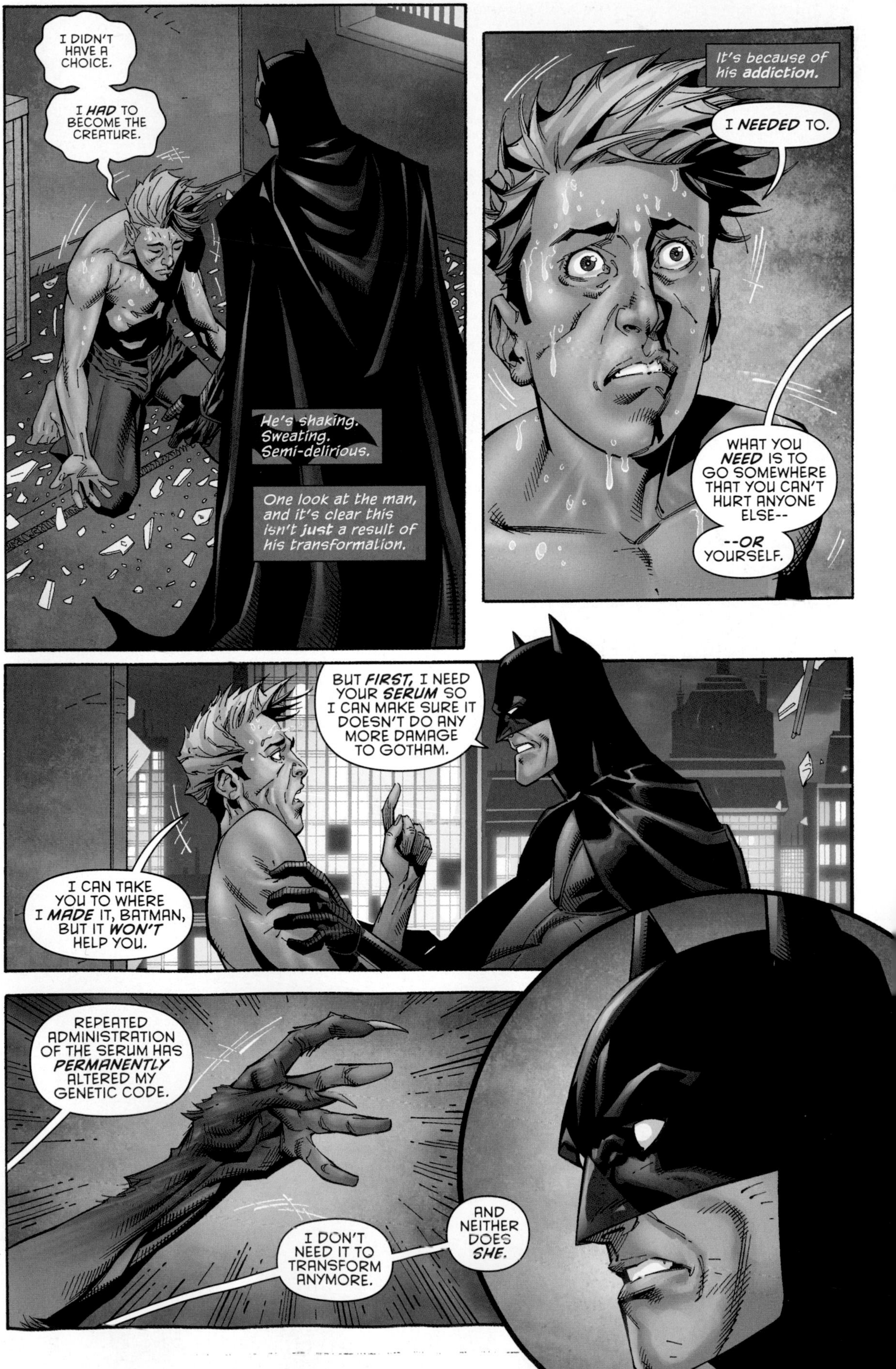
I DIDN'T HAVE A CHOICE.
I HAD TO BECOME THE CREATURE.
He's shaking. Sweating. Semi-delirious.
One look at the man, and it's clear this isn't just a result of his transformation.
It's because of his addiction.
I NEEDED TO.
WHAT YOU NEED IS TO GO SOMEWHERE THAT YOU CAN'T HURT ANYONE ELSE--
--OR YOURSELF.
BUT FIRST, I NEED YOUR SERUM SO I CAN MAKE SURE IT DOESN'T DO ANY MORE DAMAGE TO GOTHAM.
I CAN TAKE YOU TO WHERE I MADE IT, BATMAN, BUT IT WON'T HELP YOU.
REPEATED ADMINISTRATION OF THE SERUM HAS PERMANENTLY ALTERED MY GENETIC CODE.
I DON'T NEED IT TO TRANSFORM ANYMORE.
AND NEITHER DOES SHE.

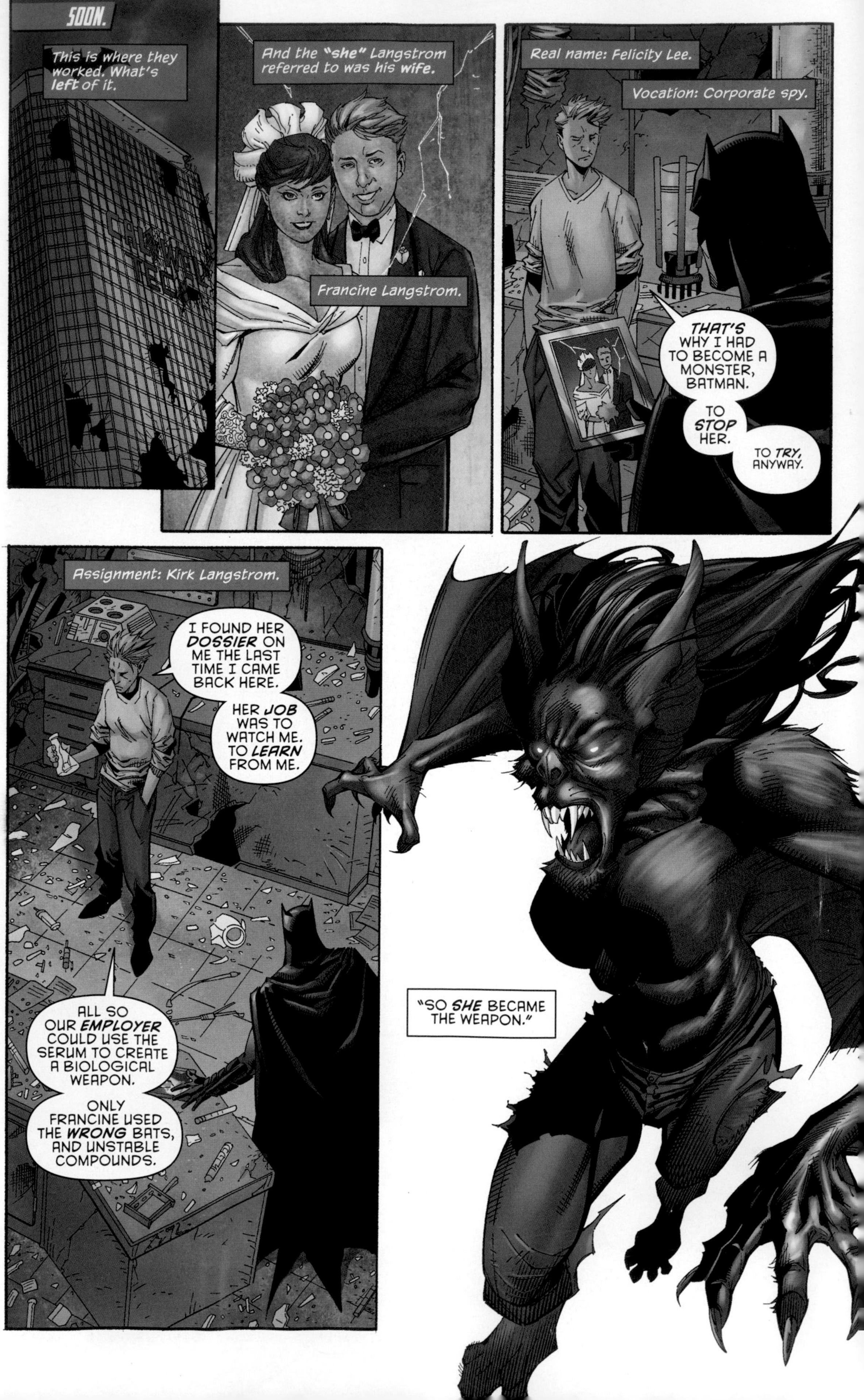
SOON.
This is where they worked. What's left of it.
And the "she" Langstrom referred to was his wife.
Francine Langstrom.
Real name: Felicity Lee.
Vocation: Corporate spy.
THAT'S WHY I HAD TO BECOME A MONSTER, BATMAN.
TO STOP HER.
TO TRY, ANYWAY.
Assignment: Kirk Langstrom.
I FOUND HER DOSSIER ON ME THE LAST TIME I CAME BACK HERE.
HER JOB WAS TO WATCH ME. TO LEARN FROM ME.
ALL SO OUR EMPLOYER COULD USE THE SERUM TO CREATE A BIOLOGICAL WEAPON.
ONLY FRANCINE USED THE WRONG BATS, AND UNSTABLE COMPOUNDS.
"SO SHE BECAME THE WEAPON."

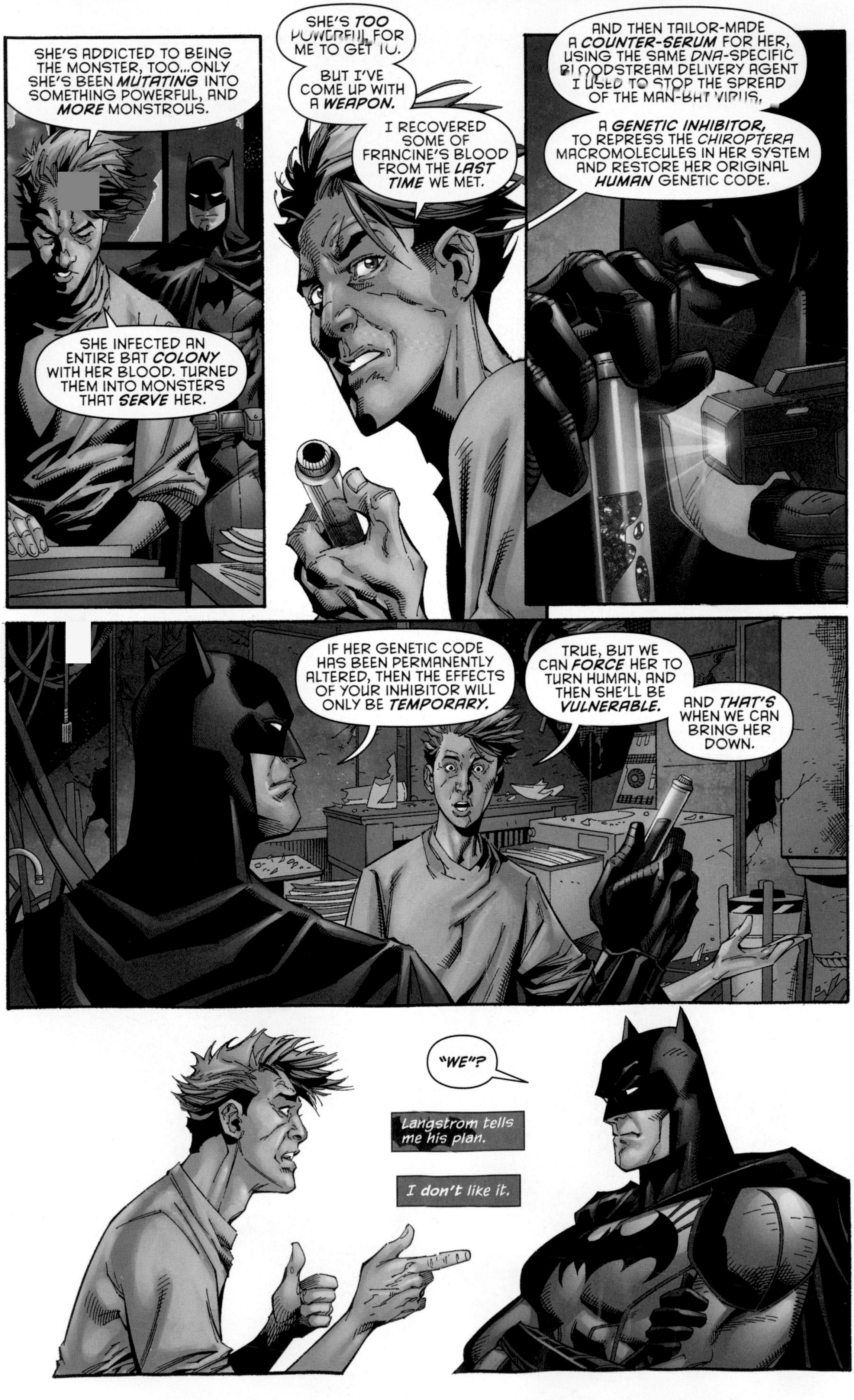
SHE'S ADDICTED TO BEING THE MONSTER, TOO...ONLY SHE'S BEEN MUTATING INTO SOMETHING POWERFUL, AND MORE MONSTROUS.
SHE INFECTED AN ENTIRE BAT COLONY WITH HER BLOOD. TURNED THEM INTO MONSTERS THAT SERVE HER.
SHE'S TOO POWERFUL FOR ME TO GET TO.
BUT I'VE COME UP WITH A WEAPON.
I RECOVERED SOME OF FRANCINE'S BLOOD FROM THE LAST TIME WE MET.
AND THEN TAILOR-MADE A COUNTER-SERUM FOR HER, USING THE SAME DNA-SPECIFIC BLOODSTREAM DELIVERY AGENT I USED TO STOP THE SPREAD OF THE MAN-BAT VIRUS.
A GENETIC INHIBITOR, TO REPRESS THE CHIROPTERA MACROMOLECULES IN HER SYSTEM AND RESTORE HER ORIGINAL HUMAN GENETIC CODE.
IF HER GENETIC CODE HAS BEEN PERMANENTLY ALTERED, THEN THE EFFECTS OF YOUR INHIBITOR WILL ONLY BE TEMPORARY.
TRUE, BUT WE CAN FORCE HER TO TURN HUMAN, AND THEN SHE'LL BE VULNERABLE.
AND THAT'S WHEN WE CAN BRING HER DOWN.
"WE"?
Langstrom tells me his plan.
I don't like it.

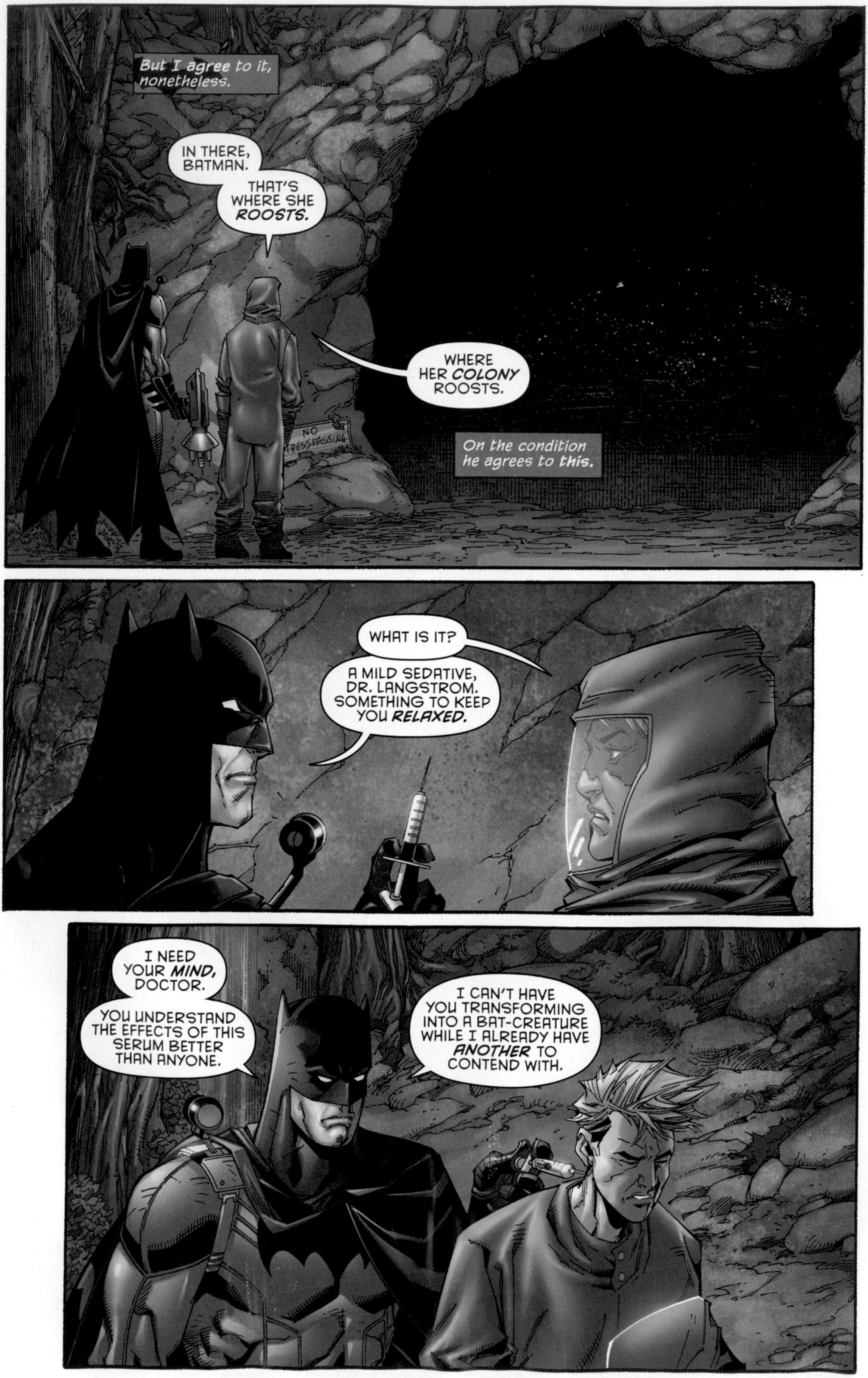
But I agree to it, nonetheless.
IN THERE, BATMAN.
THAT'S WHERE SHE ROOSTS.
WHERE HER COLONY ROOSTS.
NO TRESSPASSING
On the condition he agrees to this.
WHAT IS IT?
A MILD SEDATIVE, DR. LANGSTROM. SOMETHING TO KEEP YOU RELAXED.
I NEED YOUR MIND, DOCTOR.
YOU UNDERSTAND THE EFFECTS OF THIS SERUM BETTER THAN ANYONE.
I CAN'T HAVE YOU TRANSFORMING INTO A BAT-CREATURE WHILE I ALREADY HAVE ANOTHER TO CONTEND WITH.

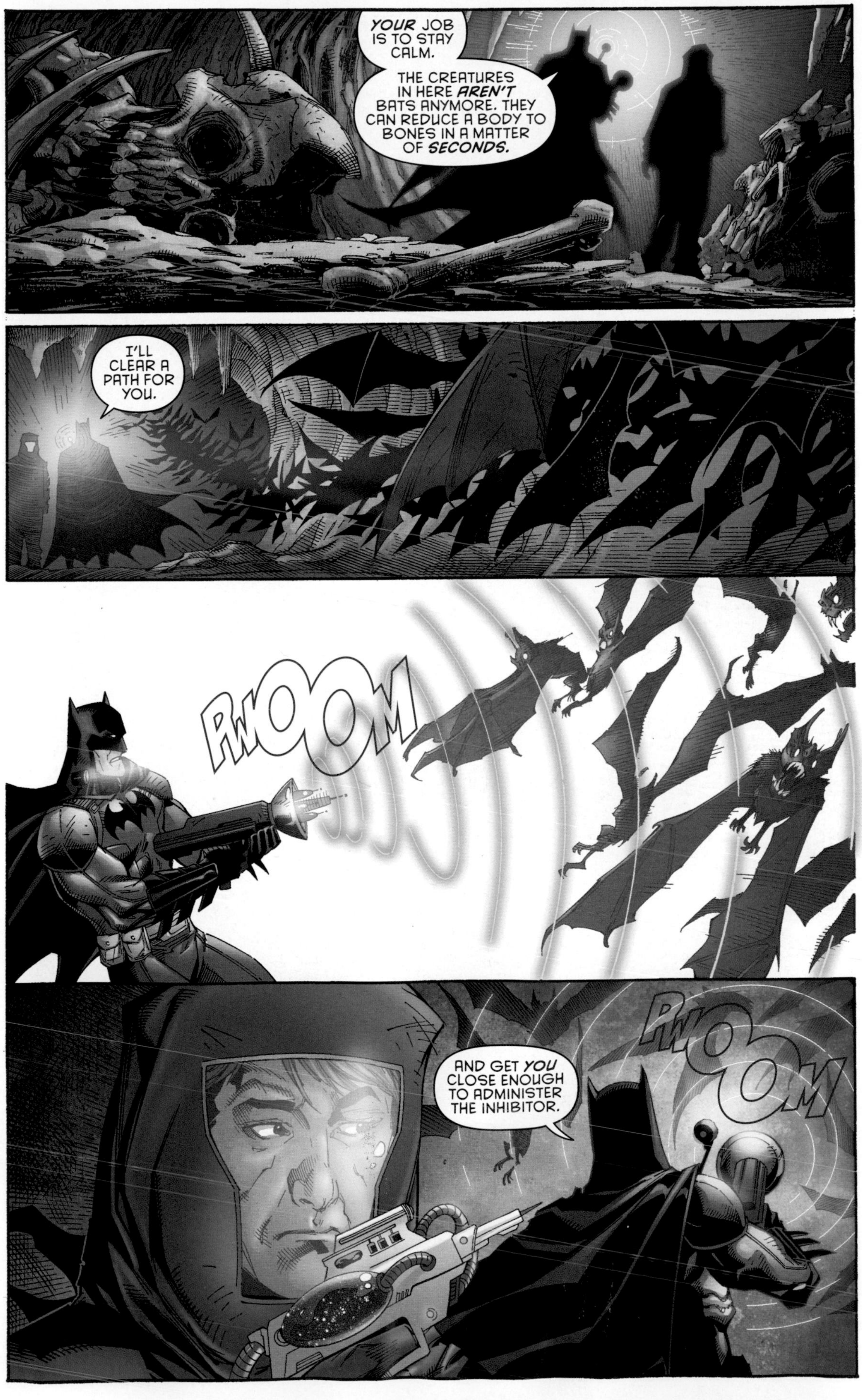
YOUR JOB IS TO STAY CALM.
THE CREATURES IN HERE AREN'T BATS ANYMORE. THEY CAN REDUCE A BODY TO BONES IN A MATTER OF SECONDS.
I'LL CLEAR A PATH FOR YOU.
PWOOM
PWOOM
AND GET YOU CLOSE ENOUGH TO ADMINISTER THE INHIBITOR.

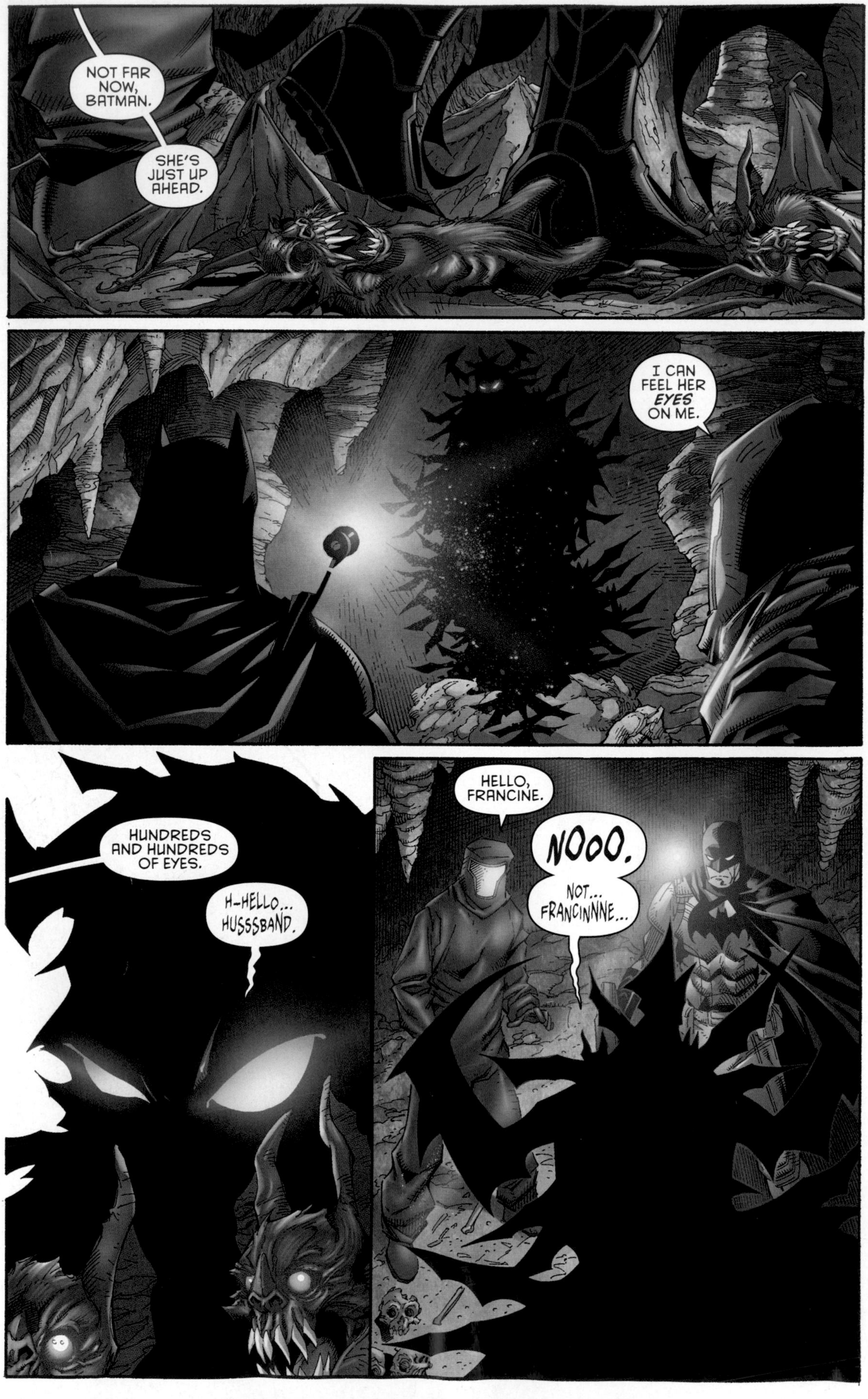
NOT FAR NOW, BATMAN.
SHE'S JUST UP AHEAD.
I CAN FEEL HER *EYES* ON ME.
HUNDREDS AND HUNDREDS OF EYES.
H-HELLO... HUSSSBAND.
HELLO, FRANCINE.
NOOO.
NOT... FRANCINNNE...

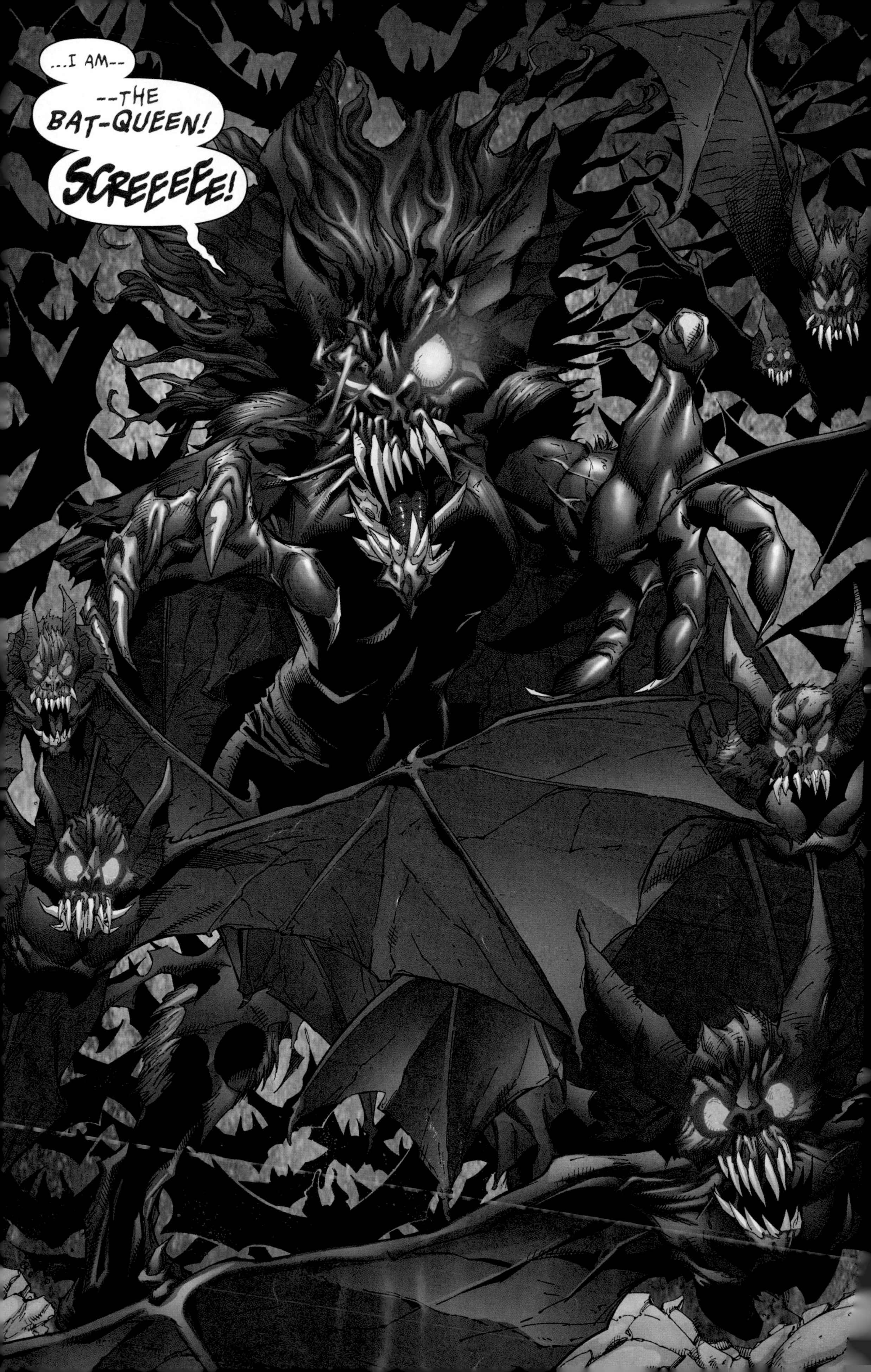
...I AM--
--THE BAT-QUEEN!
SCREEEEEE!

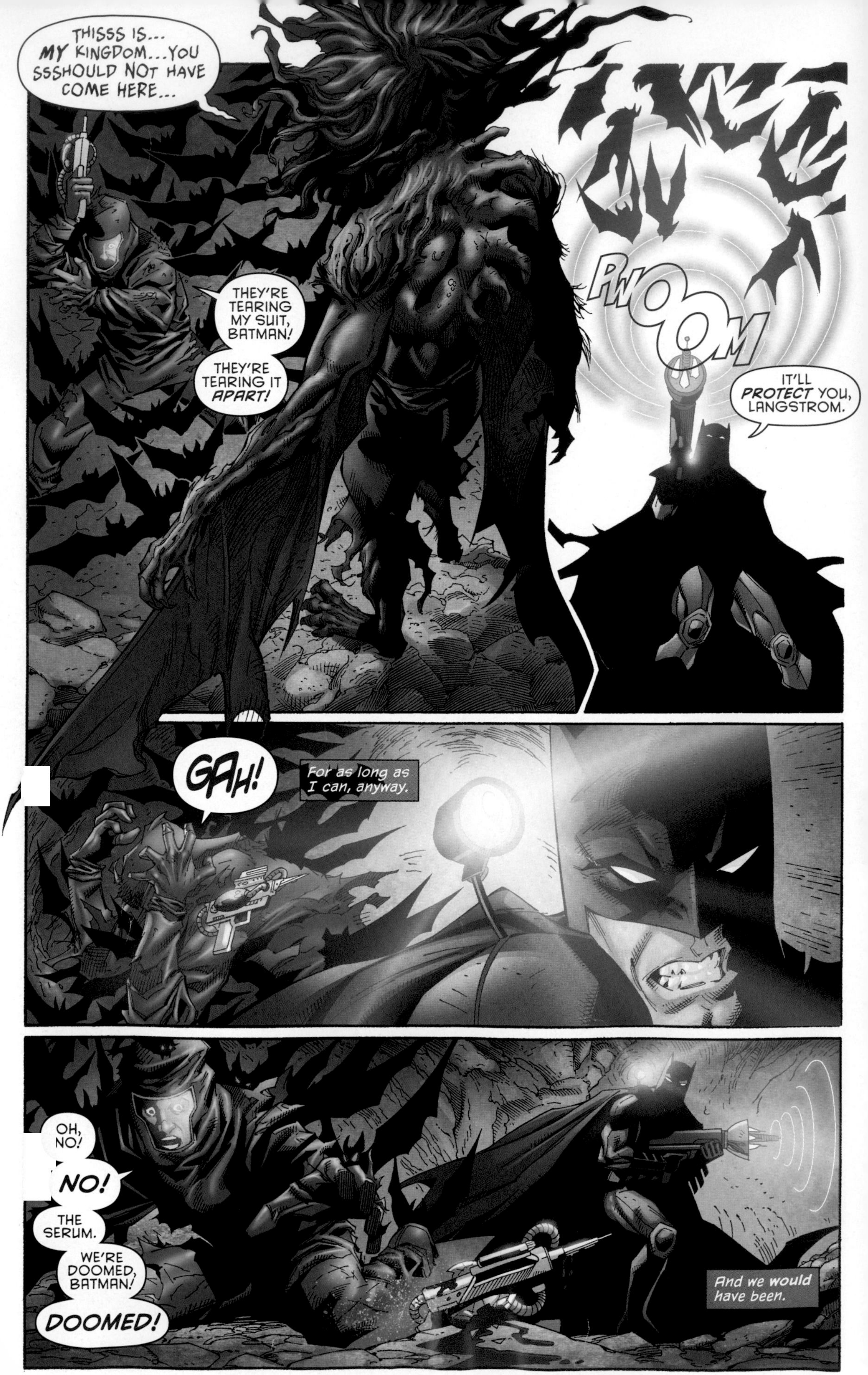
THISSS IS... MY KINGDOM...YOU SSSHOULD NOT HAVE COME HERE...
THEY'RE TEARING MY SUIT, BATMAN!
THEY'RE TEARING IT APART!
PWOOOM
IT'LL PROTECT YOU, LANGSTROM.
GAH!
For as long as I can, anyway.
OH, NO!
NO!
THE SERUM.
WE'RE DOOMED, BATMAN!
DOOMED!
And we would have been.

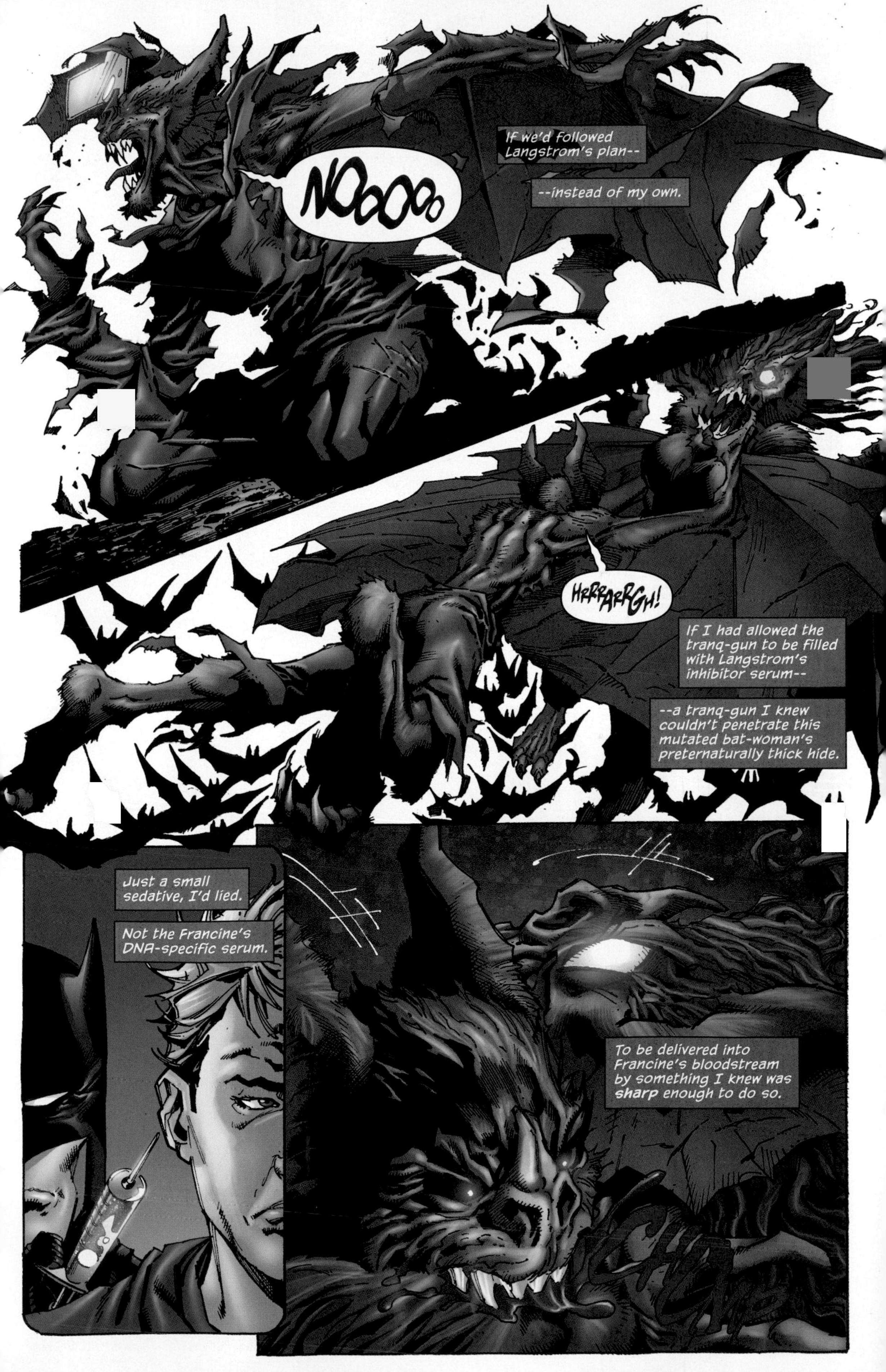
NOOOOO
If we'd followed Langstrom's plan--
--instead of my own.
HRRRARRGH!
If I had allowed the tranq-gun to be filled with Langstrom's inhibitor serum--
--a tranq-gun I knew couldn't penetrate this mutated bat-woman's preternaturally thick hide.
Just a small sedative, I'd lied.
Not the Francine's DNA-specific serum.
To be delivered into Francine's bloodstream by something I knew was **sharp** enough to do so.

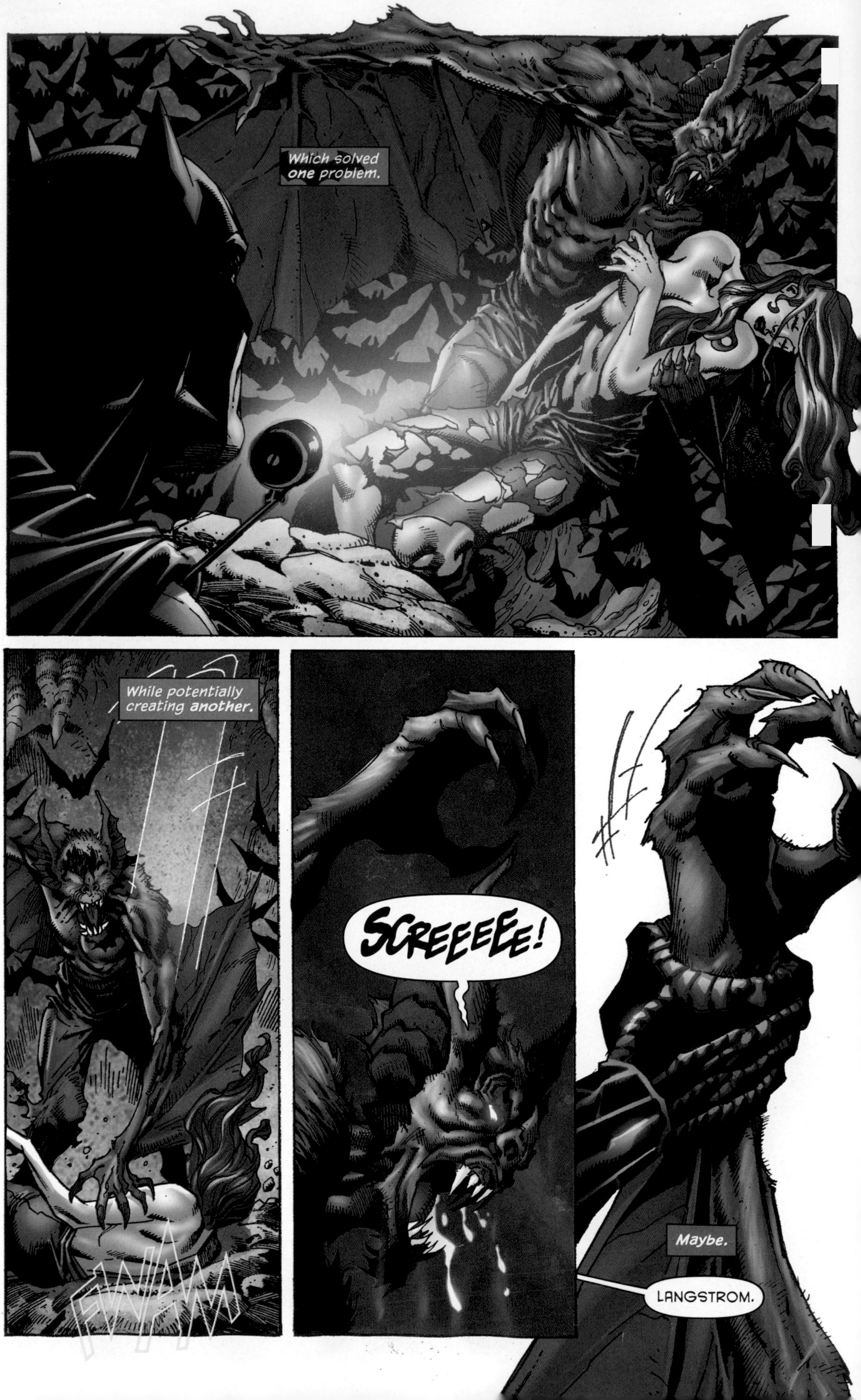
Which solved one problem.
While potentially creating another.
FWAM
SCREEEEEe!
Maybe.
LANGSTROM.

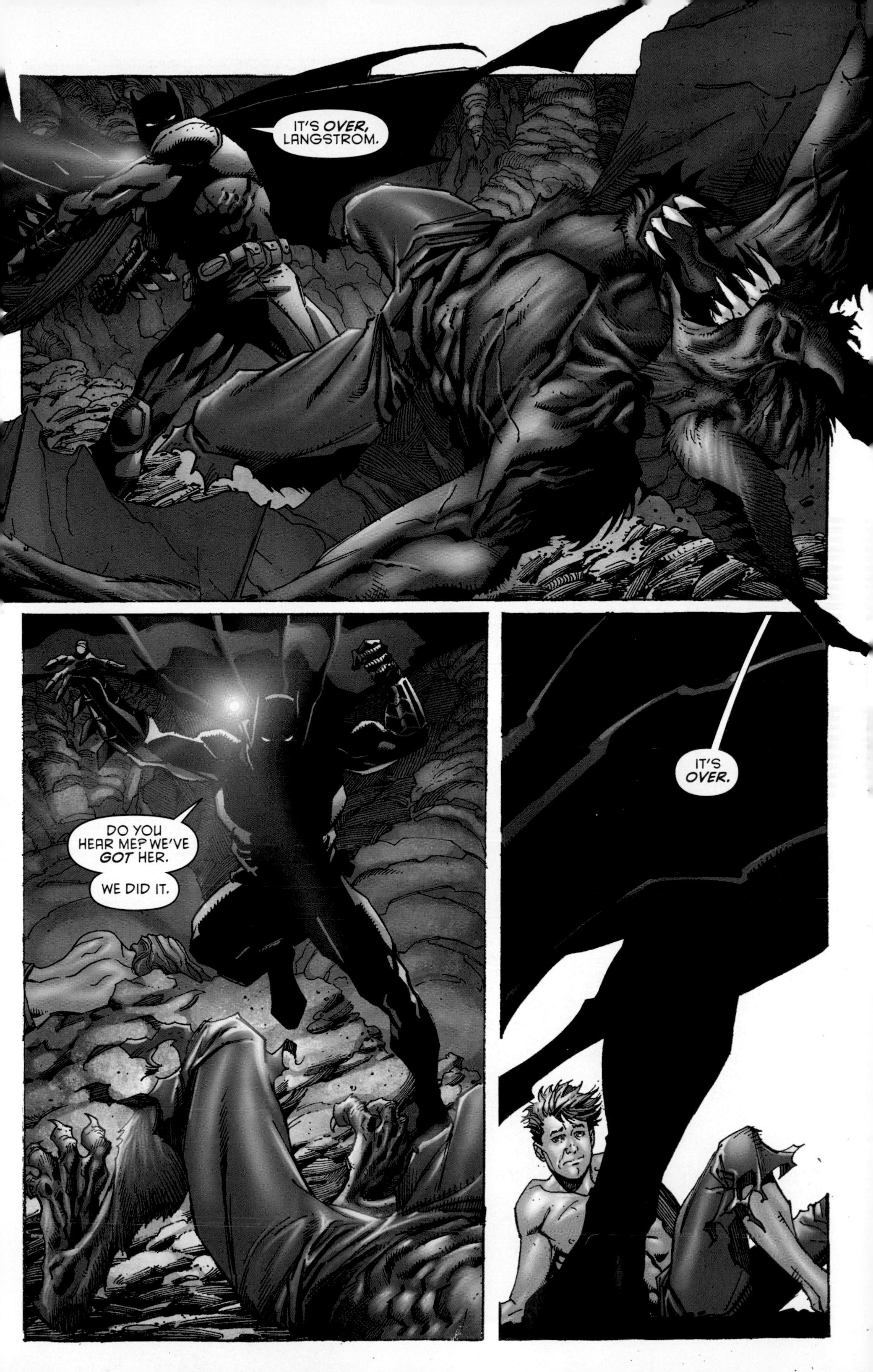
IT'S OVER, LANGSTROM.
DO YOU HEAR ME? WE'VE GOT HER.
WE DID IT.
IT'S OVER.

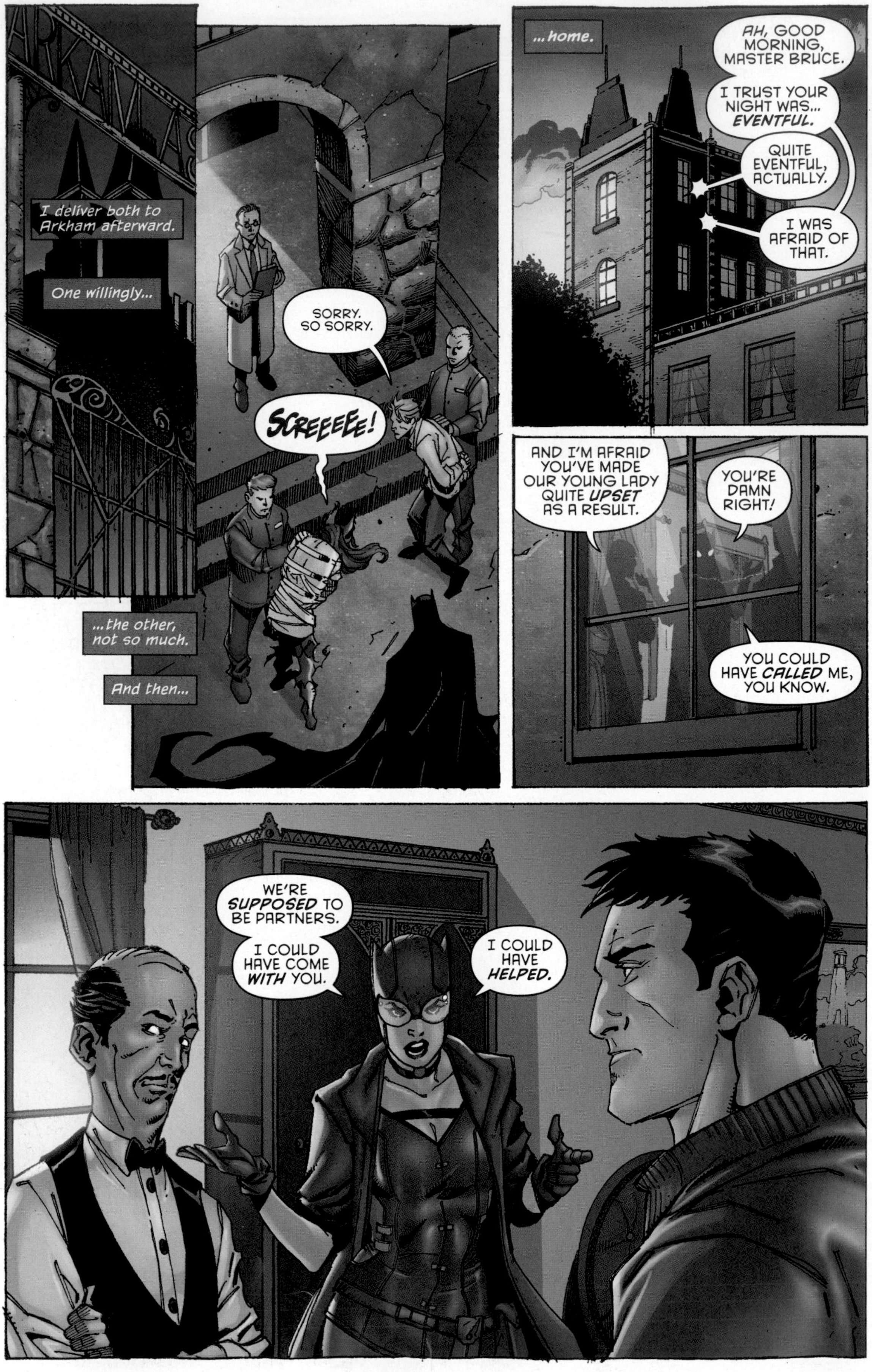
I deliver both to Arkham afterward.
One willingly...
SORRY. SO SORRY.
SCREEEEEE!
...the other, not so much.
And then...
...home.
AH, GOOD MORNING, MASTER BRUCE.
I TRUST YOUR NIGHT WAS... EVENTFUL.
QUITE EVENTFUL, ACTUALLY.
I WAS AFRAID OF THAT.
AND I'M AFRAID YOU'VE MADE OUR YOUNG LADY QUITE UPSET AS A RESULT.
YOU'RE DAMN RIGHT!
YOU COULD HAVE CALLED ME, YOU KNOW.
WE'RE SUPPOSED TO BE PARTNERS.
I COULD HAVE COME WITH YOU.
I COULD HAVE HELPED.

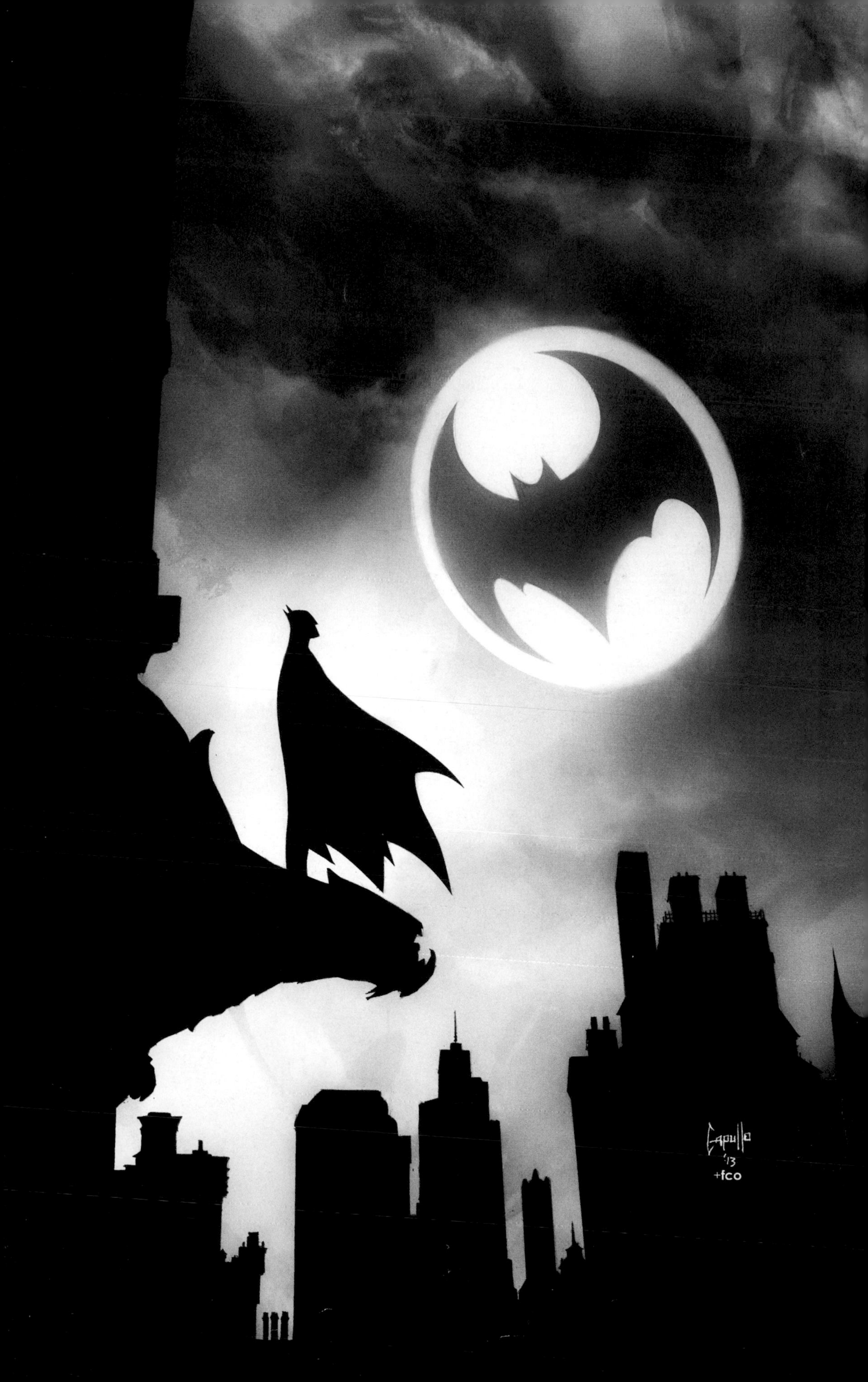
Capullo
'13
+fco

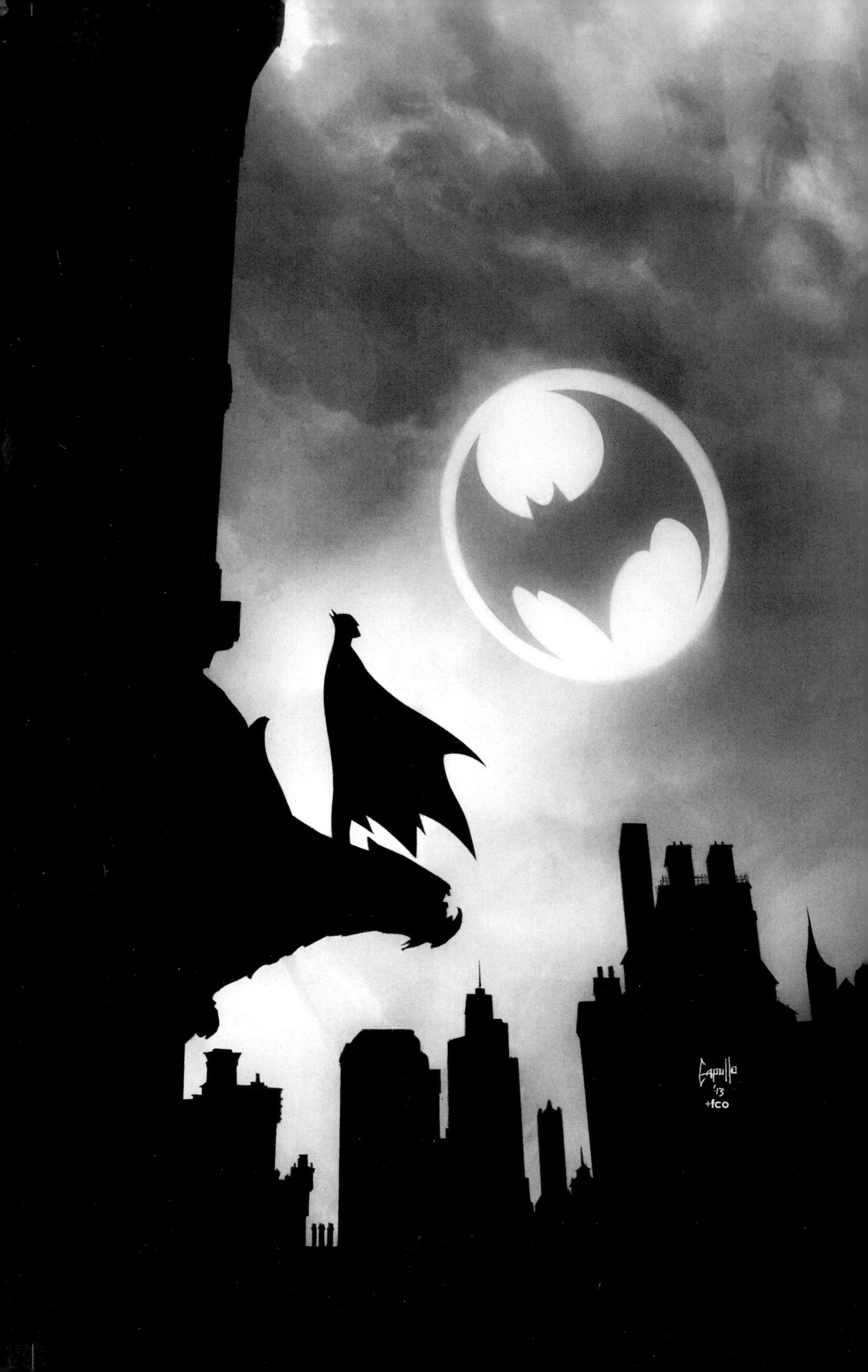
Capullo
'13
+fco

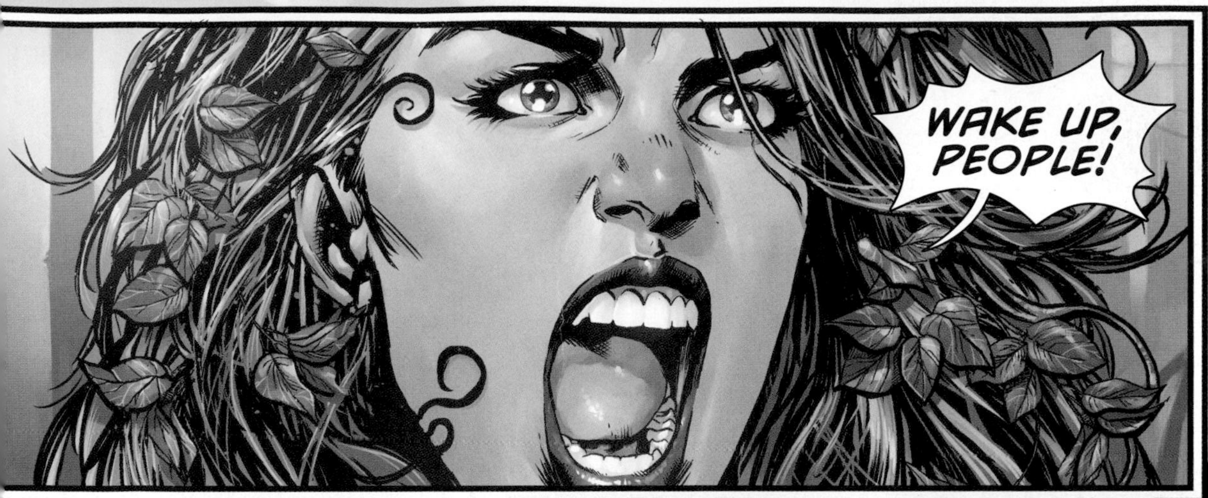
WAKE UP, PEOPLE!

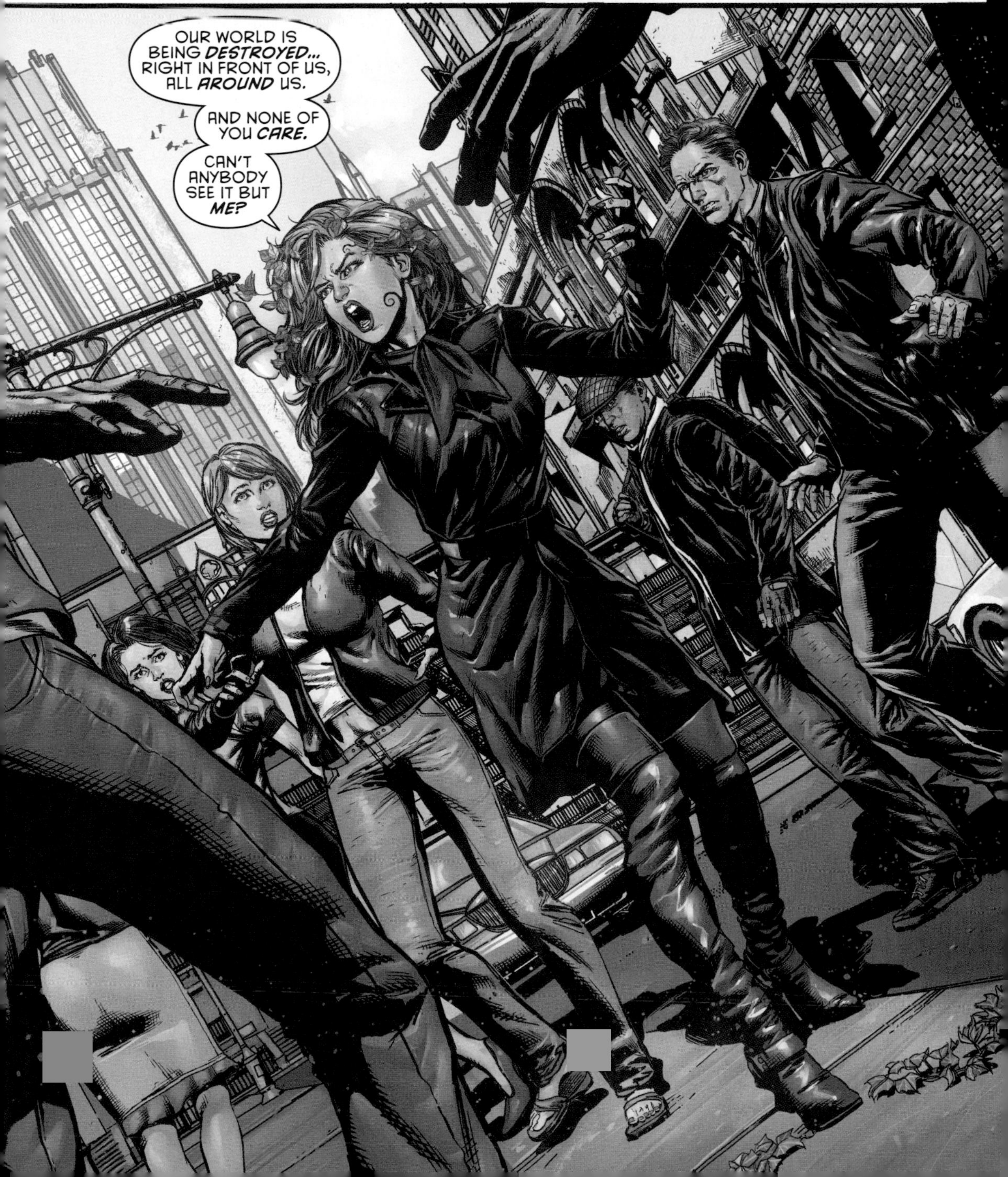
OUR WORLD IS BEING DESTROYED... RIGHT IN FRONT OF US, ALL AROUND US.
AND NONE OF YOU CARE.
CAN'T ANYBODY SEE IT BUT ME?

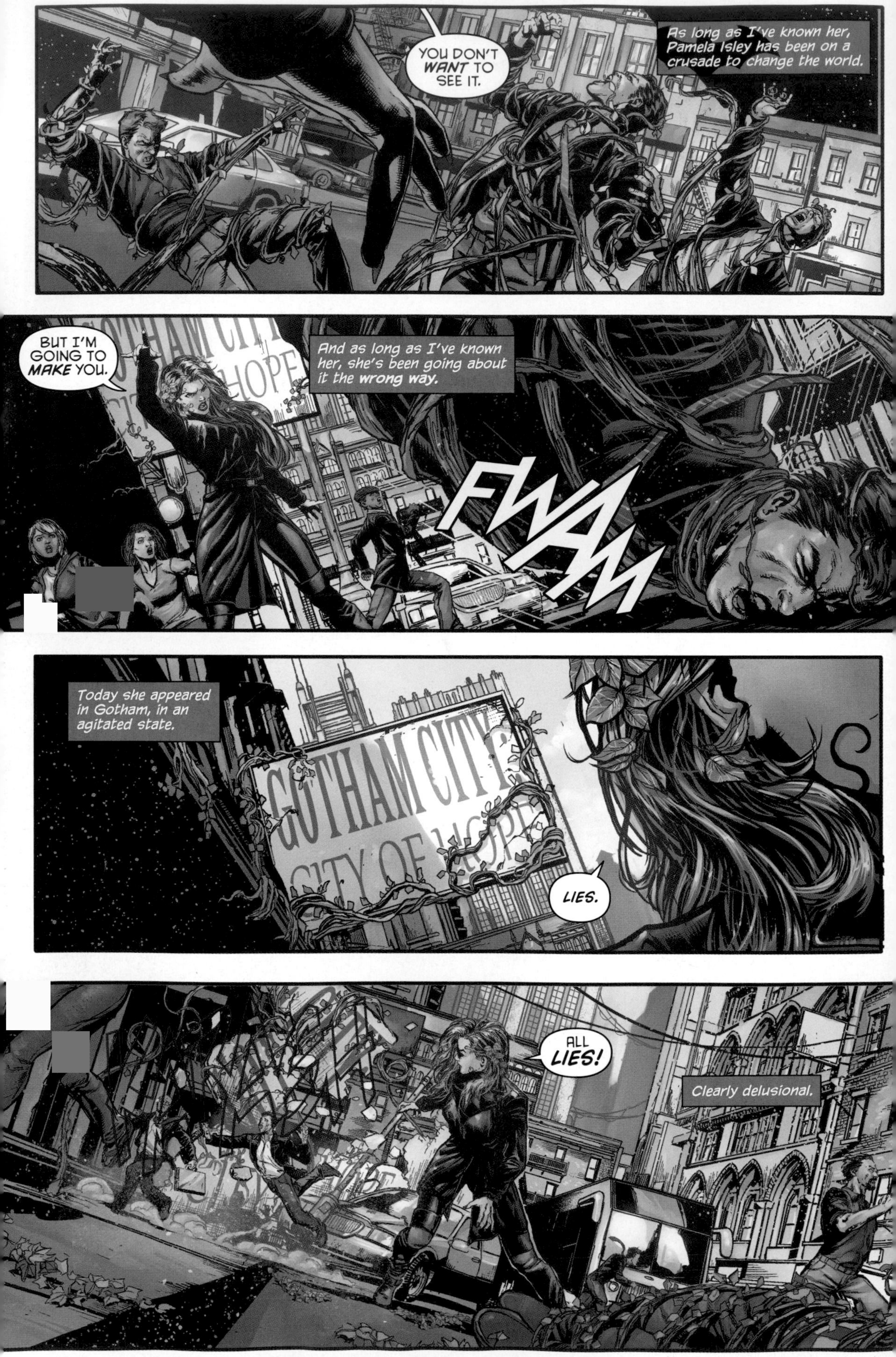
YOU DON'T *WANT* TO SEE IT.
As long as I've known her, Pamela Isley has been on a crusade to change the world.
BUT I'M GOING TO *MAKE* YOU.
And as long as I've known her, she's been going about it the **wrong way.**
FWAM
Today she appeared in Gotham, in an agitated state.
GOTHAM CITY
LIES.
ALL *LIES!*
Clearly delusional.

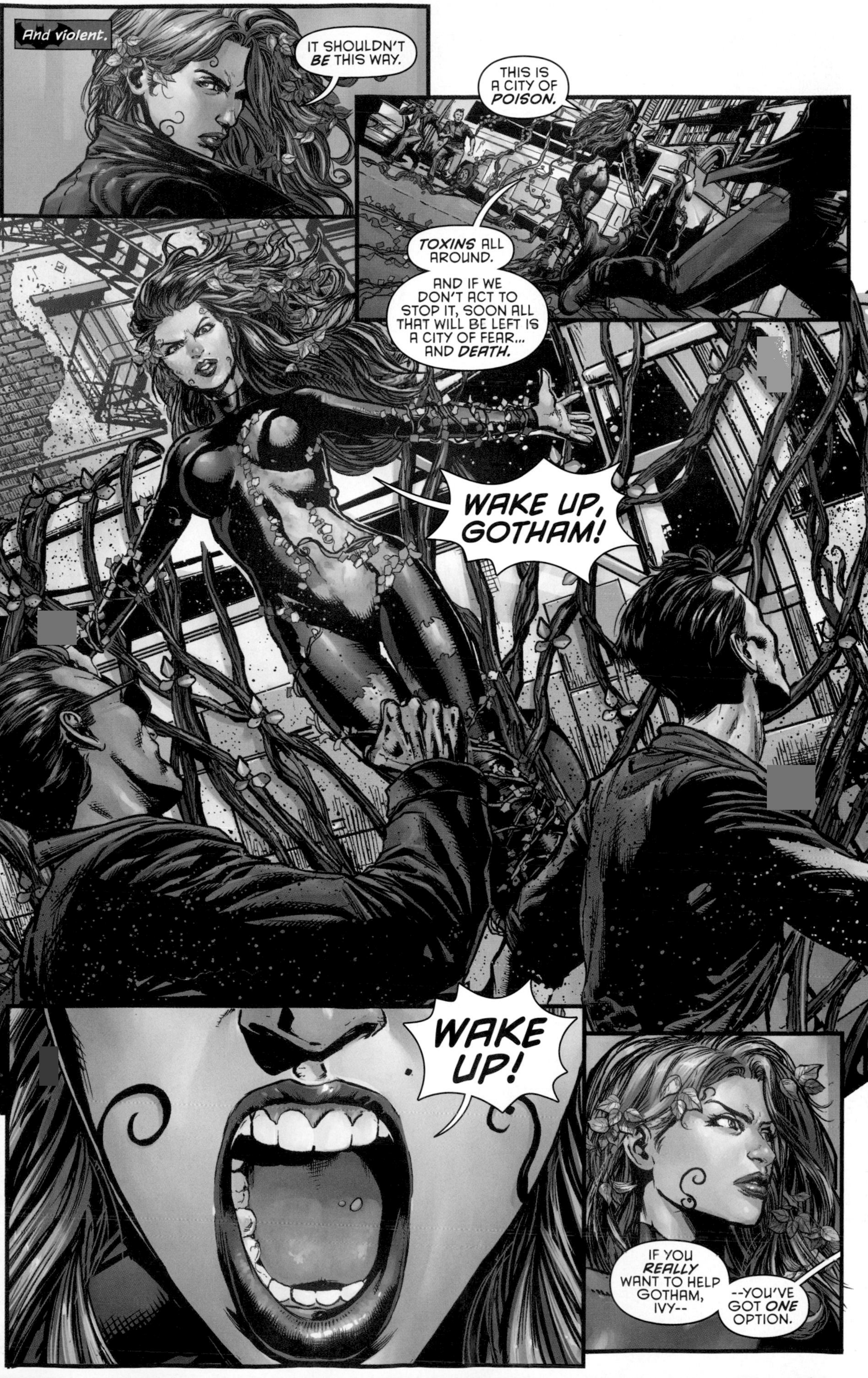
And violent.
IT SHOULDN'T *BE* THIS WAY.
THIS IS A CITY OF *POISON.*
TOXINS ALL AROUND.
AND IF WE DON'T ACT TO STOP IT, SOON ALL THAT WILL BE LEFT IS A CITY OF FEAR... AND *DEATH.*
WAKE UP, GOTHAM!
WAKE UP!
IF YOU *REALLY* WANT TO HELP GOTHAM, IVY--
--YOU'VE GOT *ONE* OPTION.

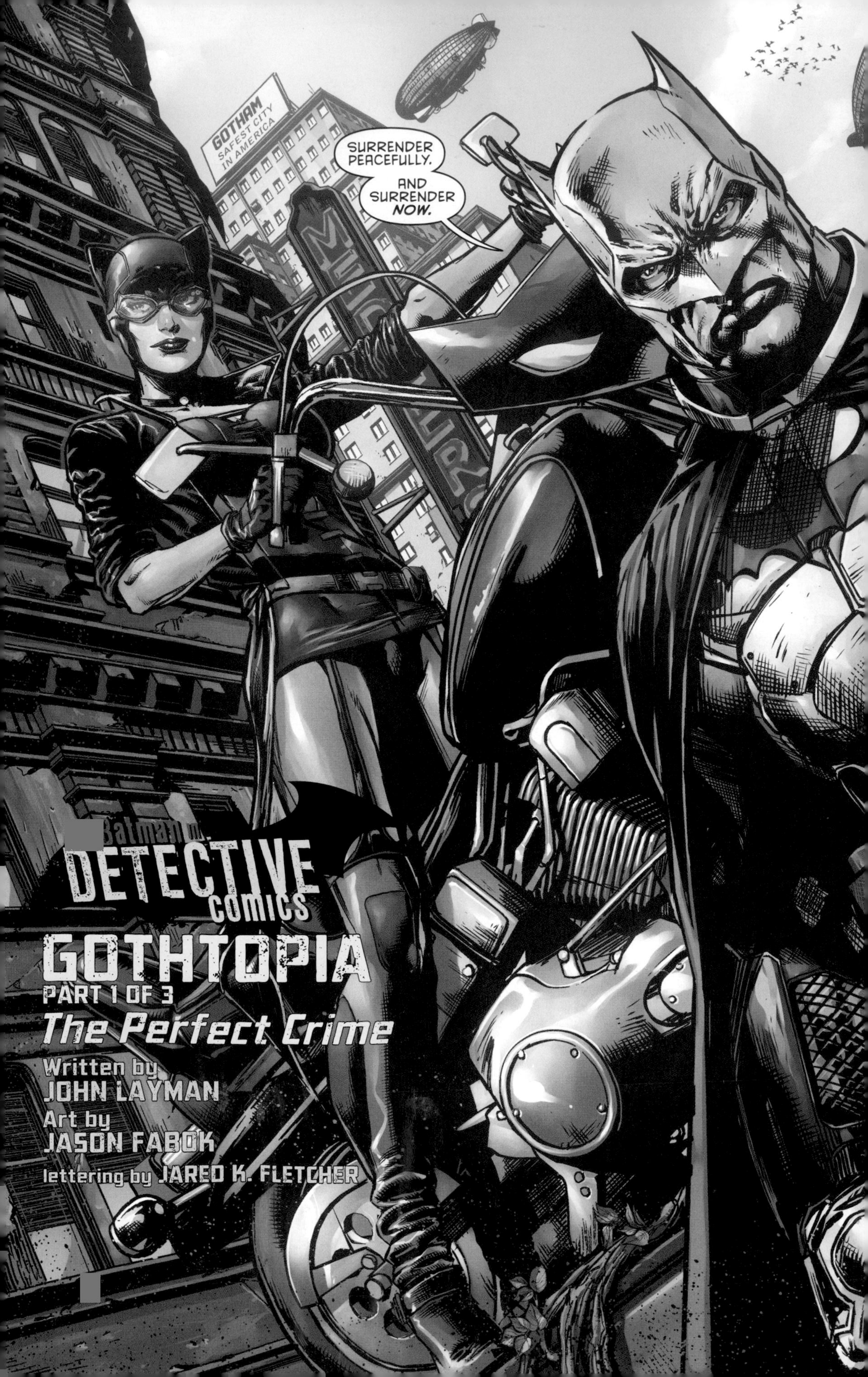
GOTHAM SAFEST CITY IN AMERICA
SURRENDER PEACEFULLY.
AND SURRENDER *NOW.*
Batman in
DETECTIVE COMICS
GOTHTOPIA
PART 1 OF 3
The Perfect Crime
Written by JOHN LAYMAN
Art by JASON FABOK
lettering by JARED K. FLETCHER

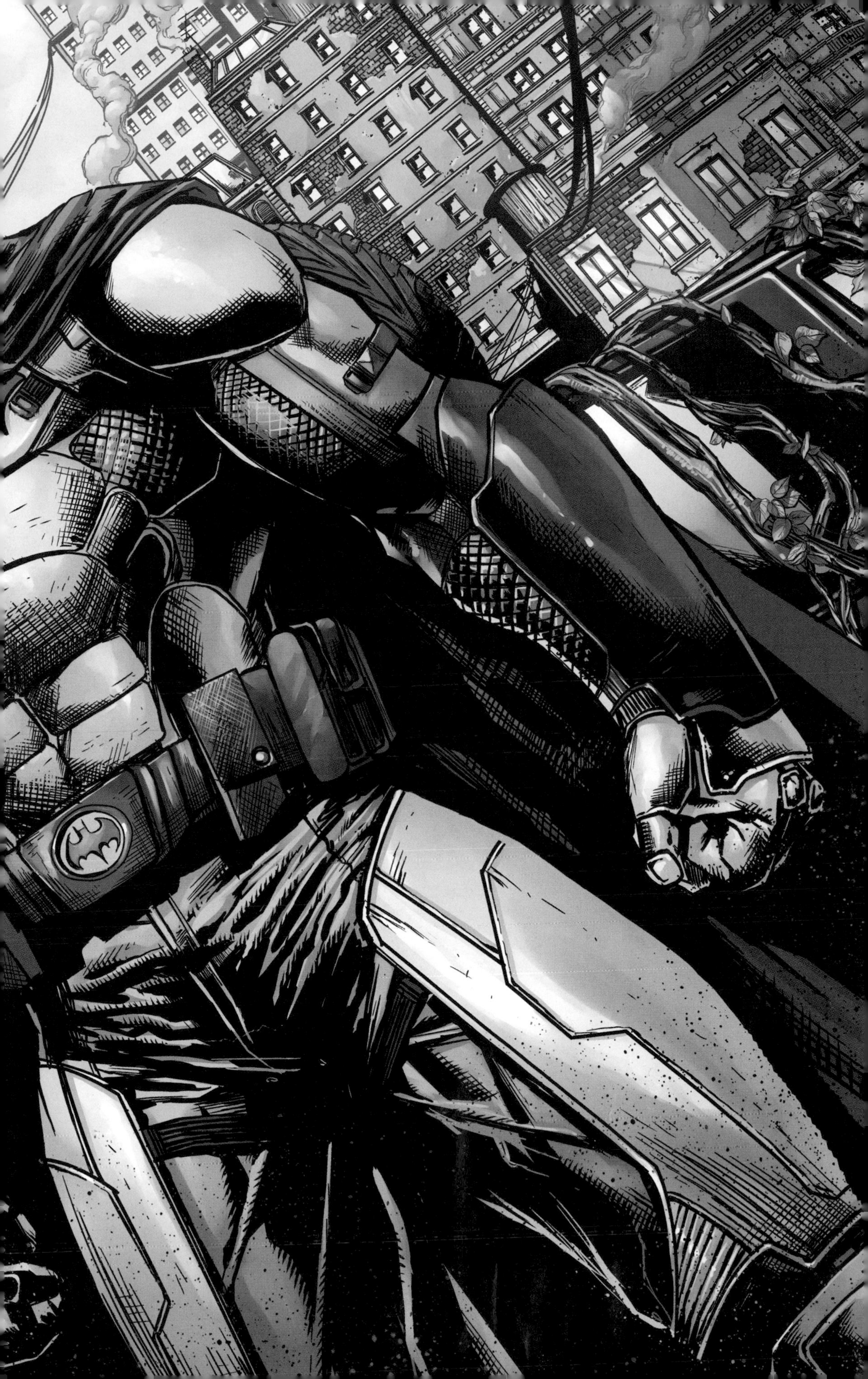

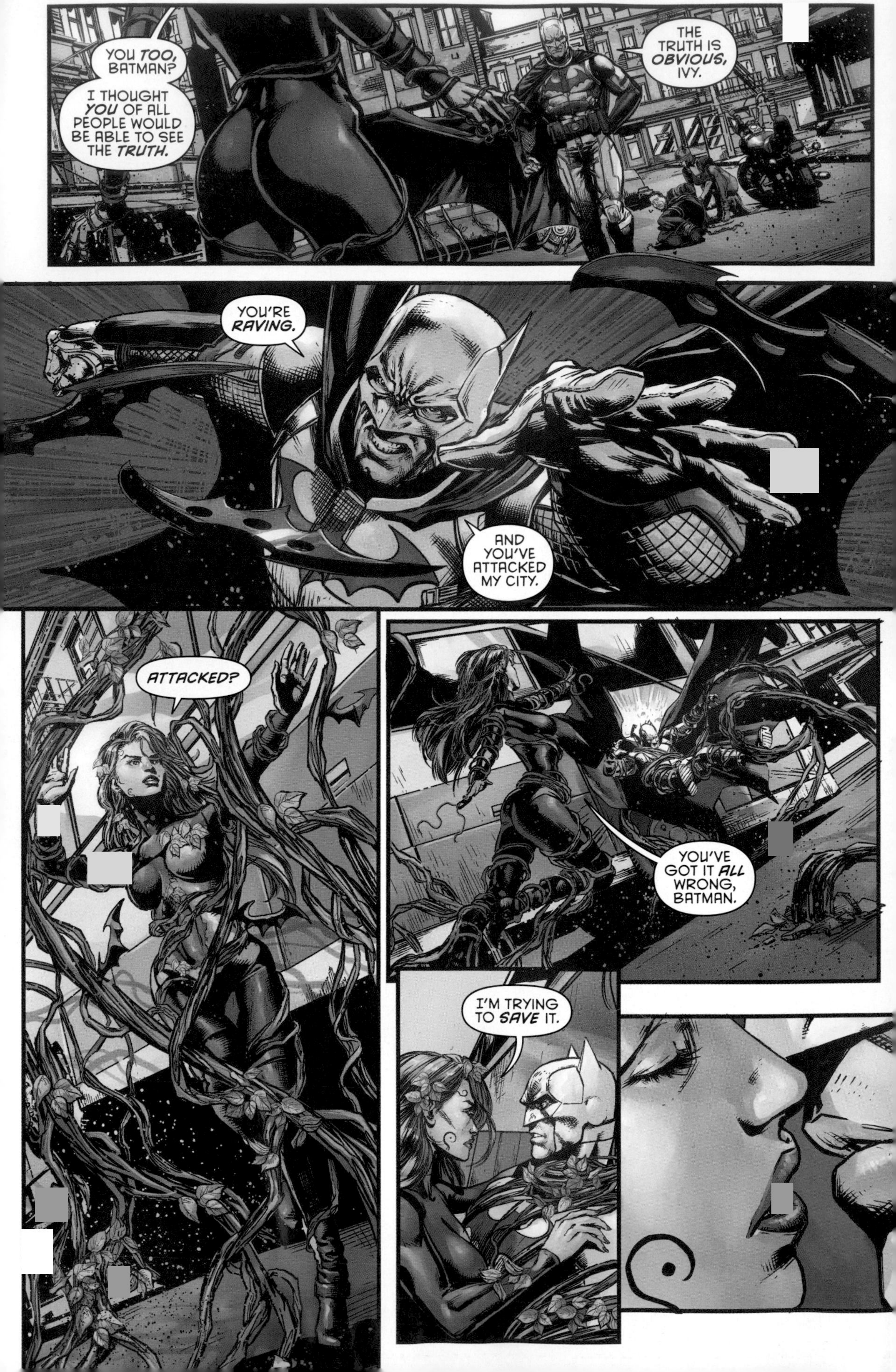
YOU *TOO*, BATMAN?
I THOUGHT *YOU* OF ALL PEOPLE WOULD BE ABLE TO SEE THE *TRUTH*.
THE TRUTH IS *OBVIOUS*, IVY.
YOU'RE *RAVING*.
AND YOU'VE ATTACKED MY CITY.
ATTACKED?
YOU'VE GOT IT *ALL* WRONG, BATMAN.
I'M TRYING TO *SAVE* IT.

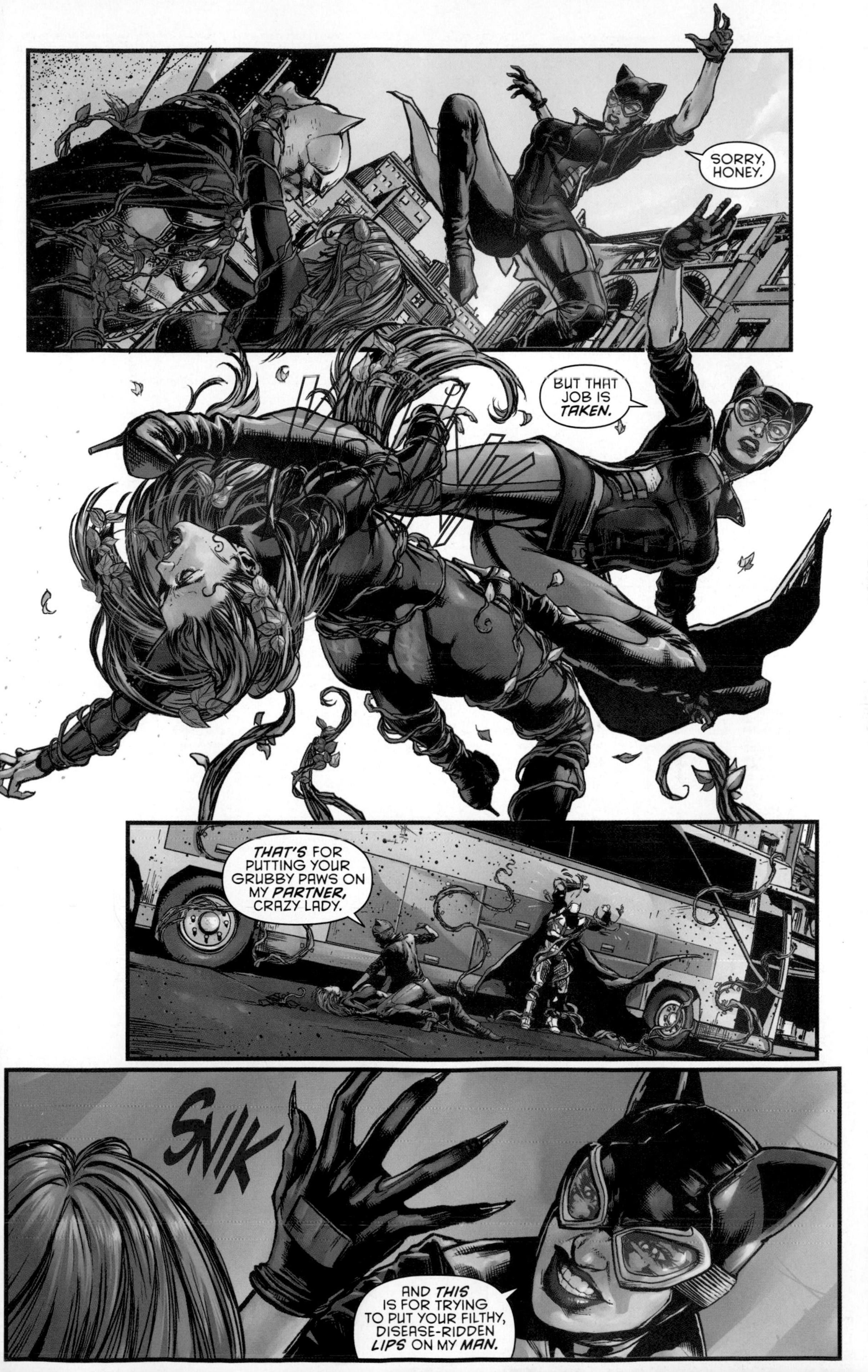
SORRY, HONEY.
BUT THAT JOB IS *TAKEN.*
THAT'S FOR PUTTING YOUR GRUBBY PAWS ON MY *PARTNER,* CRAZY LADY.
SNIK
AND *THIS* IS FOR TRYING TO PUT YOUR FILTHY, DISEASE-RIDDEN *LIPS* ON MY *MAN.*

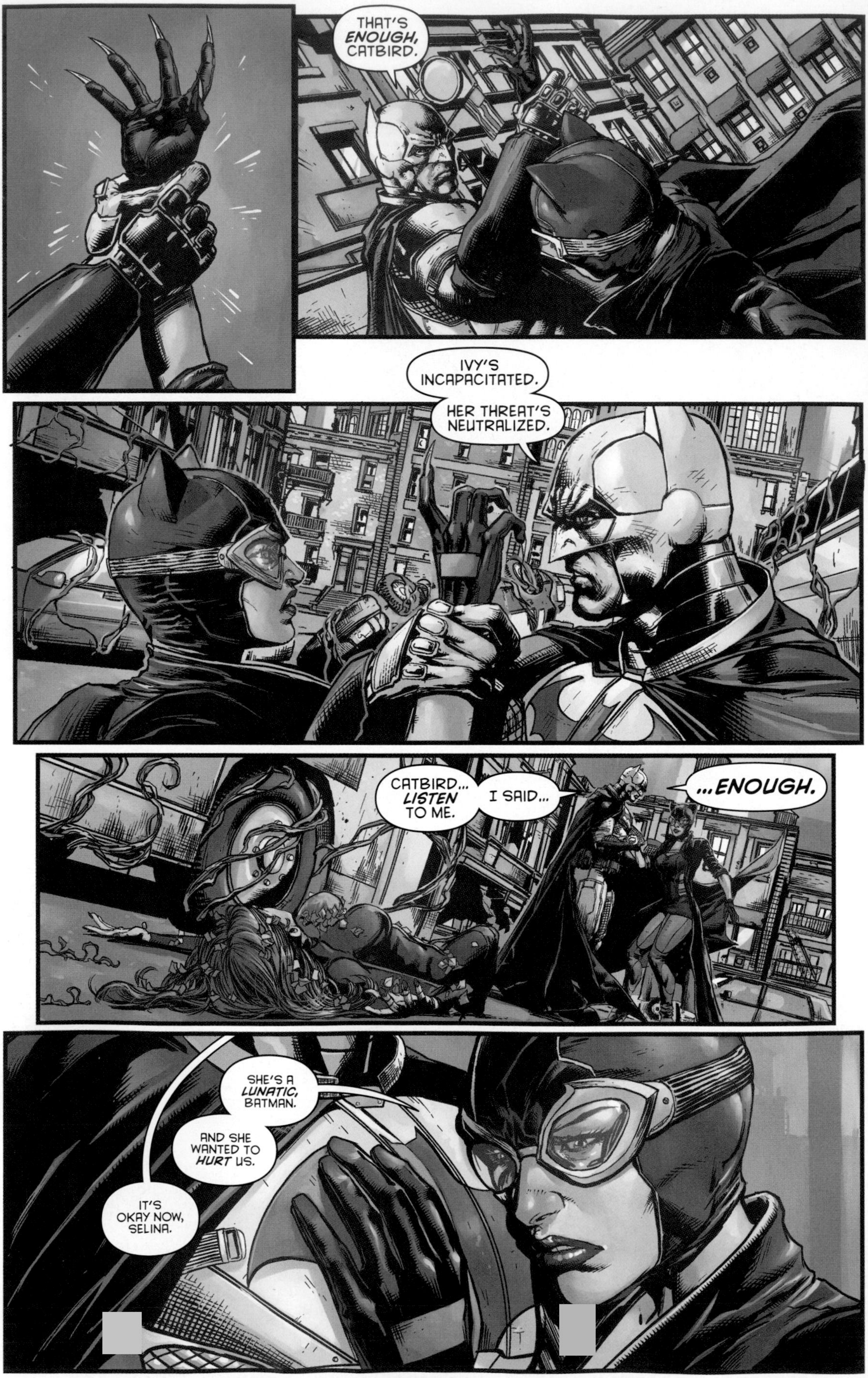
THAT'S ENOUGH, CATBIRD.
IVY'S INCAPACITATED.
HER THREAT'S NEUTRALIZED.
CATBIRD... LISTEN TO ME.
I SAID...
...ENOUGH.
SHE'S A LUNATIC, BATMAN.
AND SHE WANTED TO HURT US.
IT'S OKAY NOW, SELINA.

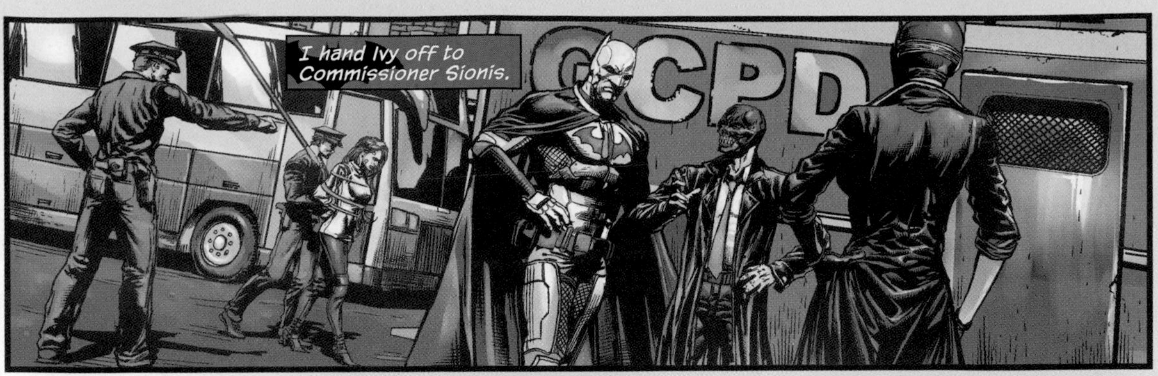
I hand Ivy off to Commissioner Sionis.
GCPD

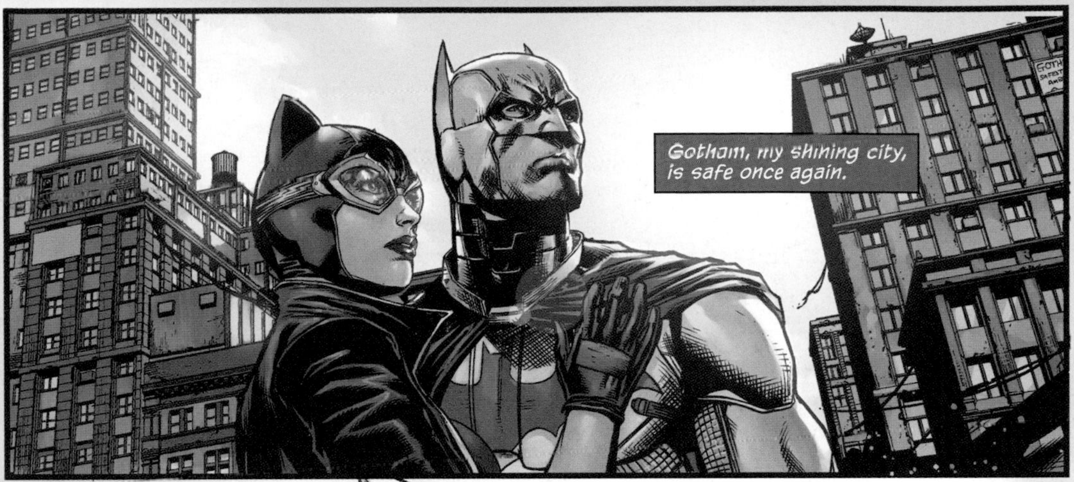
Gotham, my shining city, is safe once again.

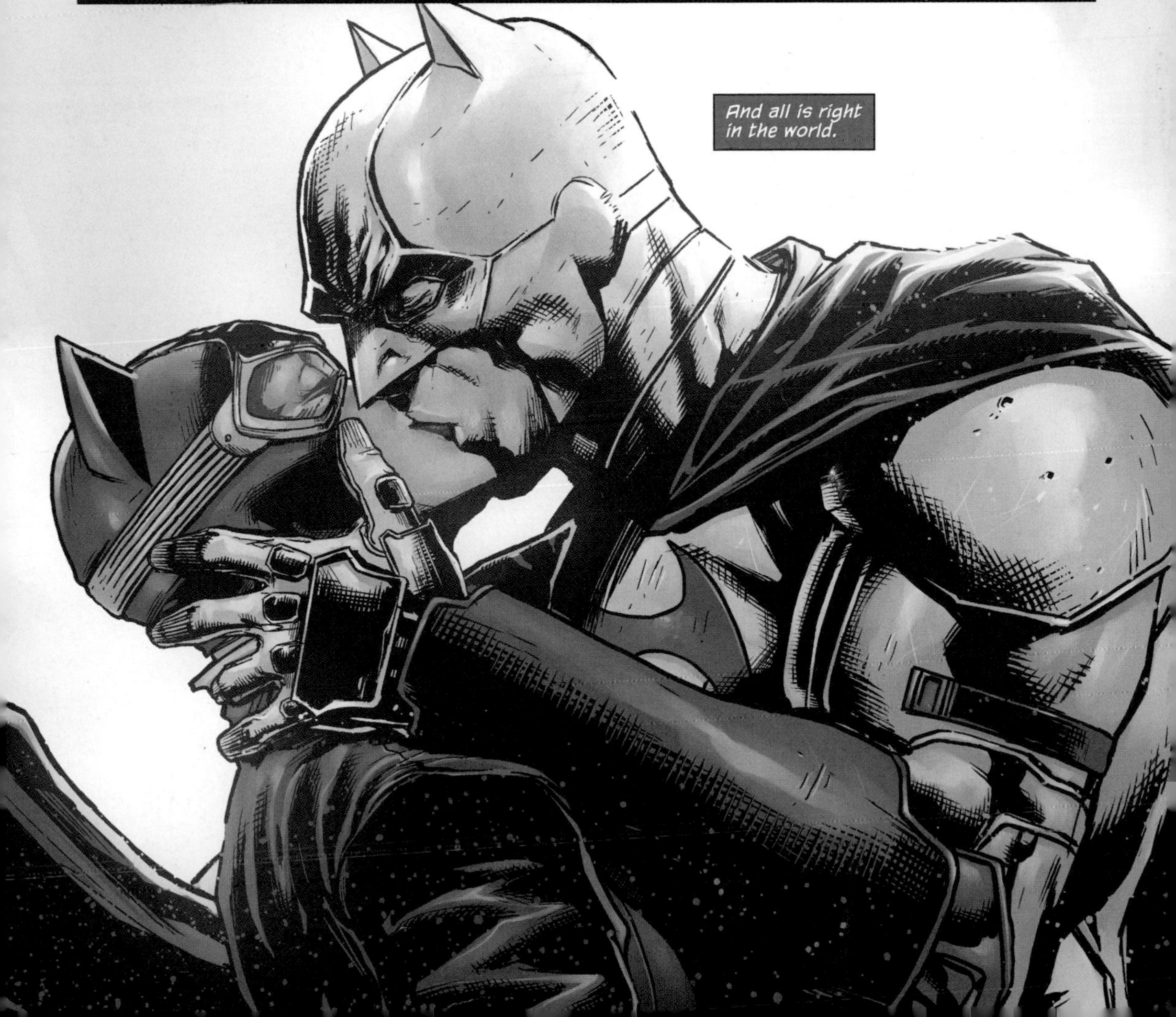
And all is right in the world.

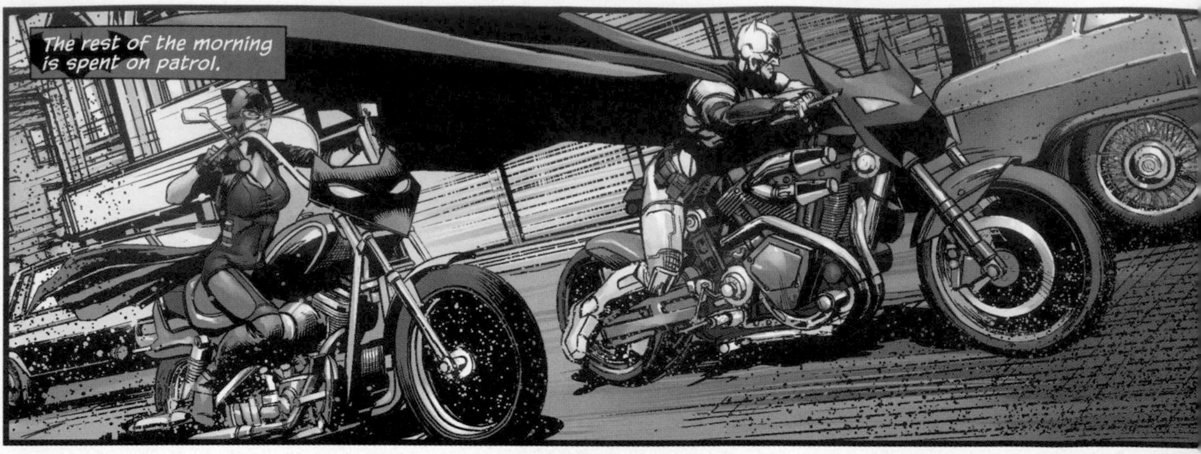
The rest of the morning is spent on patrol.

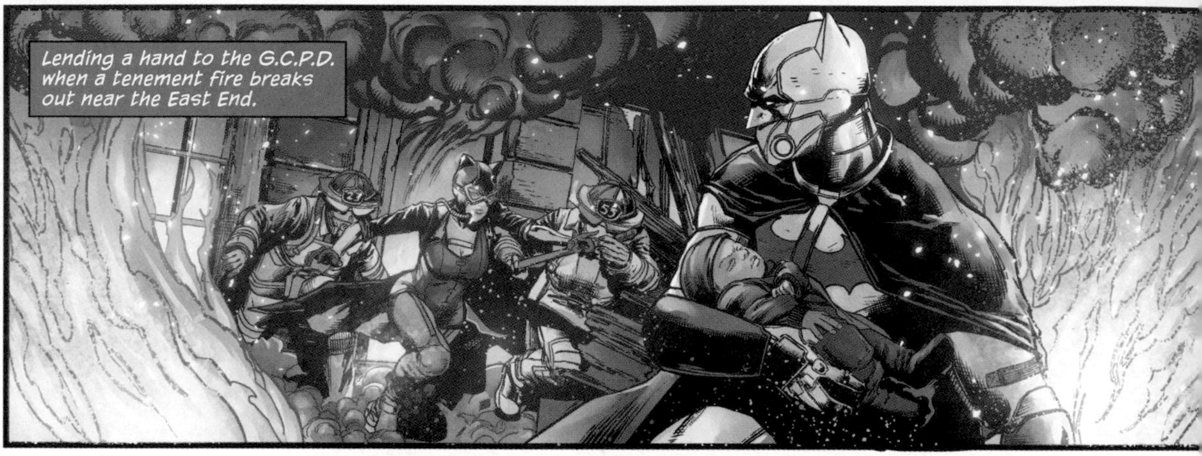
Lending a hand to the G.C.P.D. when a tenement fire breaks out near the East End.

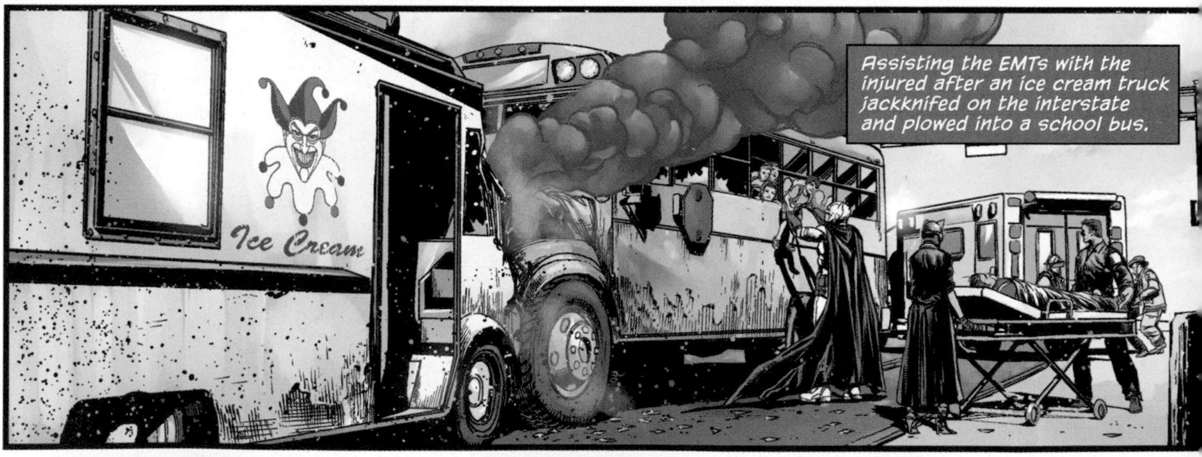
Ice Cream
Assisting the EMTs with the injured after an ice cream truck jackknifed on the interstate and plowed into a school bus.

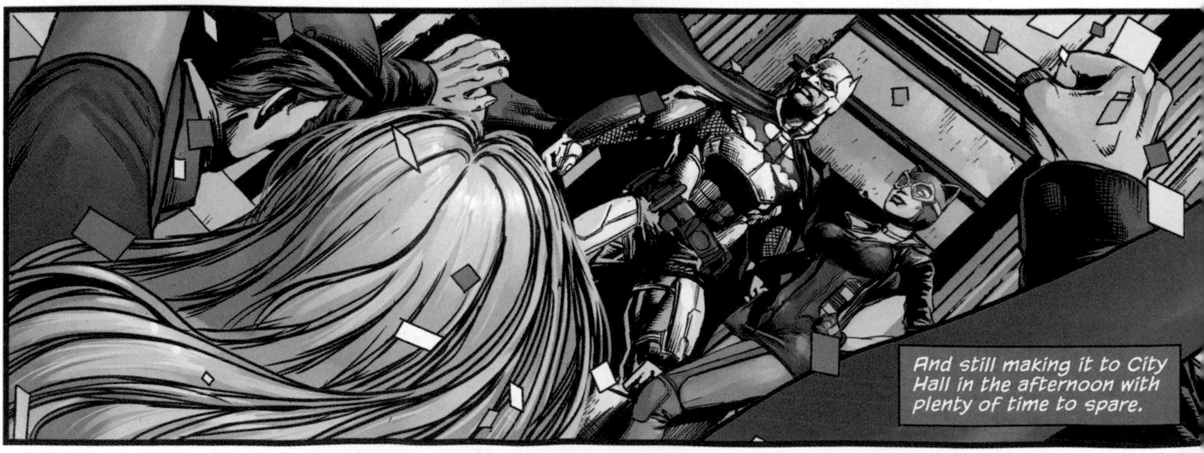
And still making it to City Hall in the afternoon with plenty of time to spare.

Bluebelle and *Brightbat* joined shortly thereafter.

And we put on a good show for the cameras as Mayor Cobblepot gave us our commendations.

WE'VE DONE GREAT THINGS IN GOTHAM, MY FRIENDS.

THIS IS SOMETHING WE CAN ALL BE *PROUD* OF.

Gotham has seen a ninety percent drop in crime over the last few months.

Other than today's incident with Ivy, Gotham is almost crime-free.

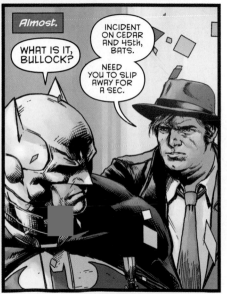

Almost.

WHAT IS IT, BULLOCK?

INCIDENT ON CEDAR AND 45th, BATS. NEED YOU TO SLIP AWAY FOR A SEC.

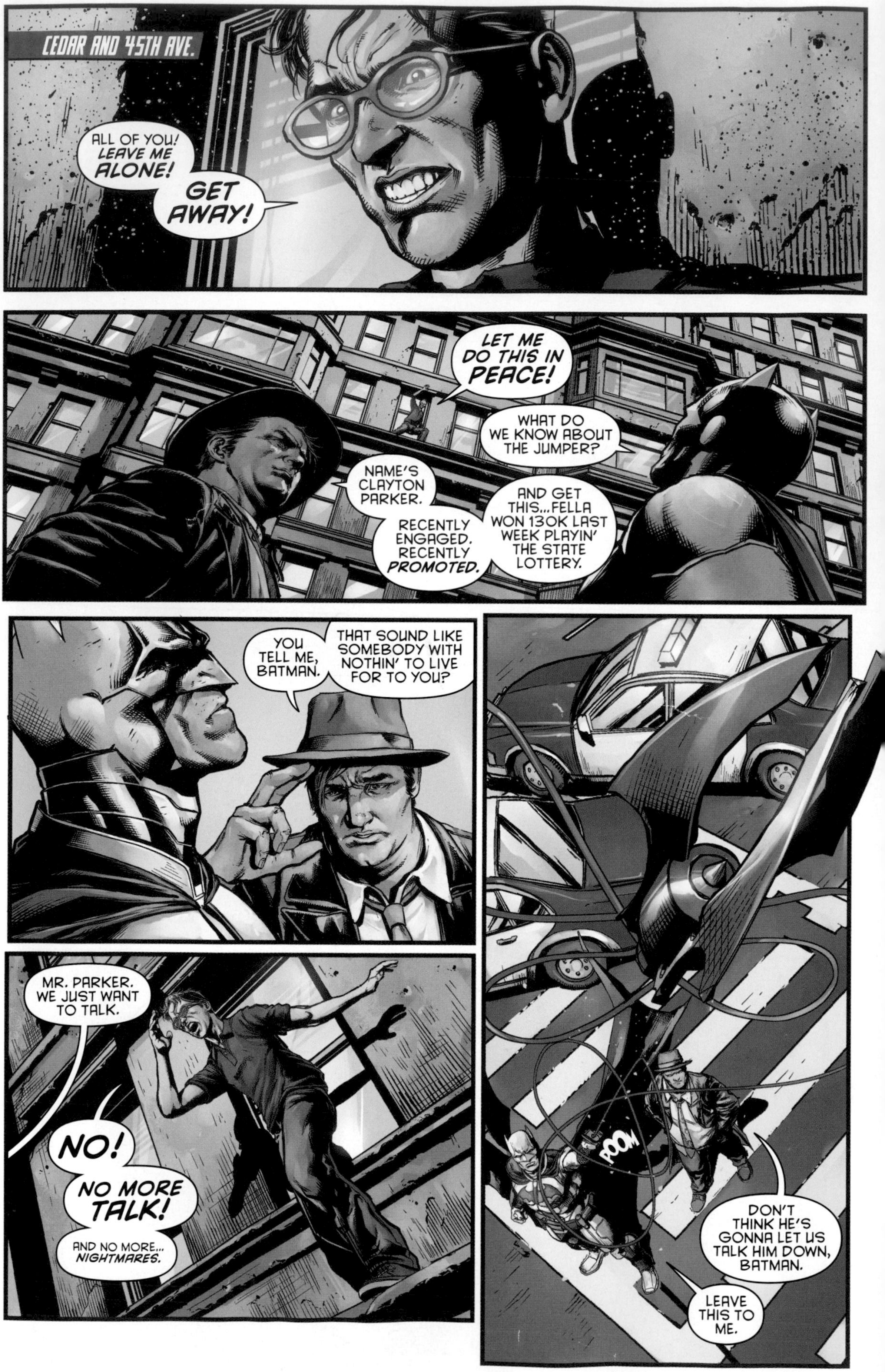
CEDAR AND 45TH AVE.
ALL OF YOU! LEAVE ME ALONE!
GET AWAY!
LET ME DO THIS IN PEACE!
WHAT DO WE KNOW ABOUT THE JUMPER?
NAME'S CLAYTON PARKER.
RECENTLY ENGAGED. RECENTLY PROMOTED.
AND GET THIS...FELLA WON 130K LAST WEEK PLAYIN' THE STATE LOTTERY.
YOU TELL ME, BATMAN.
THAT SOUND LIKE SOMEBODY WITH NOTHIN' TO LIVE FOR TO YOU?
MR. PARKER. WE JUST WANT TO TALK.
NO!
NO MORE TALK!
AND NO MORE... NIGHTMARES.
POOM
DON'T THINK HE'S GONNA LET US TALK HIM DOWN, BATMAN.
LEAVE THIS TO ME.

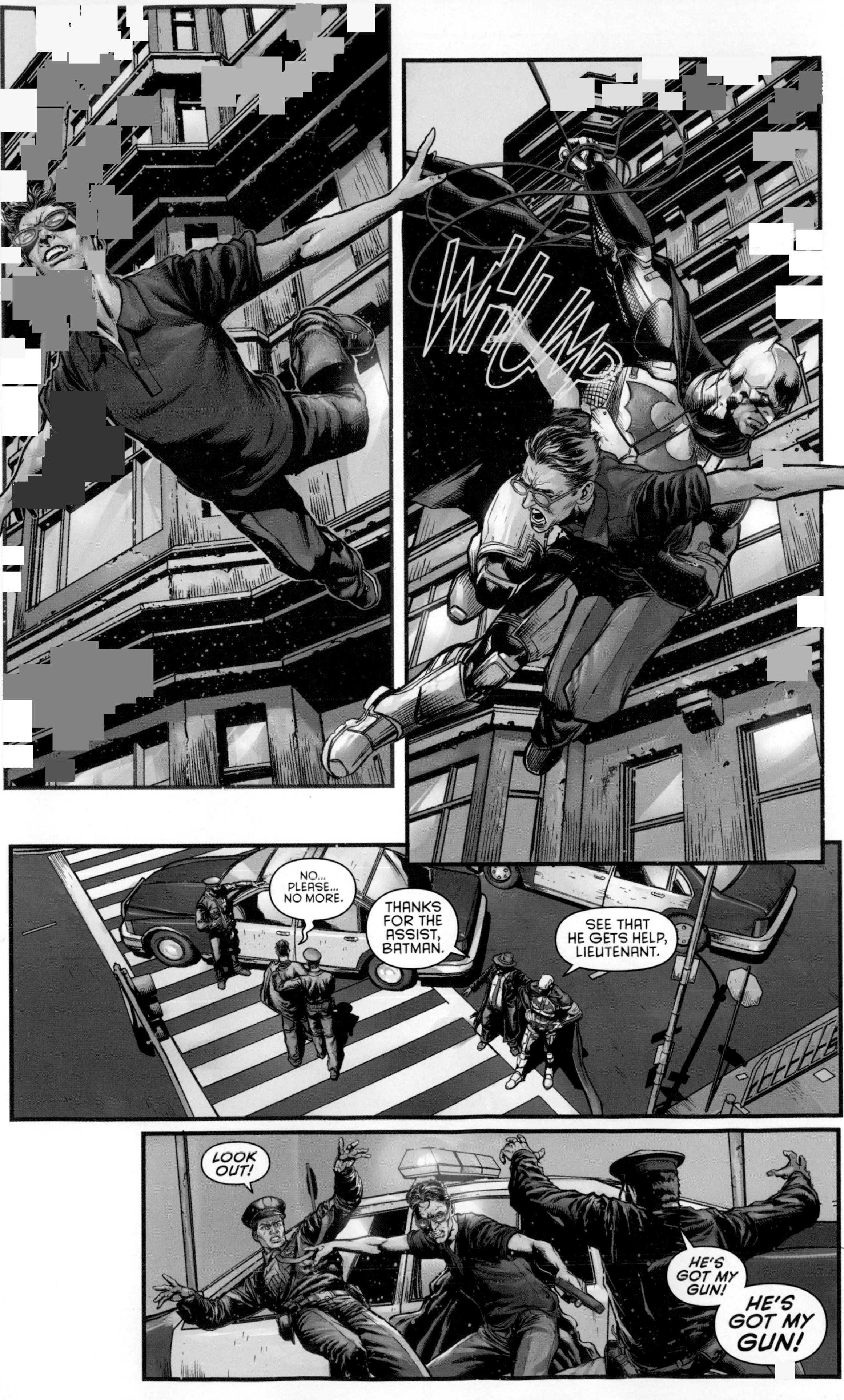
WHUMP
NO... PLEASE... NO MORE.
THANKS FOR THE ASSIST, BATMAN.
SEE THAT HE GETS HELP, LIEUTENANT.
LOOK OUT!
HE'S GOT MY GUN!
HE'S GOT MY GUN!

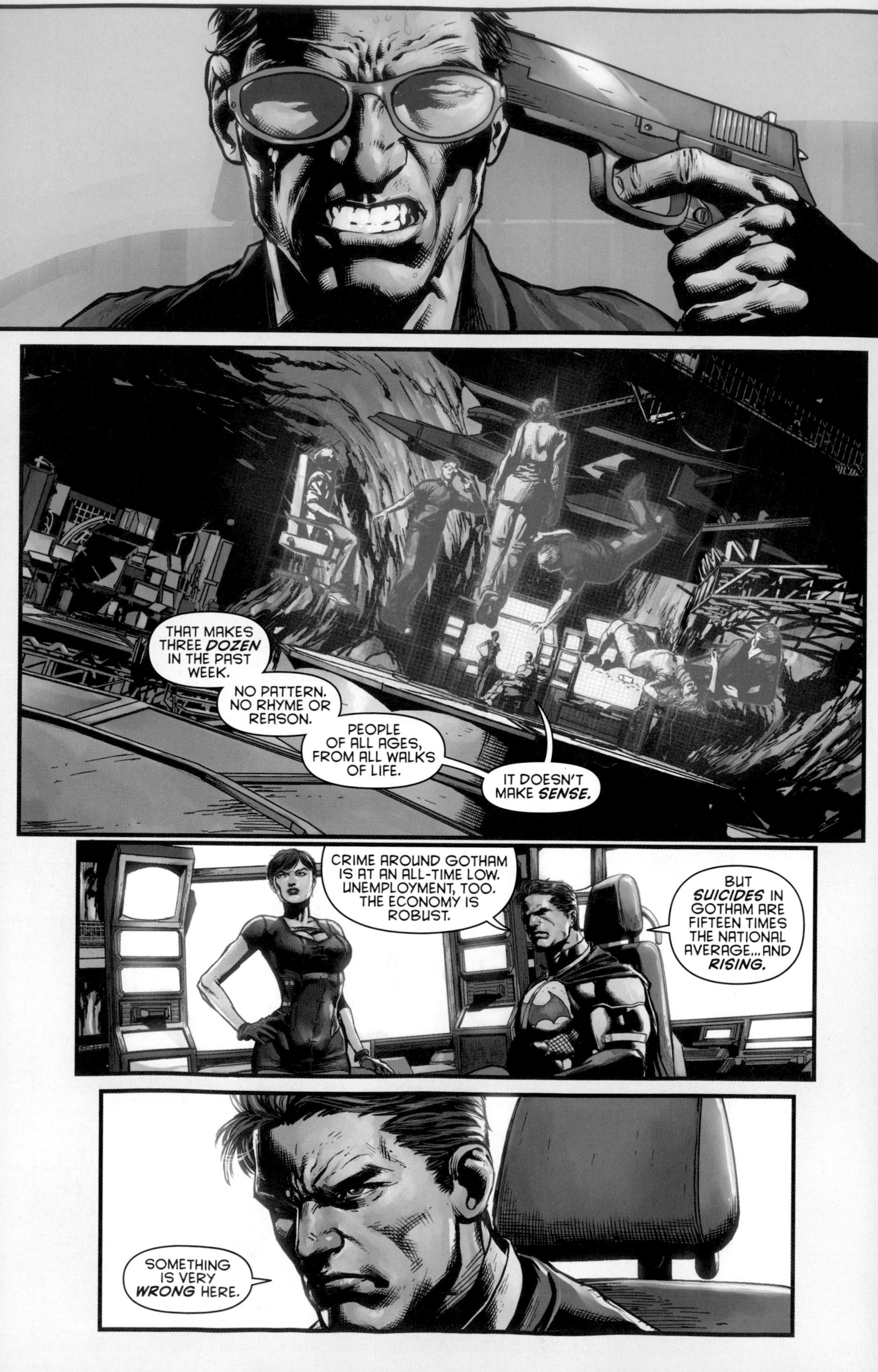
THAT MAKES THREE *DOZEN* IN THE PAST WEEK.
NO PATTERN. NO RHYME OR REASON.
PEOPLE OF ALL AGES, FROM ALL WALKS OF LIFE.
IT DOESN'T MAKE *SENSE.*
CRIME AROUND GOTHAM IS AT AN ALL-TIME LOW. UNEMPLOYMENT, TOO. THE ECONOMY IS ROBUST.
BUT *SUICIDES* IN GOTHAM ARE FIFTEEN TIMES THE NATIONAL AVERAGE...AND *RISING.*
SOMETHING IS VERY *WRONG* HERE.

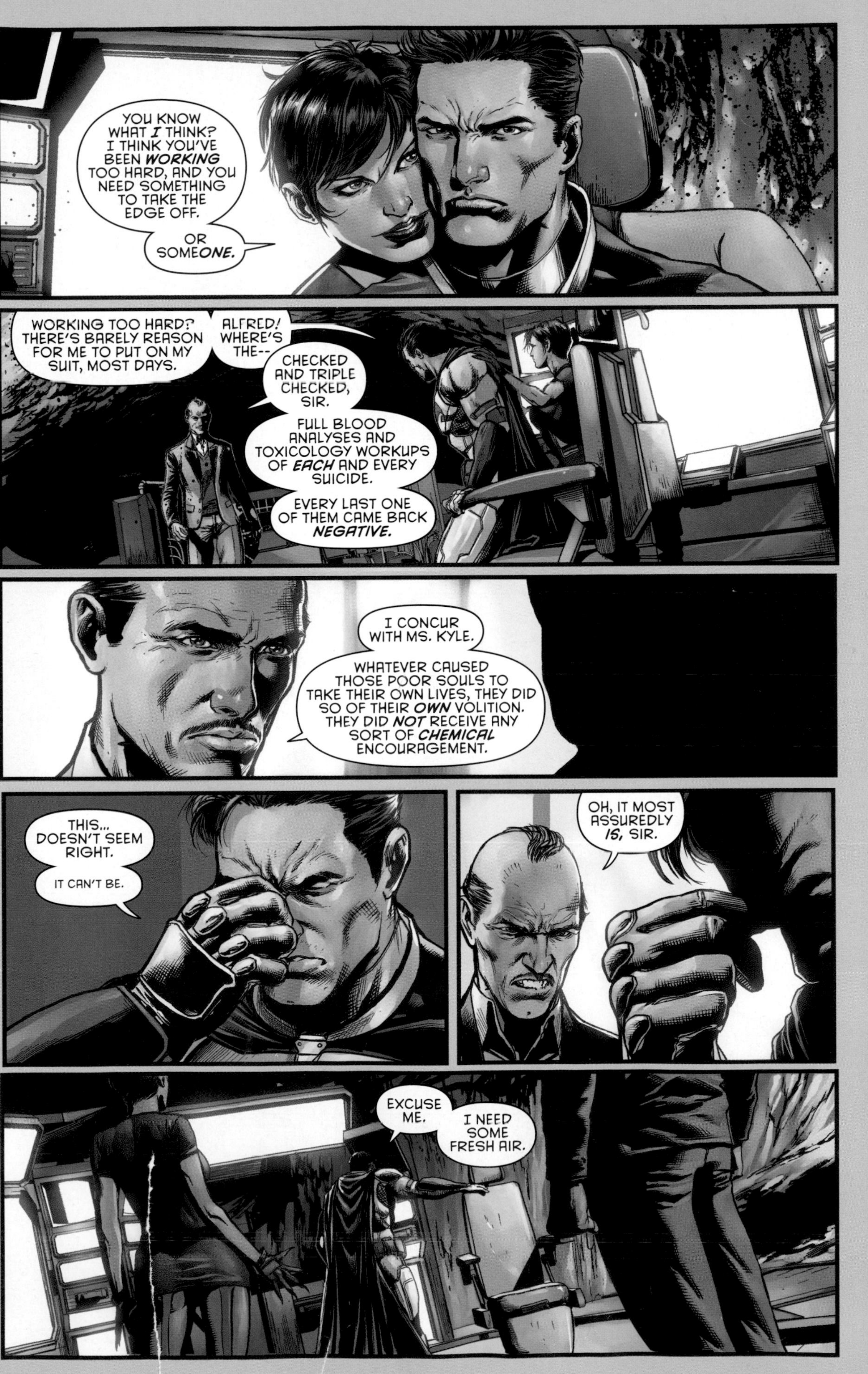
YOU KNOW WHAT *I* THINK? I THINK YOU'VE BEEN *WORKING* TOO HARD, AND YOU NEED SOMETHING TO TAKE THE EDGE OFF.
OR SOME*ONE.*
WORKING TOO HARD? THERE'S BARELY REASON FOR ME TO PUT ON MY SUIT, MOST DAYS.
ALFRED! WHERE'S THE--
CHECKED AND TRIPLE CHECKED, SIR.
FULL BLOOD ANALYSES AND TOXICOLOGY WORKUPS OF *EACH* AND EVERY SUICIDE.
EVERY LAST ONE OF THEM CAME BACK *NEGATIVE.*
I CONCUR WITH MS. KYLE.
WHATEVER CAUSED THOSE POOR SOULS TO TAKE THEIR OWN LIVES, THEY DID SO OF THEIR *OWN* VOLITION. THEY DID *NOT* RECEIVE ANY SORT OF *CHEMICAL* ENCOURAGEMENT.
THIS... DOESN'T SEEM RIGHT.
IT CAN'T BE.
OH, IT MOST ASSUREDLY *IS,* SIR.
EXCUSE ME.
I NEED SOME FRESH AIR.

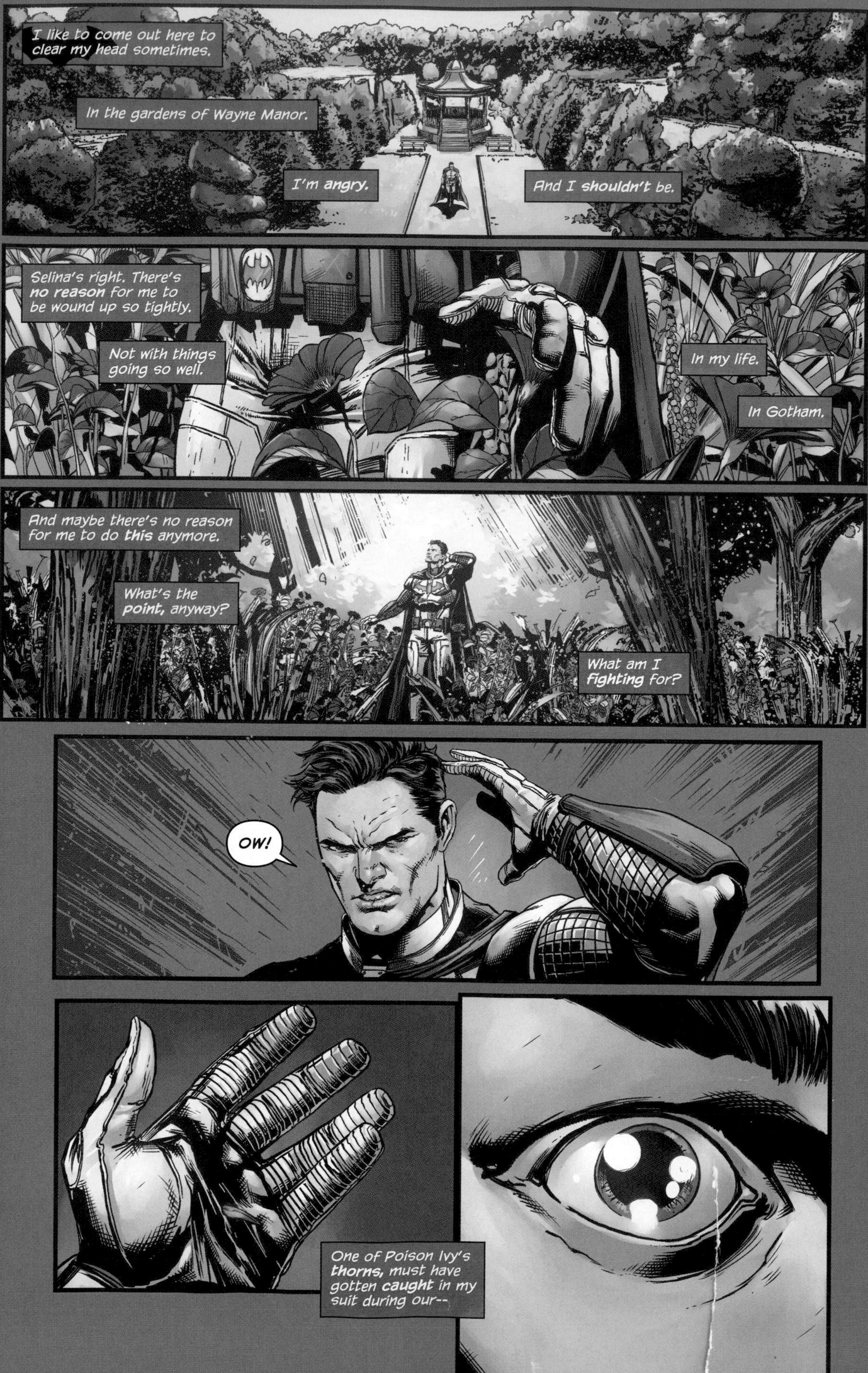
I like to come out here to clear my head sometimes.
In the gardens of Wayne Manor.
I'm angry.
And I shouldn't be.
Selina's right. There's no reason for me to be wound up so tightly.
Not with things going so well.
In my life.
In Gotham.
And maybe there's no reason for me to do this anymore.
What's the point, anyway?
What am I fighting for?
OW!
One of Poison Ivy's thorns, must have gotten caught in my suit during our--

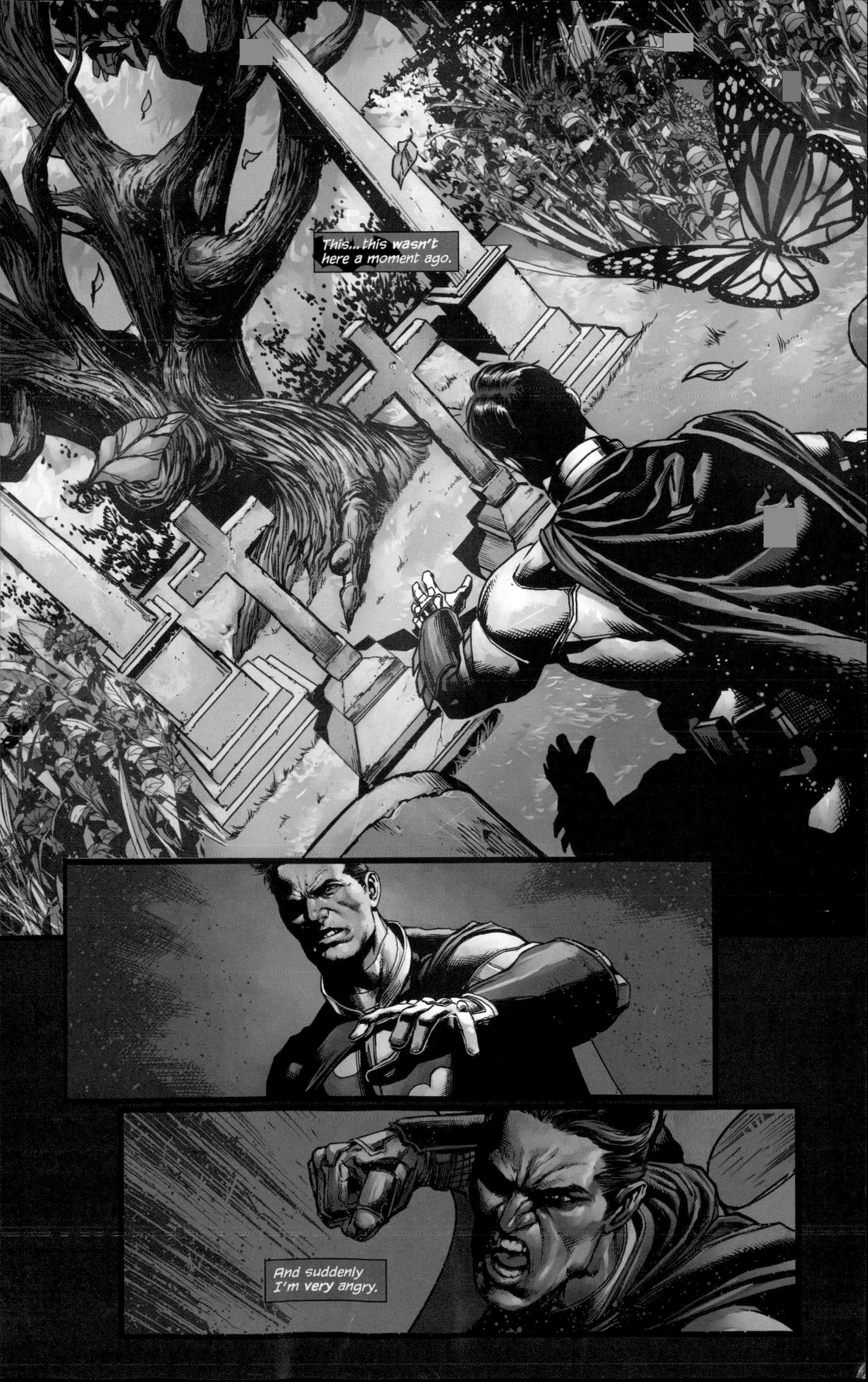
This...this wasn't here a moment ago.
And suddenly I'm very angry.

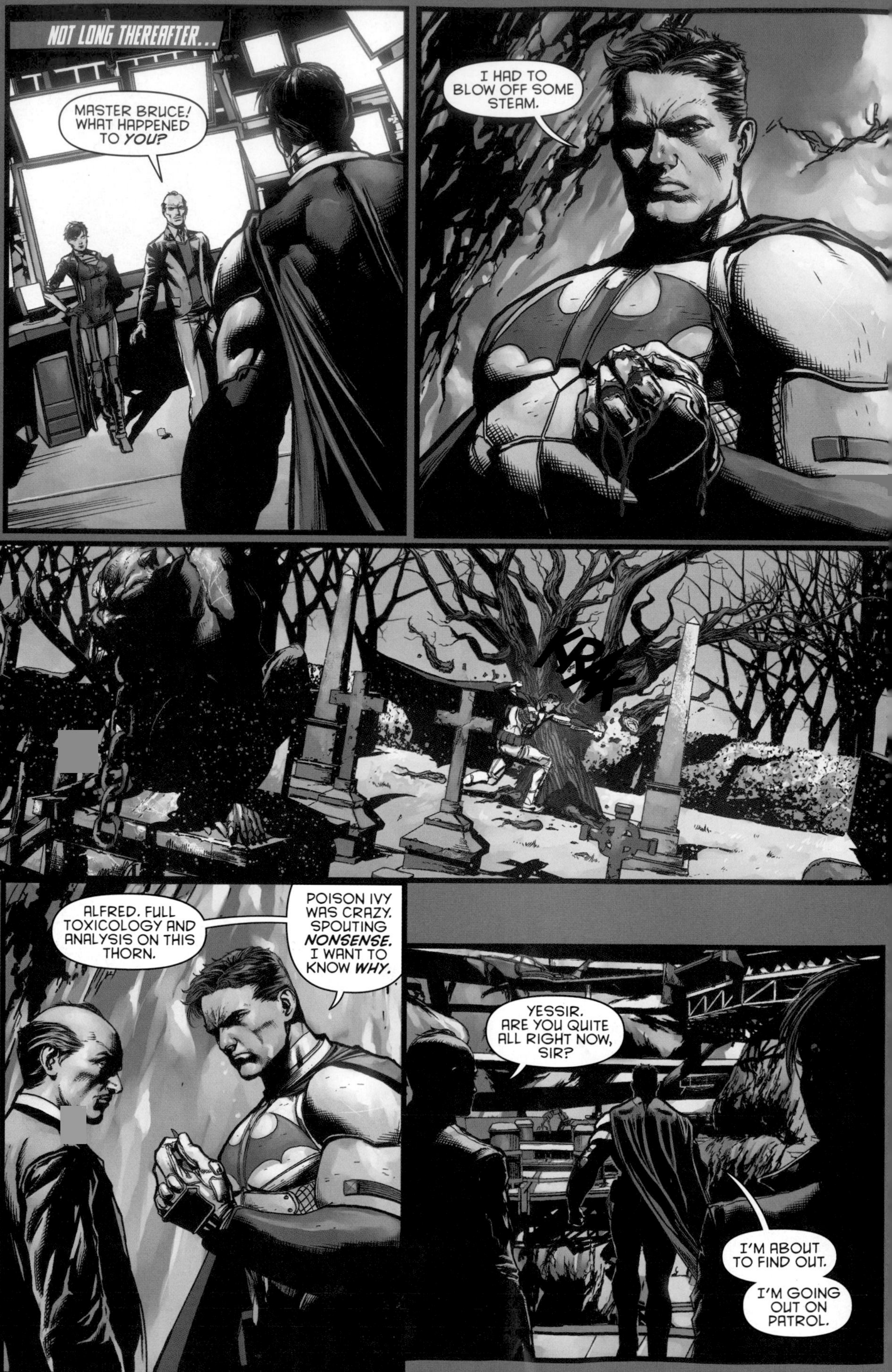
NOT LONG THEREAFTER...
MASTER BRUCE! WHAT HAPPENED TO *YOU?*
I HAD TO BLOW OFF SOME STEAM.
KRAK
ALFRED. FULL TOXICOLOGY AND ANALYSIS ON THIS THORN.
POISON IVY WAS CRAZY. SPOUTING *NONSENSE.* I WANT TO KNOW *WHY.*
YESSIR. ARE YOU QUITE ALL RIGHT NOW, SIR?
I'M ABOUT TO FIND OUT.
I'M GOING OUT ON PATROL.

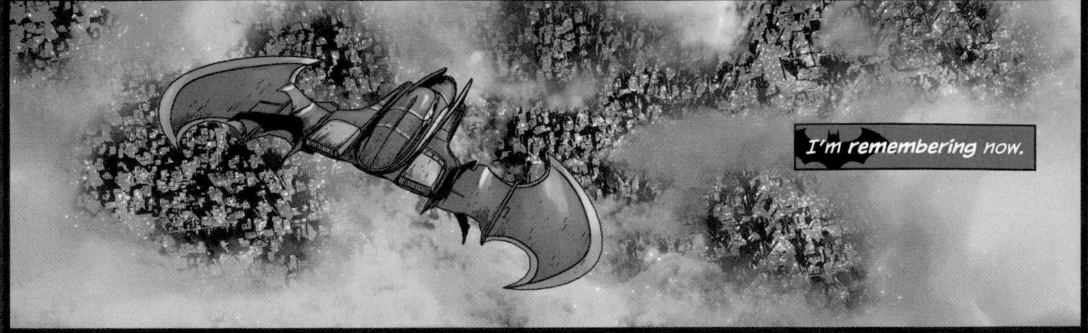
I'm remembering now.

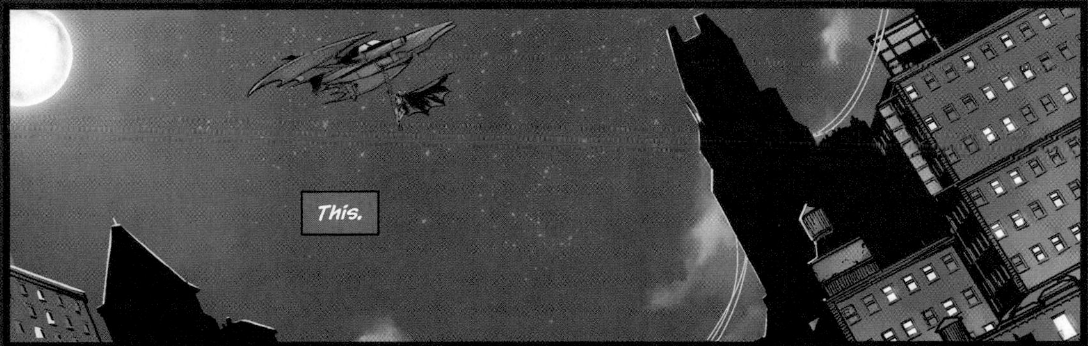
This.

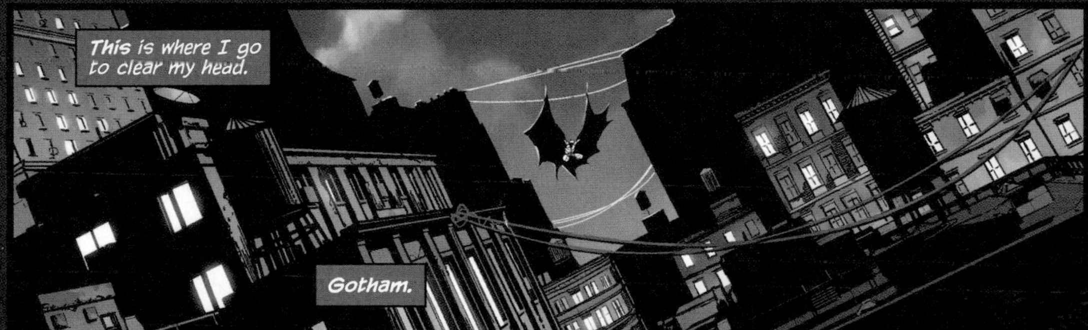
This is where I go to clear my head.
Gotham.

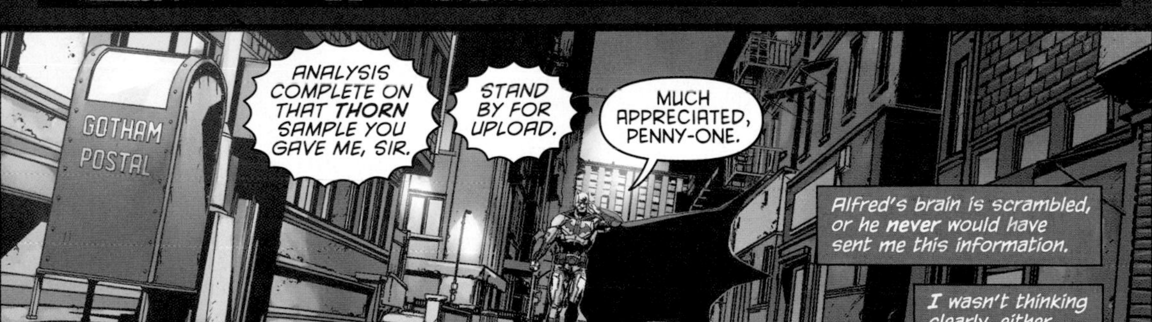
GOTHAM POSTAL
ANALYSIS COMPLETE ON THAT THORN SAMPLE YOU GAVE ME, SIR.
STAND BY FOR UPLOAD.
MUCH APPRECIATED, PENNY-ONE.
Alfred's brain is scrambled, or he never would have sent me this information.
I wasn't thinking clearly, either.

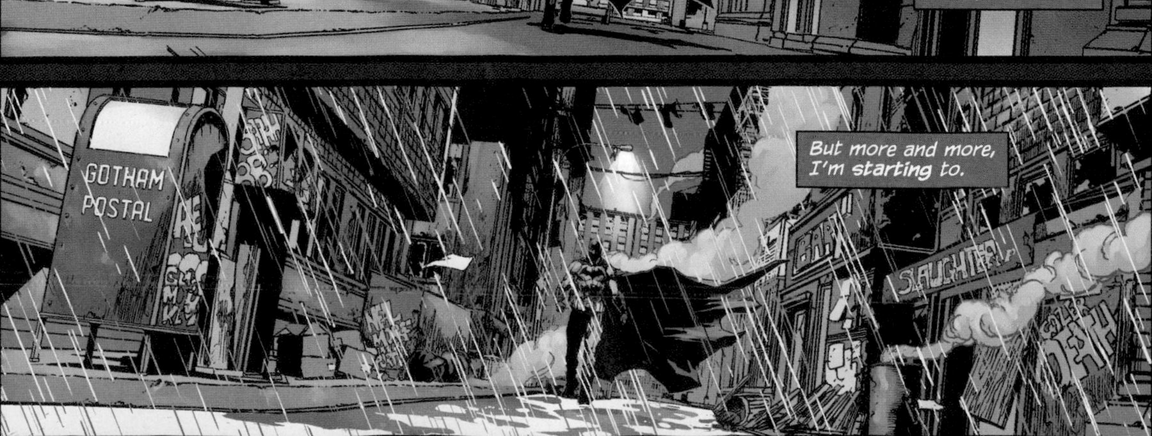
GOTHAM POSTAL
But more and more, I'm starting to.

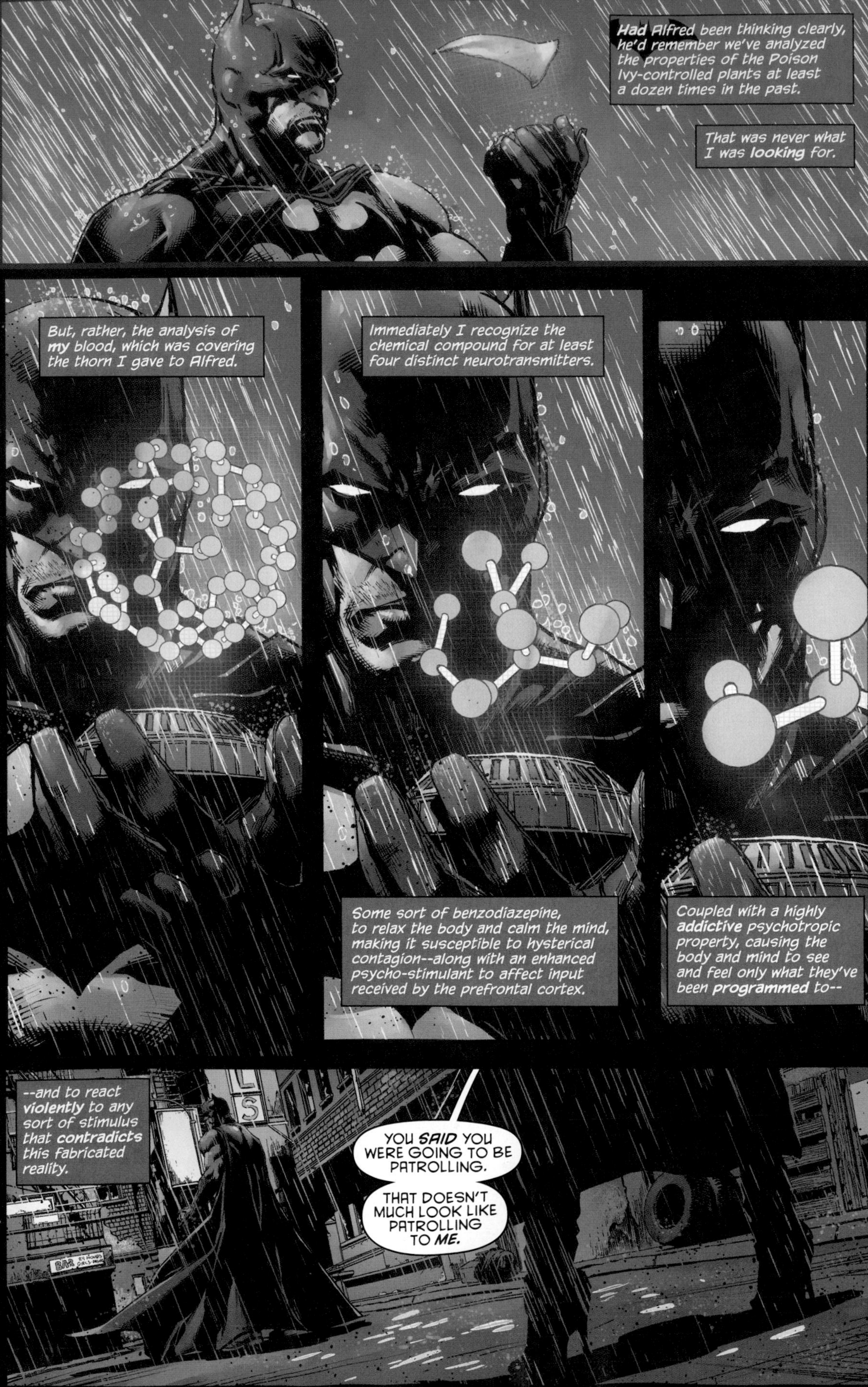
Had Alfred been thinking clearly, he'd remember we've analyzed the properties of the Poison Ivy-controlled plants at least a dozen times in the past.
That was never what I was looking for.
But, rather, the analysis of my blood, which was covering the thorn I gave to Alfred.
Immediately I recognize the chemical compound for at least four distinct neurotransmitters.
Some sort of benzodiazepine, to relax the body and calm the mind, making it susceptible to hysterical contagion--along with an enhanced psycho-stimulant to affect input received by the prefrontal cortex.
Coupled with a highly addictive psychotropic property, causing the body and mind to see and feel only what they've been programmed to--
--and to react violently to any sort of stimulus that contradicts this fabricated reality.
YOU SAID YOU WERE GOING TO BE PATROLLING.
THAT DOESN'T MUCH LOOK LIKE PATROLLING TO ME.

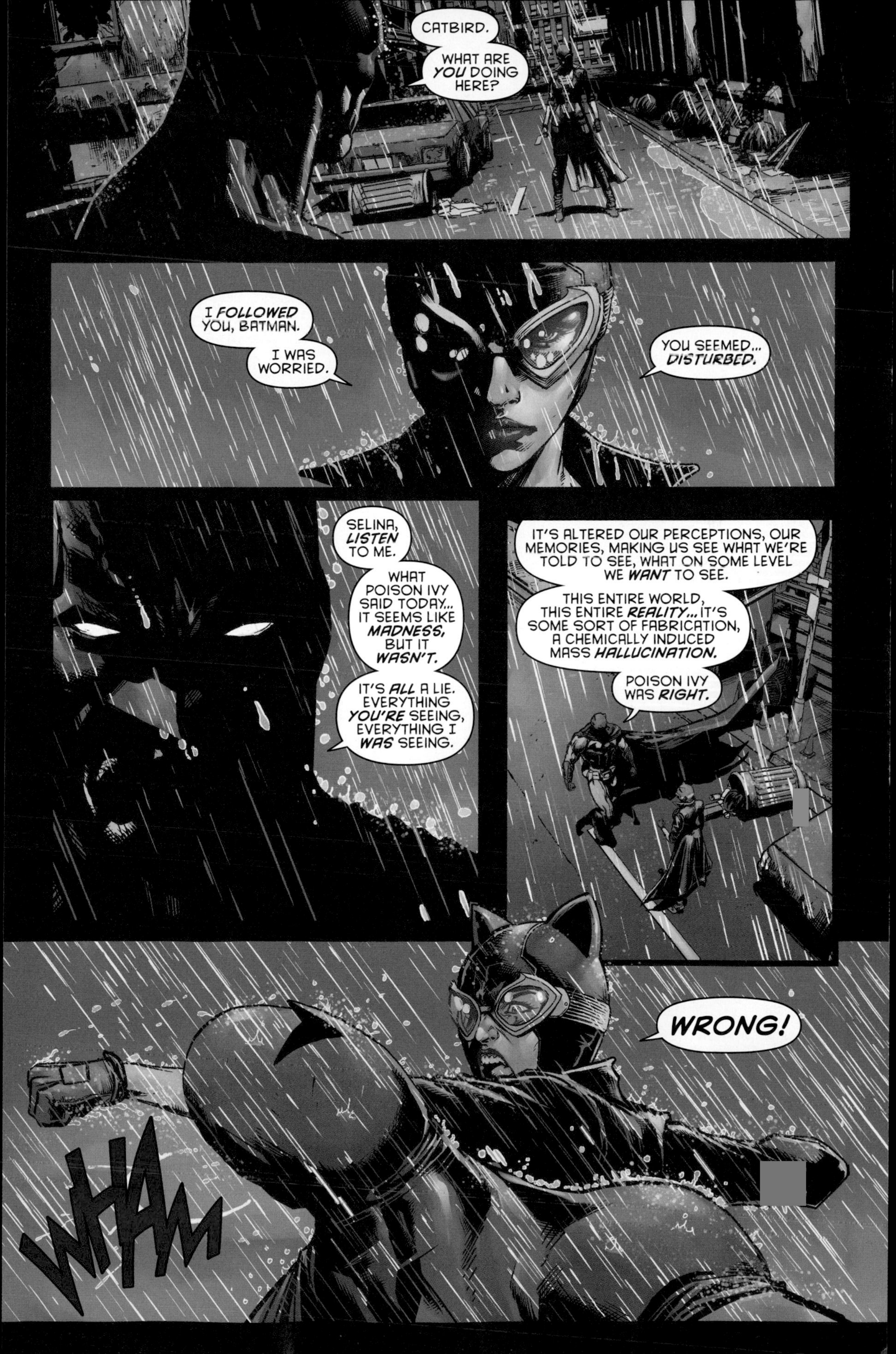
CATBIRD.
WHAT ARE *YOU* DOING HERE?
I *FOLLOWED* YOU, BATMAN.
I WAS WORRIED.
YOU SEEMED... *DISTURBED.*
SELINA, *LISTEN* TO ME.
WHAT POISON IVY SAID TODAY... IT SEEMS LIKE *MADNESS,* BUT IT *WASN'T.*
IT'S *ALL* A LIE. EVERYTHING *YOU'RE* SEEING, EVERYTHING I *WAS* SEEING.
IT'S ALTERED OUR PERCEPTIONS, OUR MEMORIES, MAKING US SEE WHAT WE'RE TOLD TO SEE, WHAT ON SOME LEVEL WE *WANT* TO SEE.
THIS ENTIRE WORLD, THIS ENTIRE *REALITY...* IT'S SOME SORT OF FABRICATION, A CHEMICALLY INDUCED MASS *HALLUCINATION.*
POISON IVY WAS *RIGHT.*
WRONG!
WHAM

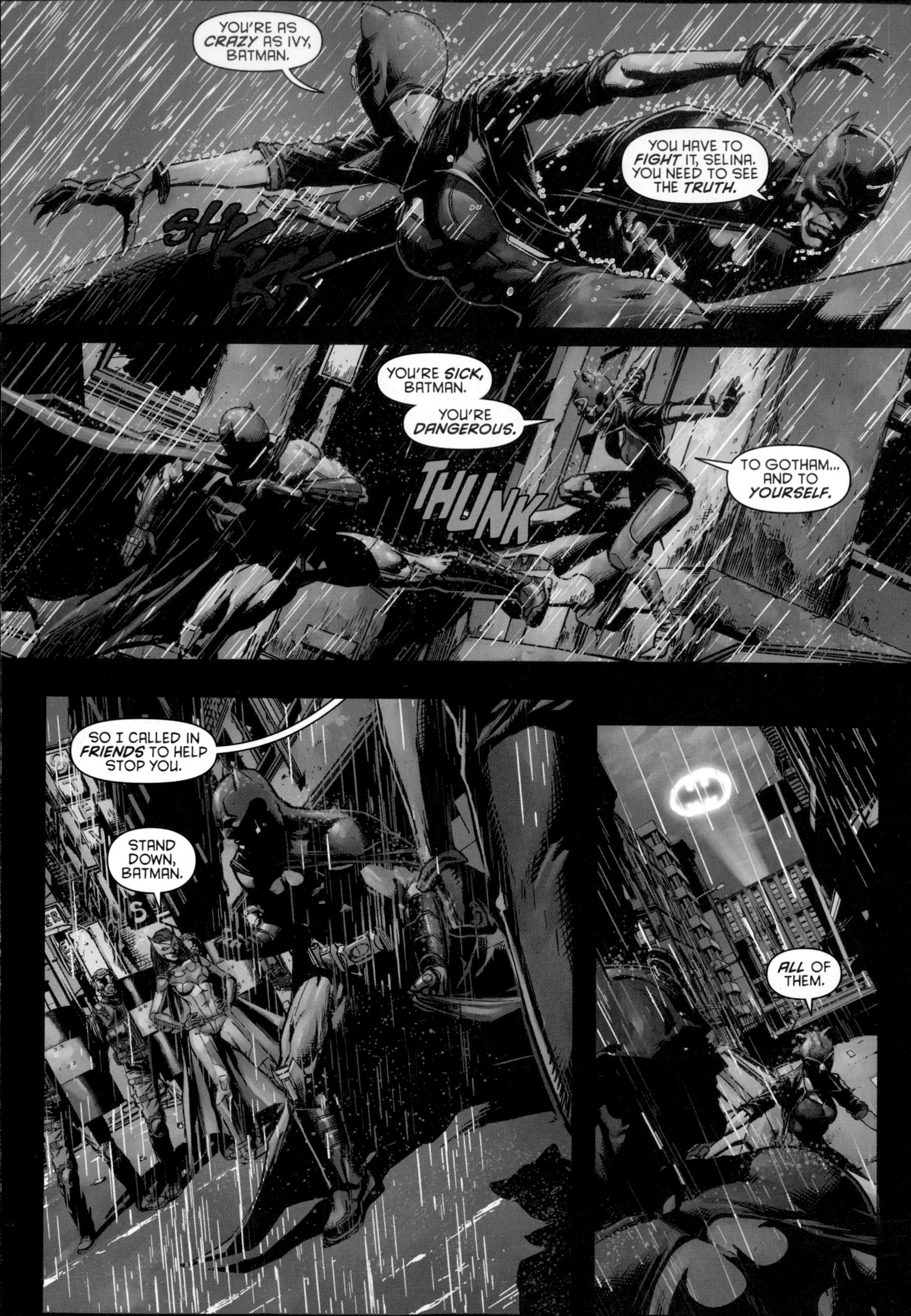
YOU'RE AS *CRAZY* AS IVY, BATMAN.
YOU HAVE TO *FIGHT* IT, SELINA. YOU NEED TO SEE THE *TRUTH*.
YOU'RE *SICK*, BATMAN.
YOU'RE *DANGEROUS*.
THUNK
TO GOTHAM... AND TO *YOURSELF*.
SO I CALLED IN *FRIENDS* TO HELP STOP YOU.
STAND DOWN, BATMAN.
ALL OF THEM.

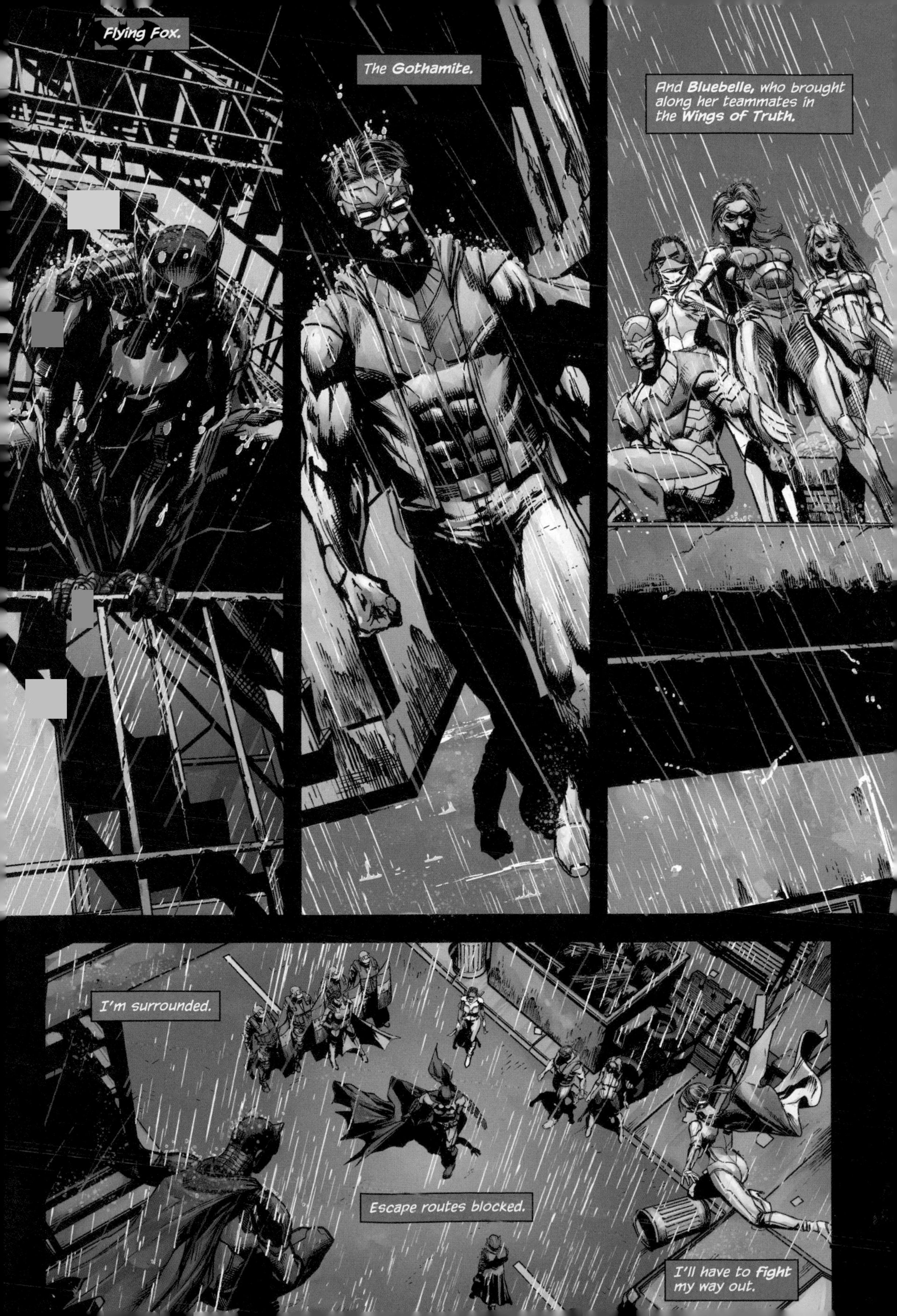
Flying Fox.
The Gothamite.
And Bluebelle, who brought along her teammates in the Wings of Truth.
I'm surrounded.
Escape routes blocked.
I'll have to fight my way out.

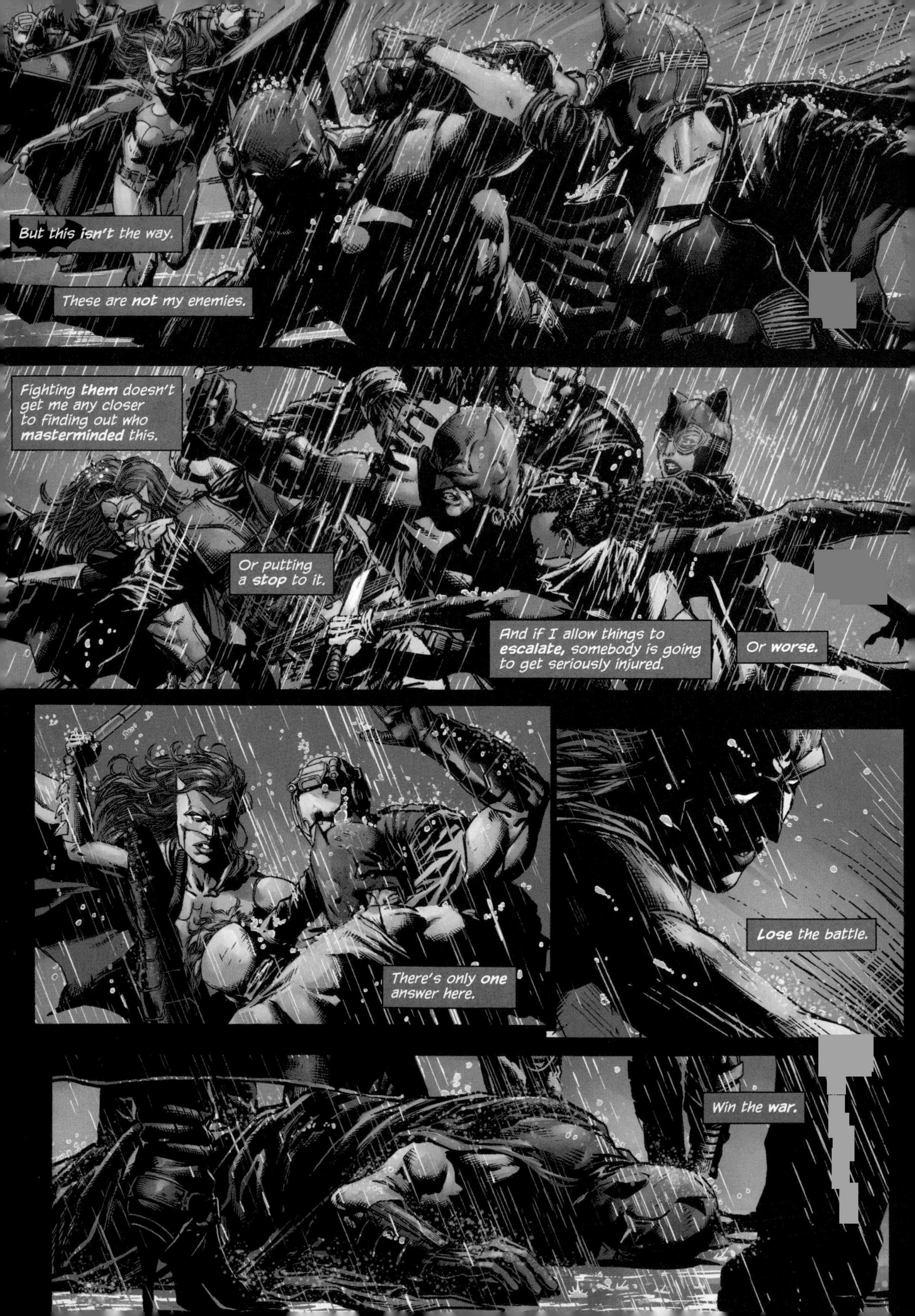
But this isn't the way.
These are not my enemies.
Fighting them doesn't get me any closer to finding out who masterminded this.
Or putting a stop to it.
And if I allow things to escalate, somebody is going to get seriously injured.
Or worse.
There's only one answer here.
Lose the battle.
Win the war.

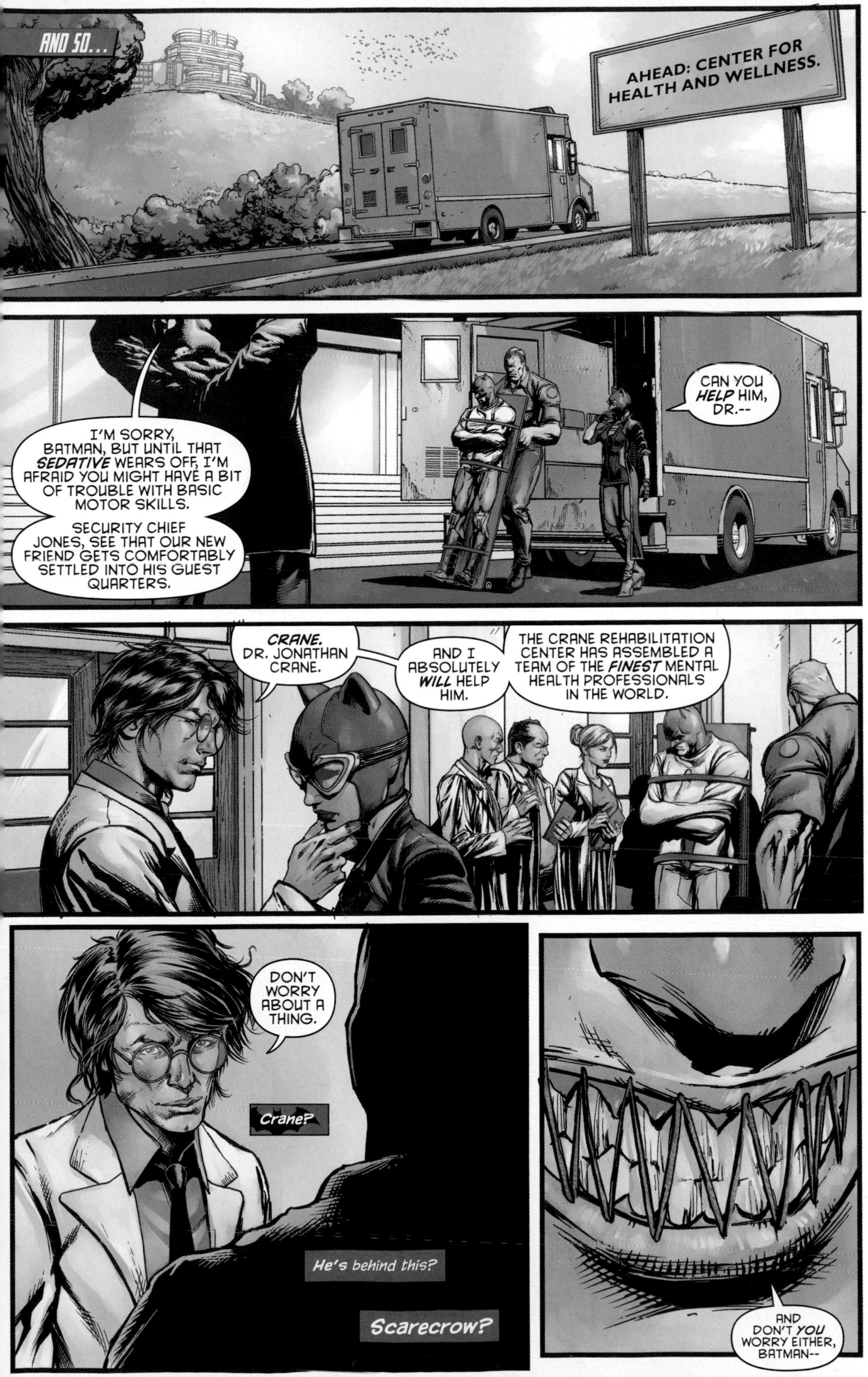
AND SO...
AHEAD: CENTER FOR HEALTH AND WELLNESS.
I'M SORRY, BATMAN, BUT UNTIL THAT SEDATIVE WEARS OFF, I'M AFRAID YOU MIGHT HAVE A BIT OF TROUBLE WITH BASIC MOTOR SKILLS.
SECURITY CHIEF JONES, SEE THAT OUR NEW FRIEND GETS COMFORTABLY SETTLED INTO HIS GUEST QUARTERS.
CAN YOU HELP HIM, DR.--
CRANE. DR. JONATHAN CRANE.
AND I ABSOLUTELY WILL HELP HIM.
THE CRANE REHABILITATION CENTER HAS ASSEMBLED A TEAM OF THE FINEST MENTAL HEALTH PROFESSIONALS IN THE WORLD.
DON'T WORRY ABOUT A THING.
Crane?
He's behind this?
Scarecrow?
AND DON'T YOU WORRY EITHER, BATMAN--

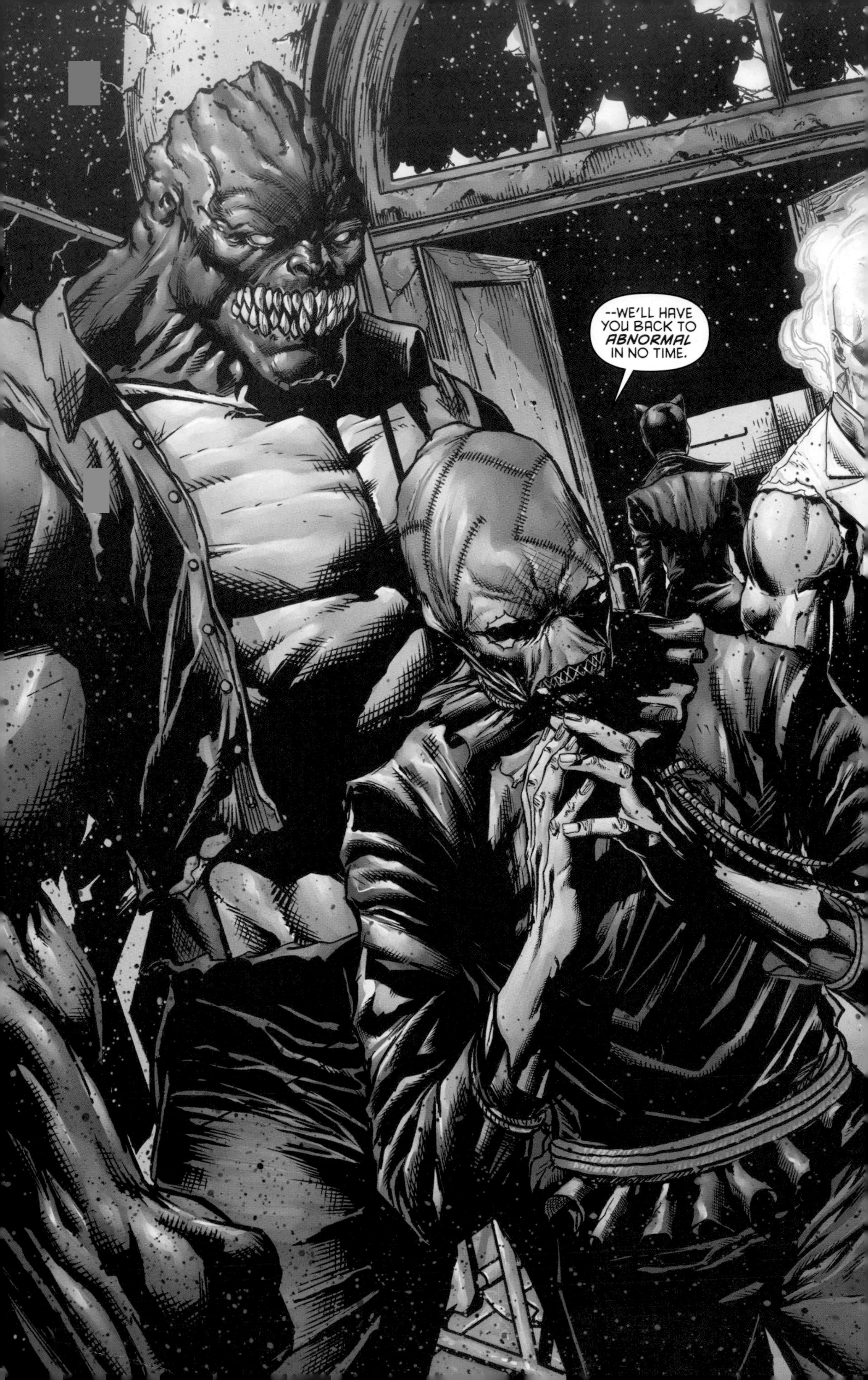
--WE'LL HAVE YOU BACK TO *ABNORMAL* IN NO TIME.

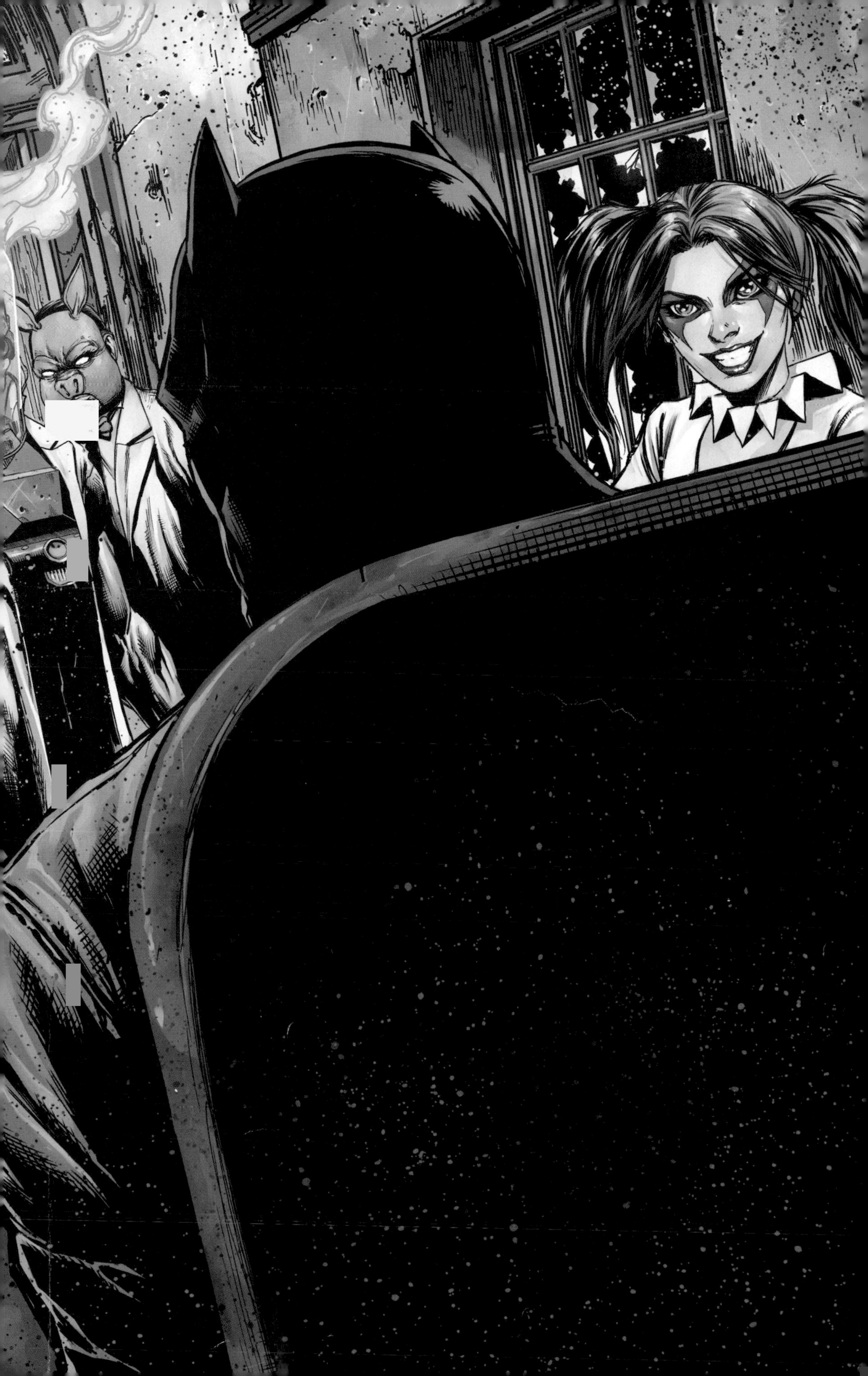

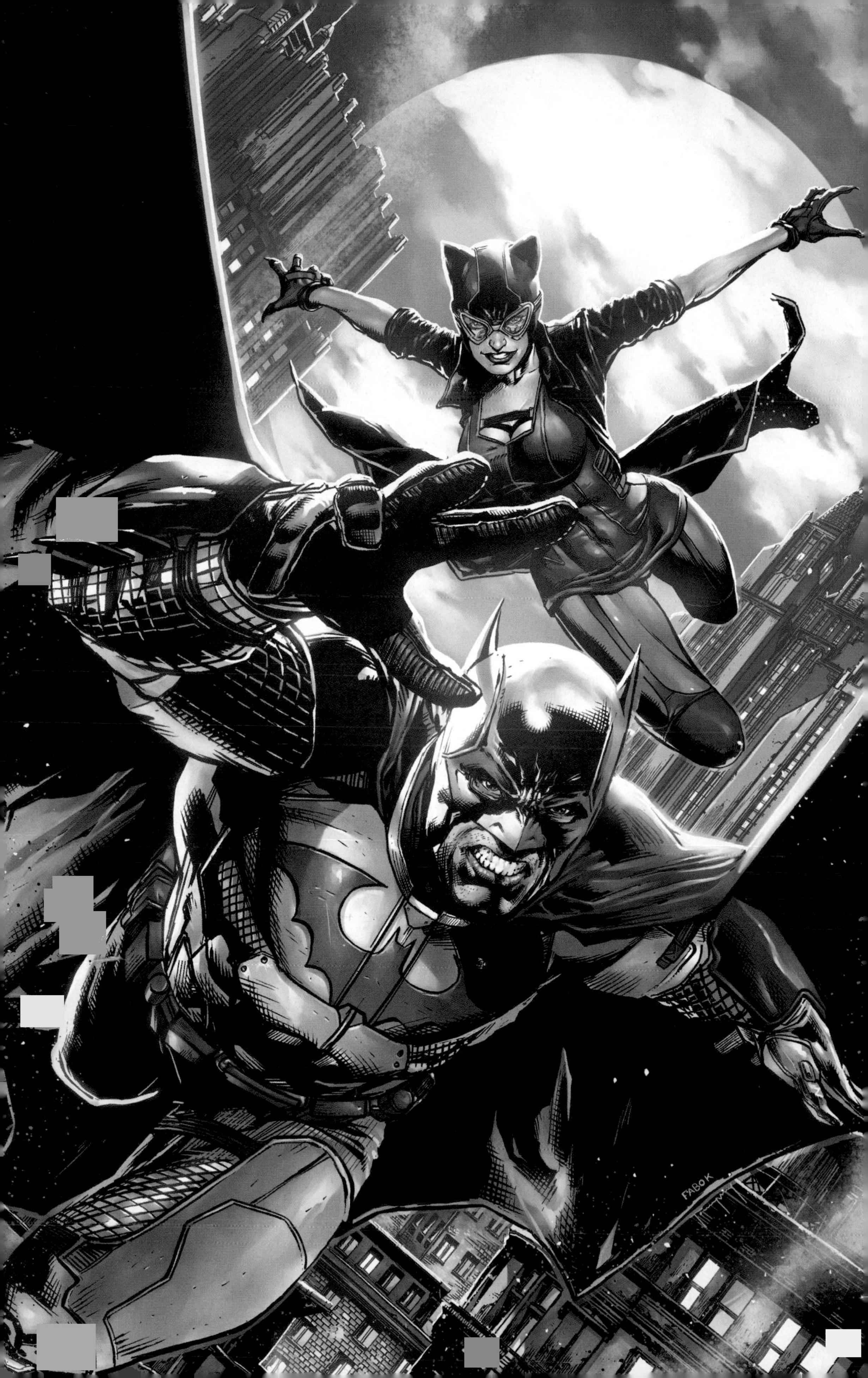
FABOK

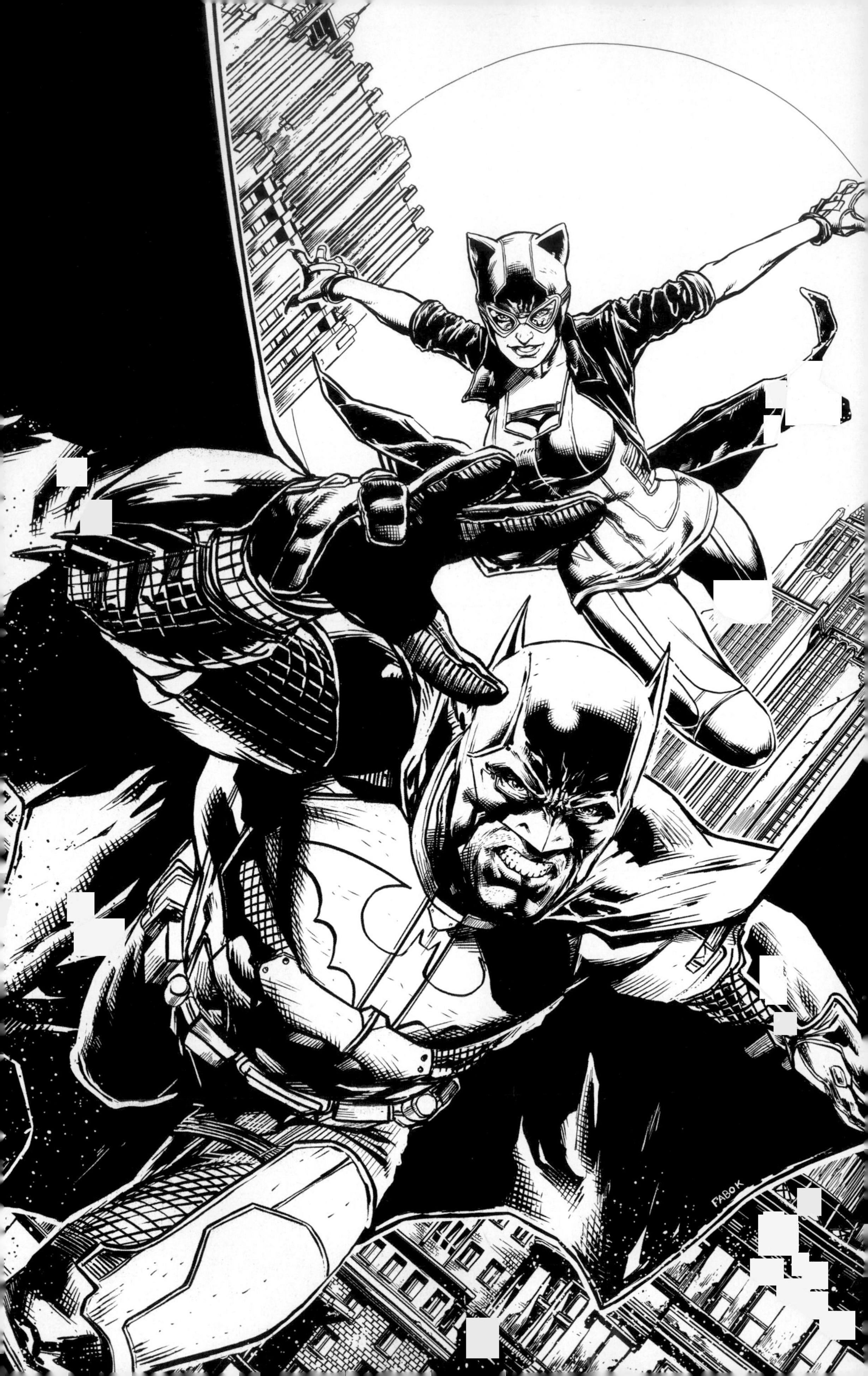
FABOK

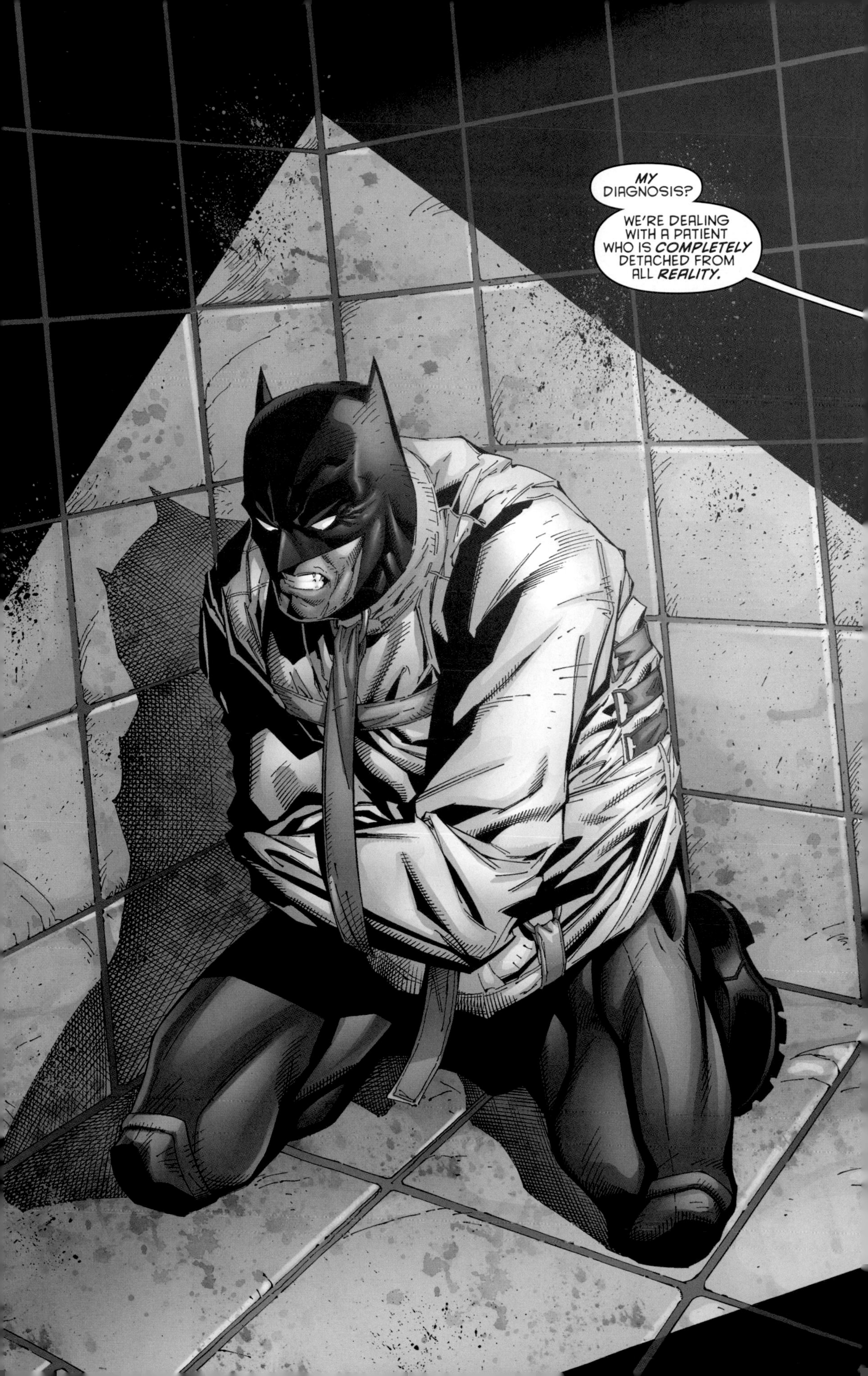
MY DIAGNOSIS?
WE'RE DEALING WITH A PATIENT WHO IS COMPLETELY DETACHED FROM ALL REALITY.

THE SUBJECT IS SUFFERING FROM NOT JUST VIVID AND PERSISTENT *HALLUCINATIONS,* BUT HE'S FABRICATED AN ENTIRE *UNIVERSE* BASED ON HIS ERRONEOUS PERCEPTIONS.

AND THIS CONFABULATION APPEARS TO EXTEND TO BOTH VISION AND *MEMORY,* WITH THE PATIENT'S SUBCONSCIOUS DEVISING A SERIES OF DISTORTED *RECOLLECTIONS* TO REINFORCE HIS FICTITIOUS WORLD-VIEW.

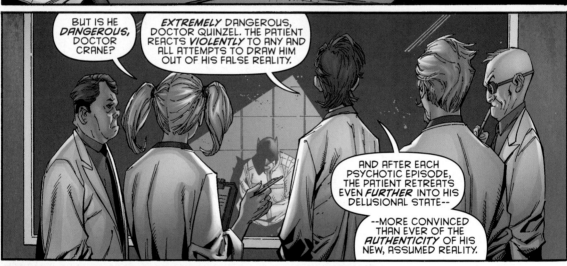

BUT IS HE *DANGEROUS,* DOCTOR CRANE?

EXTREMELY DANGEROUS, DOCTOR QUINZEL. THE PATIENT REACTS *VIOLENTLY* TO ANY AND ALL ATTEMPTS TO DRAW HIM OUT OF HIS FALSE REALITY.

AND AFTER EACH PSYCHOTIC EPISODE, THE PATIENT RETREATS EVEN *FURTHER* INTO HIS DELUSIONAL STATE--

--MORE CONVINCED THAN EVER OF THE *AUTHENTICITY* OF HIS NEW, ASSUMED REALITY.

THE PATIENT SEES WHAT HE *WANTS* TO SEE, IT'S AS SIMPLE AS THAT.

THE QUESTION I POSE TO YOU, MY ESTEEMED MEDICAL STAFF, IS HOW SHOULD WE *DEAL* WITH HIM?

Dr. Jonathan Crane.

Chief administrator, The Crane Center for Health and Wellness.

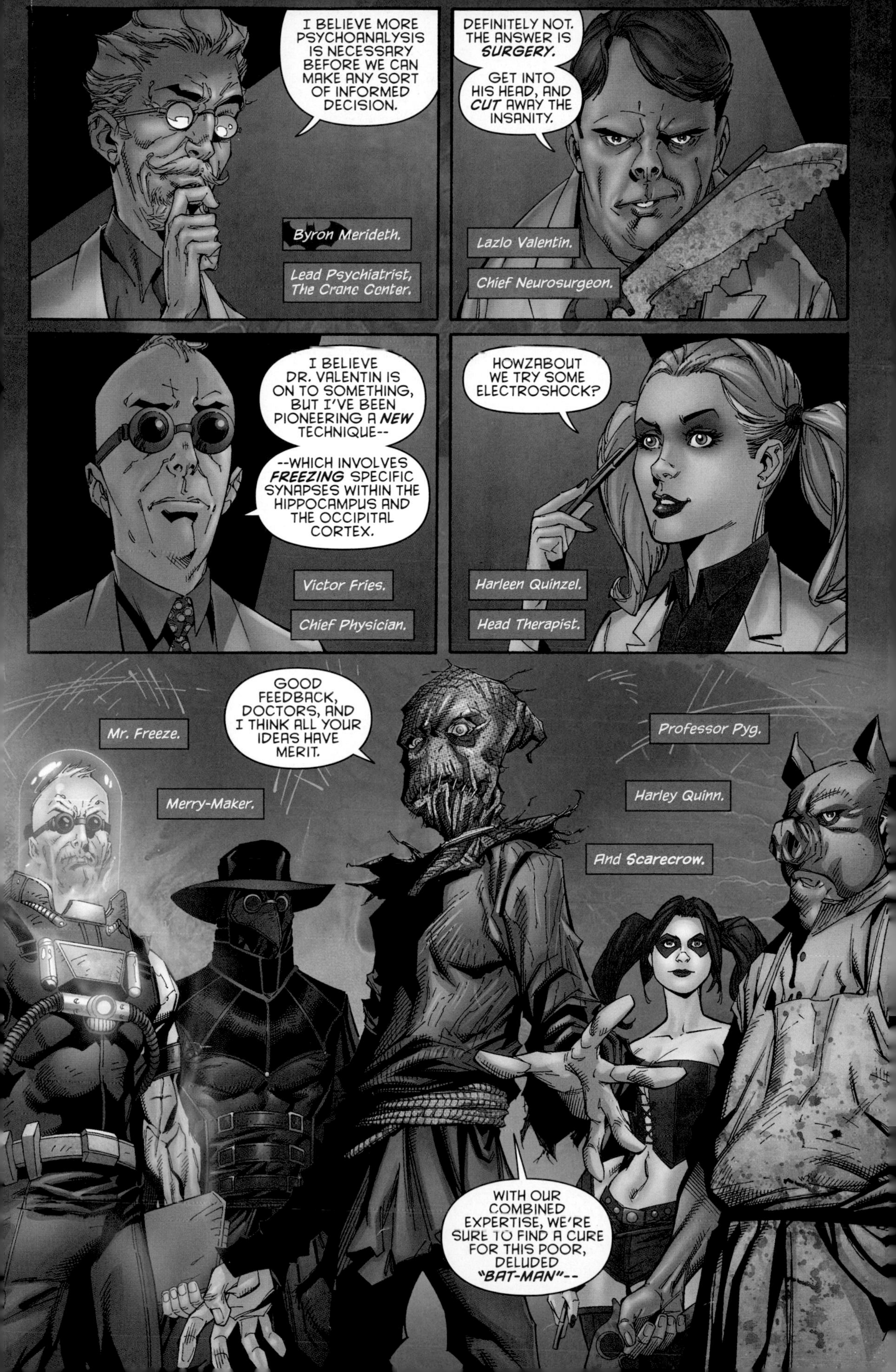
I BELIEVE MORE PSYCHOANALYSIS IS NECESSARY BEFORE WE CAN MAKE ANY SORT OF INFORMED DECISION.
Byron Merideth.
Lead Psychiatrist, The Crane Center.
DEFINITELY NOT. THE ANSWER IS SURGERY.
GET INTO HIS HEAD, AND CUT AWAY THE INSANITY.
Lazlo Valentin.
Chief Neurosurgeon.
I BELIEVE DR. VALENTIN IS ON TO SOMETHING, BUT I'VE BEEN PIONEERING A NEW TECHNIQUE--
--WHICH INVOLVES FREEZING SPECIFIC SYNAPSES WITHIN THE HIPPOCAMPUS AND THE OCCIPITAL CORTEX.
Victor Fries.
Chief Physician.
HOWZABOUT WE TRY SOME ELECTROSHOCK?
Harleen Quinzel.
Head Therapist.
Mr. Freeze.
Merry-Maker.
GOOD FEEDBACK, DOCTORS, AND I THINK ALL YOUR IDEAS HAVE MERIT.
Professor Pyg.
Harley Quinn.
And Scarecrow.
WITH OUR COMBINED EXPERTISE, WE'RE SURE TO FIND A CURE FOR THIS POOR, DELUDED "BAT-MAN"--

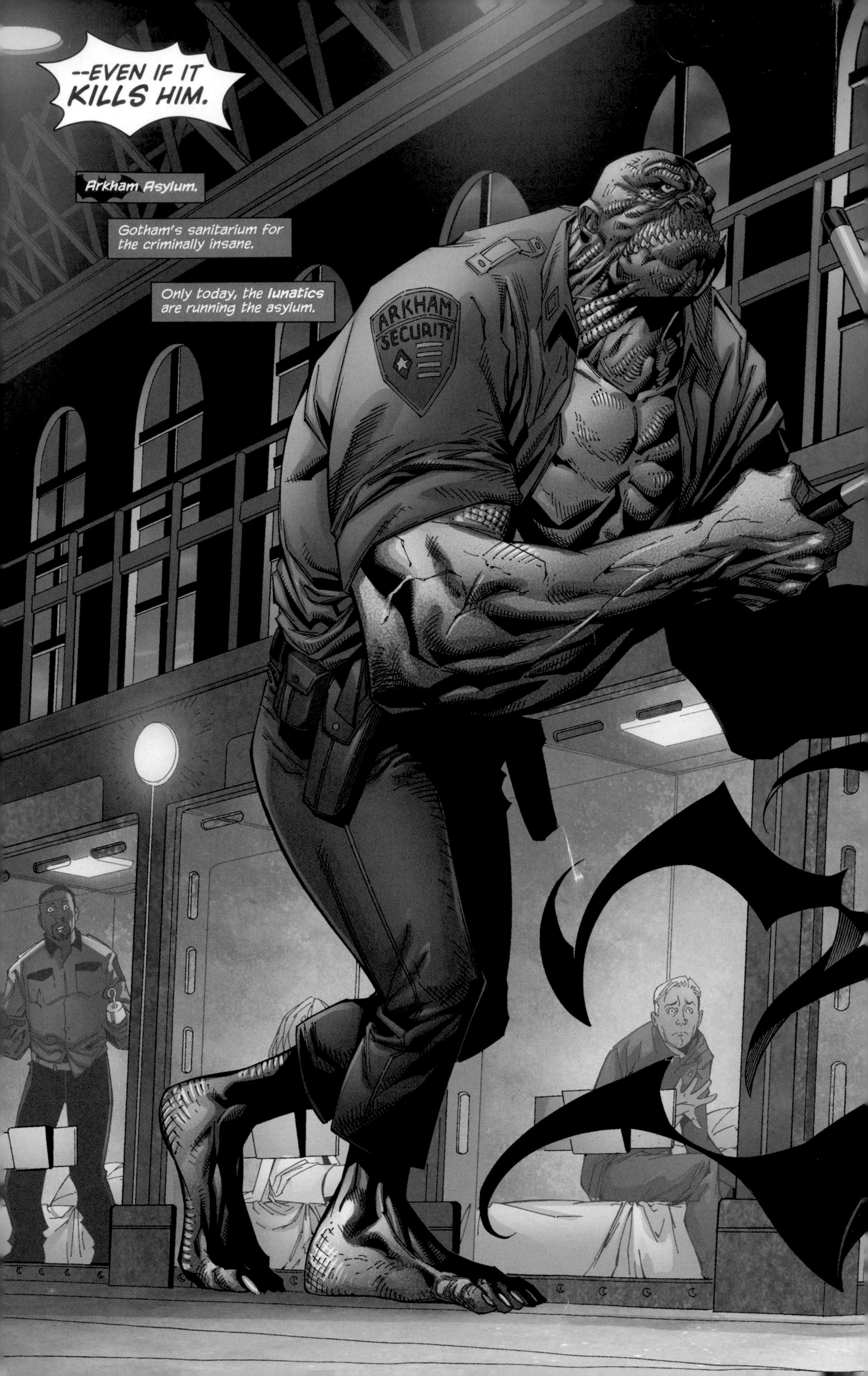
--EVEN IF IT KILLS HIM.
Arkham Asylum.
Gotham's sanitarium for the criminally insane.
Only today, the lunatics are running the asylum.
ARKHAM SECURITY

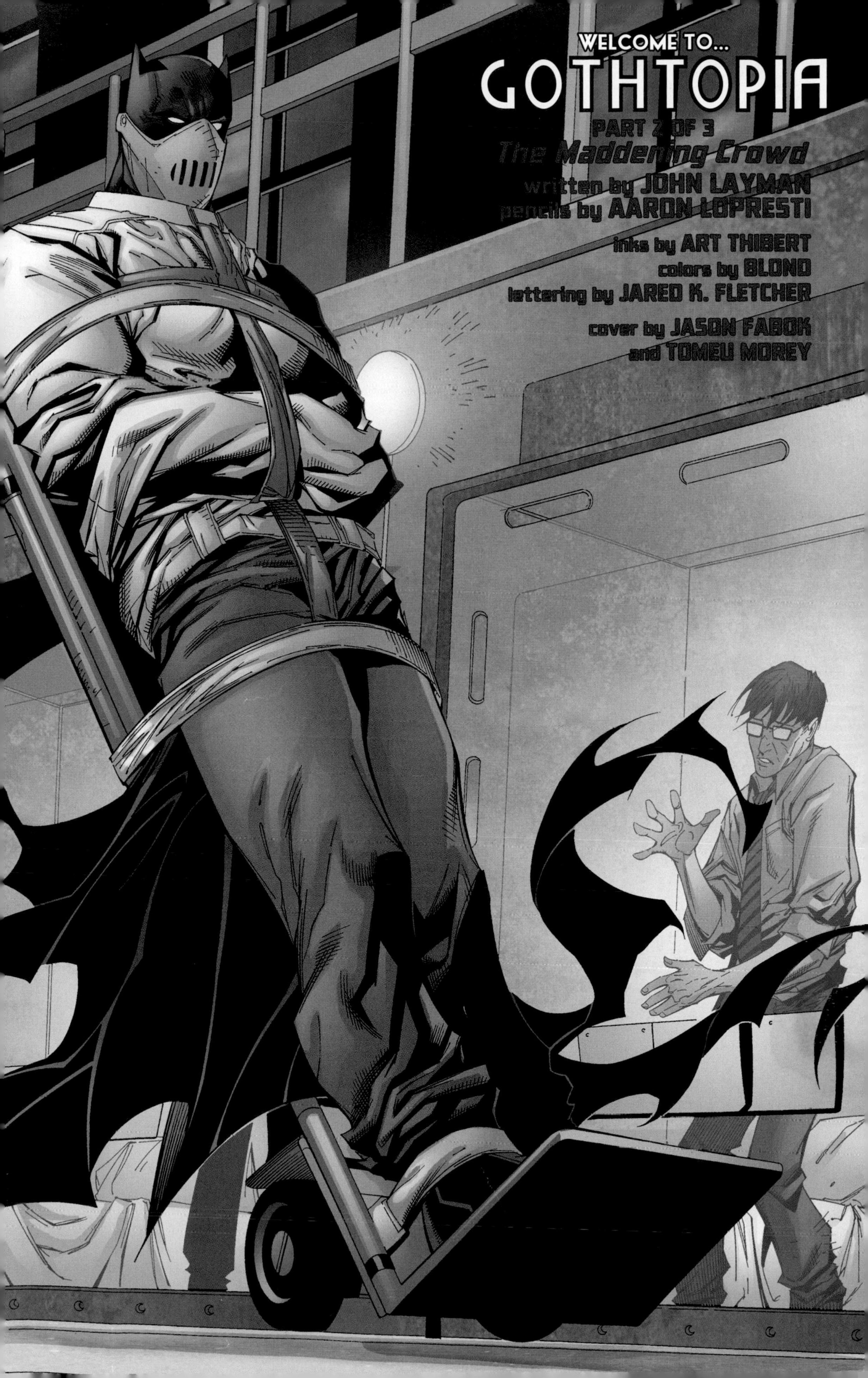

WELCOME TO...
GOTHTOPIA
PART 2 OF 3
The Maddening Crowd
written by JOHN LAYMAN
pencils by AARON LOPRESTI
inks by ART THIBERT
colors by BLOND
lettering by JARED K. FLETCHER
cover by JASON FABOK
and TOMEU MOREY

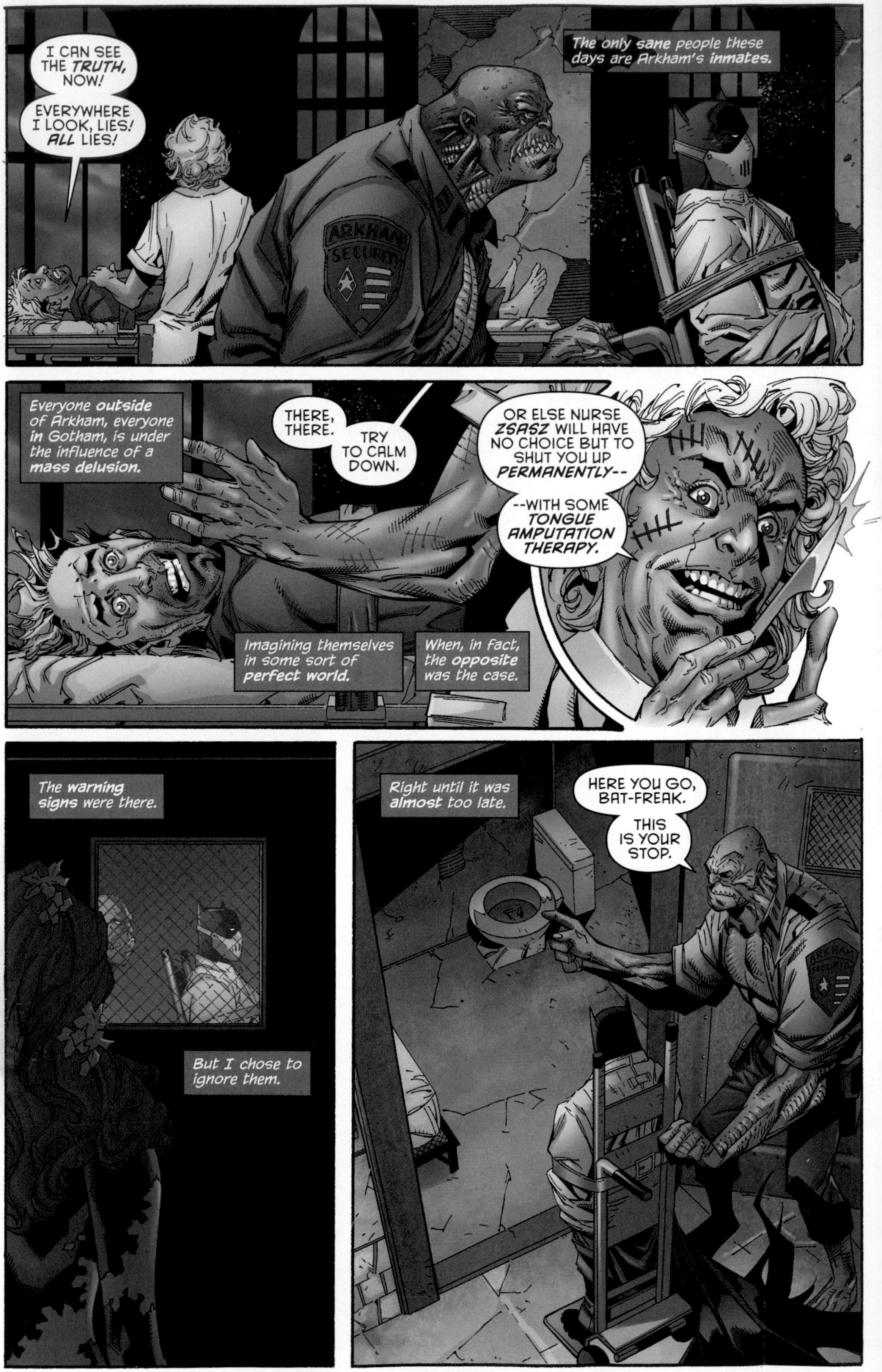
I CAN SEE THE TRUTH, NOW!
EVERYWHERE I LOOK, LIES! ALL LIES!
The only sane people these days are Arkham's inmates.
ARKHAM SECURITY
Everyone outside of Arkham, everyone in Gotham, is under the influence of a mass delusion.
THERE, THERE.
TRY TO CALM DOWN.
OR ELSE NURSE ZSASZ WILL HAVE NO CHOICE BUT TO SHUT YOU UP PERMANENTLY--
--WITH SOME TONGUE AMPUTATION THERAPY.
Imagining themselves in some sort of perfect world.
When, in fact, the opposite was the case.
The warning signs were there.
But I chose to ignore them.
Right until it was almost too late.
HERE YOU GO, BAT-FREAK.
THIS IS YOUR STOP.

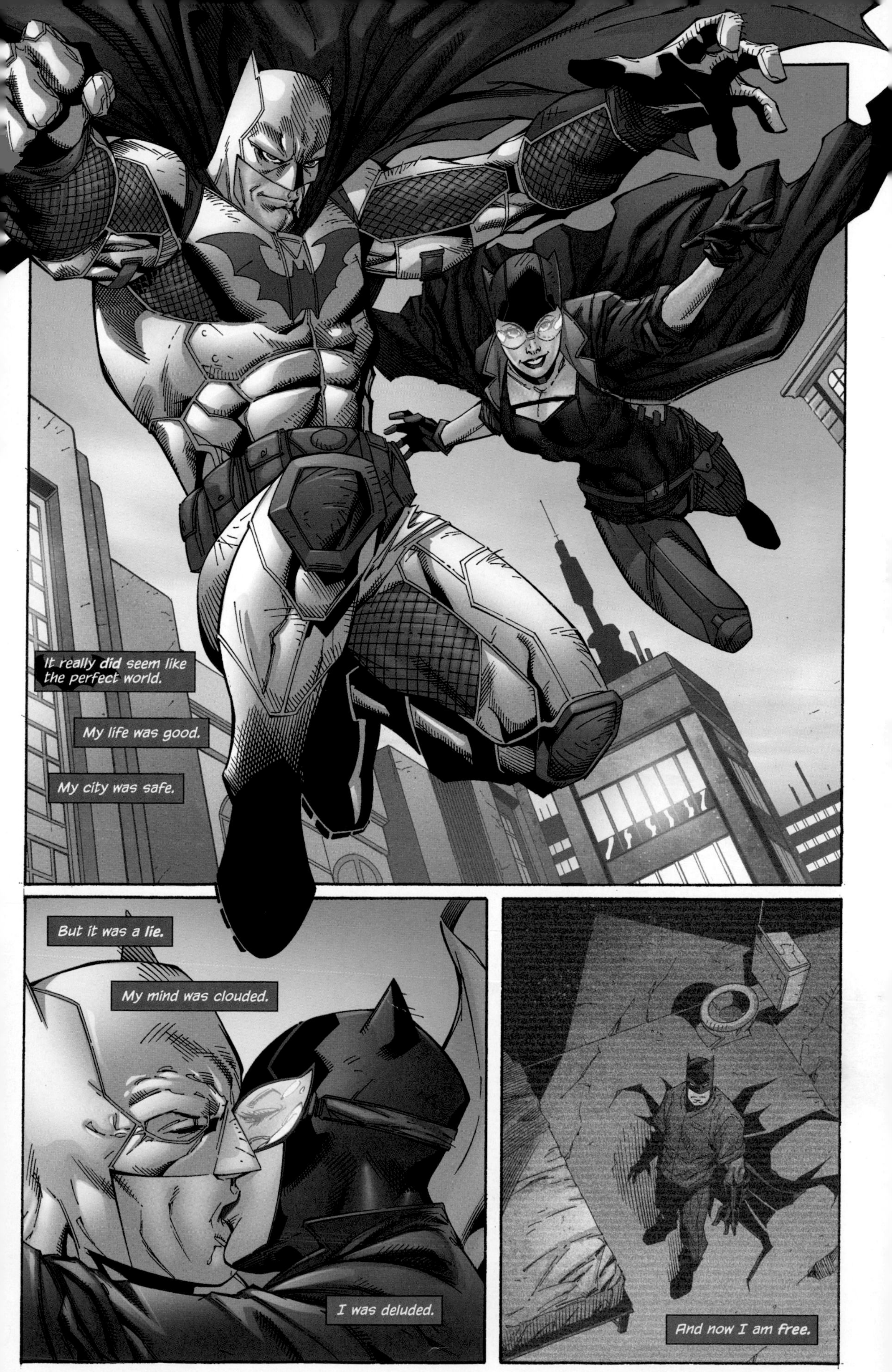
It really did seem like the perfect world.
My life was good.
My city was safe.
But it was a lie.
My mind was clouded.
I was deluded.
And now I am free.

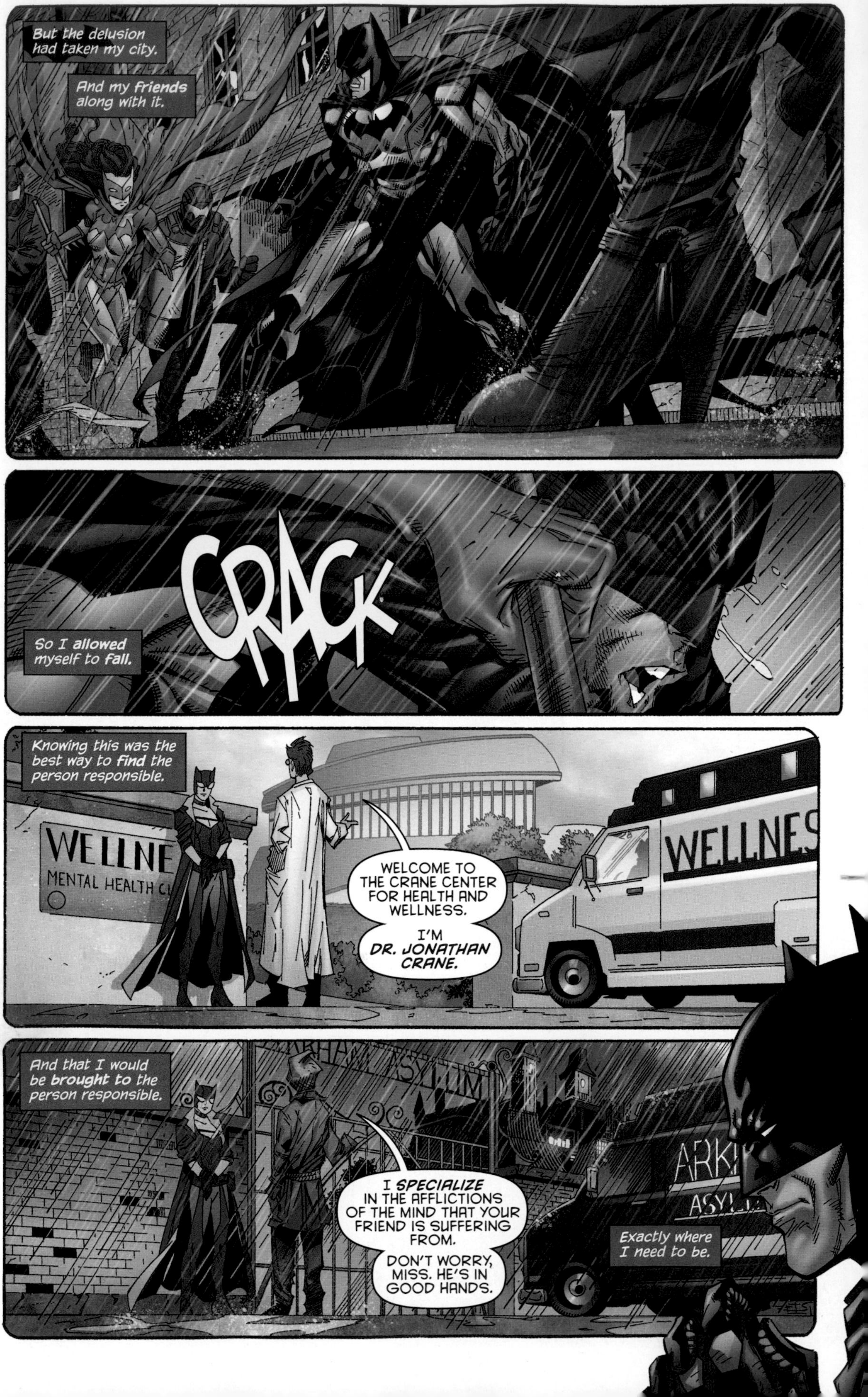
But the delusion had taken my city.
And my friends along with it.
CRACK
So I allowed myself to fall.
Knowing this was the best way to find the person responsible.
WELLNE
MENTAL HEALTH C
WELLNES
WELCOME TO THE CRANE CENTER FOR HEALTH AND WELLNESS.
I'M DR. JONATHAN CRANE.
And that I would be brought to the person responsible.
I SPECIALIZE IN THE AFFLICTIONS OF THE MIND THAT YOUR FRIEND IS SUFFERING FROM.
DON'T WORRY, MISS. HE'S IN GOOD HANDS.
Exactly where I need to be.

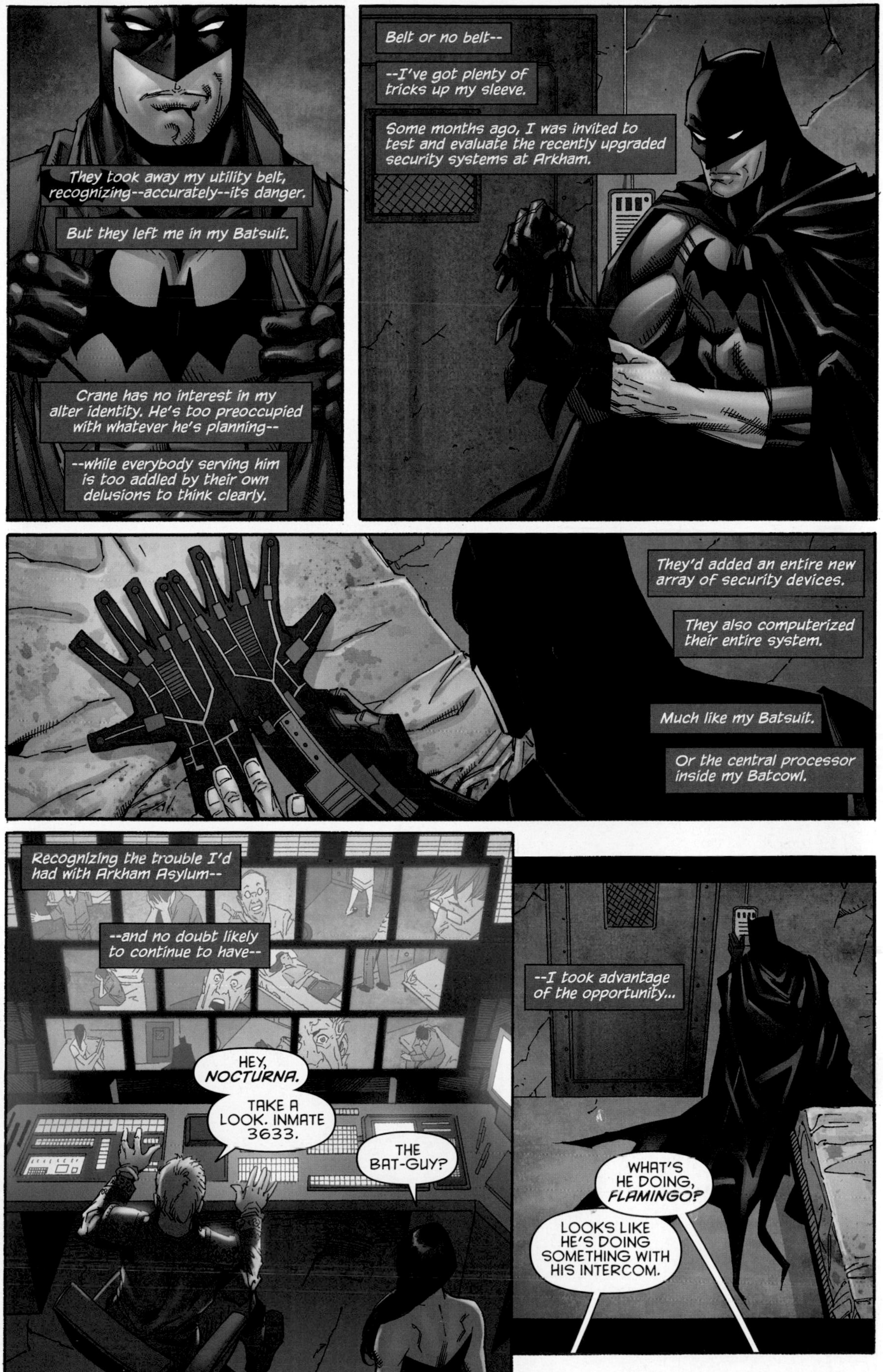
They took away my utility belt, recognizing--accurately--its danger.
But they left me in my Batsuit.
Crane has no interest in my alter identity. He's too preoccupied with whatever he's planning--
--while everybody serving him is too addled by their own delusions to think clearly.
Belt or no belt--
--I've got plenty of tricks up my sleeve.
Some months ago, I was invited to test and evaluate the recently upgraded security systems at Arkham.
They'd added an entire new array of security devices.
They also computerized their entire system.
Much like my Batsuit.
Or the central processor inside my Batcowl.
Recognizing the trouble I'd had with Arkham Asylum--
--and no doubt likely to continue to have--
HEY, NOCTURNA.
TAKE A LOOK. INMATE 3633.
THE BAT-GUY?
--I took advantage of the opportunity...
WHAT'S HE DOING, FLAMINGO?
LOOKS LIKE HE'S DOING SOMETHING WITH HIS INTERCOM.

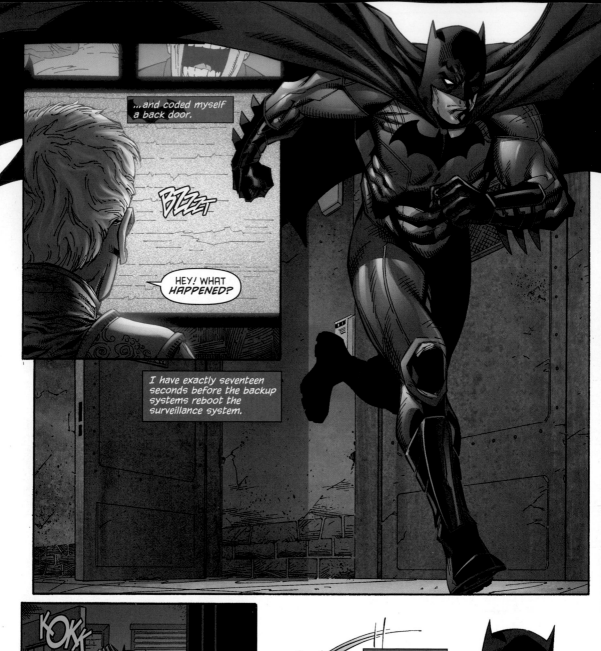

...and coded myself a back door.

BZZZT

HEY! WHAT *HAPPENED?*

I have exactly seventeen seconds before the backup systems reboot the surveillance system.

KOKK

YOU THINK WE SHOULD CALL CROC, ER... *SECURITY CHIEF JONES,* GIVE HIM A HEADS-UP THAT MAYBE THE SYSTEM IS ON THE FRITZ?

Plenty of time.

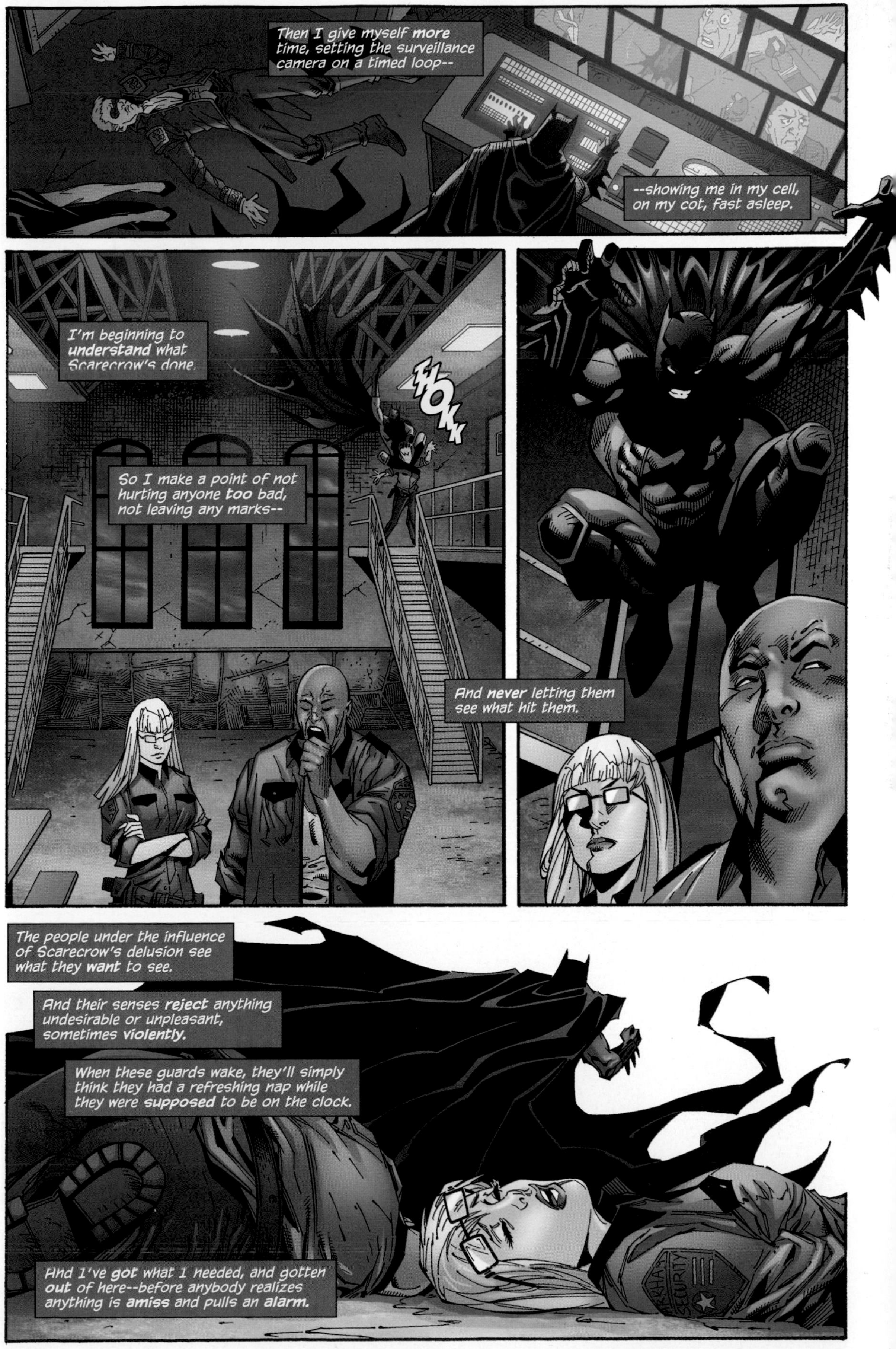
Then I give myself more time, setting the surveillance camera on a timed loop--
--showing me in my cell, on my cot, fast asleep.
I'm beginning to understand what Scarecrow's done.
THOKK
So I make a point of not hurting anyone too bad, not leaving any marks--
And never letting them see what hit them.
The people under the influence of Scarecrow's delusion see what they want to see.
And their senses reject anything undesirable or unpleasant, sometimes violently.
When these guards wake, they'll simply think they had a refreshing nap while they were supposed to be on the clock.
And I've got what I needed, and gotten out of here--before anybody realizes anything is amiss and pulls an alarm.

What I need is here.

The medical facilities in B wing--converted into some sort of makeshift lab.

Scarecrow's current base of operations.

PRIVATE

And this is where I learn **how** Scarecrow did what he did.

This **new** toxin... chemically, it's not terribly different from the Scarecrow **Fear Toxin**, causing a similar decrease in serotonergic neurons of the hypothalamus to produce hallucinatory effects.

It's the **effects** that vary so dramatically-- these are designed to produce maximum **contentment**.

Strange, considering Scarecrow's interest has always been **fear**... and **only** fear.

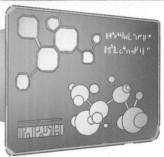

I'll need at least three more nights in the lab to create a working **antidote**.

Except I don't **have** three nights.

If **Selina** is right, I'll be dead in the morning.

EIGHT HOURS EARLIER...

YO, BAT.

YOU GOT A **VISITOR**...

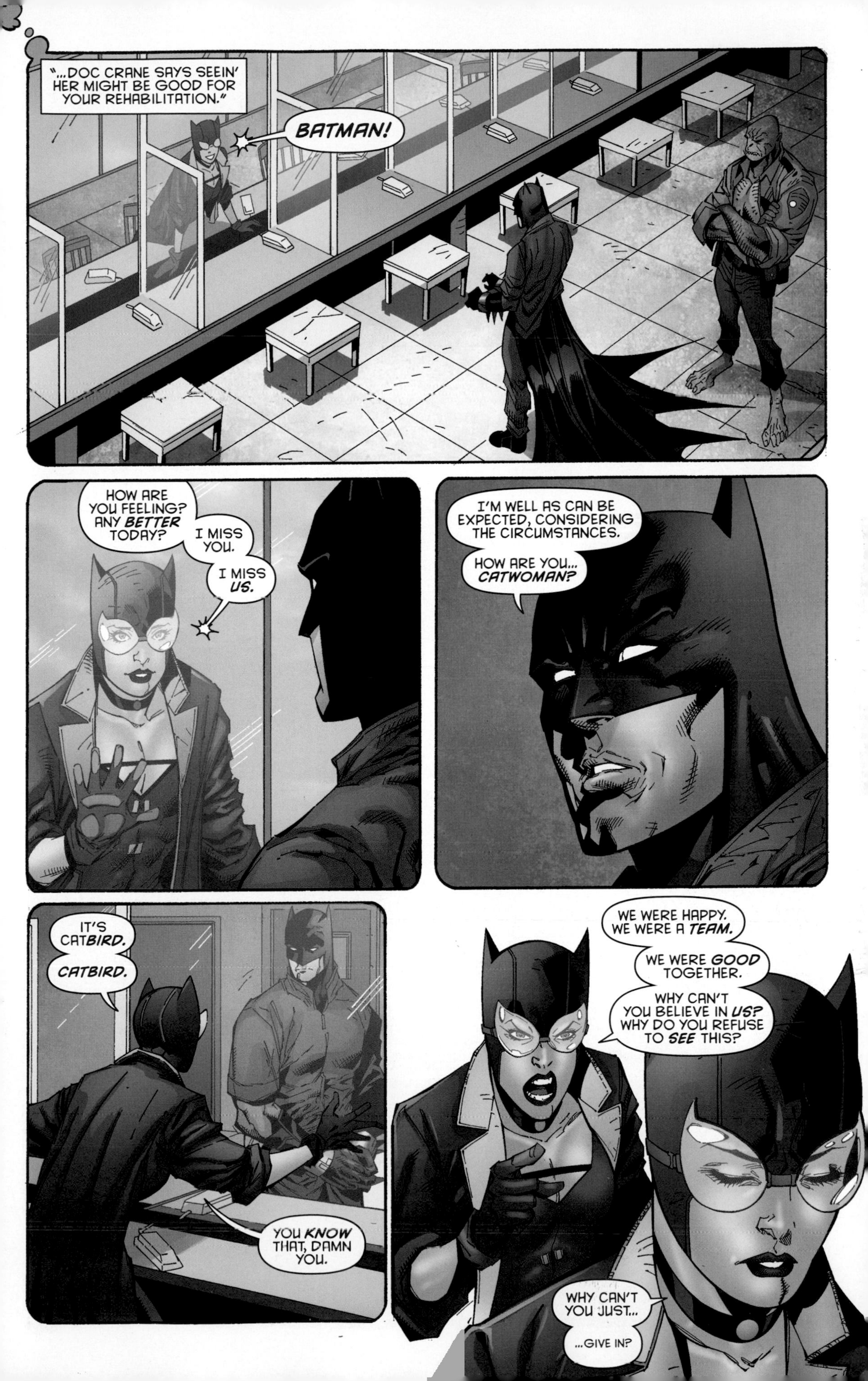
"...DOC CRANE SAYS SEEIN' HER MIGHT BE GOOD FOR YOUR REHABILITATION."
BATMAN!
HOW ARE YOU FEELING? ANY BETTER TODAY?
I MISS YOU.
I MISS US.
I'M WELL AS CAN BE EXPECTED, CONSIDERING THE CIRCUMSTANCES.
HOW ARE YOU... CATWOMAN?
IT'S CATBIRD.
CATBIRD.
YOU KNOW THAT, DAMN YOU.
WE WERE HAPPY. WE WERE A TEAM.
WE WERE GOOD TOGETHER.
WHY CAN'T YOU BELIEVE IN US? WHY DO YOU REFUSE TO SEE THIS?
WHY CAN'T YOU JUST...
...GIVE IN?

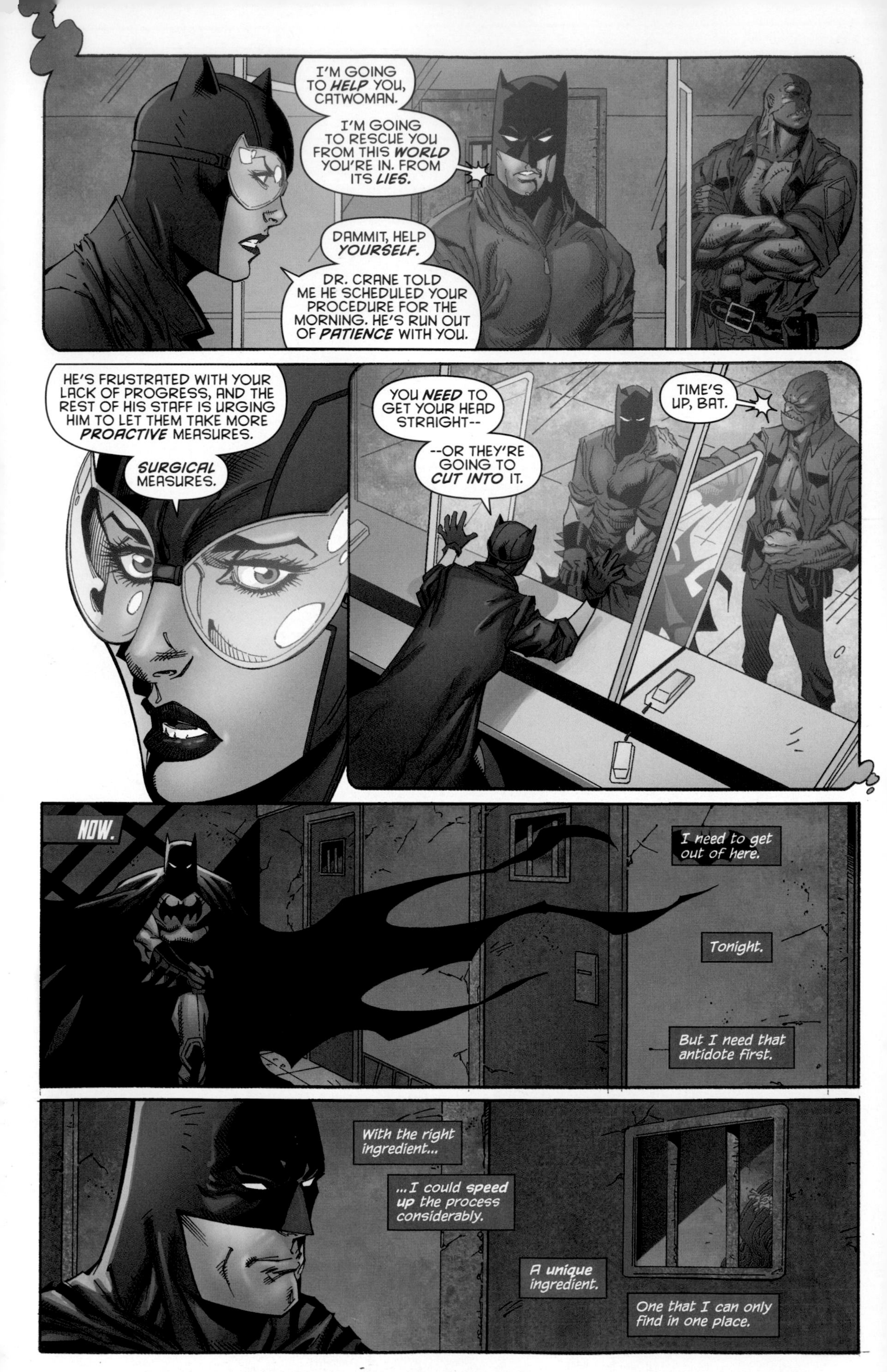
I'M GOING TO HELP YOU, CATWOMAN.
I'M GOING TO RESCUE YOU FROM THIS WORLD YOU'RE IN. FROM ITS LIES.
DAMMIT, HELP YOURSELF.
DR. CRANE TOLD ME HE SCHEDULED YOUR PROCEDURE FOR THE MORNING. HE'S RUN OUT OF PATIENCE WITH YOU.
HE'S FRUSTRATED WITH YOUR LACK OF PROGRESS, AND THE REST OF HIS STAFF IS URGING HIM TO LET THEM TAKE MORE PROACTIVE MEASURES.
SURGICAL MEASURES.
YOU NEED TO GET YOUR HEAD STRAIGHT--
--OR THEY'RE GOING TO CUT INTO IT.
TIME'S UP, BAT.
NOW.
I need to get out of here.
Tonight.
But I need that antidote first.
With the right ingredient...
...I could speed up the process considerably.
A unique ingredient.
One that I can only find in one place.

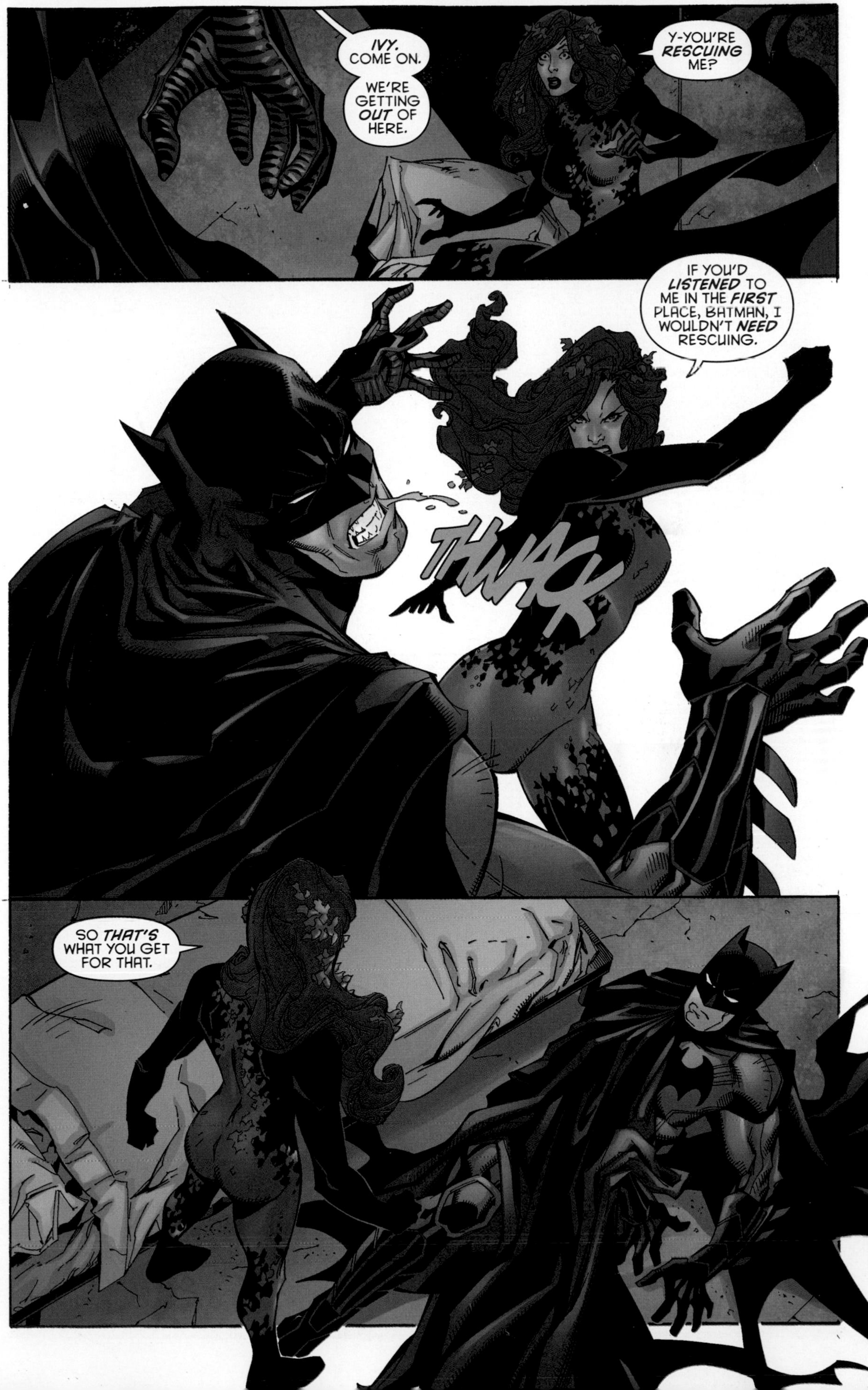
IVY. COME ON.
WE'RE GETTING *OUT* OF HERE.
Y-YOU'RE *RESCUING* ME?
IF YOU'D *LISTENED* TO ME IN THE *FIRST* PLACE, BATMAN, I WOULDN'T *NEED* RESCUING.
THWACK
SO *THAT'S* WHAT YOU GET FOR THAT.

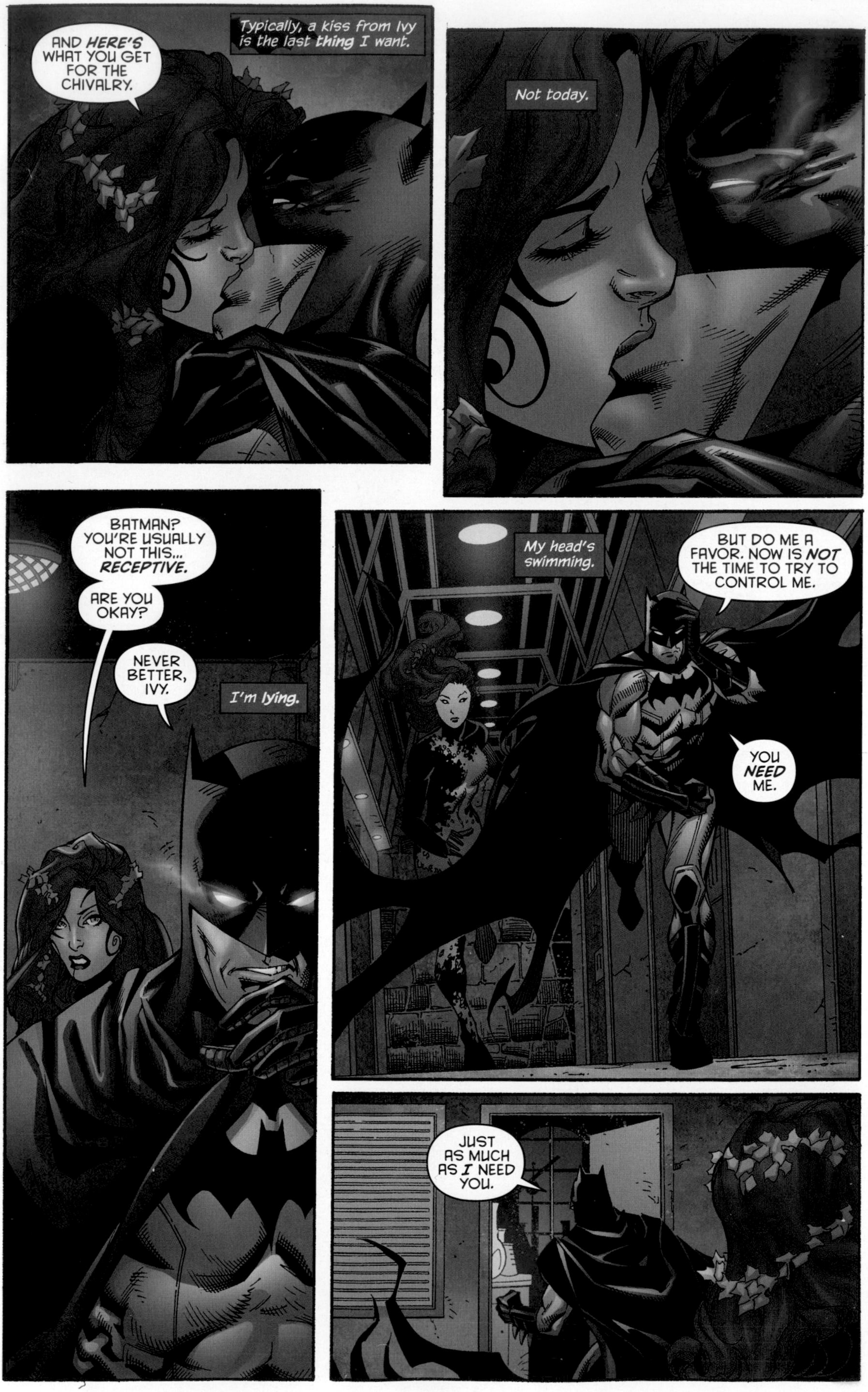
AND *HERE'S* WHAT YOU GET FOR THE CHIVALRY.
Typically, a kiss from Ivy is the last ***thing*** *I want.*
Not today.
BATMAN? YOU'RE USUALLY NOT THIS... ***RECEPTIVE.***
ARE YOU OKAY?
NEVER BETTER, IVY.
I'm ***lying.***
My head's swimming.
BUT DO ME A FAVOR. NOW IS ***NOT*** THE TIME TO TRY TO CONTROL ME.
YOU ***NEED*** ME.
JUST AS MUCH AS ***I*** NEED YOU.

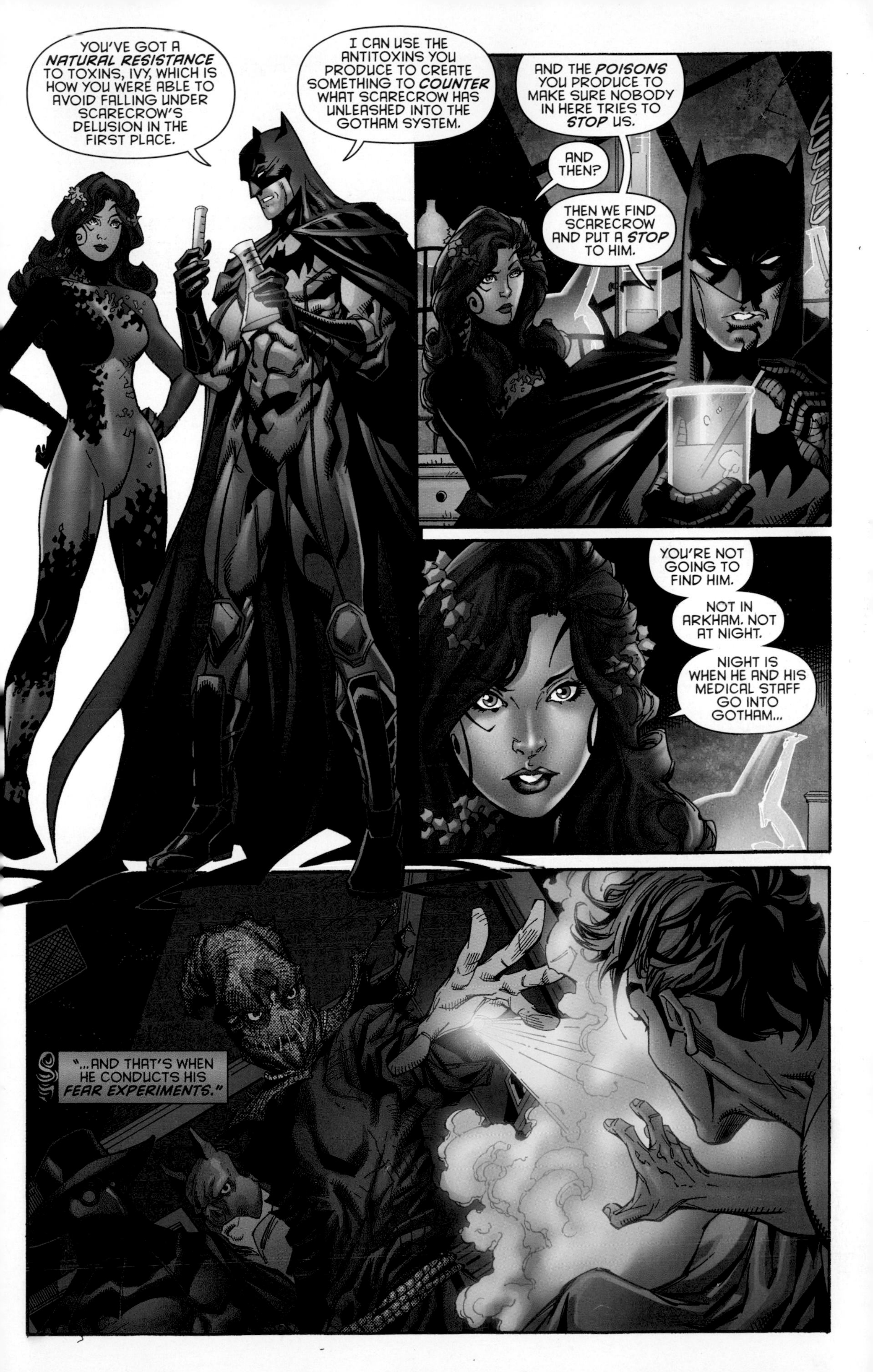
YOU'VE GOT A NATURAL RESISTANCE TO TOXINS, IVY, WHICH IS HOW YOU WERE ABLE TO AVOID FALLING UNDER SCARECROW'S DELUSION IN THE FIRST PLACE.
I CAN USE THE ANTITOXINS YOU PRODUCE TO CREATE SOMETHING TO COUNTER WHAT SCARECROW HAS UNLEASHED INTO THE GOTHAM SYSTEM.
AND THE POISONS YOU PRODUCE TO MAKE SURE NOBODY IN HERE TRIES TO STOP US.
AND THEN?
THEN WE FIND SCARECROW AND PUT A STOP TO HIM.
YOU'RE NOT GOING TO FIND HIM.
NOT IN ARKHAM. NOT AT NIGHT.
NIGHT IS WHEN HE AND HIS MEDICAL STAFF GO INTO GOTHAM...
"...AND THAT'S WHEN HE CONDUCTS HIS FEAR EXPERIMENTS."

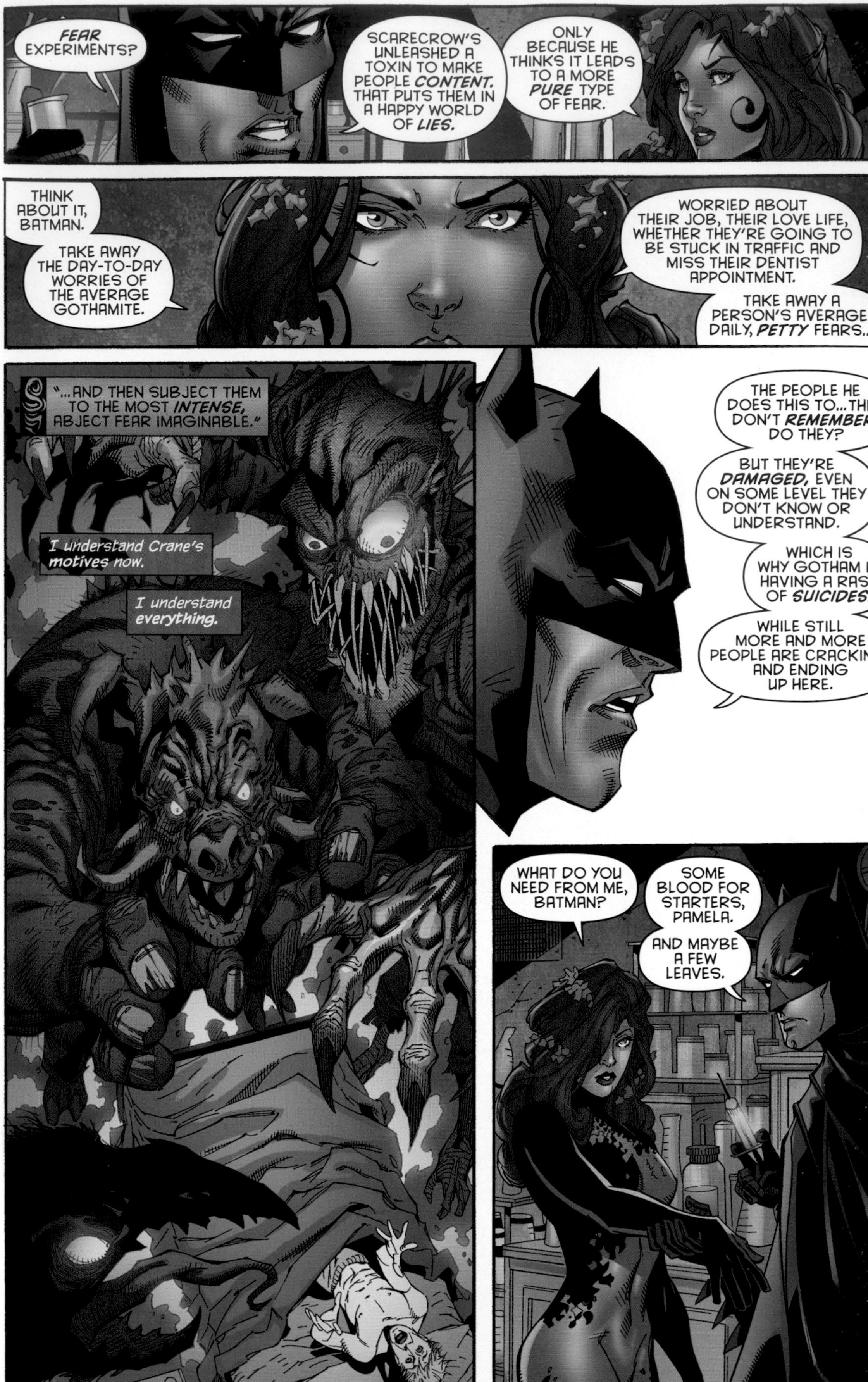
FEAR EXPERIMENTS?
SCARECROW'S UNLEASHED A TOXIN TO MAKE PEOPLE CONTENT. THAT PUTS THEM IN A HAPPY WORLD OF LIES.
ONLY BECAUSE HE THINKS IT LEADS TO A MORE PURE TYPE OF FEAR.
THINK ABOUT IT, BATMAN.
TAKE AWAY THE DAY-TO-DAY WORRIES OF THE AVERAGE GOTHAMITE.
WORRIED ABOUT THEIR JOB, THEIR LOVE LIFE, WHETHER THEY'RE GOING TO BE STUCK IN TRAFFIC AND MISS THEIR DENTIST APPOINTMENT.
TAKE AWAY A PERSON'S AVERAGE, DAILY, PETTY FEARS...
"...AND THEN SUBJECT THEM TO THE MOST INTENSE, ABJECT FEAR IMAGINABLE."
I understand Crane's motives now.
I understand everything.
THE PEOPLE HE DOES THIS TO...THEY DON'T REMEMBER, DO THEY?
BUT THEY'RE DAMAGED, EVEN ON SOME LEVEL THEY DON'T KNOW OR UNDERSTAND.
WHICH IS WHY GOTHAM IS HAVING A RASH OF SUICIDES.
WHILE STILL MORE AND MORE PEOPLE ARE CRACKING, AND ENDING UP HERE.
WHAT DO YOU NEED FROM ME, BATMAN?
SOME BLOOD FOR STARTERS, PAMELA.
AND MAYBE A FEW LEAVES.

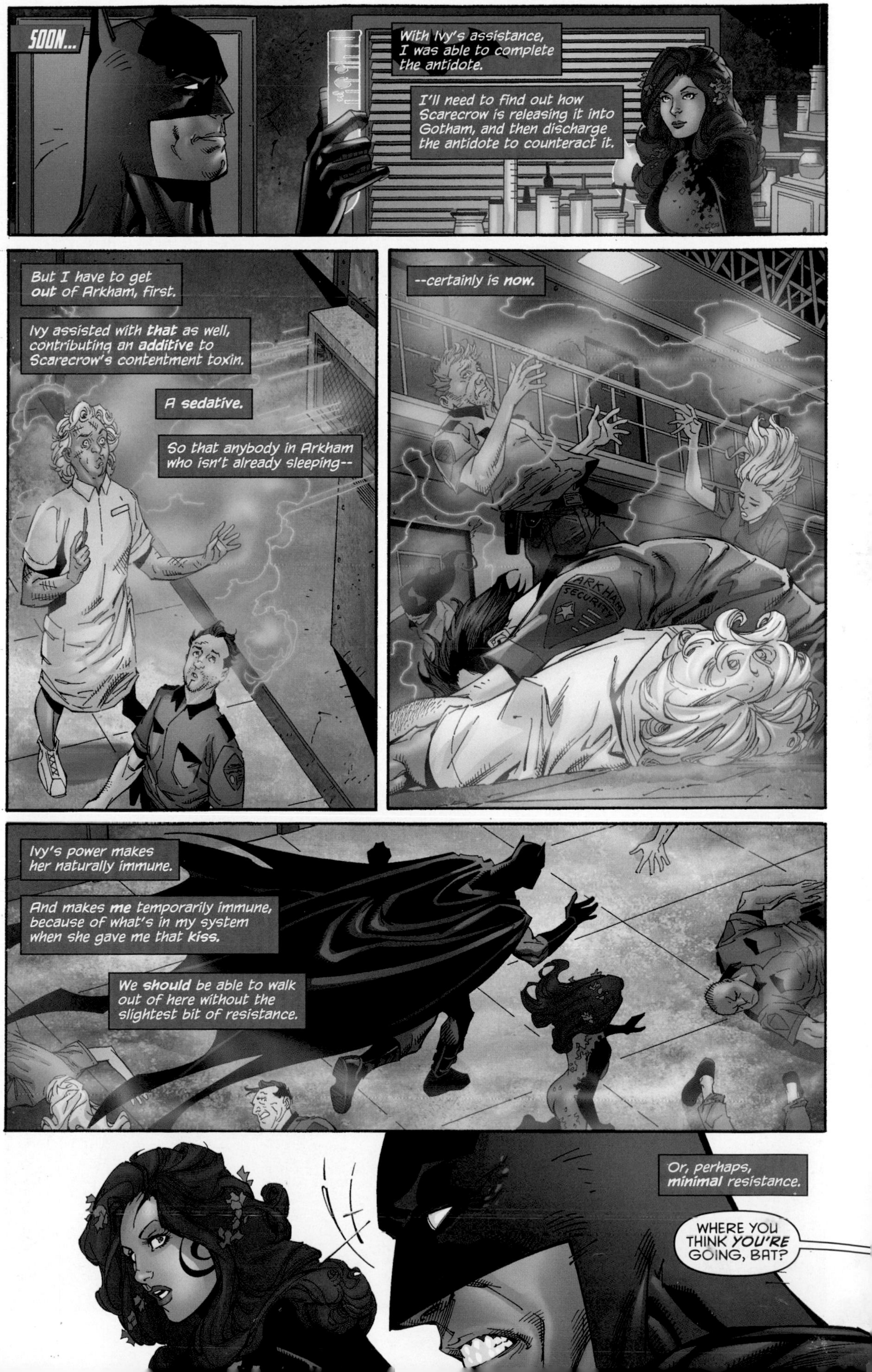
SOON...
With Ivy's assistance, I was able to complete the antidote.
I'll need to find out how Scarecrow is releasing it into Gotham, and then discharge the antidote to counteract it.
But I have to get out of Arkham, first.
Ivy assisted with that as well, contributing an additive to Scarecrow's contentment toxin.
A sedative.
So that anybody in Arkham who isn't already sleeping--
--certainly is now.
ARKHAM SECURITY
Ivy's power makes her naturally immune.
And makes me temporarily immune, because of what's in my system when she gave me that kiss.
We should be able to walk out of here without the slightest bit of resistance.
Or, perhaps, minimal resistance.
WHERE YOU THINK YOU'RE GOING, BAT?

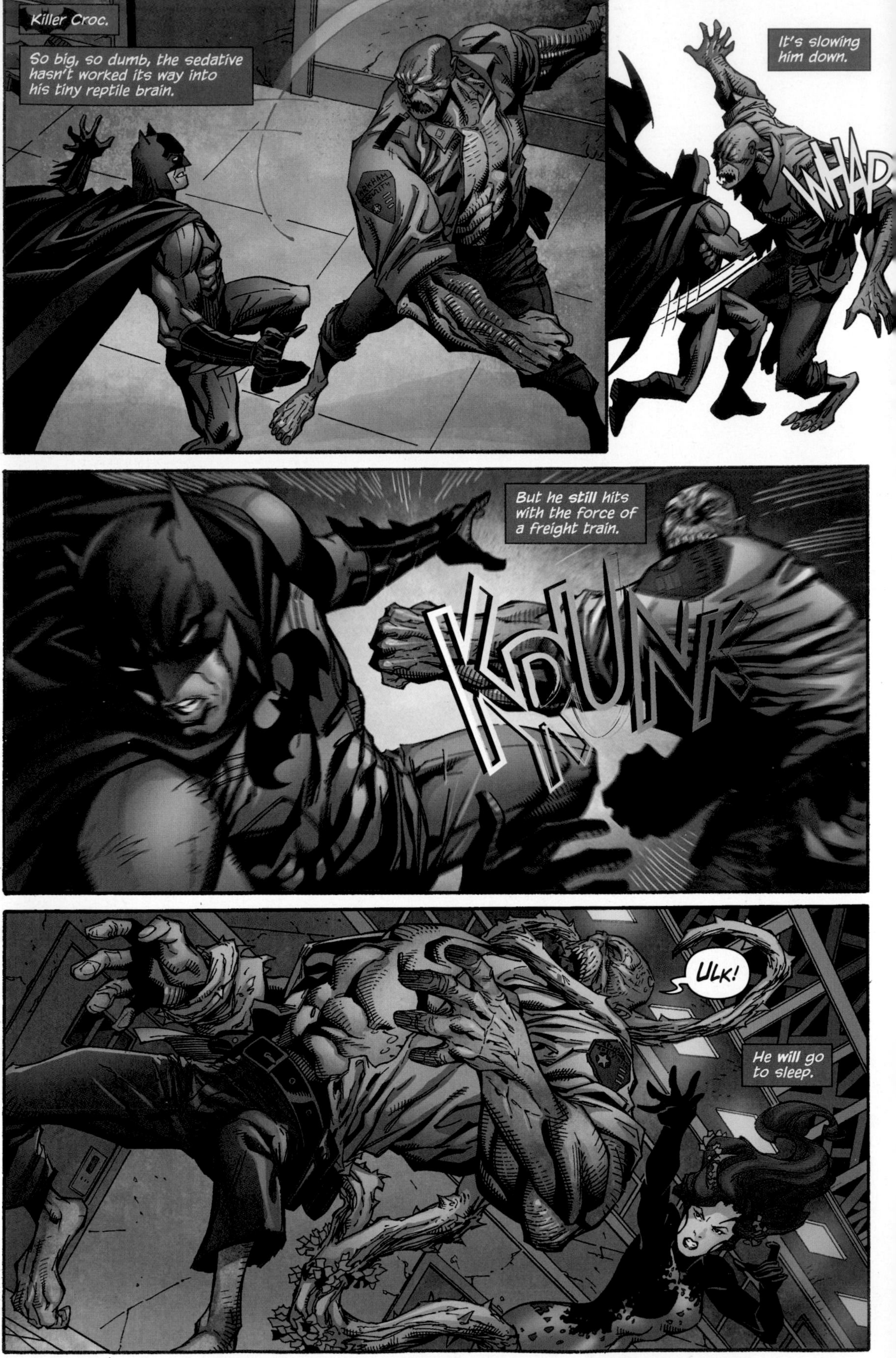
Killer Croc.
So big, so dumb, the sedative hasn't worked its way into his tiny reptile brain.
It's slowing him down.
WHAP
But he **still** hits with the force of a freight train.
KDUNK
ULK!
He **will** go to sleep.

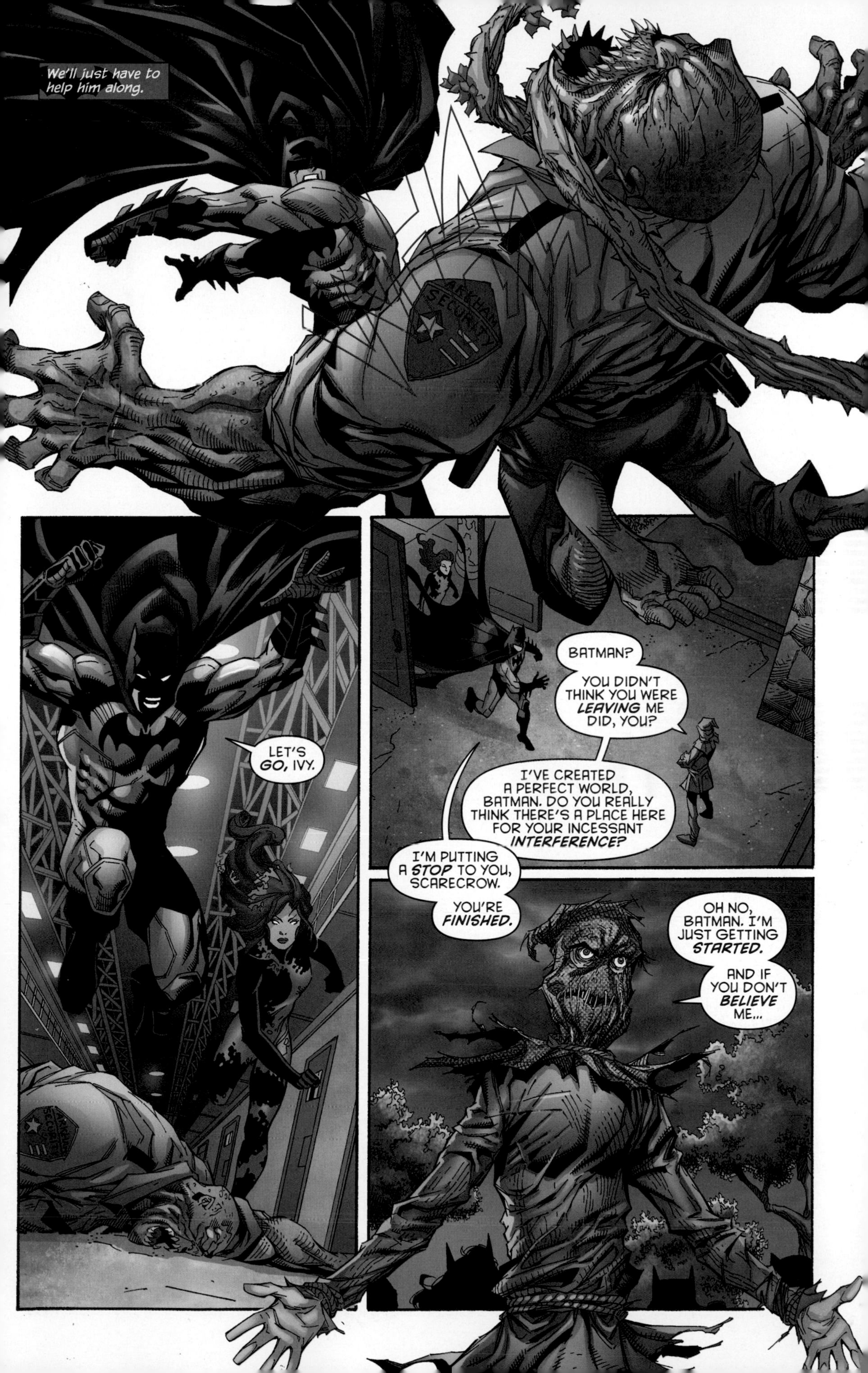
We'll just have to help him along.
LET'S *GO,* IVY.
BATMAN?
YOU DIDN'T THINK YOU WERE *LEAVING* ME DID, YOU?
I'VE CREATED A PERFECT WORLD, BATMAN. DO YOU REALLY THINK THERE'S A PLACE HERE FOR YOUR INCESSANT *INTERFERENCE?*
I'M PUTTING A *STOP* TO YOU, SCARECROW.
YOU'RE *FINISHED.*
OH NO, BATMAN. I'M JUST GETTING *STARTED.*
AND IF YOU DON'T *BELIEVE* ME...

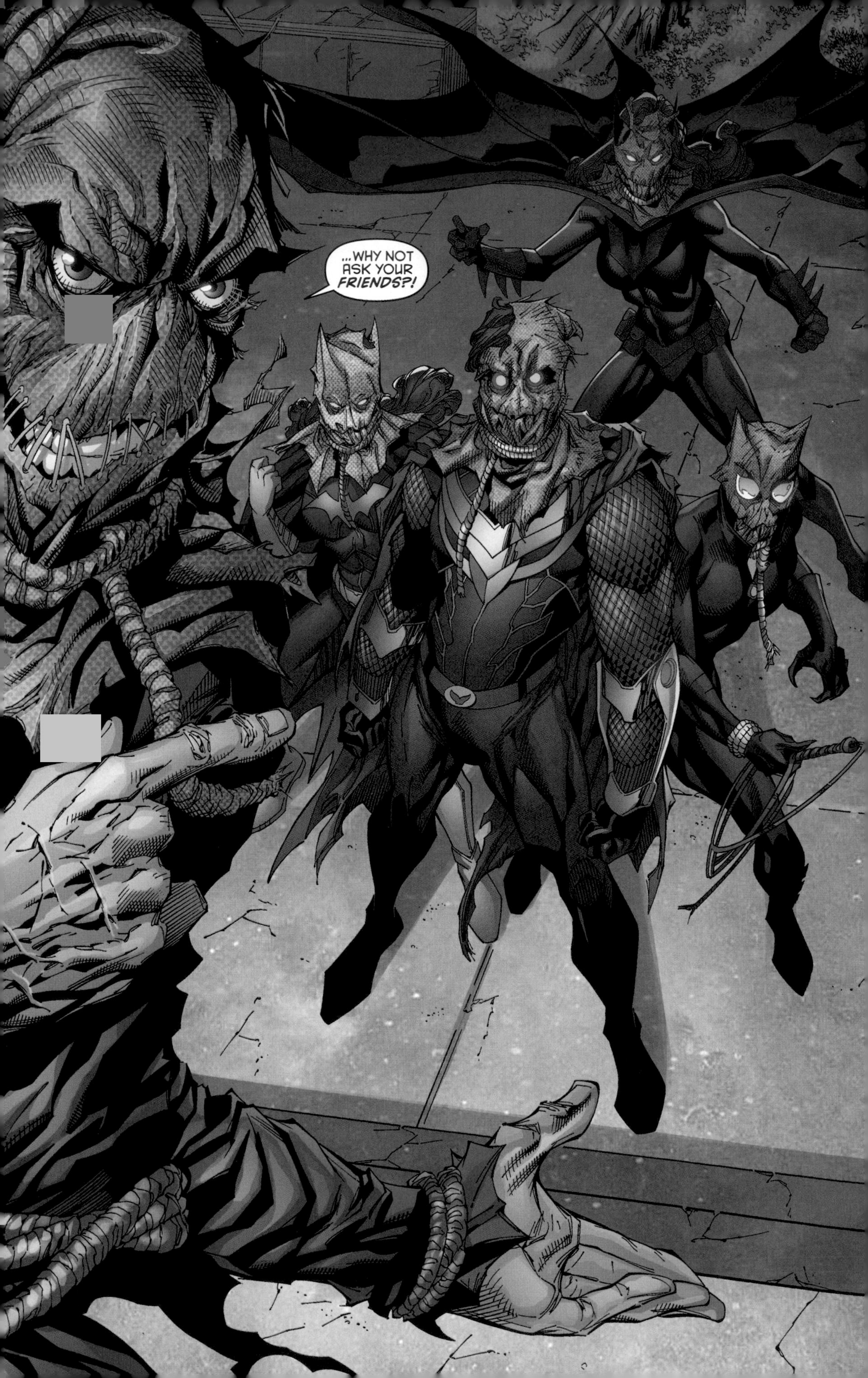
...WHY NOT ASK YOUR *FRIENDS?!*

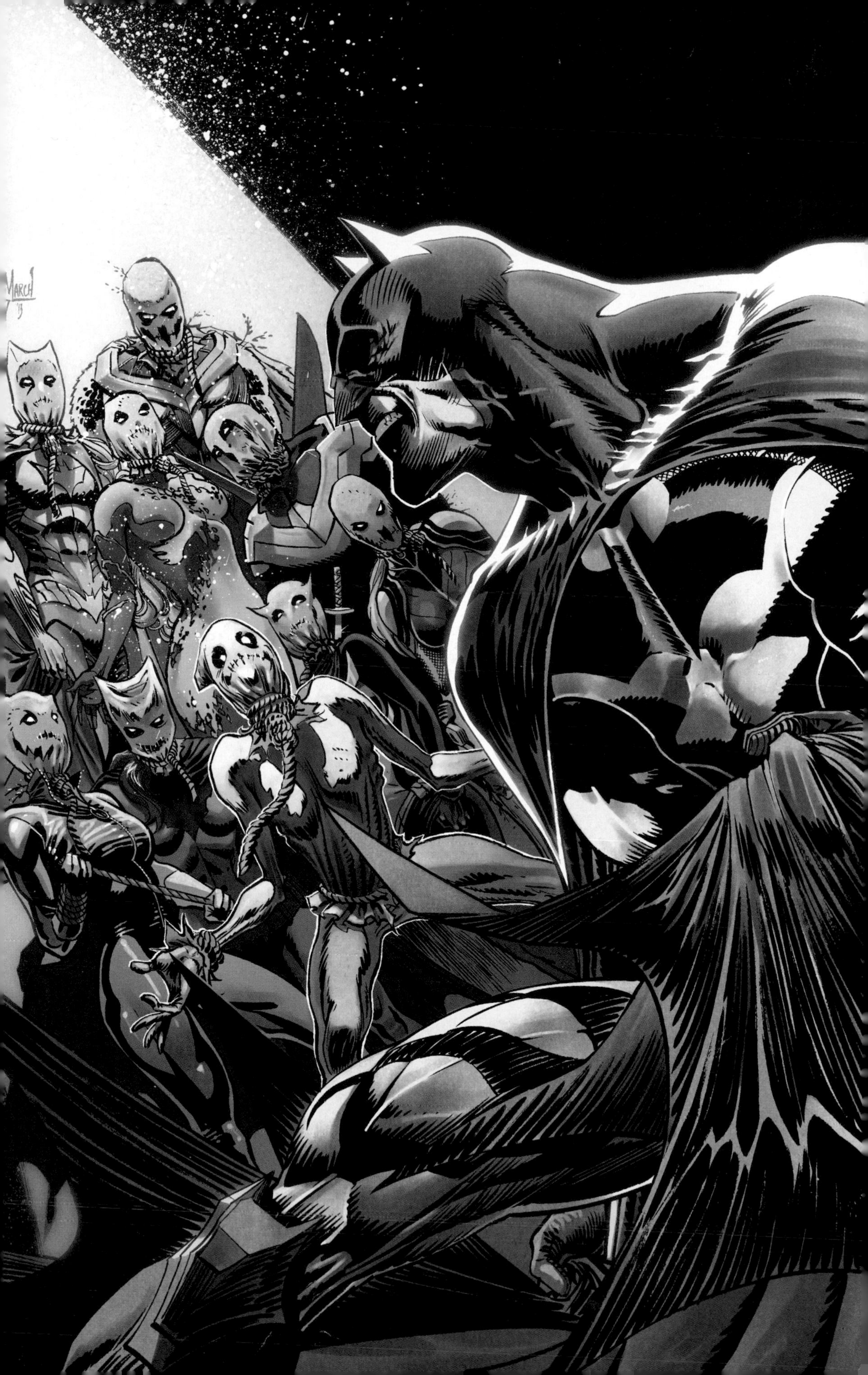

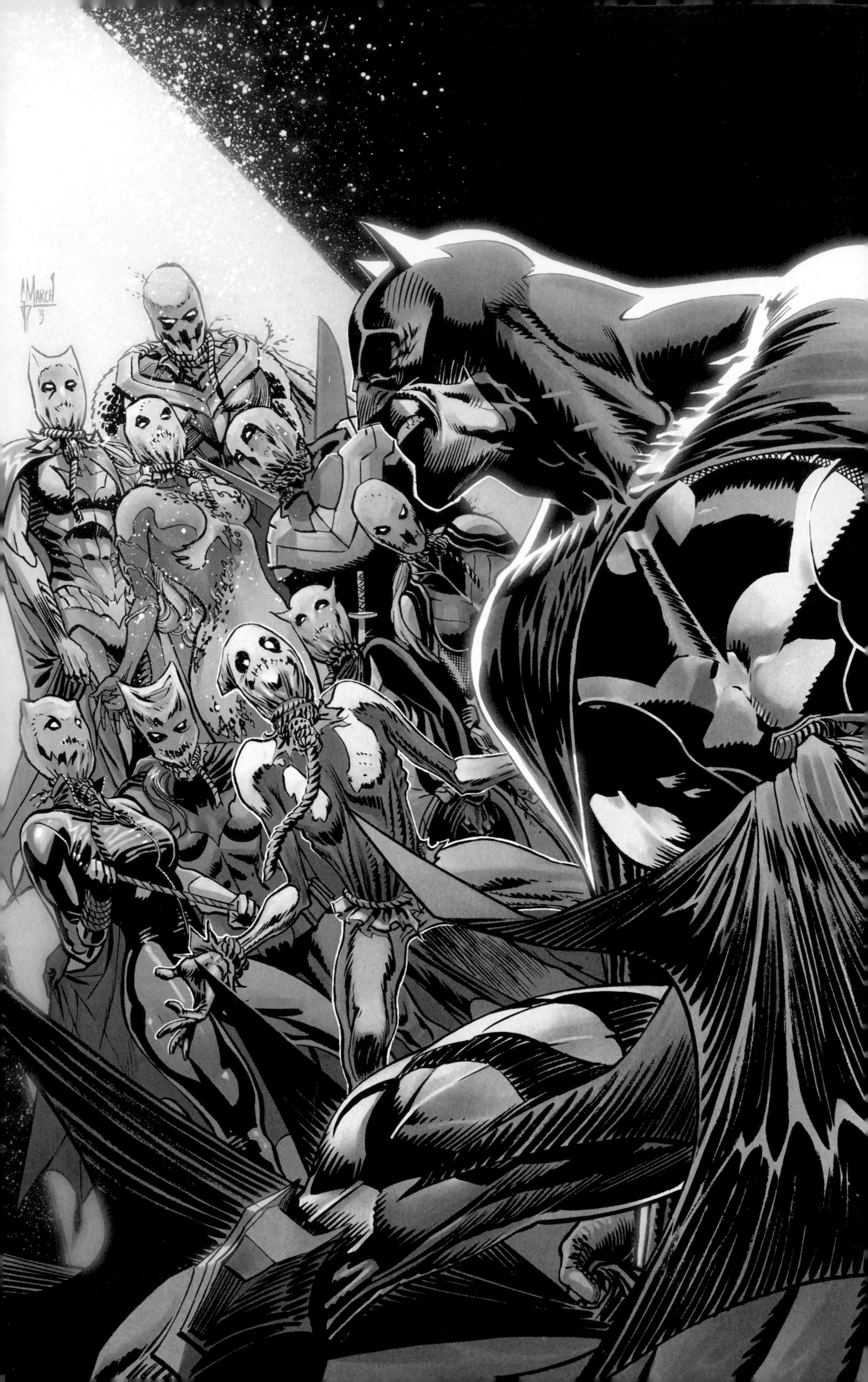
MARCH

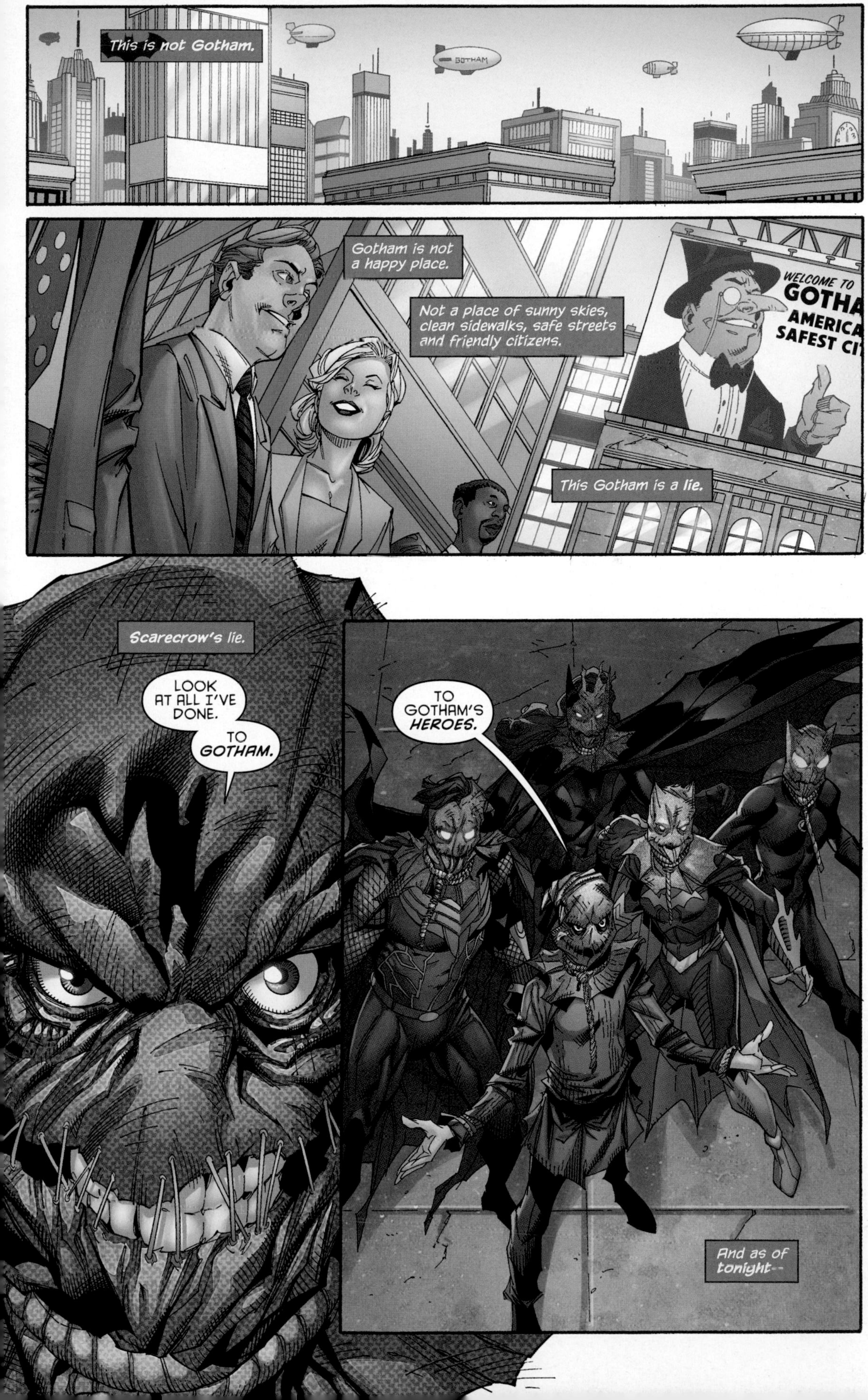
This is not Gotham.
GOTHAM
Gotham is not a happy place.
Not a place of sunny skies, clean sidewalks, safe streets and friendly citizens.
WELCOME TO
GOTHA
AMERICA
SAFEST CIT
This Gotham is a lie.
Scarecrow's lie.
LOOK AT ALL I'VE DONE.
TO GOTHAM.
TO GOTHAM'S HEROES.
And as of tonight--

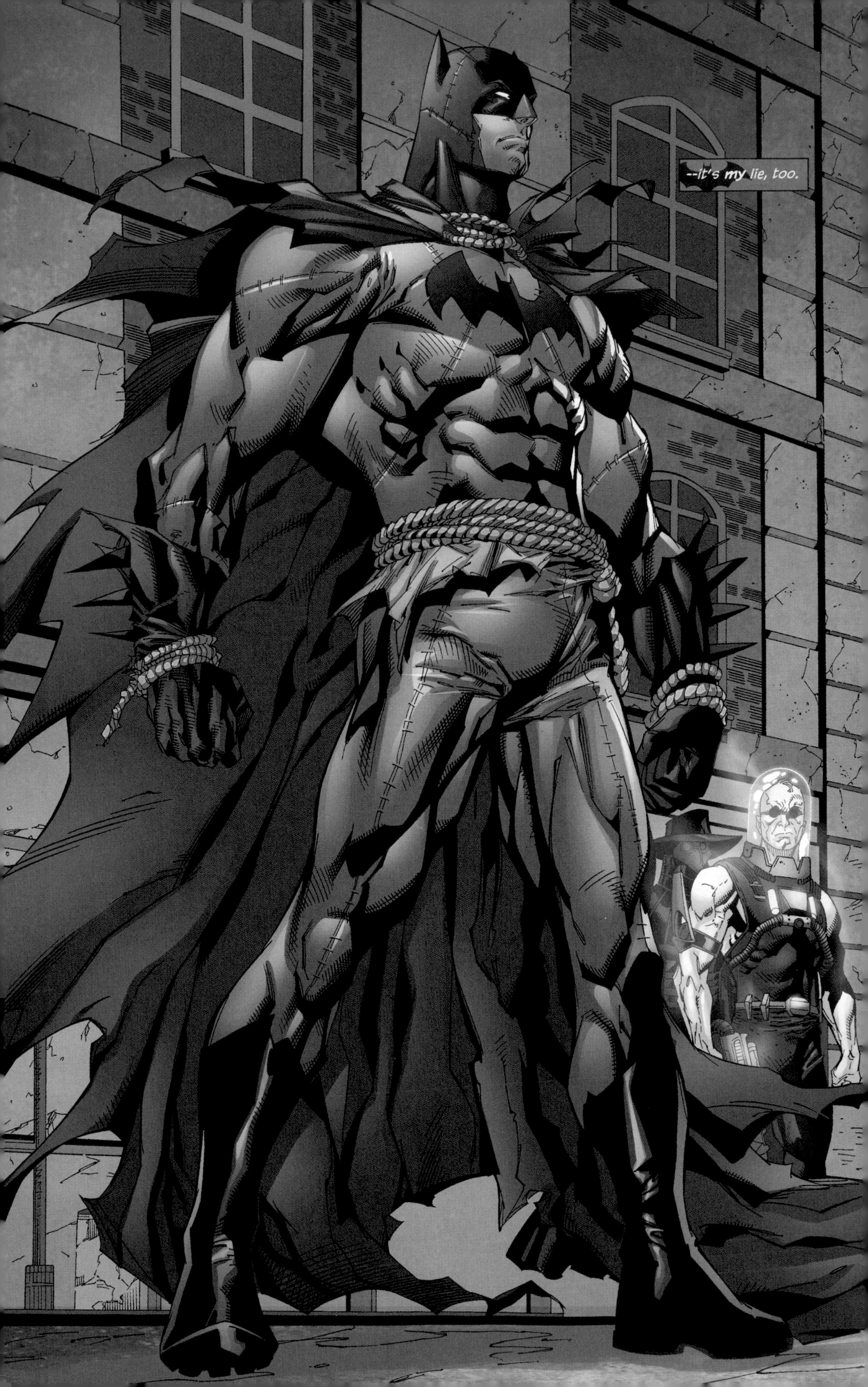
--it's my lie, too.

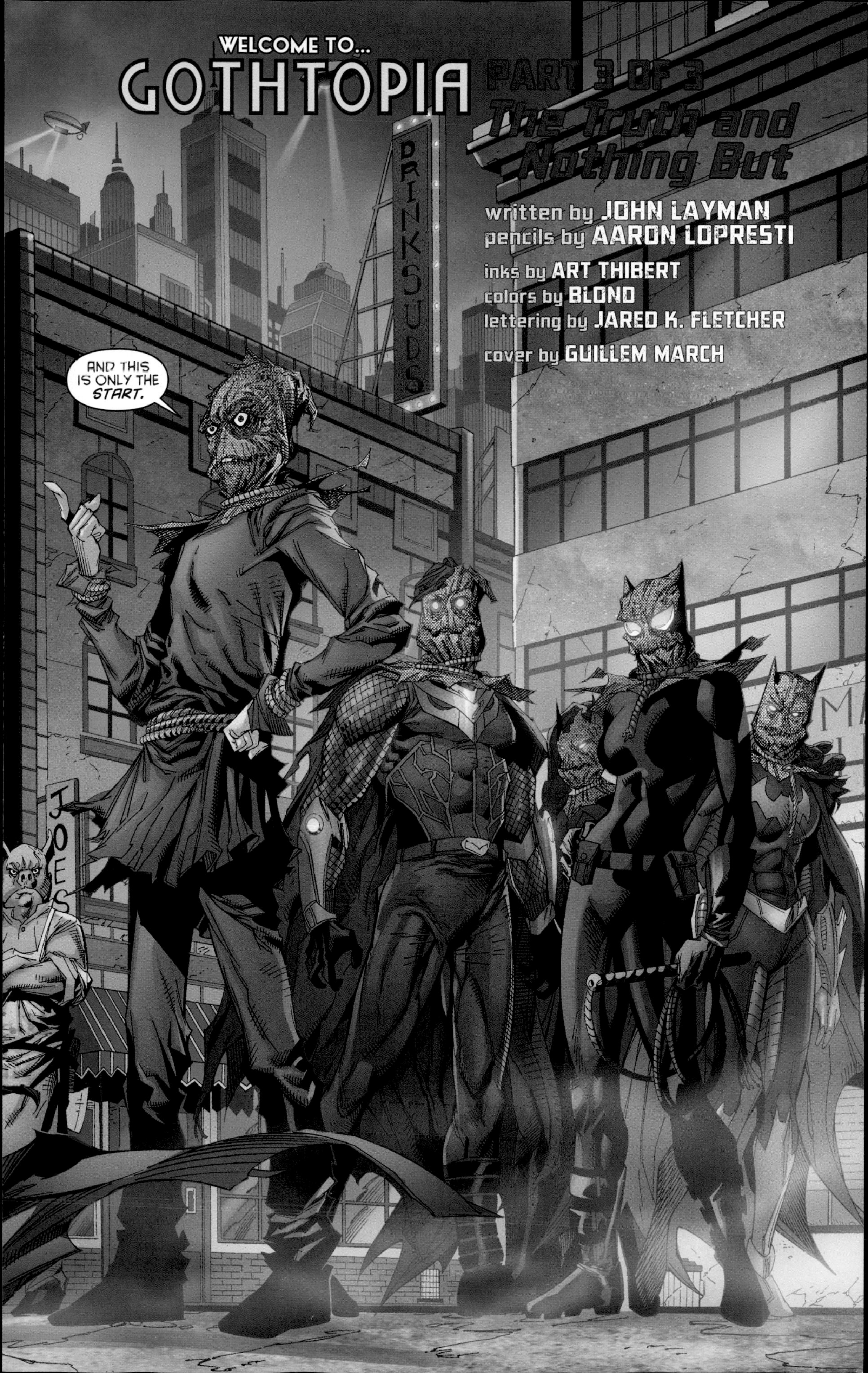
WELCOME TO...
GOTHTOPIA
PART 3 OF 3
The Truth and Nothing But
written by JOHN LAYMAN
pencils by AARON LOPRESTI
inks by ART THIBERT
colors by BLOND
lettering by JARED K. FLETCHER
cover by GUILLEM MARCH
DRINKSUDS
AND THIS IS ONLY THE START.
JOES

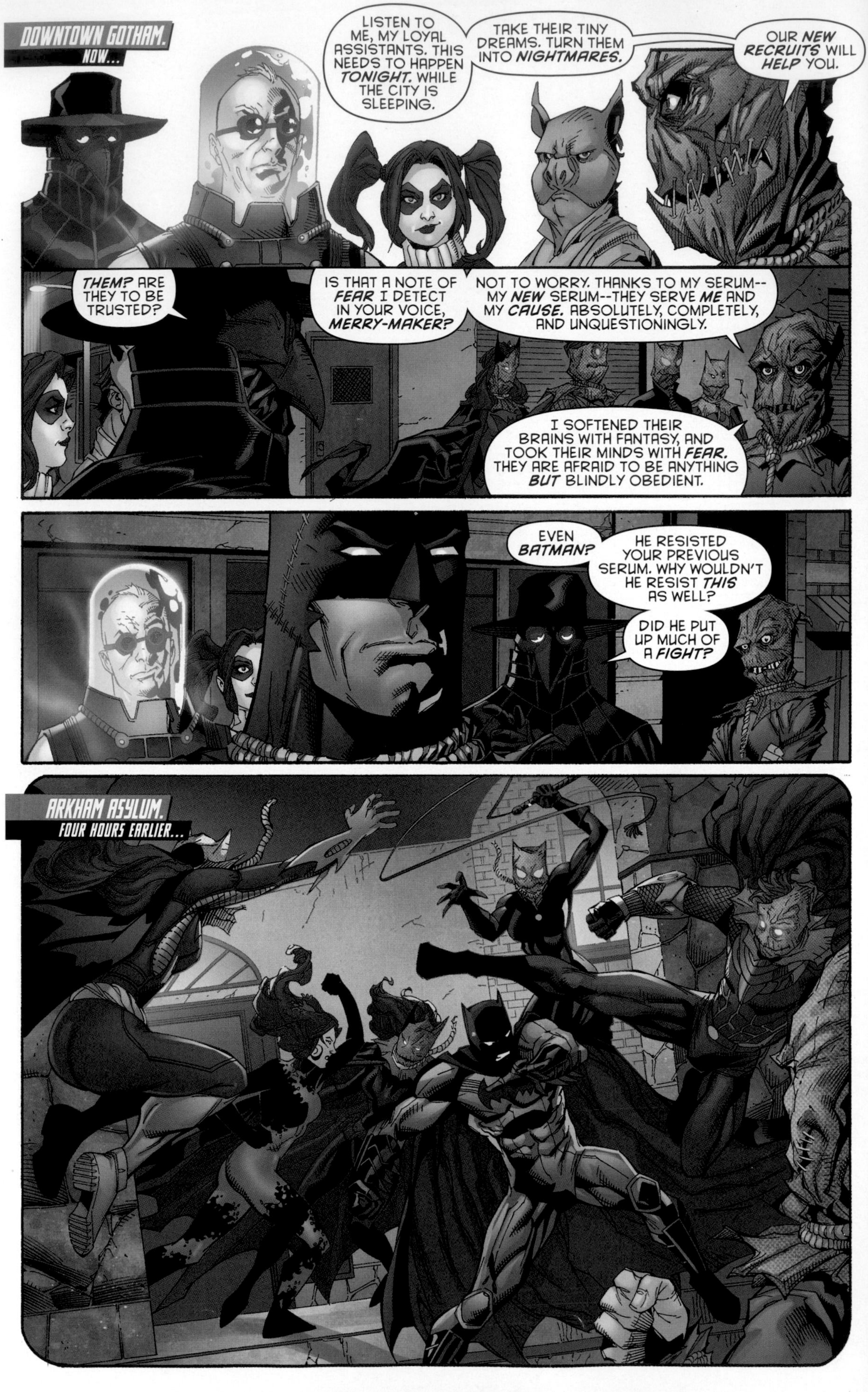
DOWNTOWN GOTHAM.
NOW...
LISTEN TO ME, MY LOYAL ASSISTANTS. THIS NEEDS TO HAPPEN TONIGHT. WHILE THE CITY IS SLEEPING.
TAKE THEIR TINY DREAMS. TURN THEM INTO NIGHTMARES.
OUR NEW RECRUITS WILL HELP YOU.
THEM? ARE THEY TO BE TRUSTED?
IS THAT A NOTE OF FEAR I DETECT IN YOUR VOICE, MERRY-MAKER?
NOT TO WORRY. THANKS TO MY SERUM-- MY NEW SERUM--THEY SERVE ME AND MY CAUSE. ABSOLUTELY, COMPLETELY, AND UNQUESTIONINGLY.
I SOFTENED THEIR BRAINS WITH FANTASY, AND TOOK THEIR MINDS WITH FEAR. THEY ARE AFRAID TO BE ANYTHING BUT BLINDLY OBEDIENT.
EVEN BATMAN?
HE RESISTED YOUR PREVIOUS SERUM. WHY WOULDN'T HE RESIST THIS AS WELL?
DID HE PUT UP MUCH OF A FIGHT?
ARKHAM ASYLUM.
FOUR HOURS EARLIER...

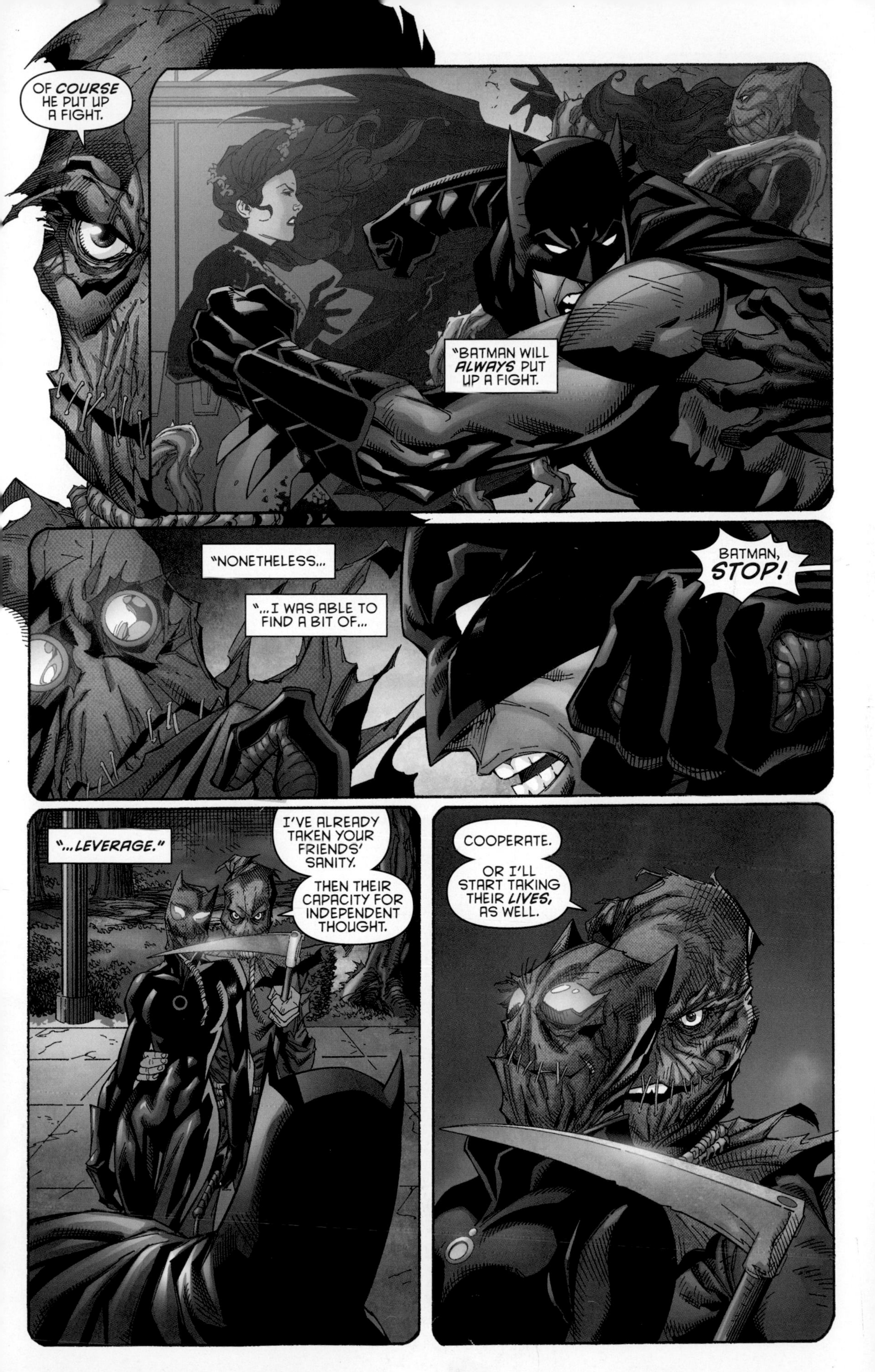
OF COURSE HE PUT UP A FIGHT.
"BATMAN WILL ALWAYS PUT UP A FIGHT.
"NONETHELESS...
"...I WAS ABLE TO FIND A BIT OF...
BATMAN, STOP!
"...LEVERAGE."
I'VE ALREADY TAKEN YOUR FRIENDS' SANITY.
THEN THEIR CAPACITY FOR INDEPENDENT THOUGHT.
COOPERATE.
OR I'LL START TAKING THEIR LIVES, AS WELL.

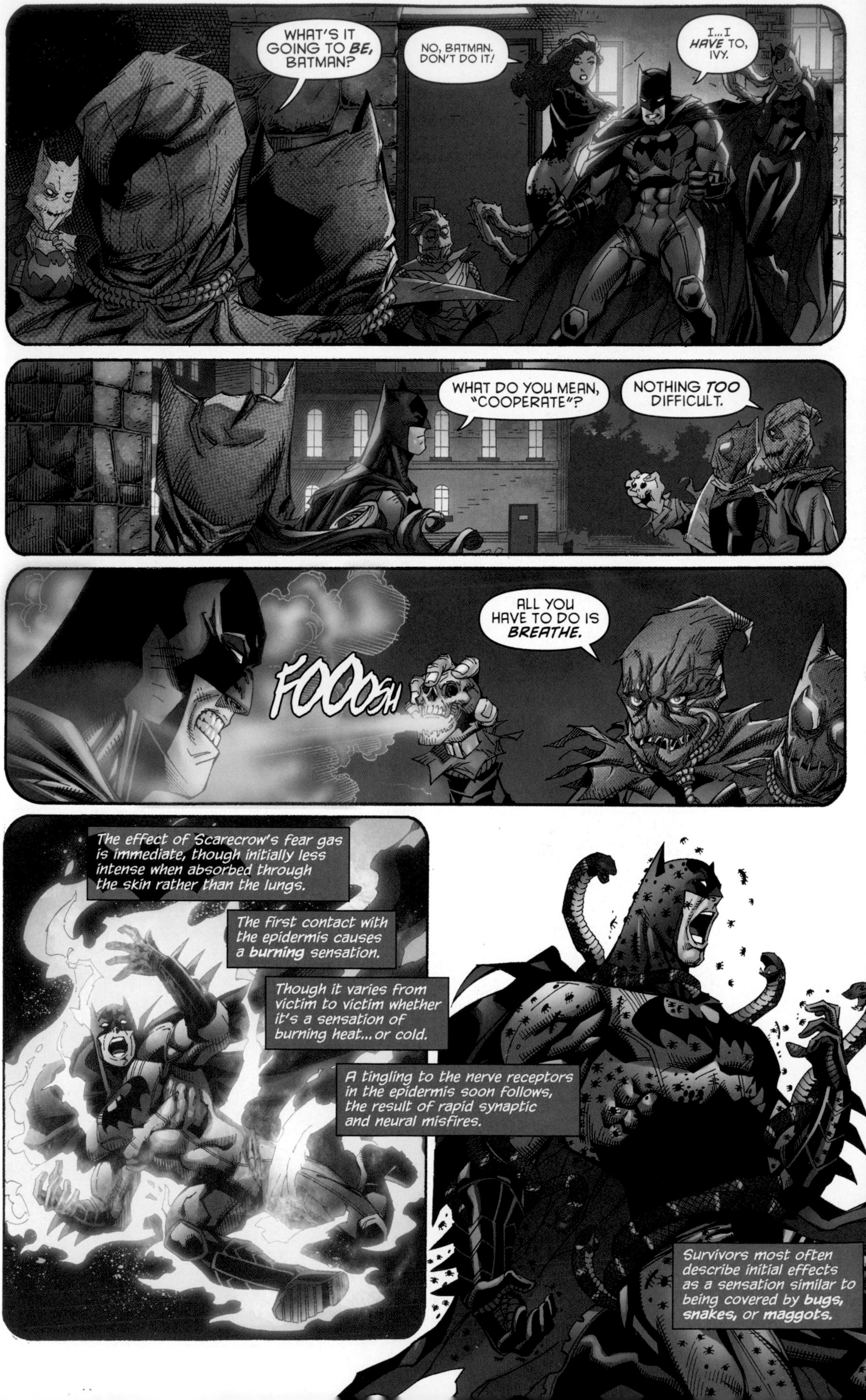
WHAT'S IT GOING TO *BE,* BATMAN?
NO, BATMAN. DON'T DO IT!
I...I *HAVE* TO, IVY.
WHAT DO YOU MEAN, "COOPERATE"?
NOTHING *TOO* DIFFICULT.
FOOOSH
ALL YOU HAVE TO DO IS *BREATHE.*
The effect of Scarecrow's fear gas is immediate, though initially less intense when absorbed through the skin rather than the lungs.
The first contact with the epidermis causes a **burning** sensation.
Though it varies from victim to victim whether it's a sensation of burning heat...or cold.
A tingling to the nerve receptors in the epidermis soon follows, the result of rapid synaptic and neural misfires.
Survivors most often describe initial effects as a sensation similar to being covered by **bugs, snakes,** or **maggots.**

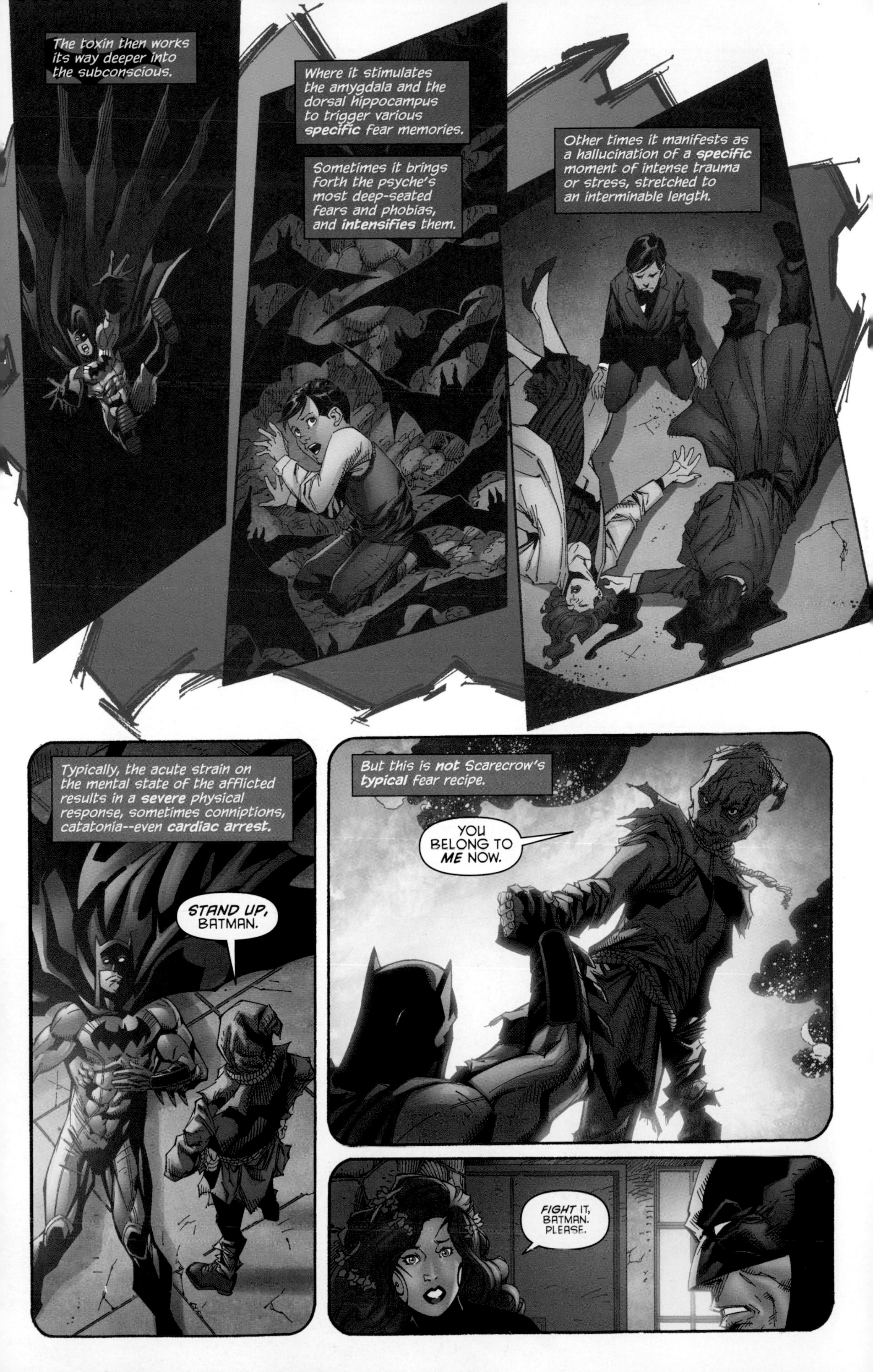
The toxin then works its way deeper into the subconscious.
Where it stimulates the amygdala and the dorsal hippocampus to trigger various specific fear memories.
Sometimes it brings forth the psyche's most deep-seated fears and phobias, and intensifies them.
Other times it manifests as a hallucination of a specific moment of intense trauma or stress, stretched to an interminable length.
Typically, the acute strain on the mental state of the afflicted results in a severe physical response, sometimes conniptions, catatonia--even cardiac arrest.
STAND UP, BATMAN.
But this is not Scarecrow's typical fear recipe.
YOU BELONG TO ME NOW.
FIGHT IT, BATMAN. PLEASE.

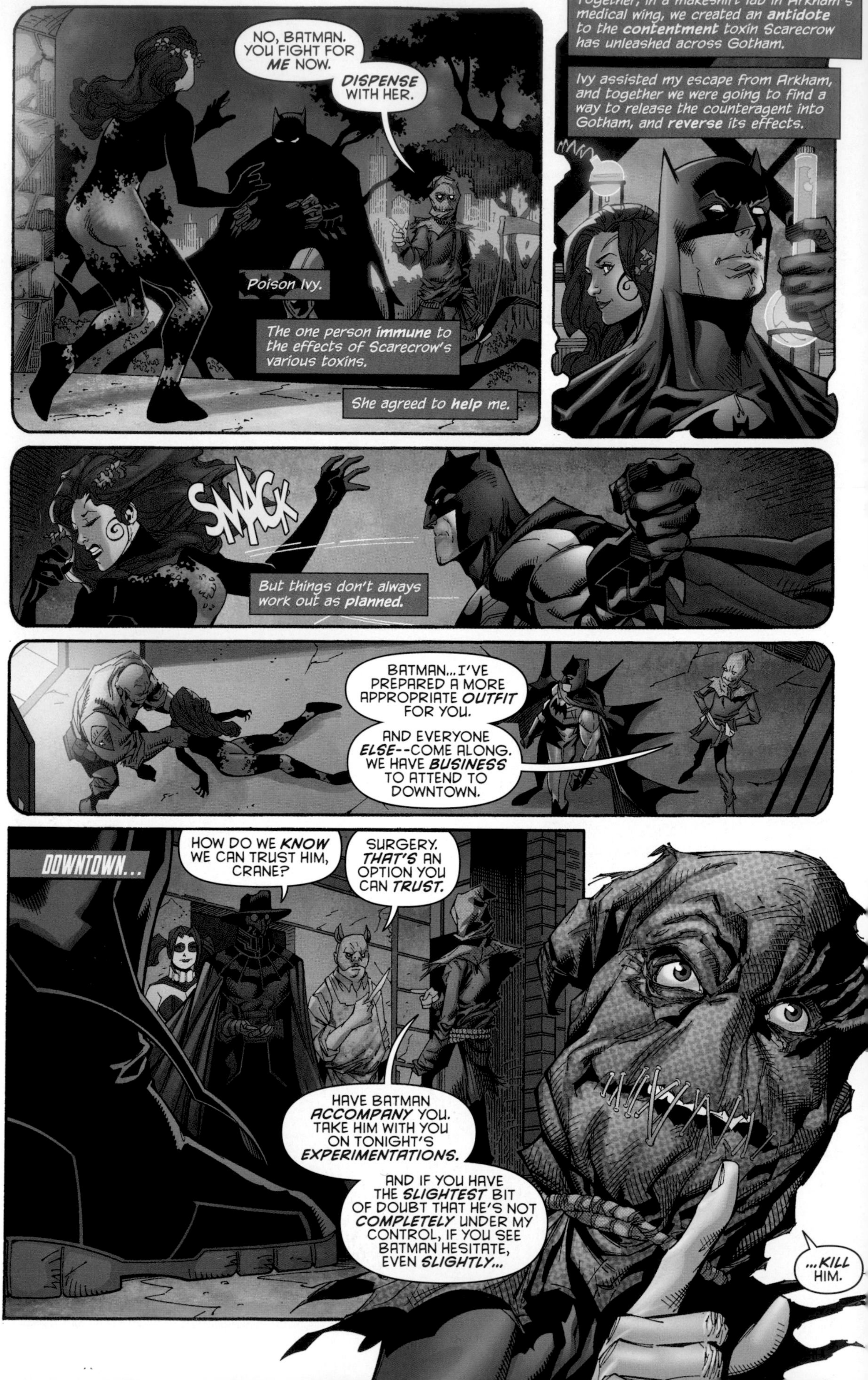
NO, BATMAN. YOU FIGHT FOR ME NOW.
DISPENSE WITH HER.
Poison Ivy.
The one person immune to the effects of Scarecrow's various toxins.
She agreed to help me.
Together, in a makeshift lab in Arkham's medical wing, we created an antidote to the contentment toxin Scarecrow has unleashed across Gotham.
Ivy assisted my escape from Arkham, and together we were going to find a way to release the counteragent into Gotham, and reverse its effects.
SMACK
But things don't always work out as planned.
BATMAN...I'VE PREPARED A MORE APPROPRIATE OUTFIT FOR YOU.
AND EVERYONE ELSE--COME ALONG. WE HAVE BUSINESS TO ATTEND TO DOWNTOWN.
DOWNTOWN...
HOW DO WE KNOW WE CAN TRUST HIM, CRANE?
SURGERY. THAT'S AN OPTION YOU CAN TRUST.
HAVE BATMAN ACCOMPANY YOU. TAKE HIM WITH YOU ON TONIGHT'S EXPERIMENTATIONS.
AND IF YOU HAVE THE SLIGHTEST BIT OF DOUBT THAT HE'S NOT COMPLETELY UNDER MY CONTROL, IF YOU SEE BATMAN HESITATE, EVEN SLIGHTLY...
...KILL HIM.

C'MON, BATS. IT'S *SHOWTIME*.

THIS WAY.

They are right not to trust me.

NO. *THIS* WAY.

WHA--?

I'm *not* under Scarecrow's control.

Crane's ego has always been his blind spot. He desperately *wants* me under his control.

But I have an *antidote*. I've *taken* the antidote.

Chemically, Scarecrow's latest toxins are not terribly different from one another. Fear, contentment... control, I'm able to resist all three.

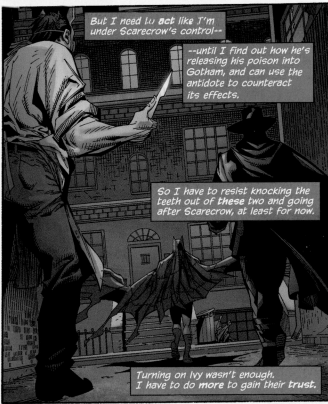

But I need to *act* like I'm under Scarecrow's control--

--until I find out how he's releasing his poison into Gotham, and can use the antidote to counteract its effects.

So I have to resist knocking the teeth out of *these* two and going after Scarecrow, at least for now.

Turning on Ivy wasn't enough. I have to do *more* to gain their *trust*.

The question is...

...how *far* am I willing to go?

LOOK AT HIM. SO COMFY AND COZY, DREAMING SUCH SWEET DREAMS.

THEY'LL BE *NIGHTMARES* SOON ENOUGH.

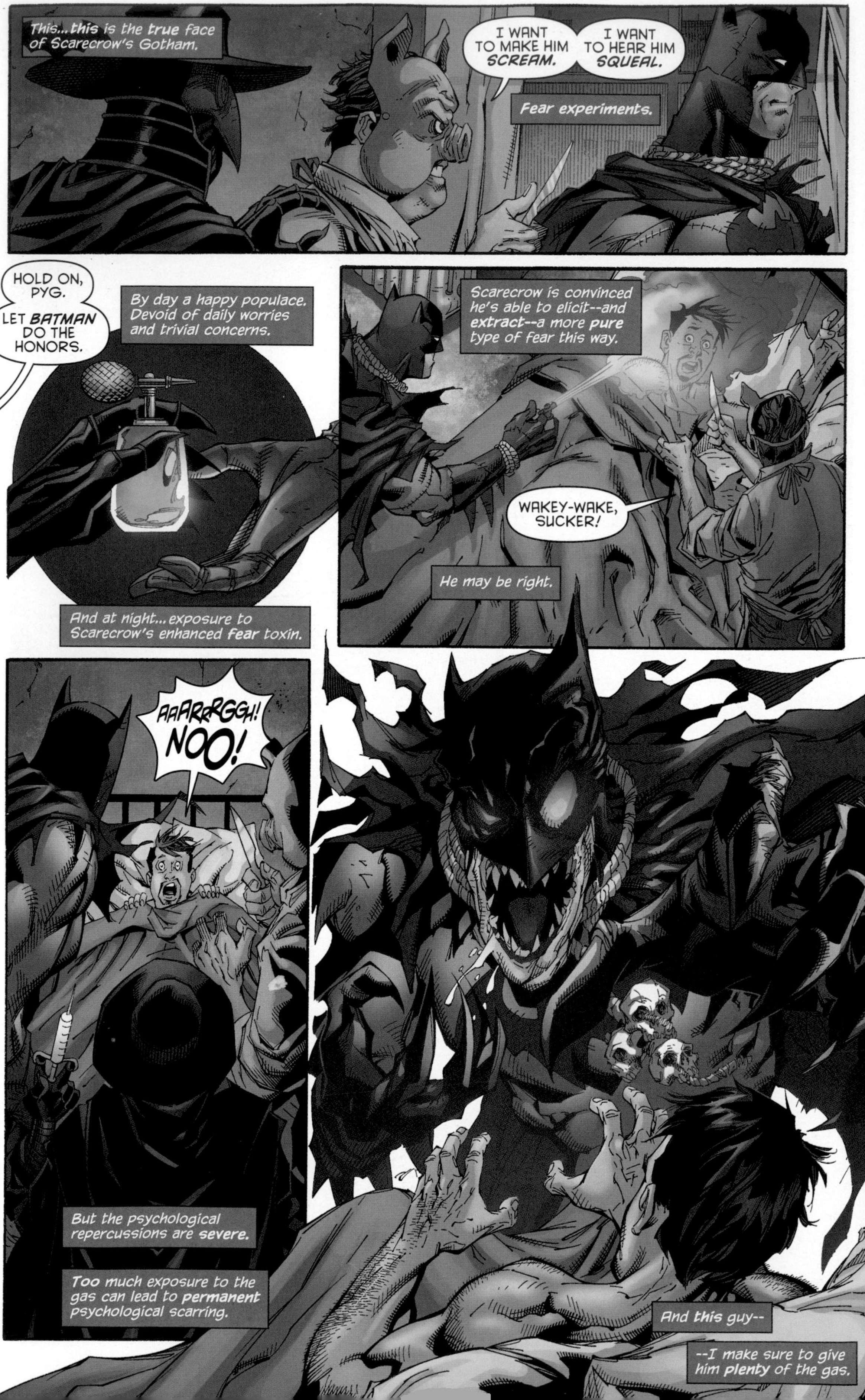
This...this is the true face of Scarecrow's Gotham.
I WANT TO MAKE HIM SCREAM.
I WANT TO HEAR HIM SQUEAL.
Fear experiments.
HOLD ON, PYG.
LET BATMAN DO THE HONORS.
By day a happy populace. Devoid of daily worries and trivial concerns.
And at night...exposure to Scarecrow's enhanced fear toxin.
Scarecrow is convinced he's able to elicit--and extract--a more pure type of fear this way.
WAKEY-WAKE, SUCKER!
He may be right.
AAARRRGGH! NOO!
But the psychological repercussions are severe.
Too much exposure to the gas can lead to permanent psychological scarring.
And this guy--
--I make sure to give him plenty of the gas.

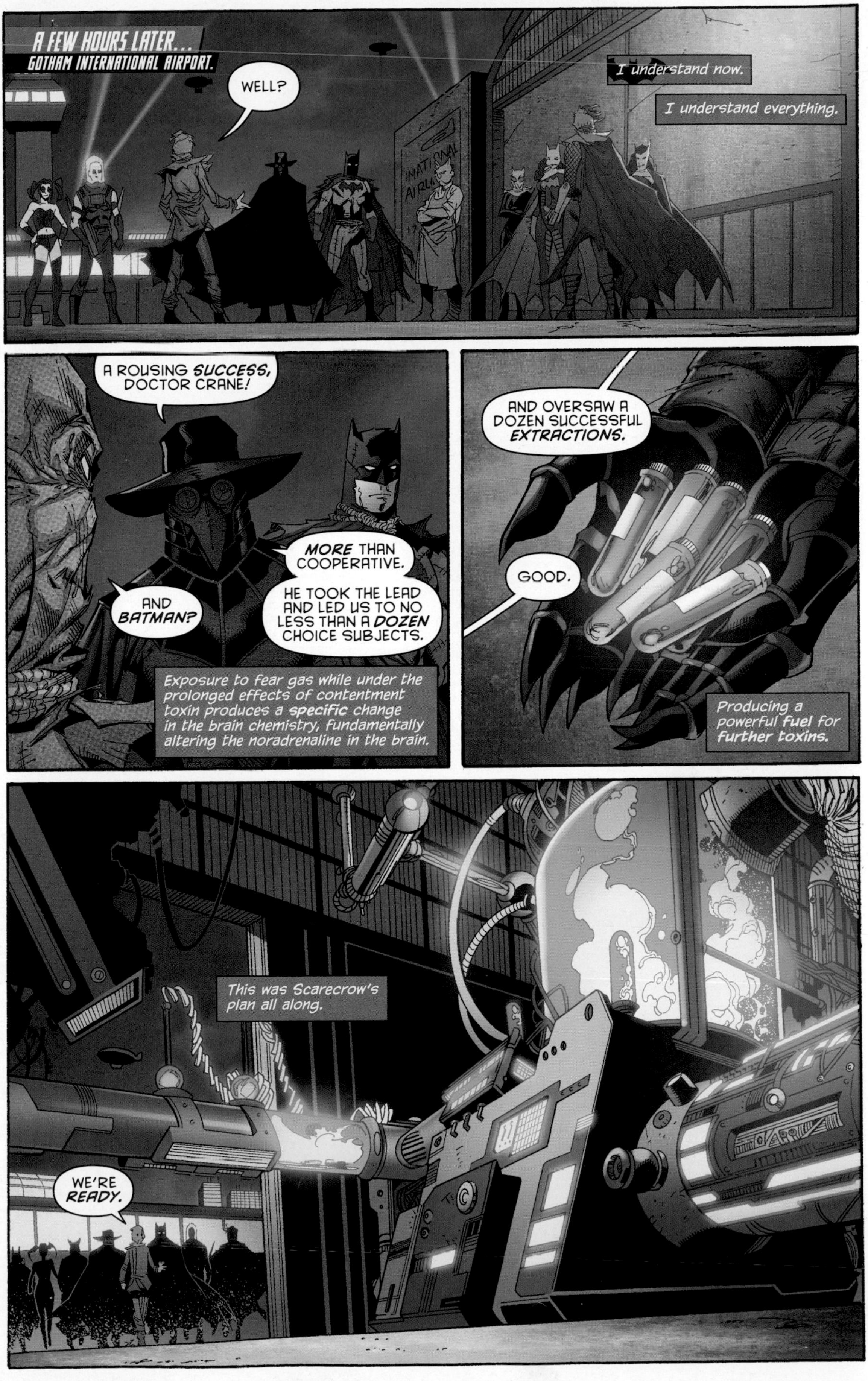
A FEW HOURS LATER...
GOTHAM INTERNATIONAL AIRPORT.
WELL?
I understand now.
I understand everything.
A ROUSING SUCCESS, DOCTOR CRANE!
AND BATMAN?
MORE THAN COOPERATIVE.
HE TOOK THE LEAD AND LED US TO NO LESS THAN A DOZEN CHOICE SUBJECTS.
Exposure to fear gas while under the prolonged effects of contentment toxin produces a specific change in the brain chemistry, fundamentally altering the noradrenaline in the brain.
AND OVERSAW A DOZEN SUCCESSFUL EXTRACTIONS.
GOOD.
Producing a powerful fuel for further toxins.
This was Scarecrow's plan all along.
WE'RE READY.

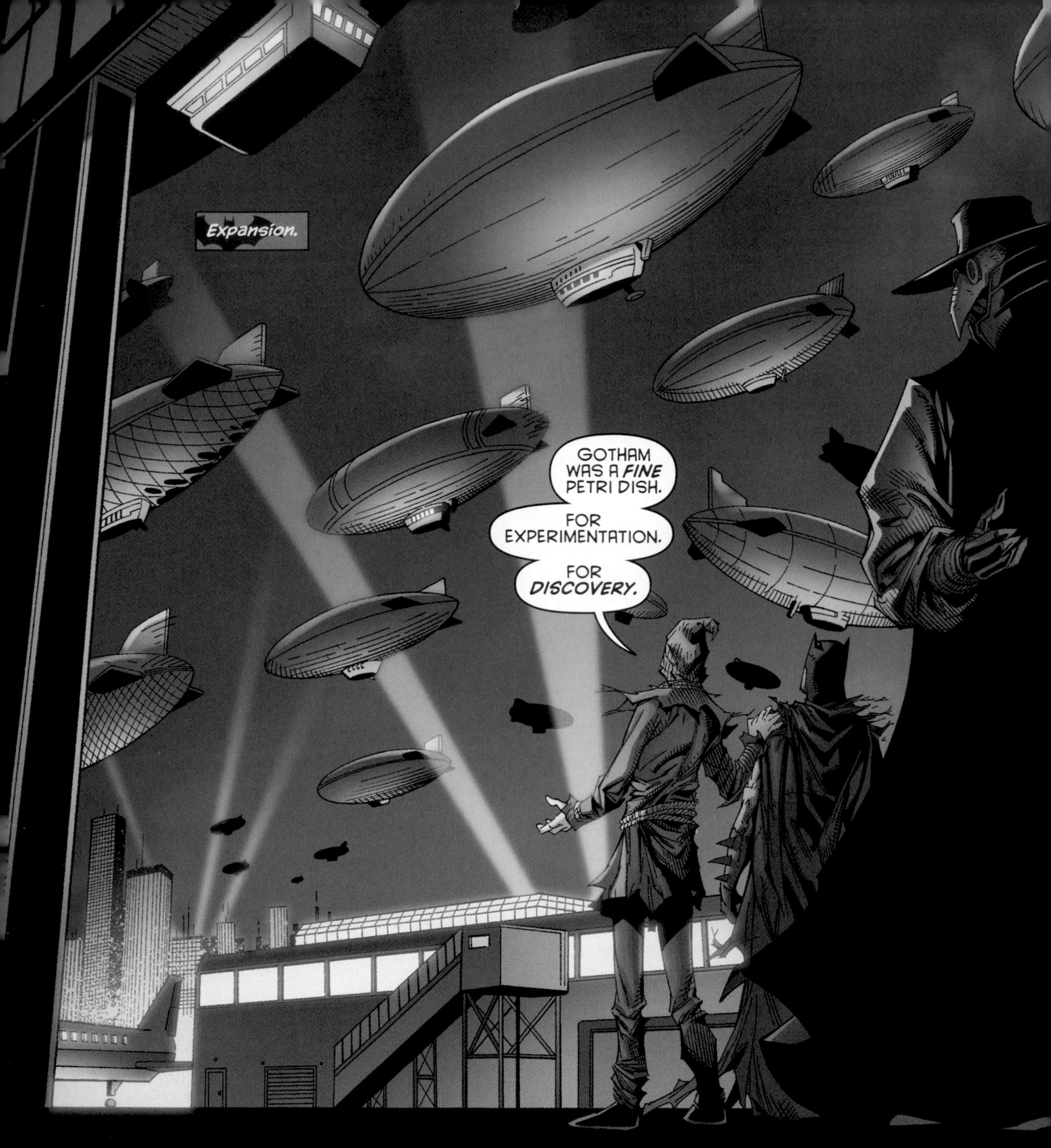
Expansion.
GOTHAM WAS A FINE PETRI DISH.
FOR EXPERIMENTATION.
FOR DISCOVERY.

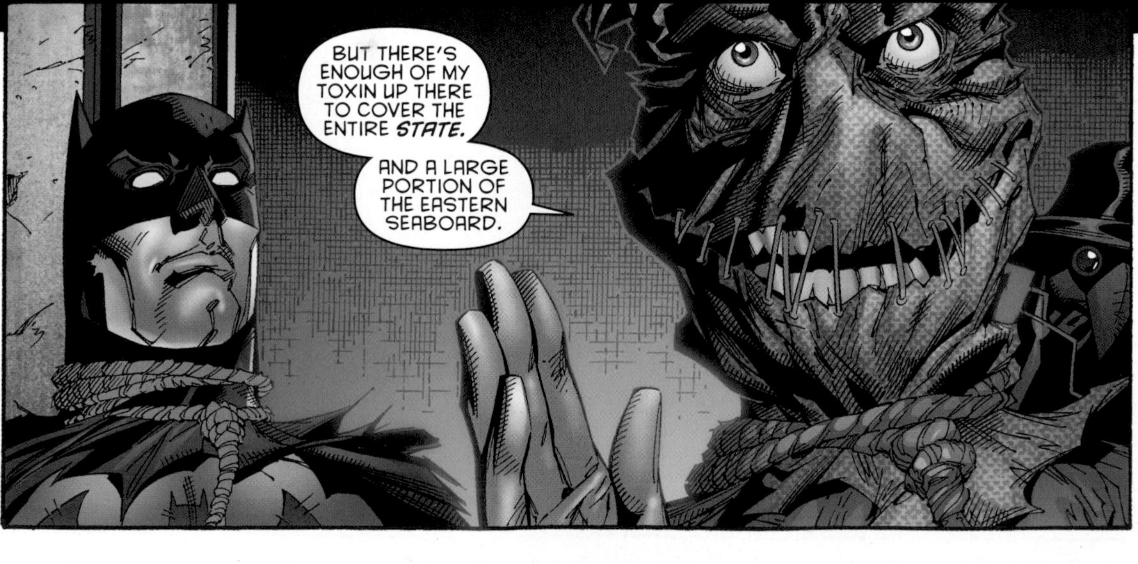
BUT THERE'S ENOUGH OF MY TOXIN UP THERE TO COVER THE ENTIRE STATE.
AND A LARGE PORTION OF THE EASTERN SEABOARD.

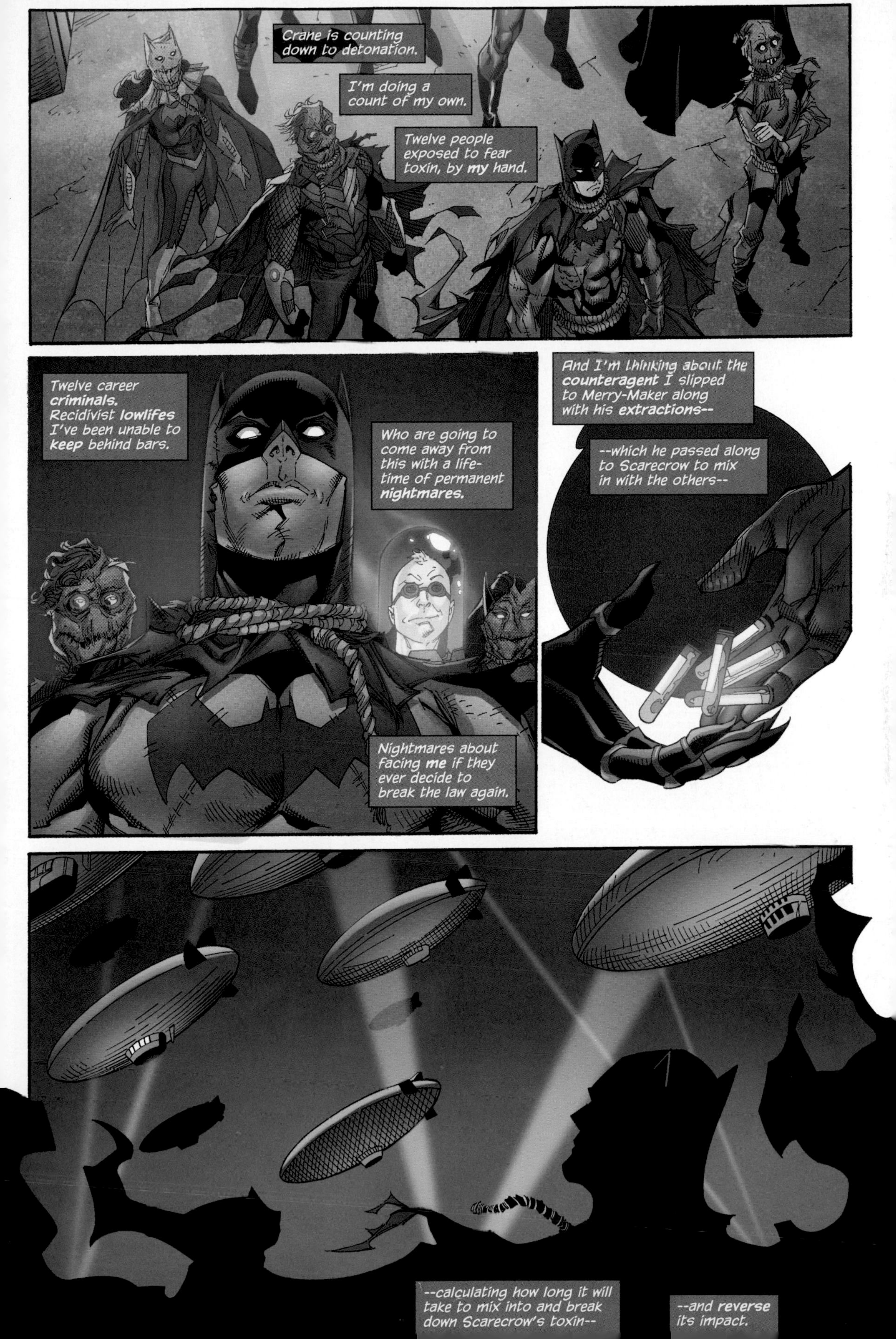
Crane is counting down to detonation.
I'm doing a count of my own.
Twelve people exposed to fear toxin, by **my** hand.
Twelve career **criminals.** Recidivist **lowlifes** I've been unable to **keep** behind bars.
Who are going to come away from this with a lifetime of permanent **nightmares.**
Nightmares about facing **me** if they ever decide to break the law again.
And I'm thinking about the **counteragent** I slipped to Merry-Maker along with his **extractions--**
--which he passed along to Scarecrow to mix in with the others--
--calculating how long it will take to mix into and break down Scarecrow's toxin--
--and **reverse** its impact.

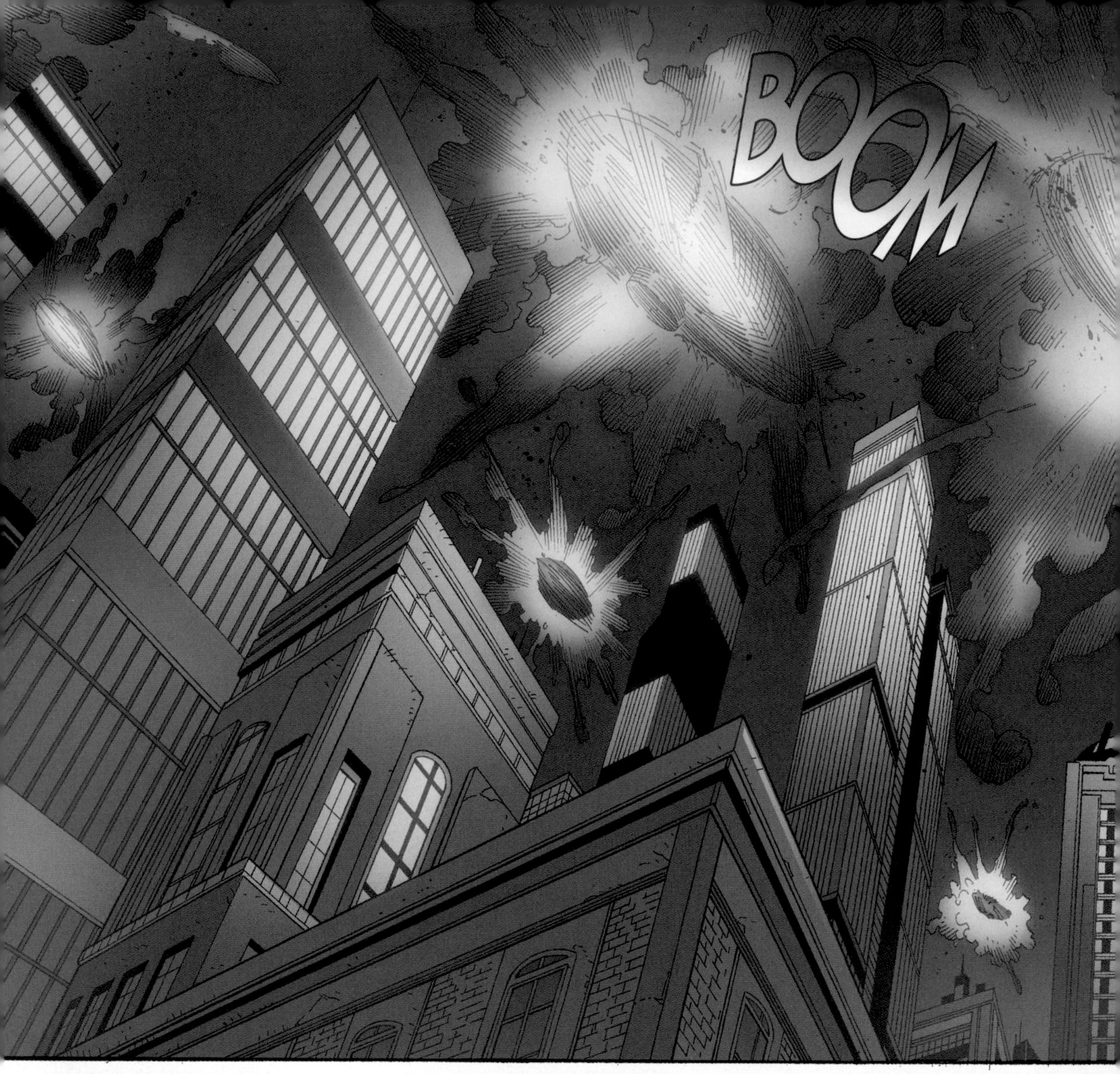
BOOM

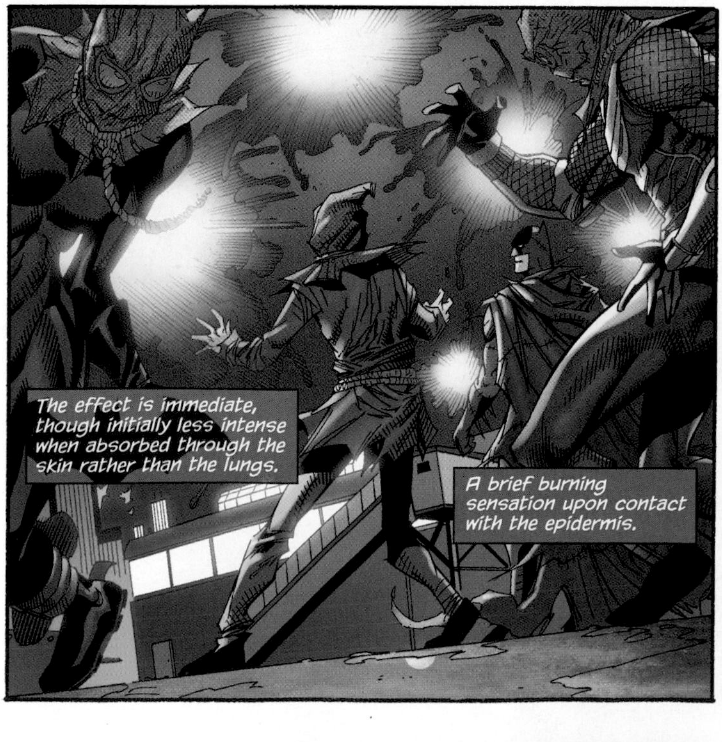
The effect is immediate, though initially less intense when absorbed through the skin rather than the lungs.
A brief burning sensation upon contact with the epidermis.

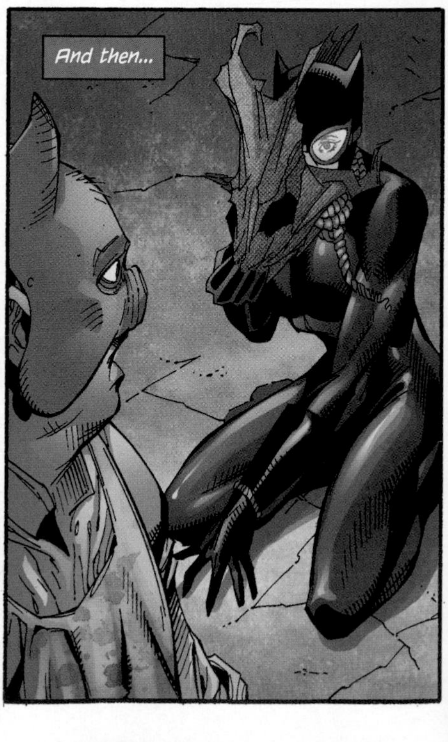
And then...

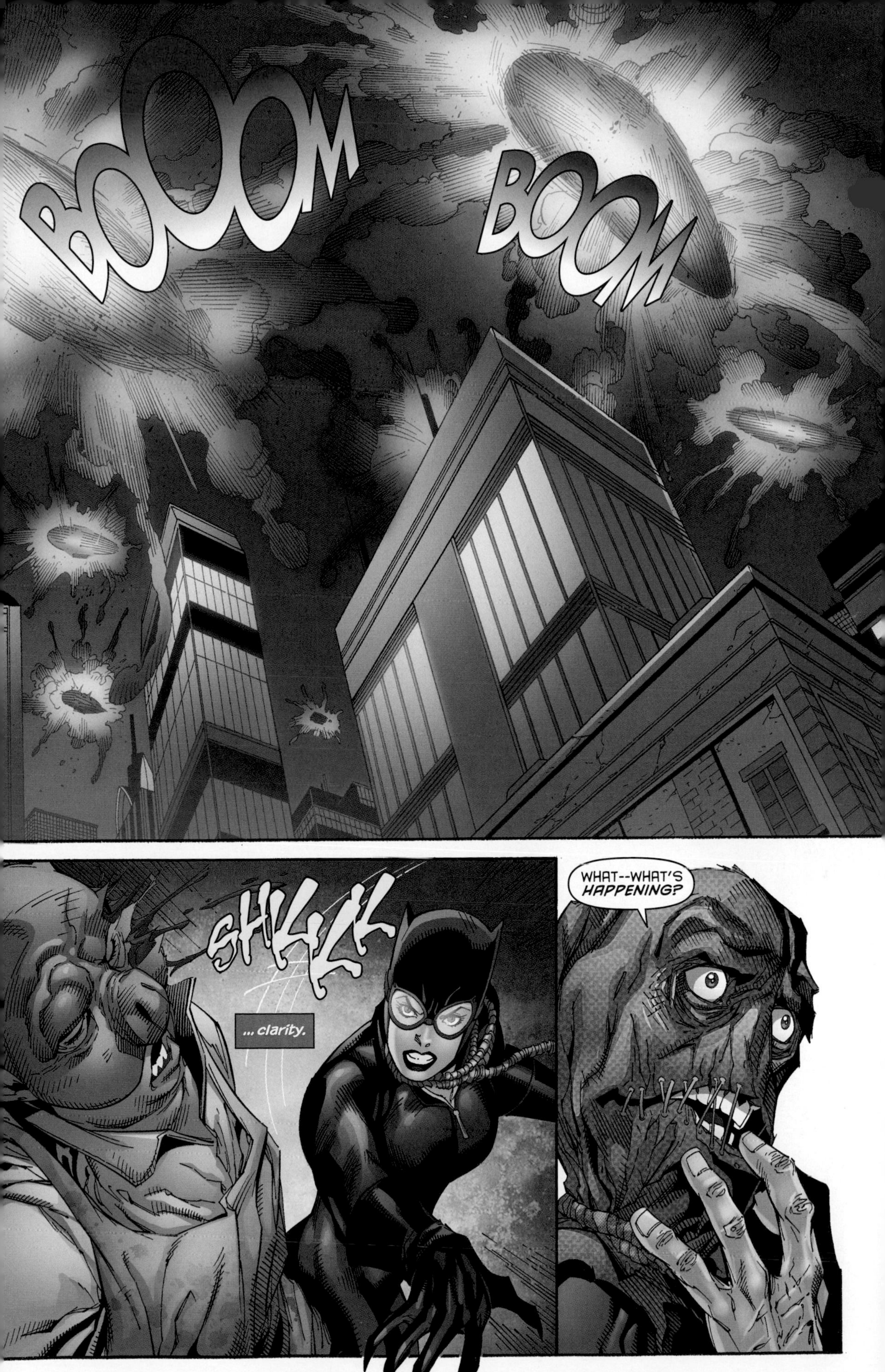
BOOOM
BOOM
...clarity.
WHAT--WHAT'S HAPPENING?

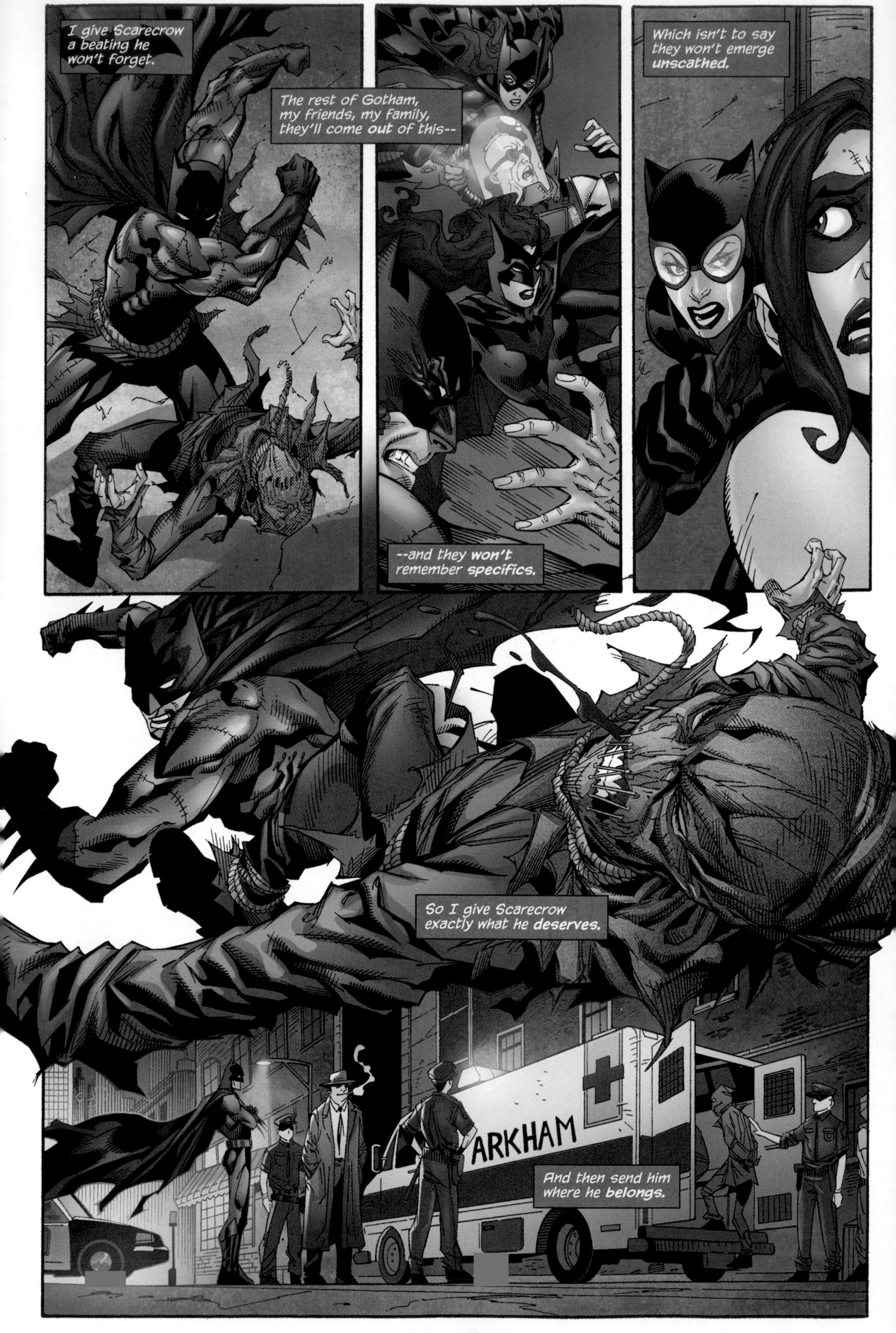
I give Scarecrow a beating he won't forget.
The rest of Gotham, my friends, my family, they'll come **out** of this--
--and they **won't** remember **specifics.**
Which isn't to say they won't emerge **unscathed.**
So I give Scarecrow exactly what he **deserves.**
ARKHAM
And then send him where he **belongs.**

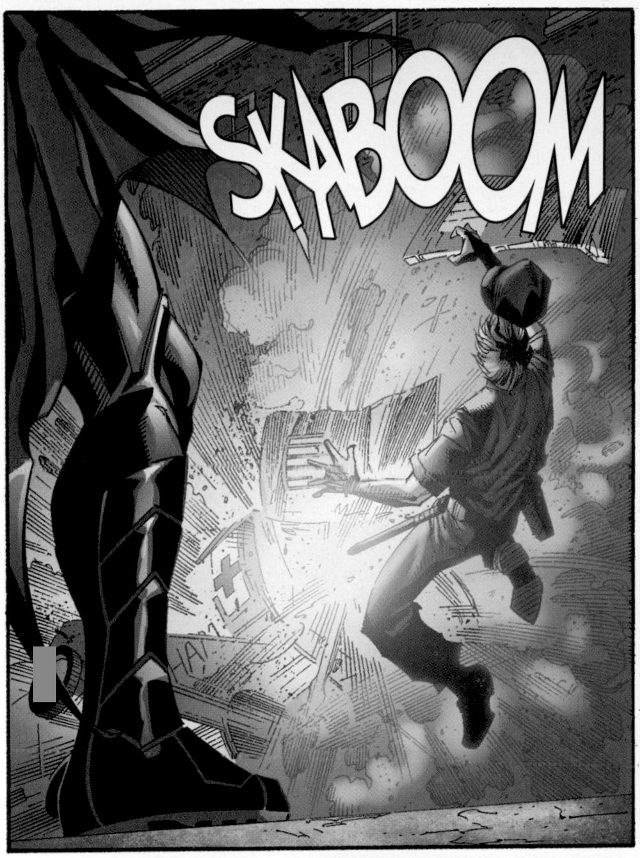
SKABOOM
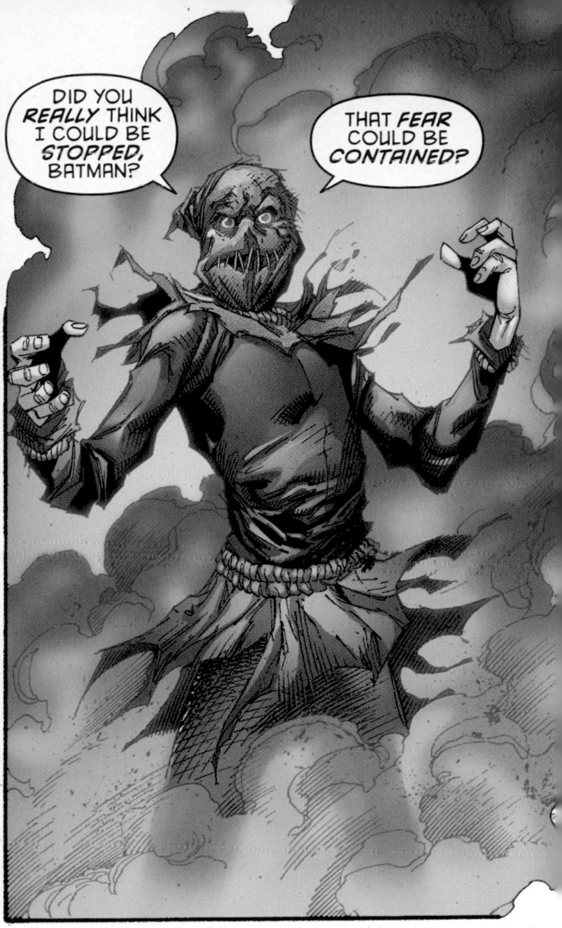
DID YOU REALLY THINK I COULD BE STOPPED, BATMAN?
THAT FEAR COULD BE CONTAINED?
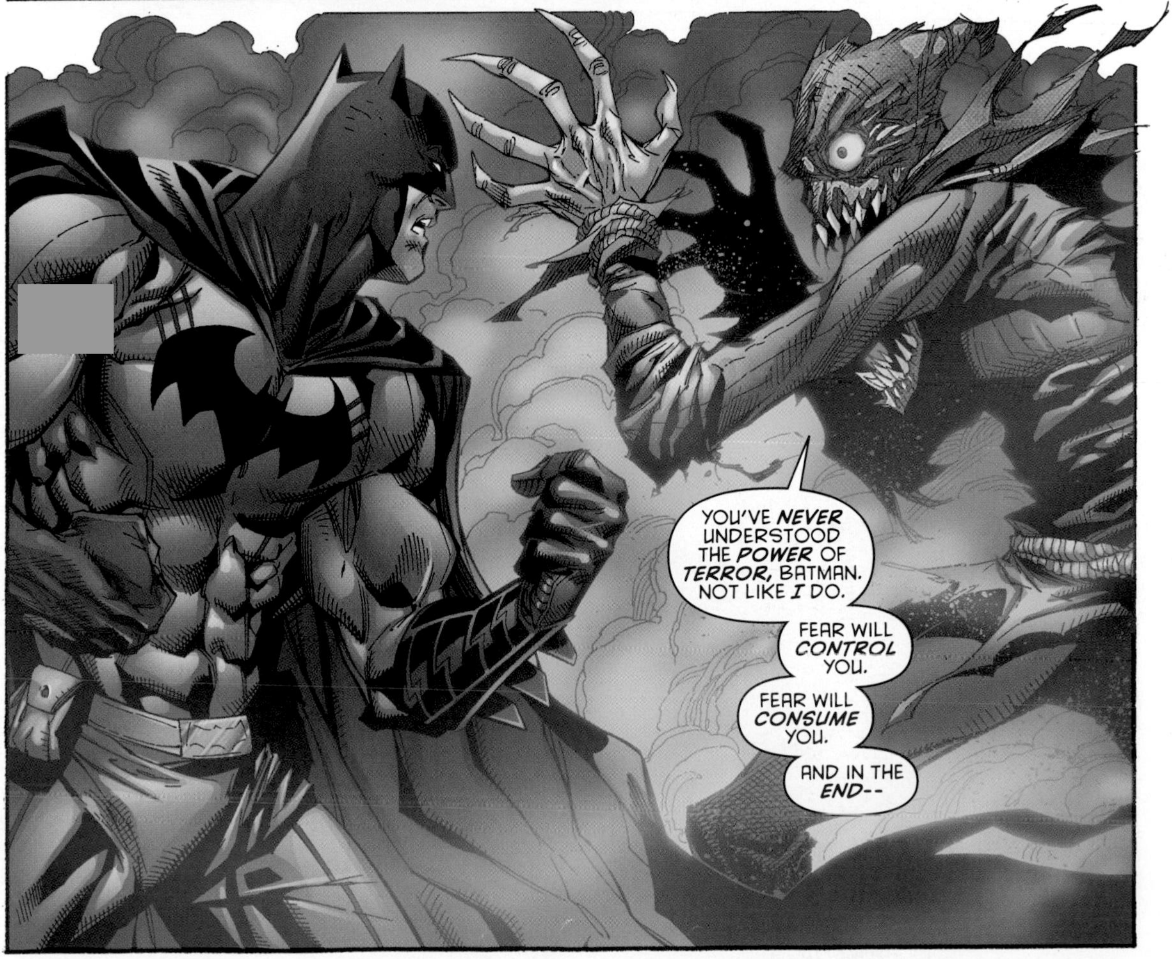
YOU'VE NEVER UNDERSTOOD THE POWER OF TERROR, BATMAN. NOT LIKE I DO.
FEAR WILL CONTROL YOU.
FEAR WILL CONSUME YOU.
AND IN THE END--

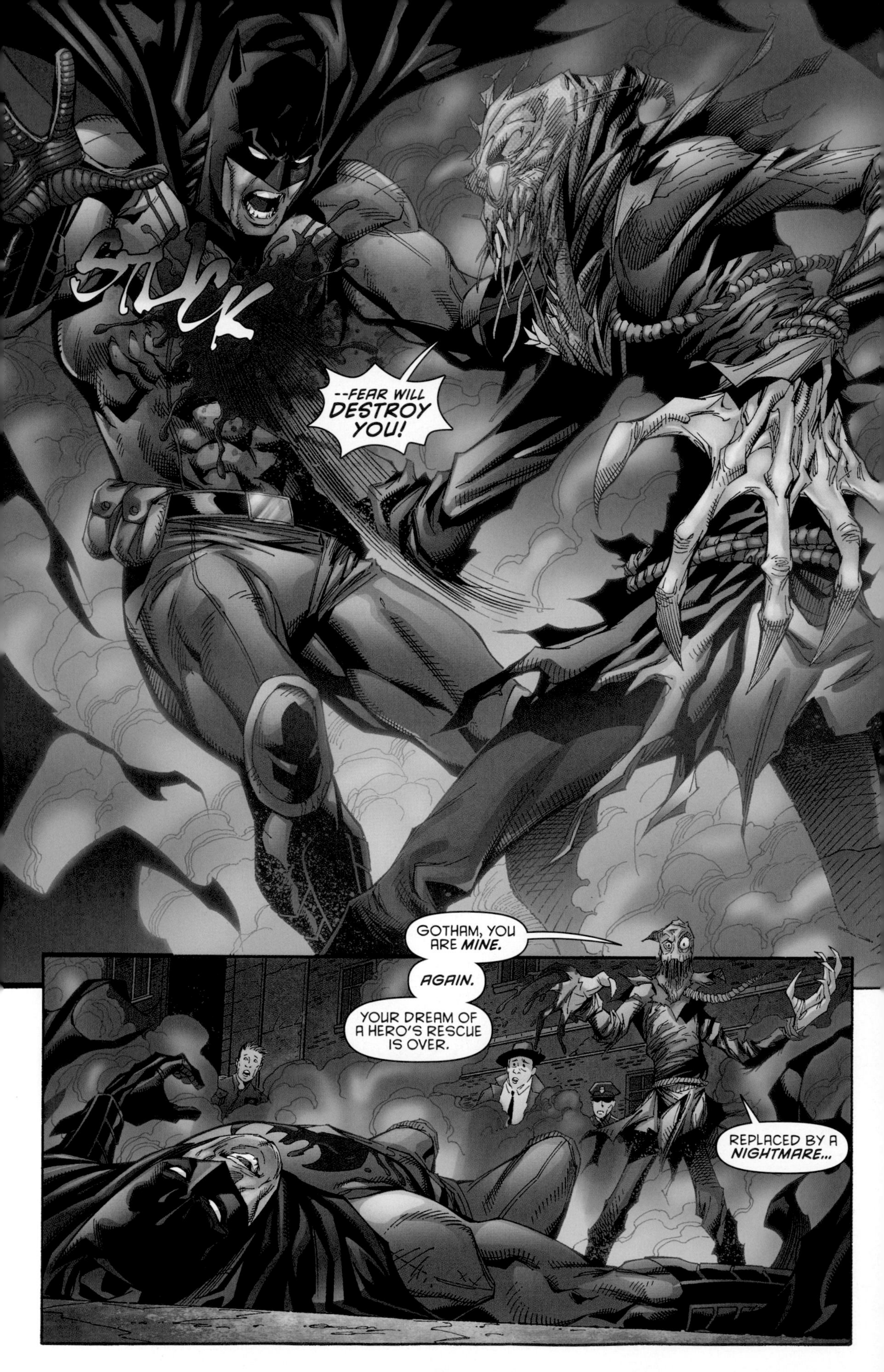
STUCK
--FEAR WILL DESTROY YOU!
GOTHAM, YOU ARE *MINE.*
AGAIN.
YOUR DREAM OF A HERO'S RESCUE IS OVER.
REPLACED BY A *NIGHTMARE...*

...OBEY ME, GOTHAM...

...FEAR ME.

WHAT'S HE *SEEING,* EXACTLY?

EXACTLY WHAT HE *WANTS* TO, COMMISSIONER.

YOU'VE HEARD THE EXPRESSION "A TASTE OF HIS OWN MEDICINE," NO DOUBT.

IT'S MY BELIEF THIS *CONTENTMENT SERUM* OF SCARECROW'S WILL GO A LONG WAY TOWARD KEEPING HIM--AND ALL THE *OTHER* MORE TROUBLESOME INMATES--FROM BECOMING TOO...*AMBITIOUS.*

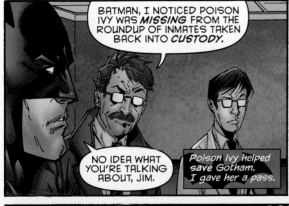

BATMAN, I NOTICED POISON IVY WAS *MISSING* FROM THE ROUNDUP OF INMATES TAKEN BACK INTO *CUSTODY.*

NO IDEA WHAT YOU'RE TALKING ABOUT, JIM.

Poison Ivy helped save Gotham. I gave her a pass.

At least, until the next time she steps out of line.

IT *WON'T* LAST, YOU KNOW.

EXCUSE ME?

CRANE'S HAD TOO MUCH EXPOSURE TO HIS OWN SERUMS. *EVENTUALLY,* HE'LL COME OUT OF IT.

"HE'LL FIGURE OUT *EXACTLY* WHERE HE IS.

ARKHAM ASYLUM REHABILITATION CEN

"HE'LL COME BACK TO REALITY--"

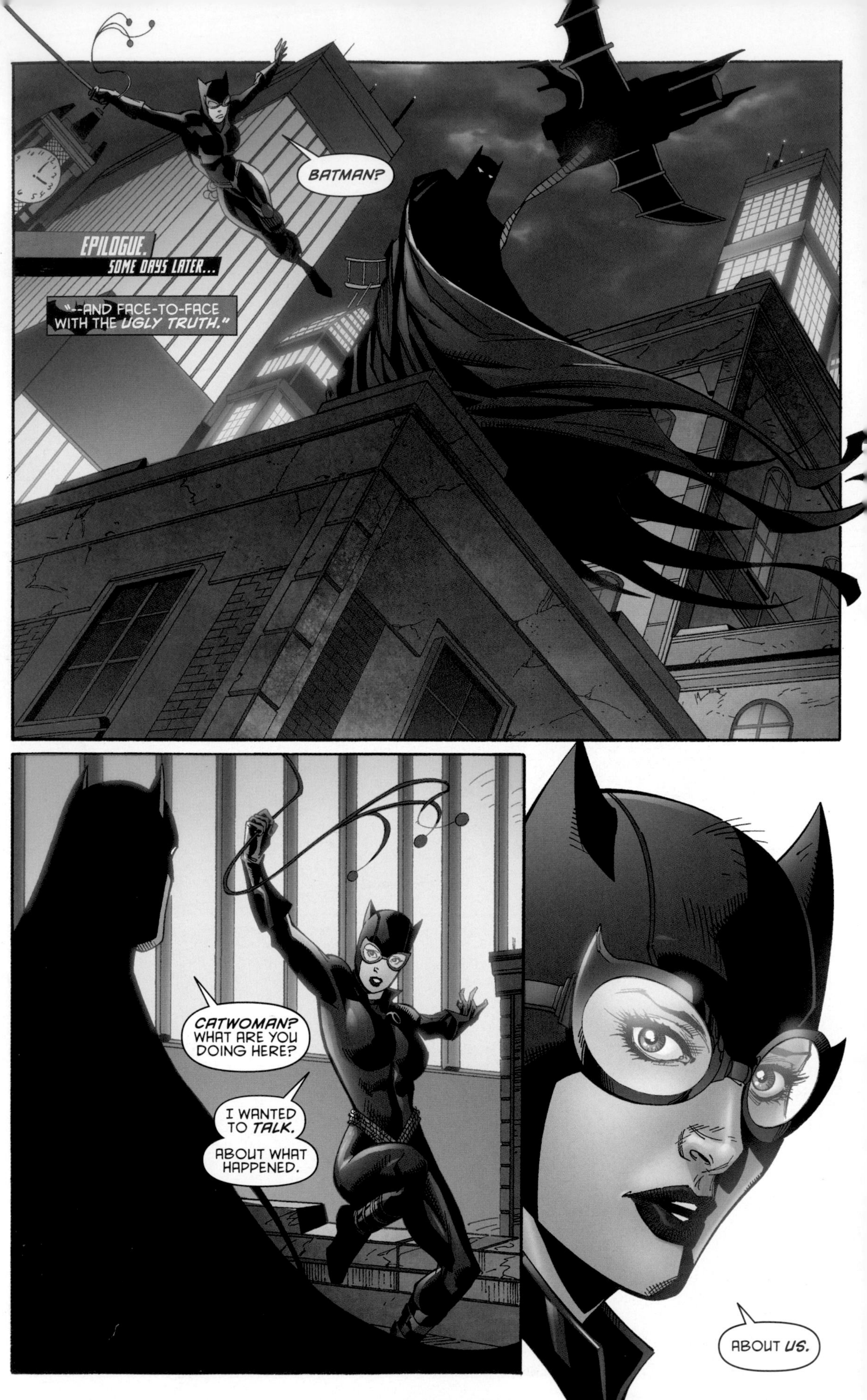
BATMAN?
EPILOGUE.
SOME DAYS LATER...
"--AND FACE-TO-FACE WITH THE UGLY TRUTH."
CATWOMAN? WHAT ARE YOU DOING HERE?
I WANTED TO TALK.
ABOUT WHAT HAPPENED.
ABOUT US.

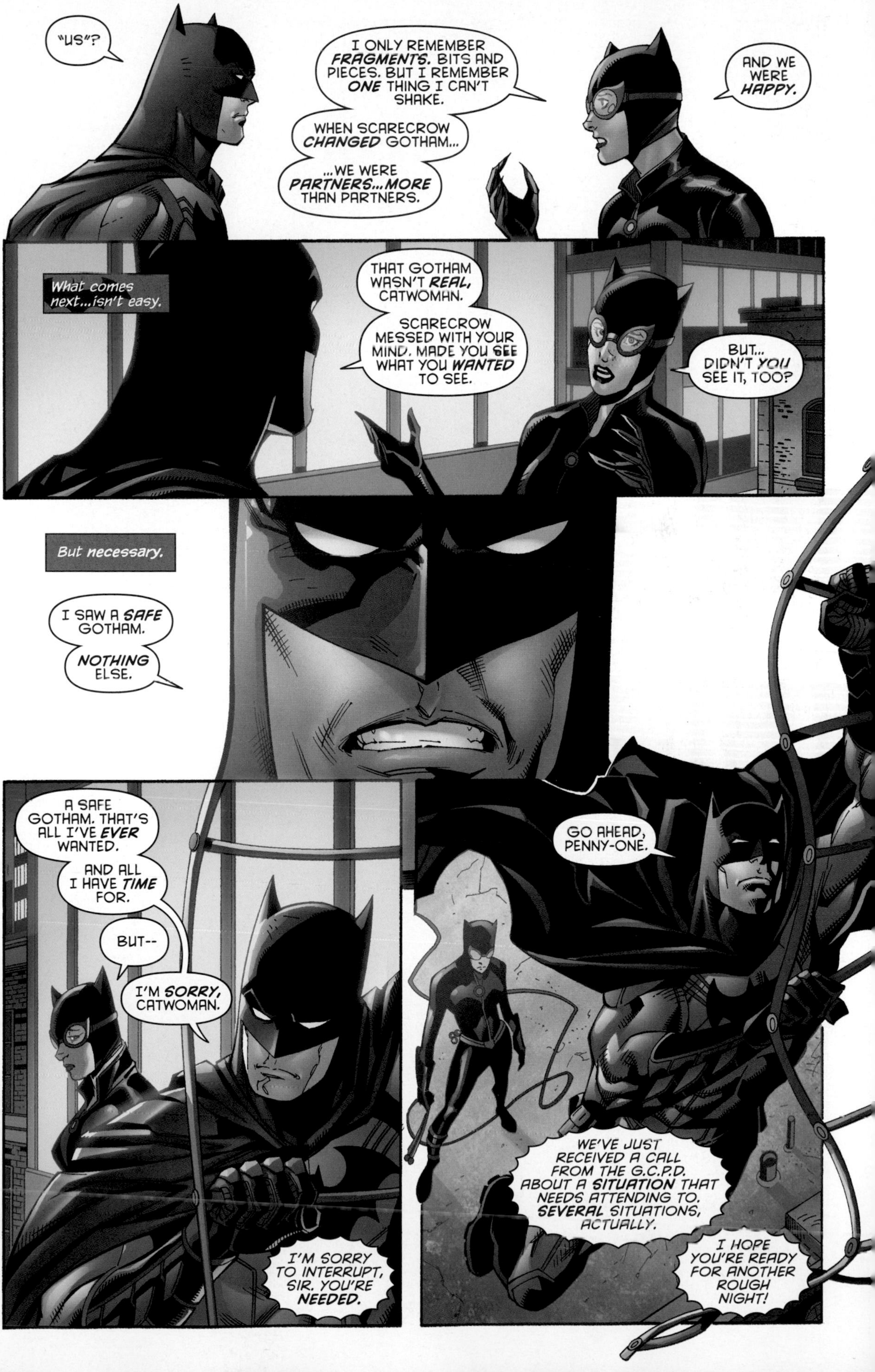
"US"?
I ONLY REMEMBER FRAGMENTS. BITS AND PIECES. BUT I REMEMBER ONE THING I CAN'T SHAKE.
WHEN SCARECROW CHANGED GOTHAM...
...WE WERE PARTNERS...MORE THAN PARTNERS.
AND WE WERE HAPPY.
What comes next...isn't easy.
THAT GOTHAM WASN'T REAL, CATWOMAN.
SCARECROW MESSED WITH YOUR MIND. MADE YOU SEE WHAT YOU WANTED TO SEE.
BUT... DIDN'T YOU SEE IT, TOO?
But necessary.
I SAW A SAFE GOTHAM.
NOTHING ELSE.
A SAFE GOTHAM. THAT'S ALL I'VE EVER WANTED.
AND ALL I HAVE TIME FOR.
BUT--
I'M SORRY, CATWOMAN.
I'M SORRY TO INTERRUPT, SIR. YOU'RE NEEDED.
GO AHEAD, PENNY-ONE.
WE'VE JUST RECEIVED A CALL FROM THE G.C.P.D. ABOUT A SITUATION THAT NEEDS ATTENDING TO. SEVERAL SITUATIONS, ACTUALLY.
I HOPE YOU'RE READY FOR ANOTHER ROUGH NIGHT!

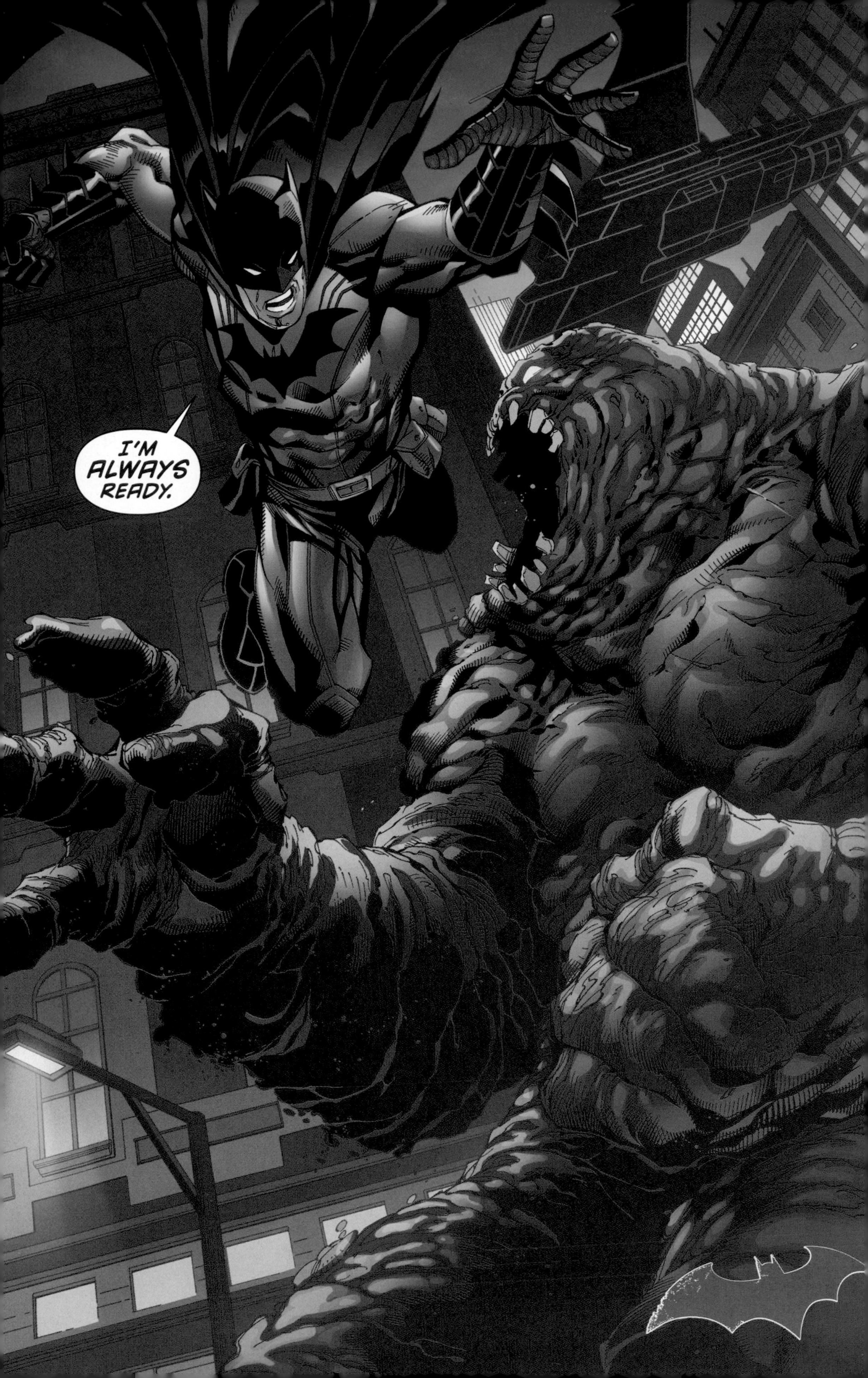
I'M ALWAYS READY.

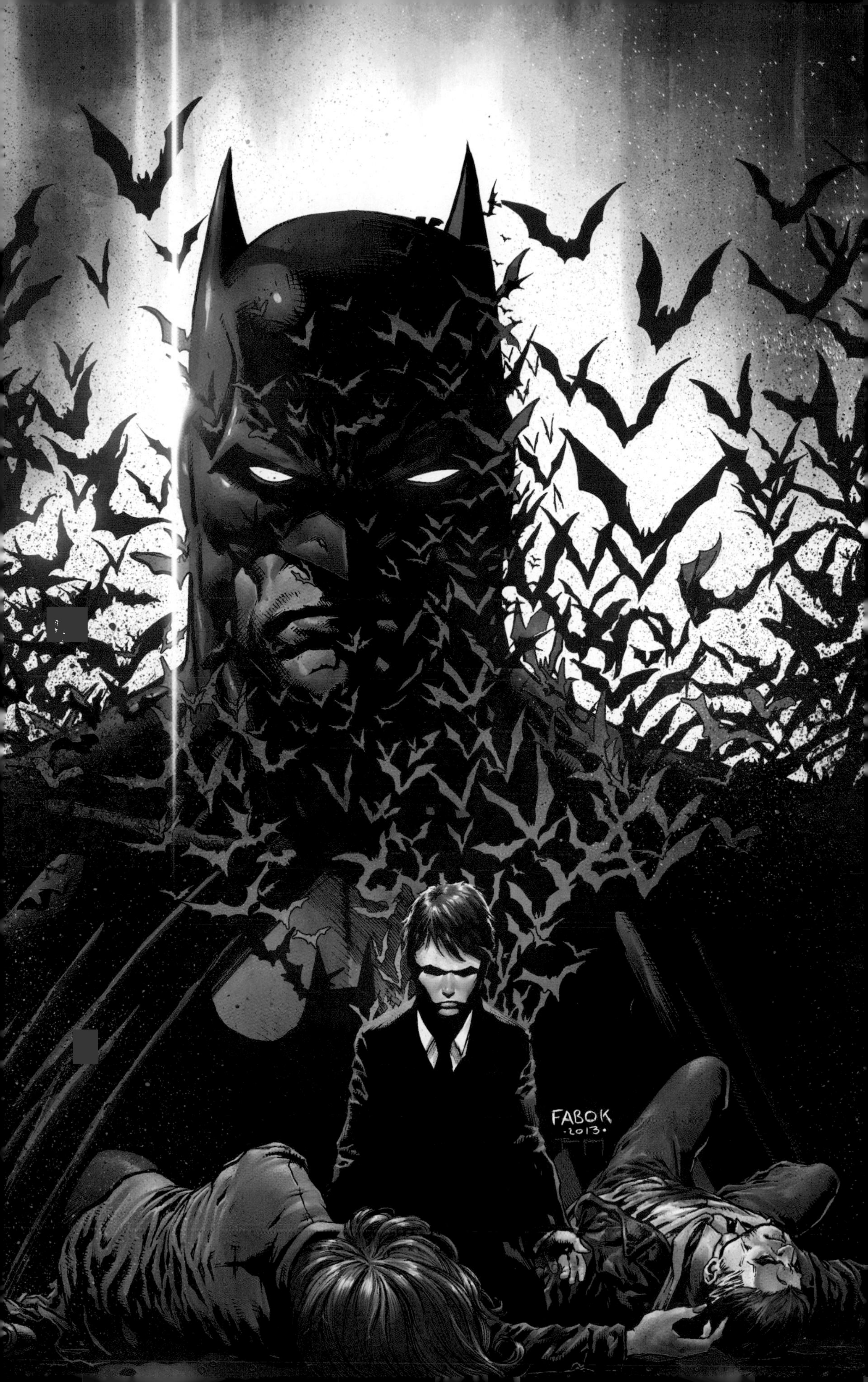
FABOK
·2013·

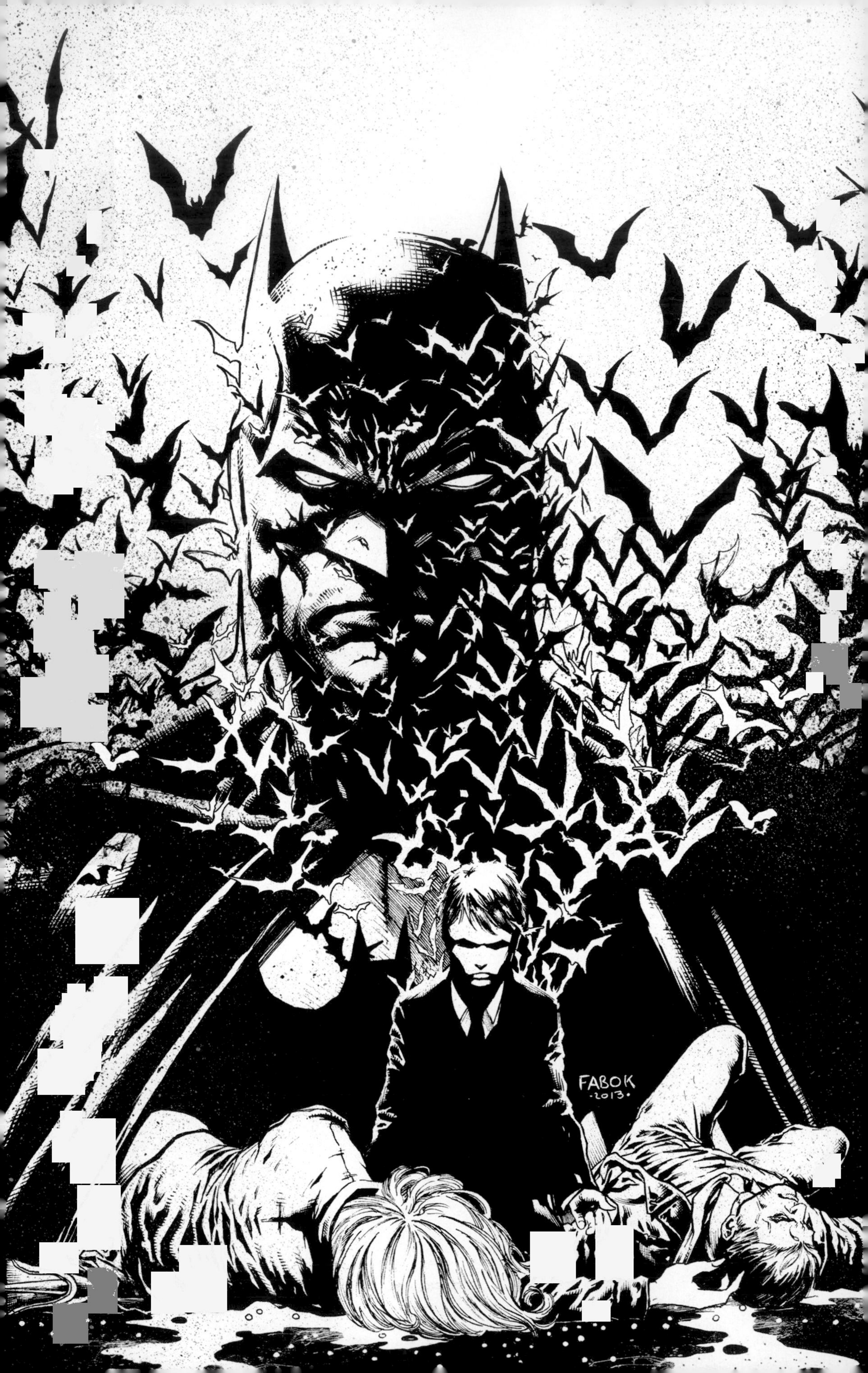
FABOK
·2013·

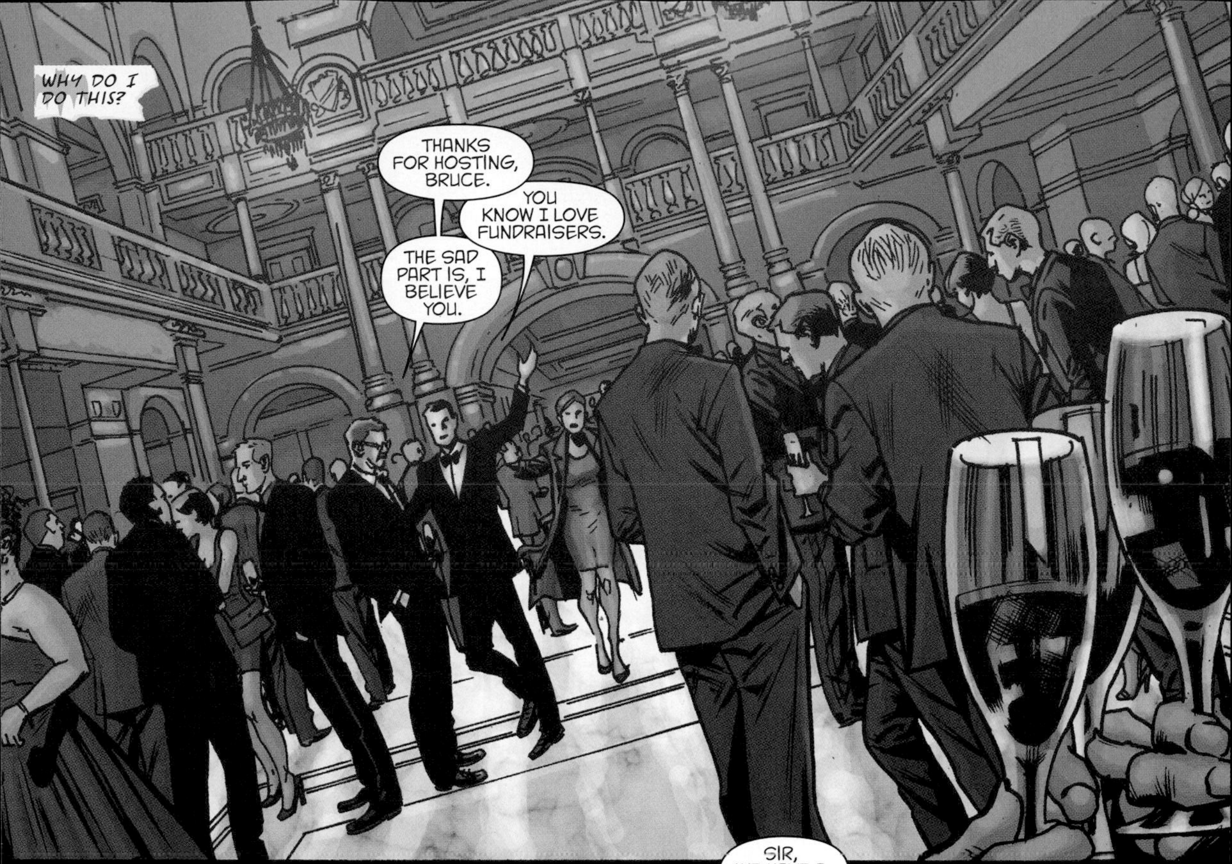
WHY DO I DO THIS?
THANKS FOR HOSTING, BRUCE.
YOU KNOW I LOVE FUNDRAISERS.
THE SAD PART IS, I BELIEVE YOU.

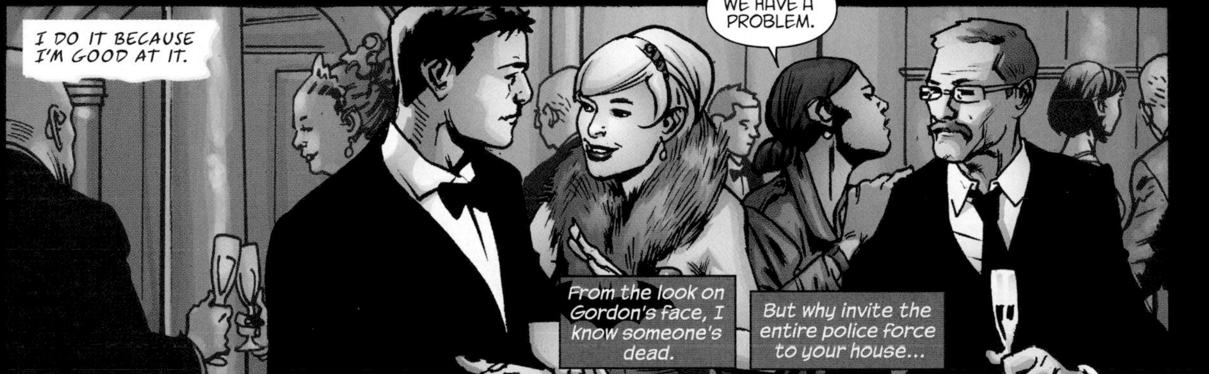
I DO IT BECAUSE I'M GOOD AT IT.
SIR, WE HAVE A PROBLEM.
From the look on Gordon's face, I know someone's dead.
But why invite the entire police force to your house...

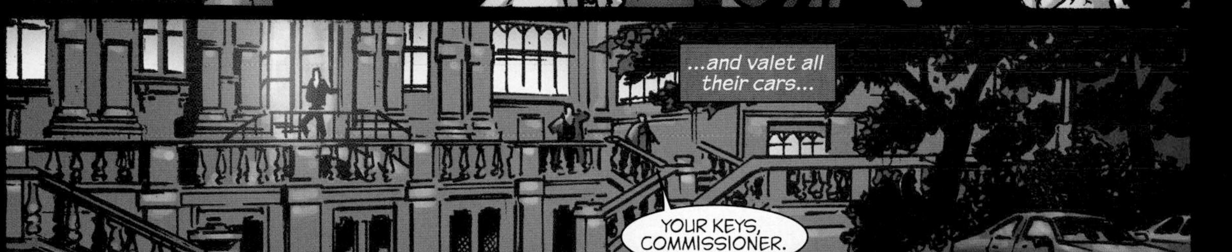
...and valet all their cars...
YOUR KEYS, COMMISSIONER.

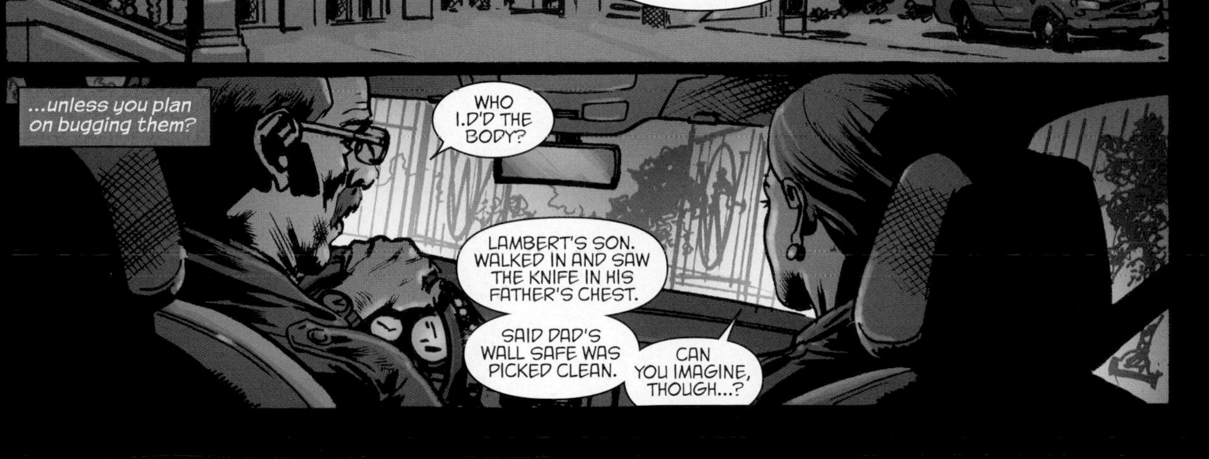
...unless you plan on bugging them?
WHO I.D'D THE BODY?
LAMBERT'S SON. WALKED IN AND SAW THE KNIFE IN HIS FATHER'S CHEST.
SAID DAD'S WALL SAFE WAS PICKED CLEAN.
CAN YOU IMAGINE, THOUGH...?

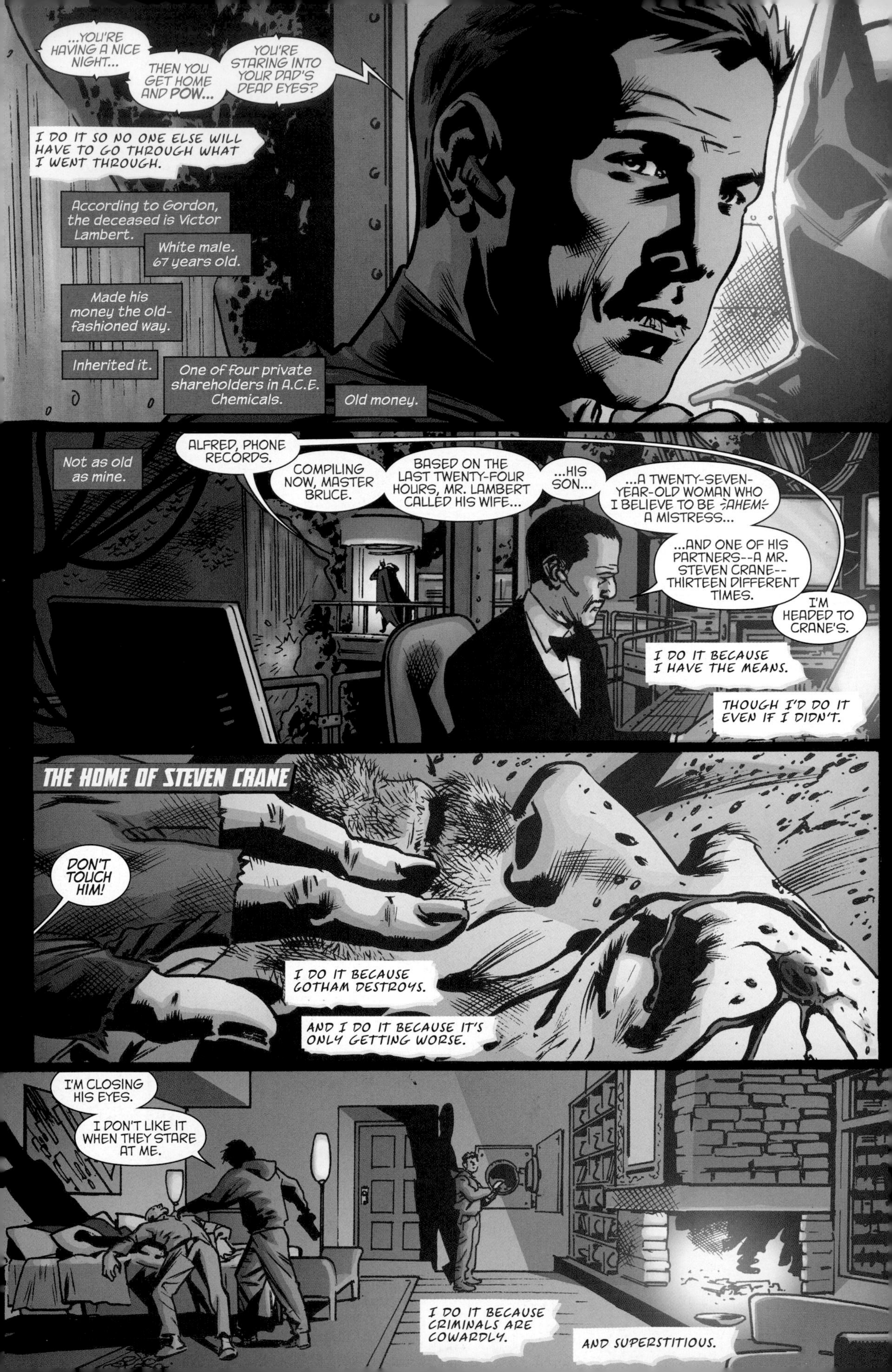
...YOU'RE HAVING A NICE NIGHT...
THEN YOU GET HOME AND POW...
YOU'RE STARING INTO YOUR DAD'S DEAD EYES?
I DO IT SO NO ONE ELSE WILL HAVE TO GO THROUGH WHAT I WENT THROUGH.
According to Gordon, the deceased is Victor Lambert.
White male. 67 years old.
Made his money the old-fashioned way.
Inherited it.
One of four private shareholders in A.C.E. Chemicals.
Old money.
Not as old as mine.
ALFRED, PHONE RECORDS.
COMPILING NOW, MASTER BRUCE.
BASED ON THE LAST TWENTY-FOUR HOURS, MR. LAMBERT CALLED HIS WIFE...
...HIS SON...
...A TWENTY-SEVEN-YEAR-OLD WOMAN WHO I BELIEVE TO BE AHEM A MISTRESS...
...AND ONE OF HIS PARTNERS--A MR. STEVEN CRANE--THIRTEEN DIFFERENT TIMES.
I'M HEADED TO CRANE'S.
I DO IT BECAUSE I HAVE THE MEANS.
THOUGH I'D DO IT EVEN IF I DIDN'T.
THE HOME OF STEVEN CRANE
DON'T TOUCH HIM!
I DO IT BECAUSE GOTHAM DESTROYS.
AND I DO IT BECAUSE IT'S ONLY GETTING WORSE.
I'M CLOSING HIS EYES.
I DON'T LIKE IT WHEN THEY STARE AT ME.
I DO IT BECAUSE CRIMINALS ARE COWARDLY.
AND SUPERSTITIOUS.

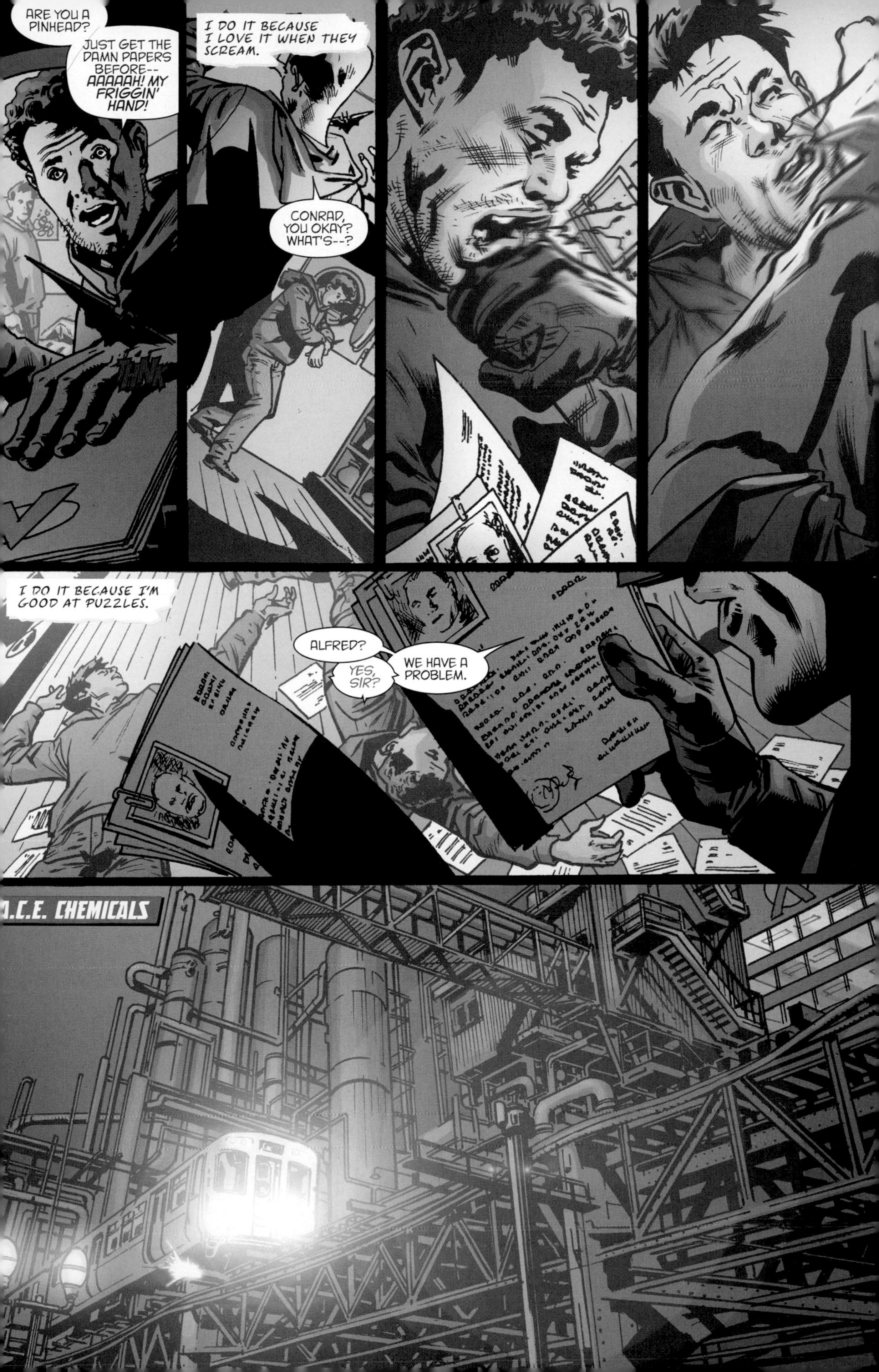
ARE YOU A PINHEAD?
JUST GET THE DAMN PAPERS BEFORE-- AAAAAH! MY FRIGGIN' HAND!
THNK
I DO IT BECAUSE I LOVE IT WHEN THEY SCREAM.
CONRAD, YOU OKAY? WHAT'S--?
I DO IT BECAUSE I'M GOOD AT PUZZLES.
ALFRED?
YES, SIR?
WE HAVE A PROBLEM.
A.C.E. CHEMICALS

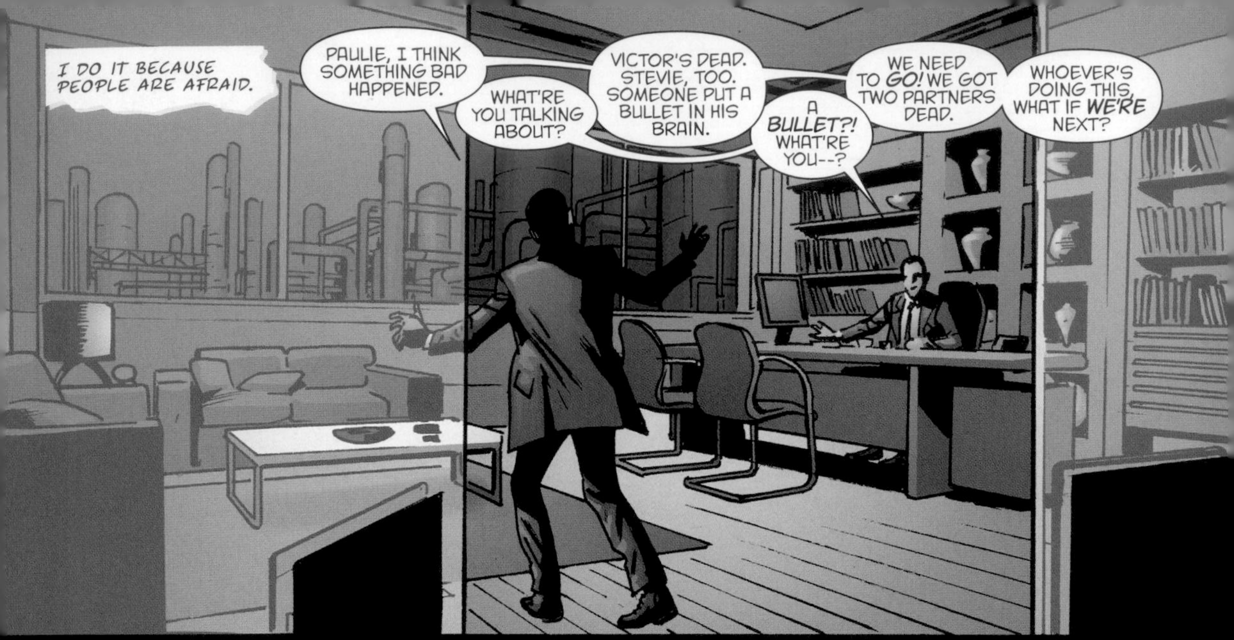
I DO IT BECAUSE PEOPLE ARE AFRAID.
PAULIE, I THINK SOMETHING BAD HAPPENED.
WHAT'RE YOU TALKING ABOUT?
VICTOR'S DEAD. STEVIE, TOO. SOMEONE PUT A BULLET IN HIS BRAIN.
A *BULLET?!* WHAT'RE YOU--?
WE NEED TO *GO!* WE GOT TWO PARTNERS DEAD.
WHOEVER'S DOING THIS, WHAT IF *WE'RE* NEXT?

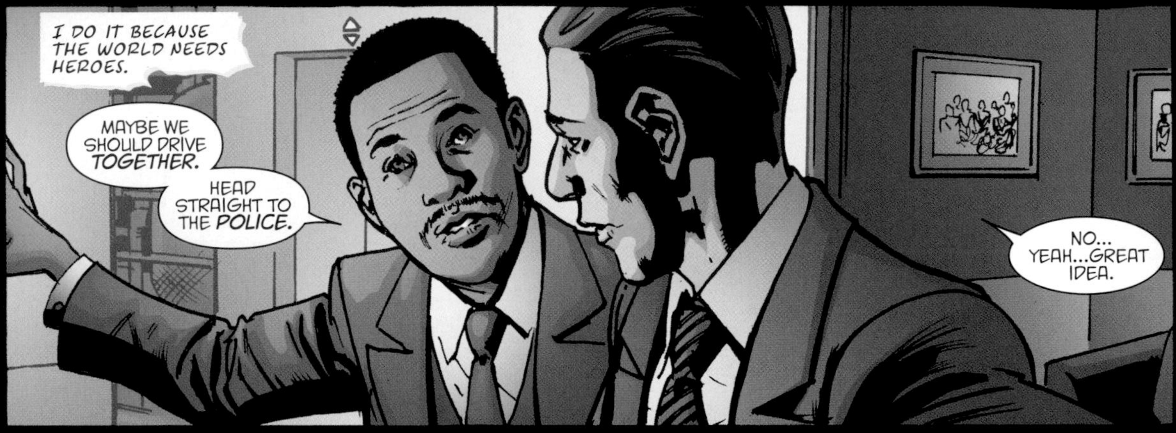
I DO IT BECAUSE THE WORLD NEEDS HEROES.
MAYBE WE SHOULD DRIVE *TOGETHER.*
HEAD STRAIGHT TO THE *POLICE.*
NO... YEAH...GREAT IDEA.

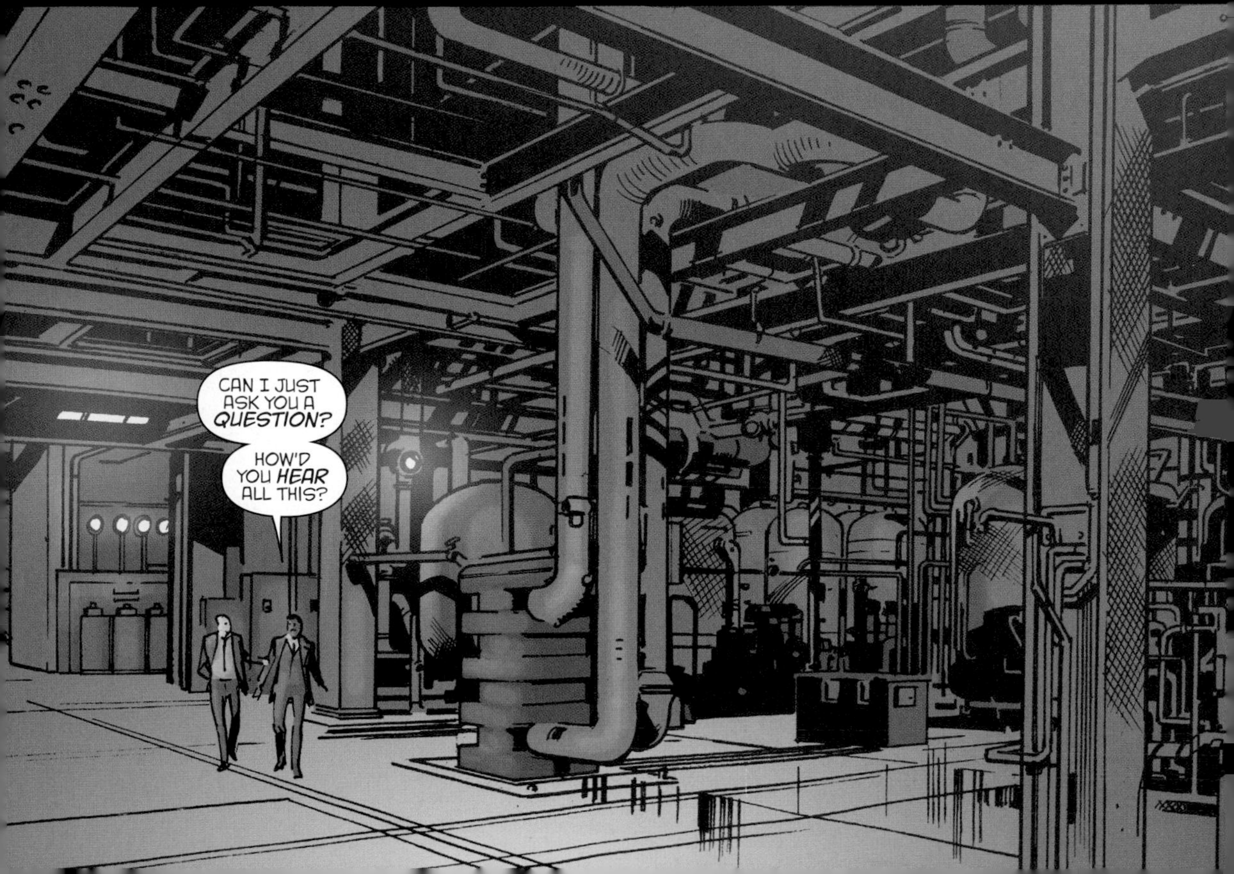
CAN I JUST ASK YOU A *QUESTION?*
HOW'D YOU *HEAR* ALL THIS?

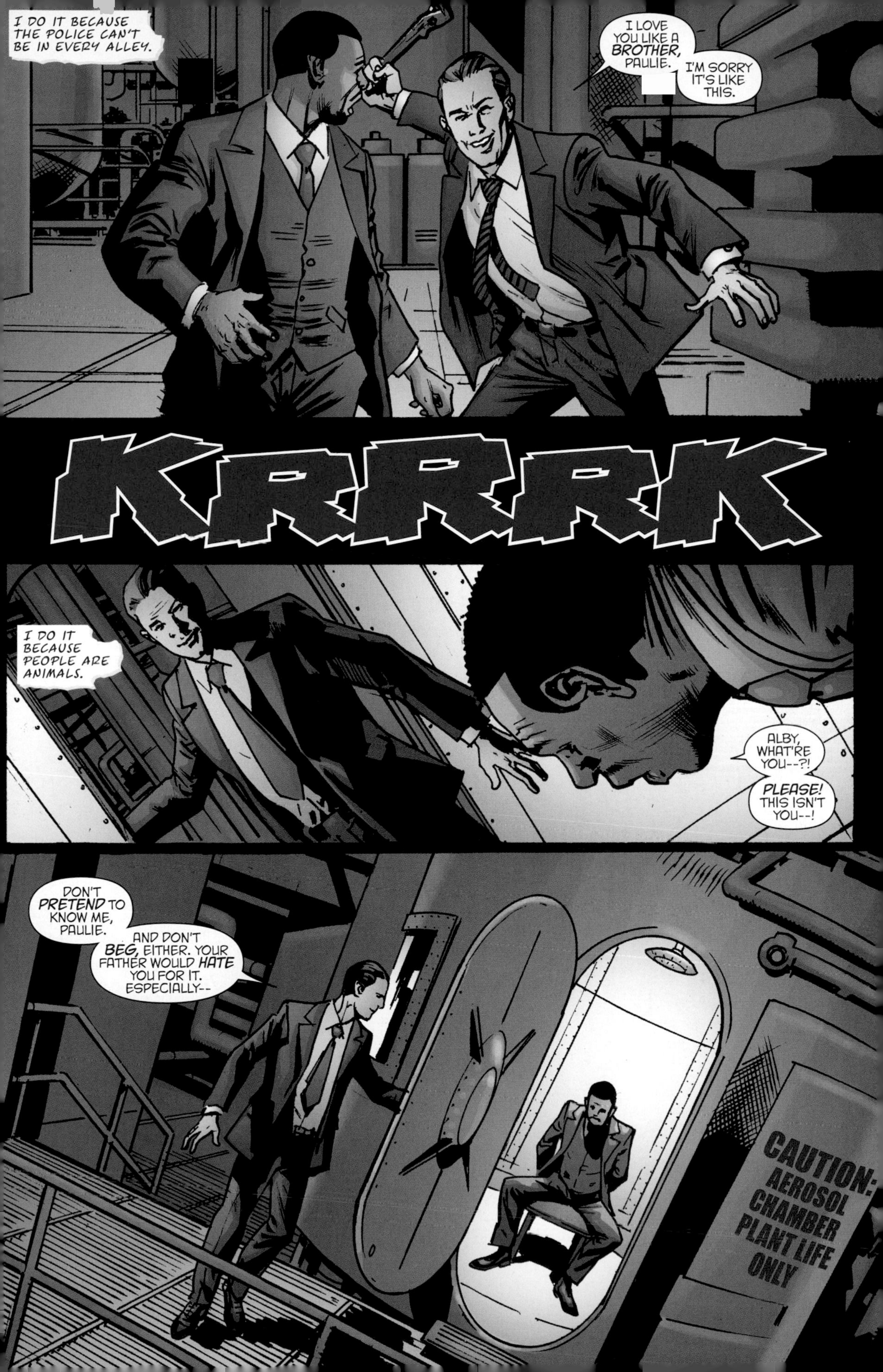
I DO IT BECAUSE THE POLICE CAN'T BE IN EVERY ALLEY.
I LOVE YOU LIKE A BROTHER, PAULIE.
I'M SORRY IT'S LIKE THIS.
KRRRK
I DO IT BECAUSE PEOPLE ARE ANIMALS.
ALBY, WHAT'RE YOU--?!
PLEASE! THIS ISN'T YOU--!
DON'T PRETEND TO KNOW ME, PAULIE.
AND DON'T BEG, EITHER. YOUR FATHER WOULD HATE YOU FOR IT. ESPECIALLY--
CAUTION: AEROSOL CHAMBER PLANT LIFE ONLY

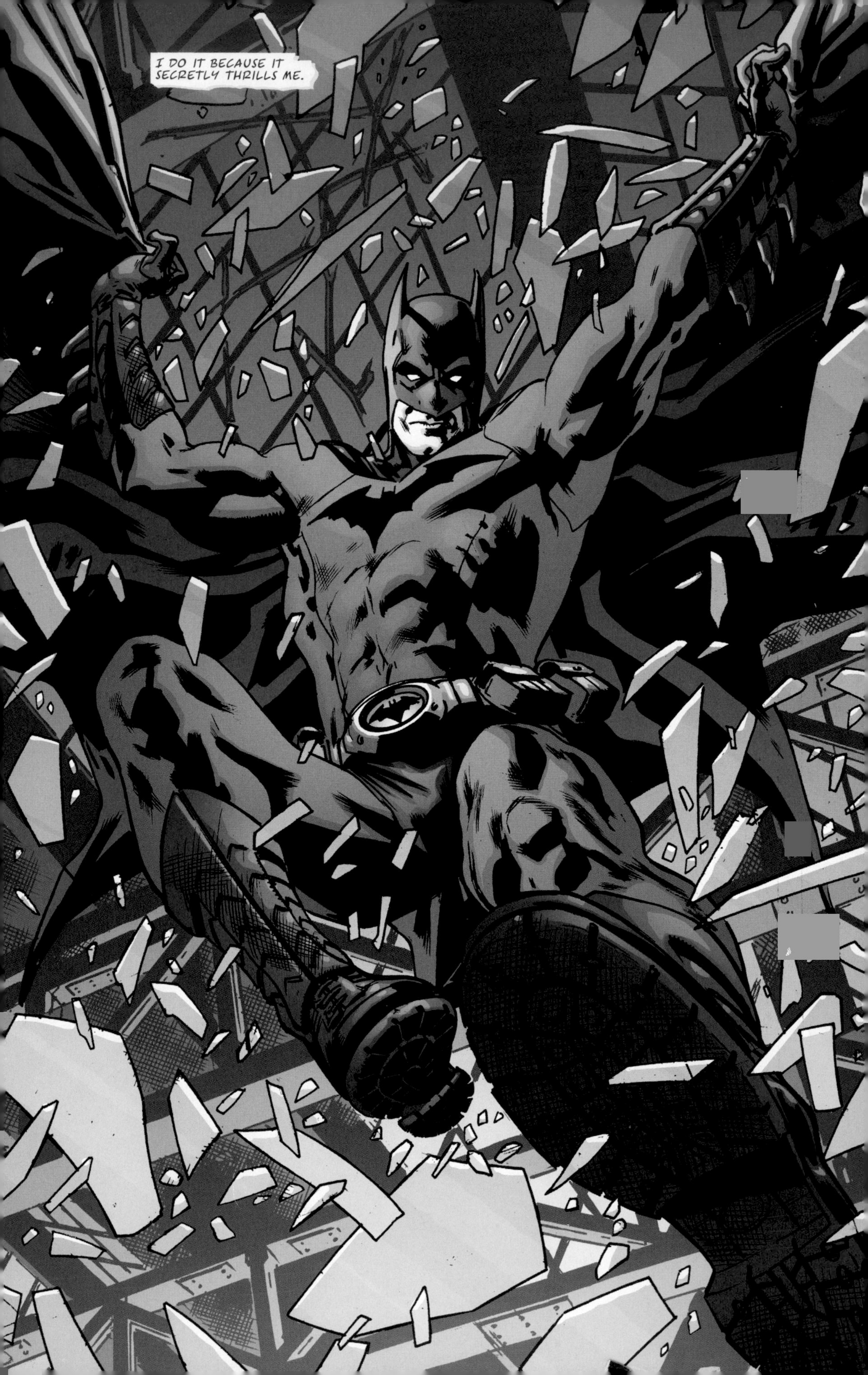
I DO IT BECAUSE IT SECRETLY THRILLS ME.

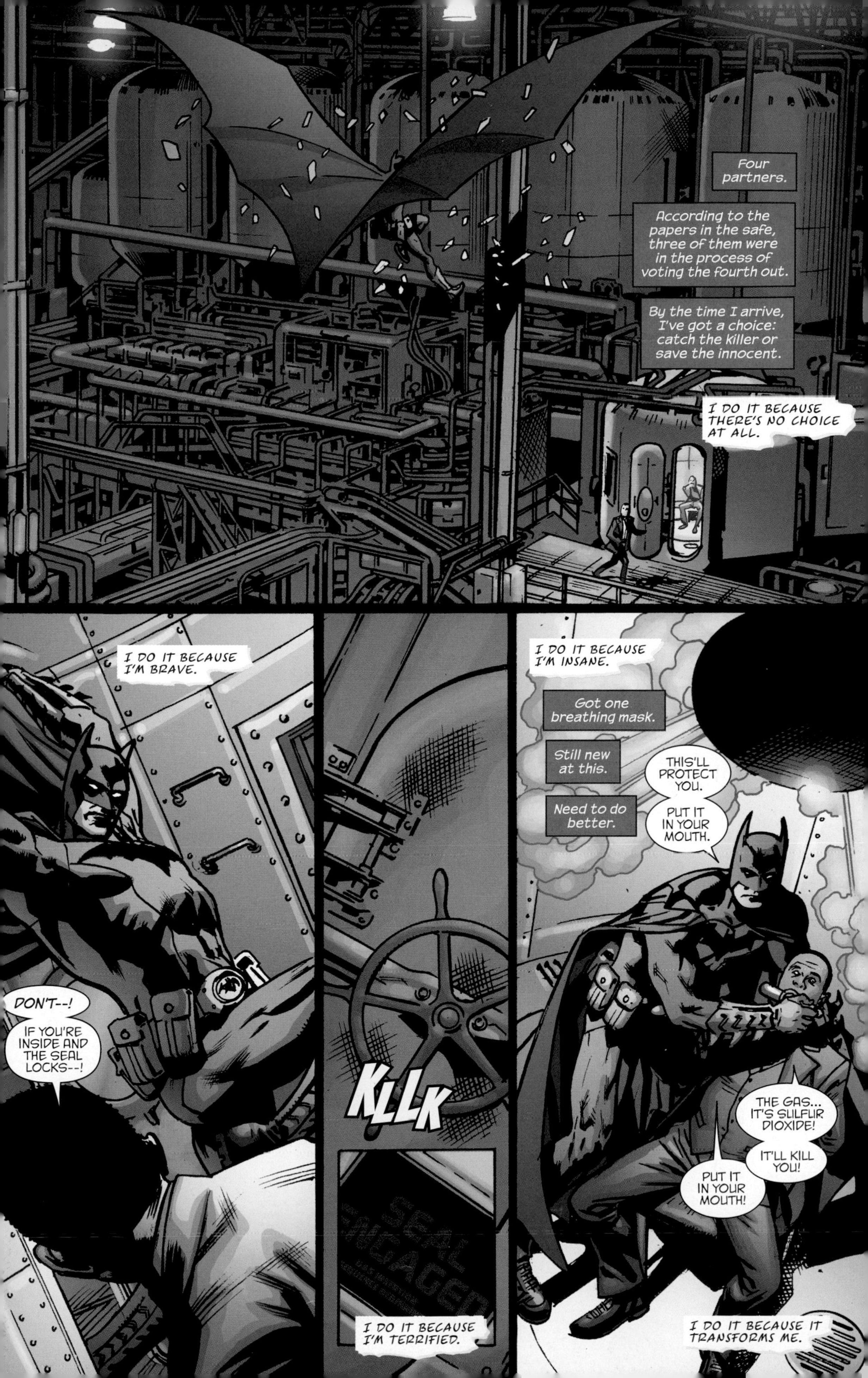

Four partners.
According to the papers in the safe, three of them were in the process of voting the fourth out.
By the time I arrive, I've got a choice: catch the killer or save the innocent.
I DO IT BECAUSE THERE'S NO CHOICE AT ALL.
I DO IT BECAUSE I'M BRAVE.
DON'T--!
IF YOU'RE INSIDE AND THE SEAL LOCKS--!
KLLK
I DO IT BECAUSE I'M TERRIFIED.
I DO IT BECAUSE I'M INSANE.
Got one breathing mask.
Still new at this.
Need to do better.
THIS'LL PROTECT YOU.
PUT IT IN YOUR MOUTH.
THE GAS... IT'S SULFUR DIOXIDE!
IT'LL KILL YOU!
PUT IT IN YOUR MOUTH!
I DO IT BECAUSE IT TRANSFORMS ME.

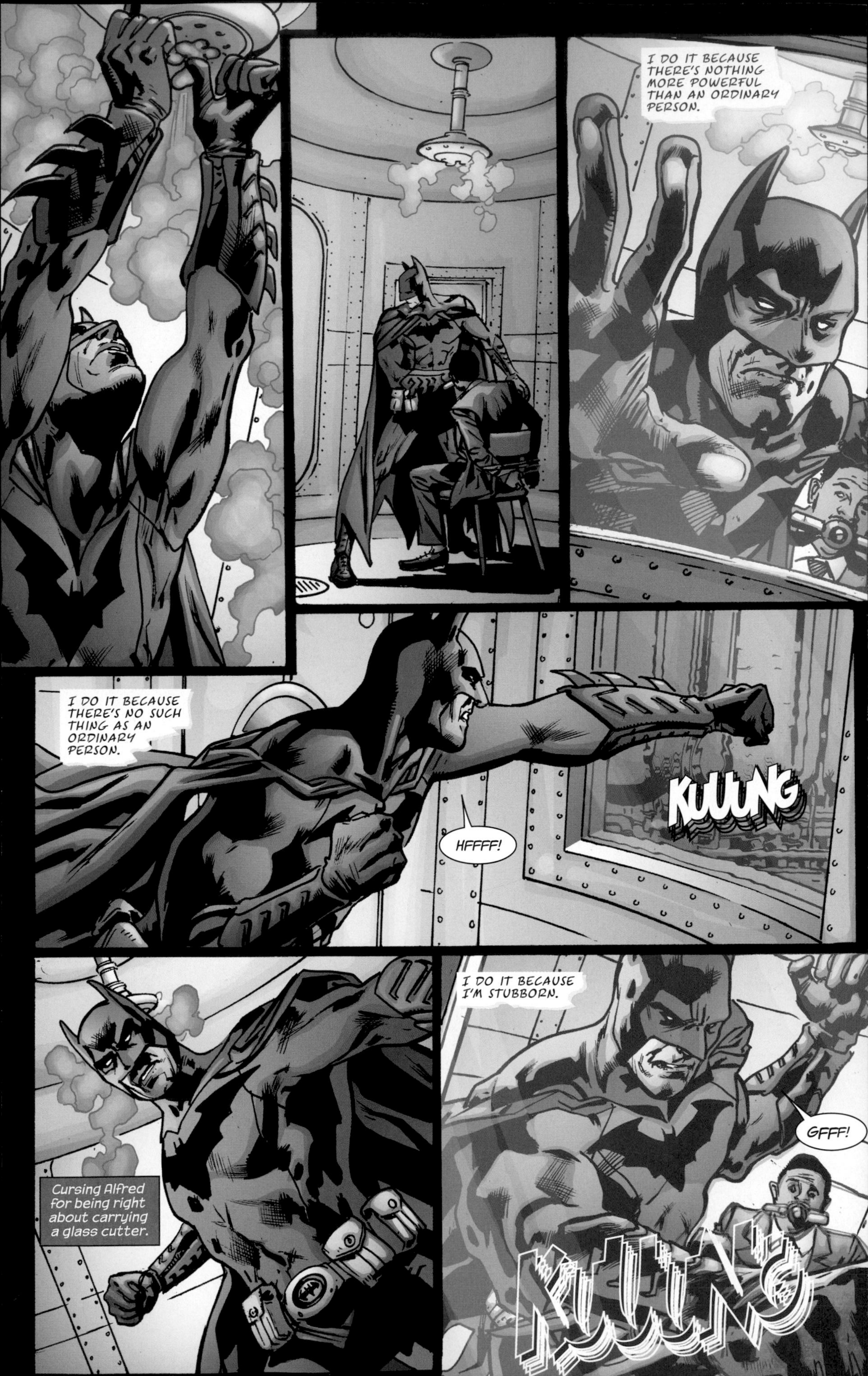
I DO IT BECAUSE THERE'S NOTHING MORE POWERFUL THAN AN ORDINARY PERSON.
I DO IT BECAUSE THERE'S NO SUCH THING AS AN ORDINARY PERSON.
HFFFF!
KUUUNG
Cursing Alfred for being right about carrying a glass cutter.
I DO IT BECAUSE I'M STUBBORN.
GFFF!

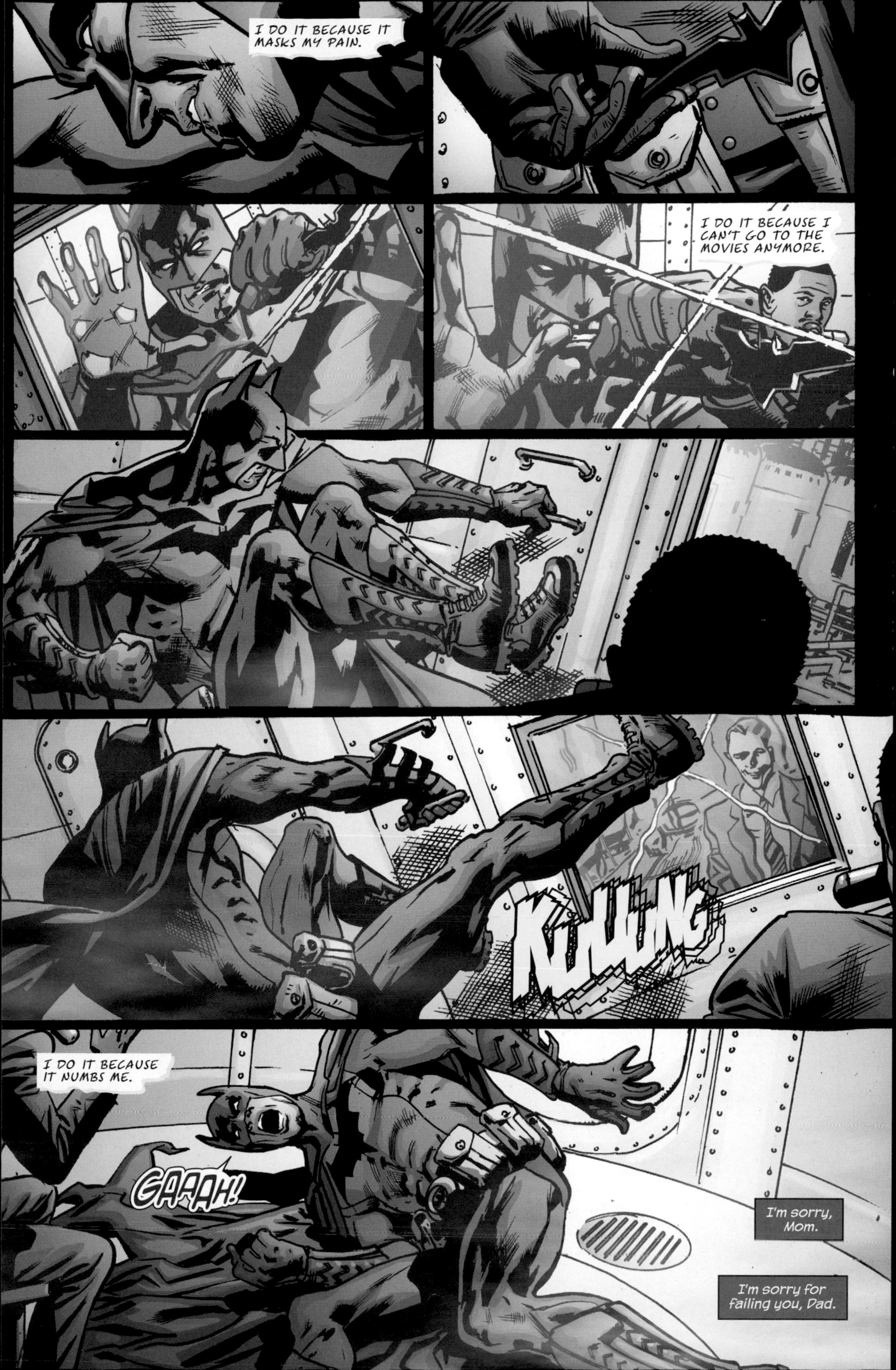
I DO IT BECAUSE IT MASKS MY PAIN.
I DO IT BECAUSE I CAN'T GO TO THE MOVIES ANYMORE.
KLUUNG
I DO IT BECAUSE IT NUMBS ME.
GAAAH!
I'm sorry, Mom.
I'm sorry for failing you, Dad.

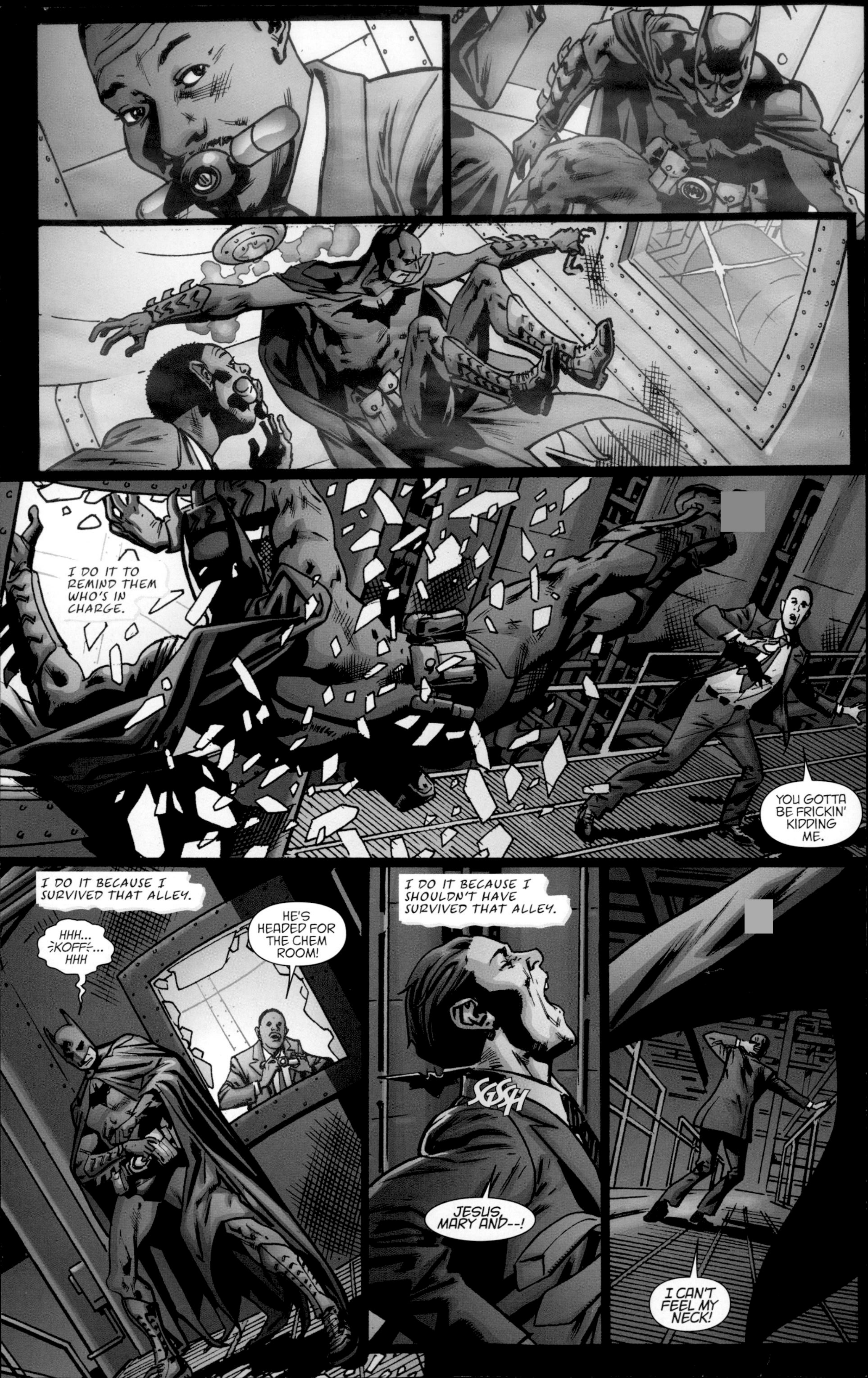
I DO IT TO REMIND THEM WHO'S IN CHARGE.
YOU GOTTA BE FRICKIN' KIDDING ME.
I DO IT BECAUSE I SURVIVED THAT ALLEY.
HHH... KOFF... HHH
HE'S HEADED FOR THE CHEM ROOM!
I DO IT BECAUSE I SHOULDN'T HAVE SURVIVED THAT ALLEY.
SGSH
JESUS, MARY AND--!
I CAN'T FEEL MY NECK!

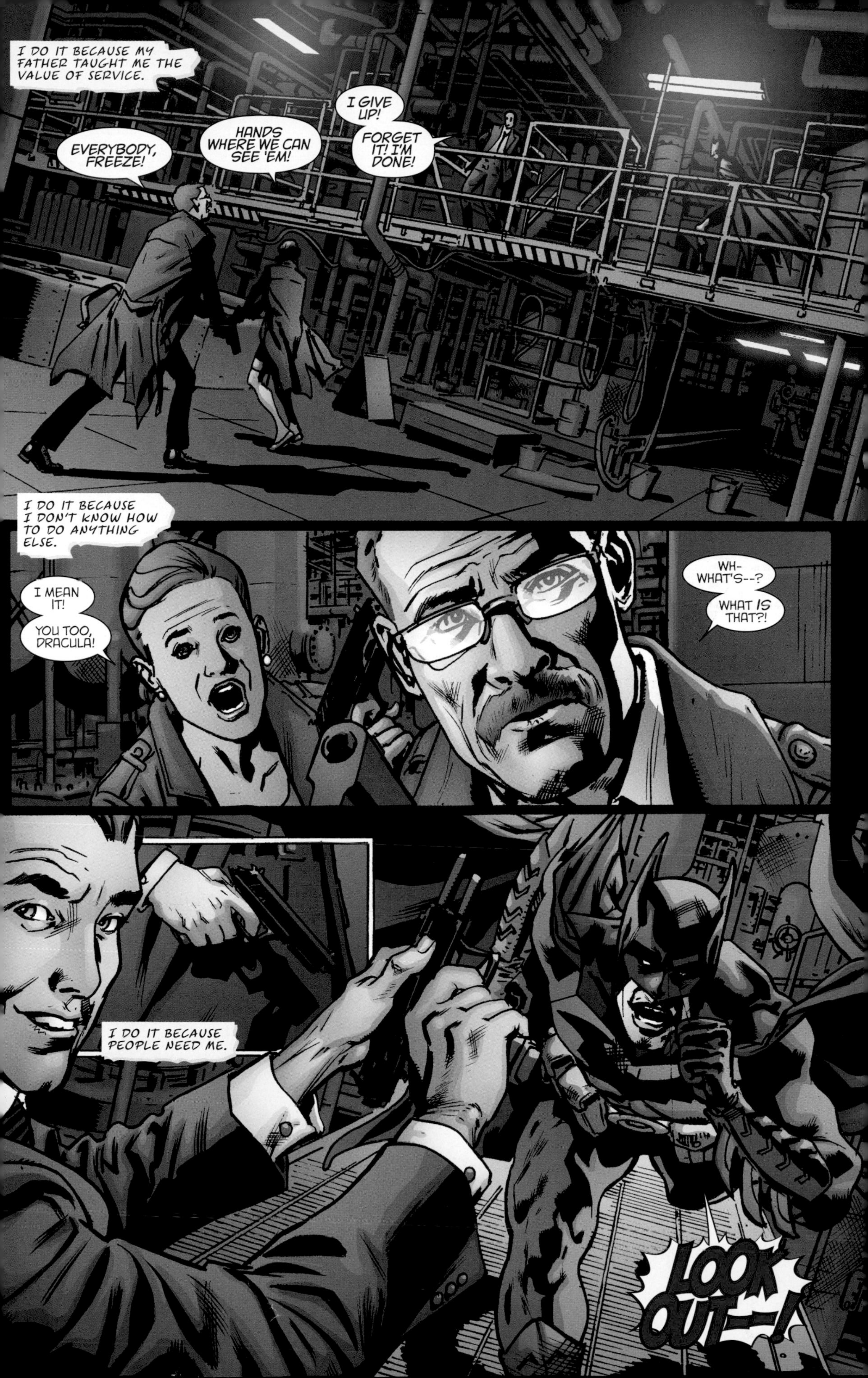
I DO IT BECAUSE MY FATHER TAUGHT ME THE VALUE OF SERVICE.
EVERYBODY, FREEZE!
HANDS WHERE WE CAN SEE 'EM!
I GIVE UP!
FORGET IT! I'M DONE!
I DO IT BECAUSE I DON'T KNOW HOW TO DO ANYTHING ELSE.
I MEAN IT!
YOU TOO, DRACULA!
WH- WHAT'S--?
WHAT *IS* THAT?!
I DO IT BECAUSE PEOPLE NEED ME.
LOOK OUT--!

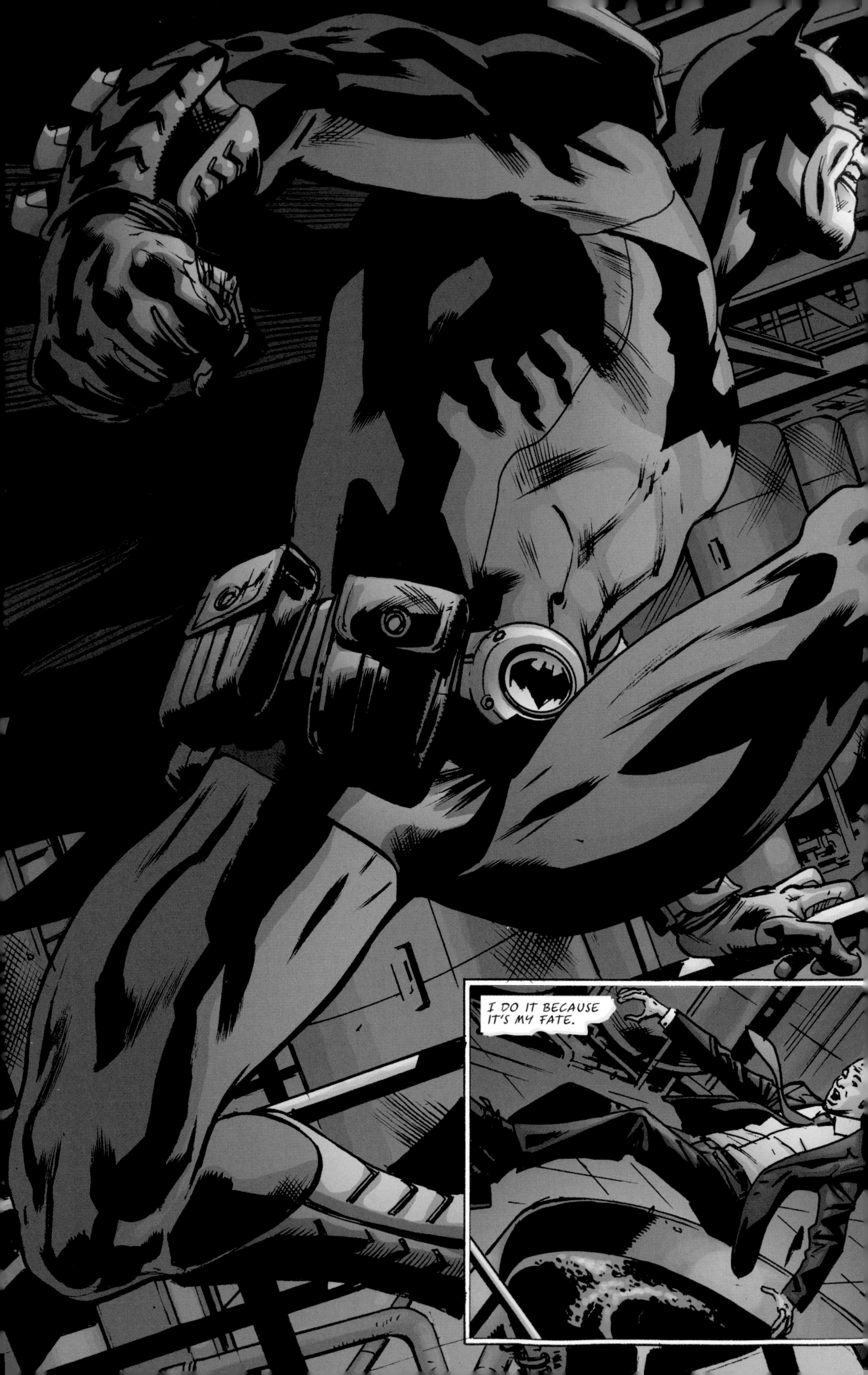
I DO IT BECAUSE IT'S MY FATE.

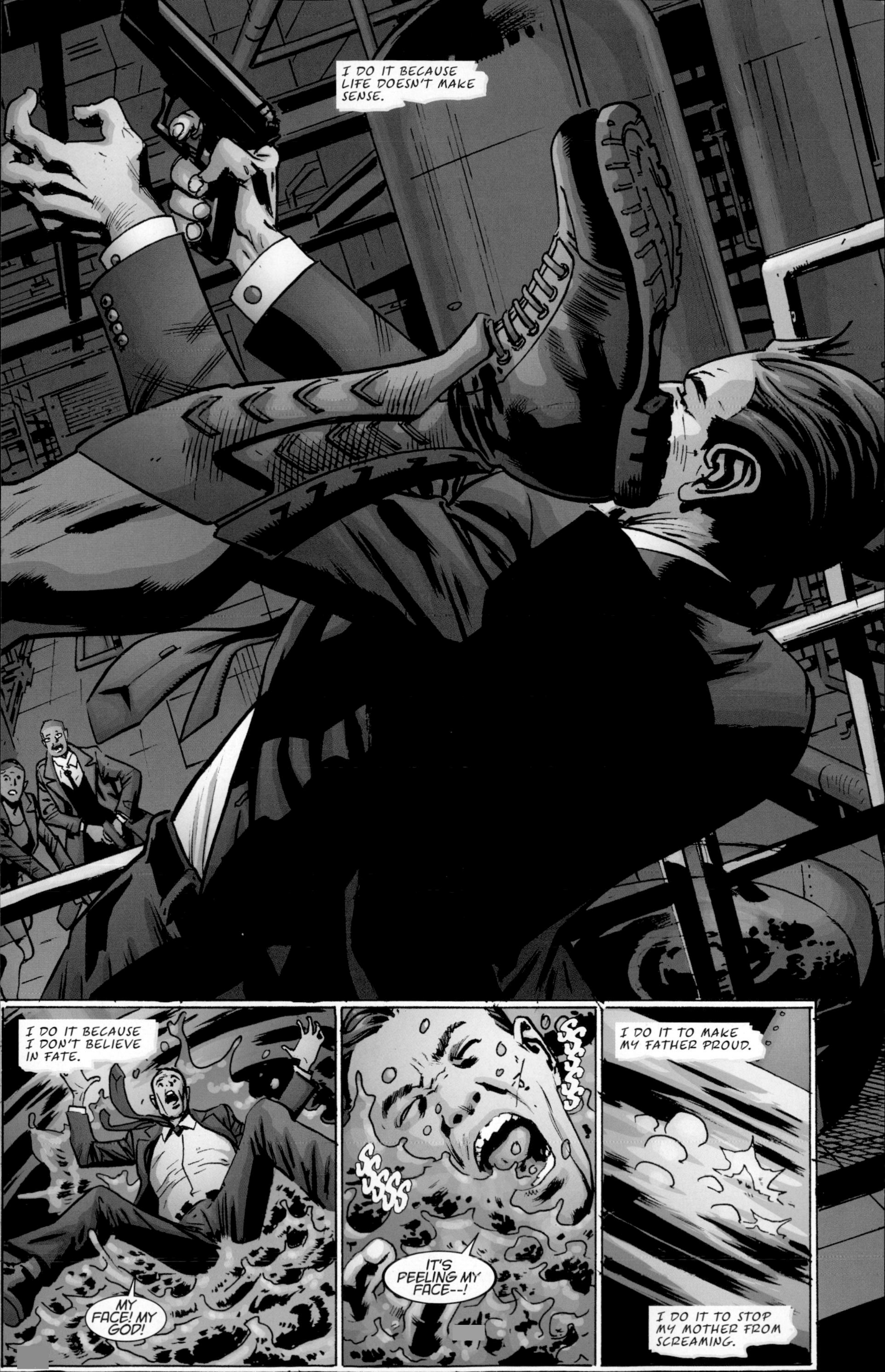
I DO IT BECAUSE LIFE DOESN'T MAKE SENSE.
I DO IT BECAUSE I DON'T BELIEVE IN FATE.
MY FACE! MY GOD!
SSSSS
SSSSS
IT'S PEELING MY FACE--!
I DO IT TO MAKE MY FATHER PROUD.
I DO IT TO STOP MY MOTHER FROM SCREAMING.

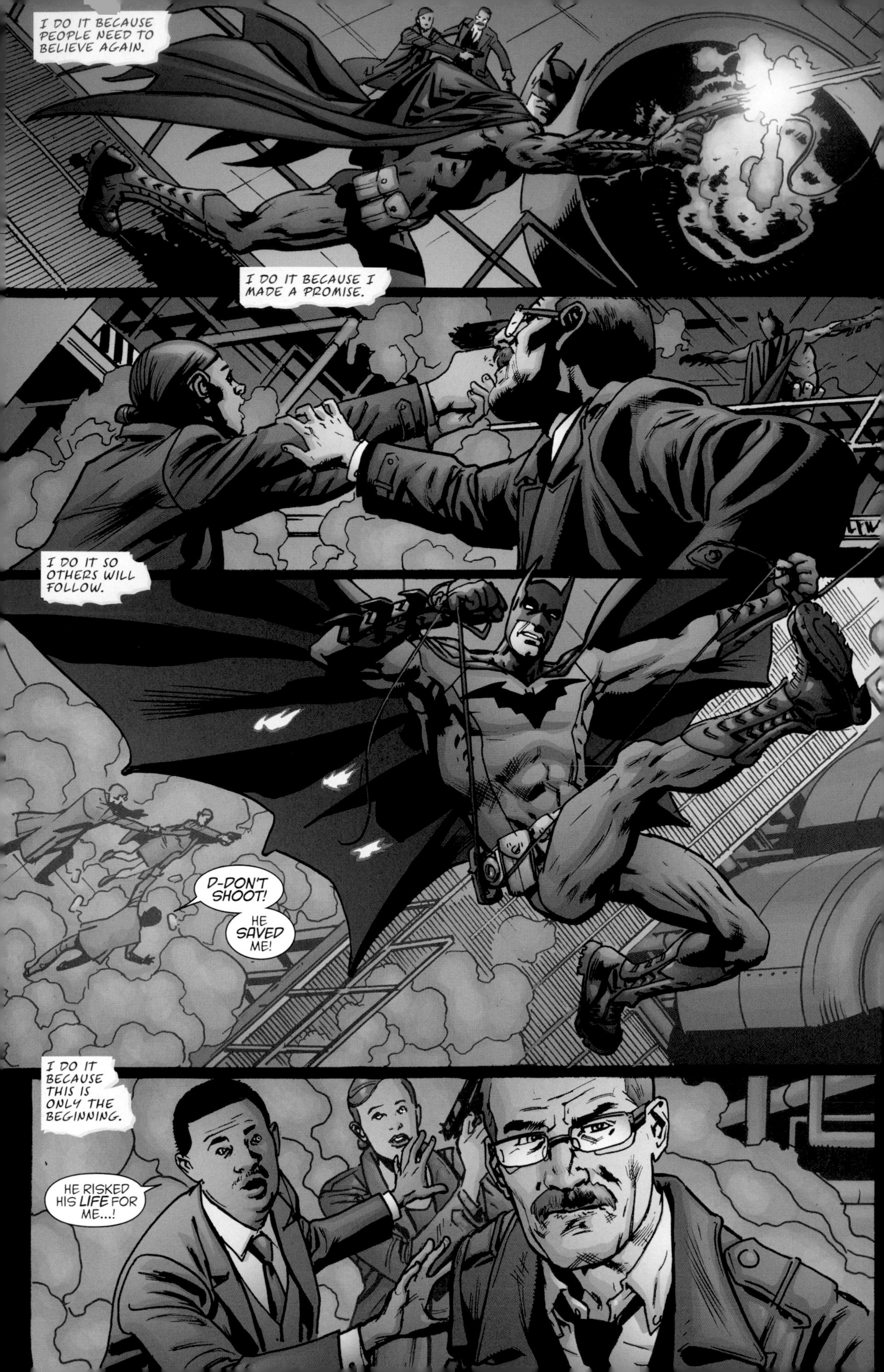
I DO IT BECAUSE PEOPLE NEED TO BELIEVE AGAIN.
I DO IT BECAUSE I MADE A PROMISE.
I DO IT SO OTHERS WILL FOLLOW.
D-DON'T SHOOT!
HE SAVED ME!
I DO IT BECAUSE THIS IS ONLY THE BEGINNING.
HE RISKED HIS LIFE FOR ME...!

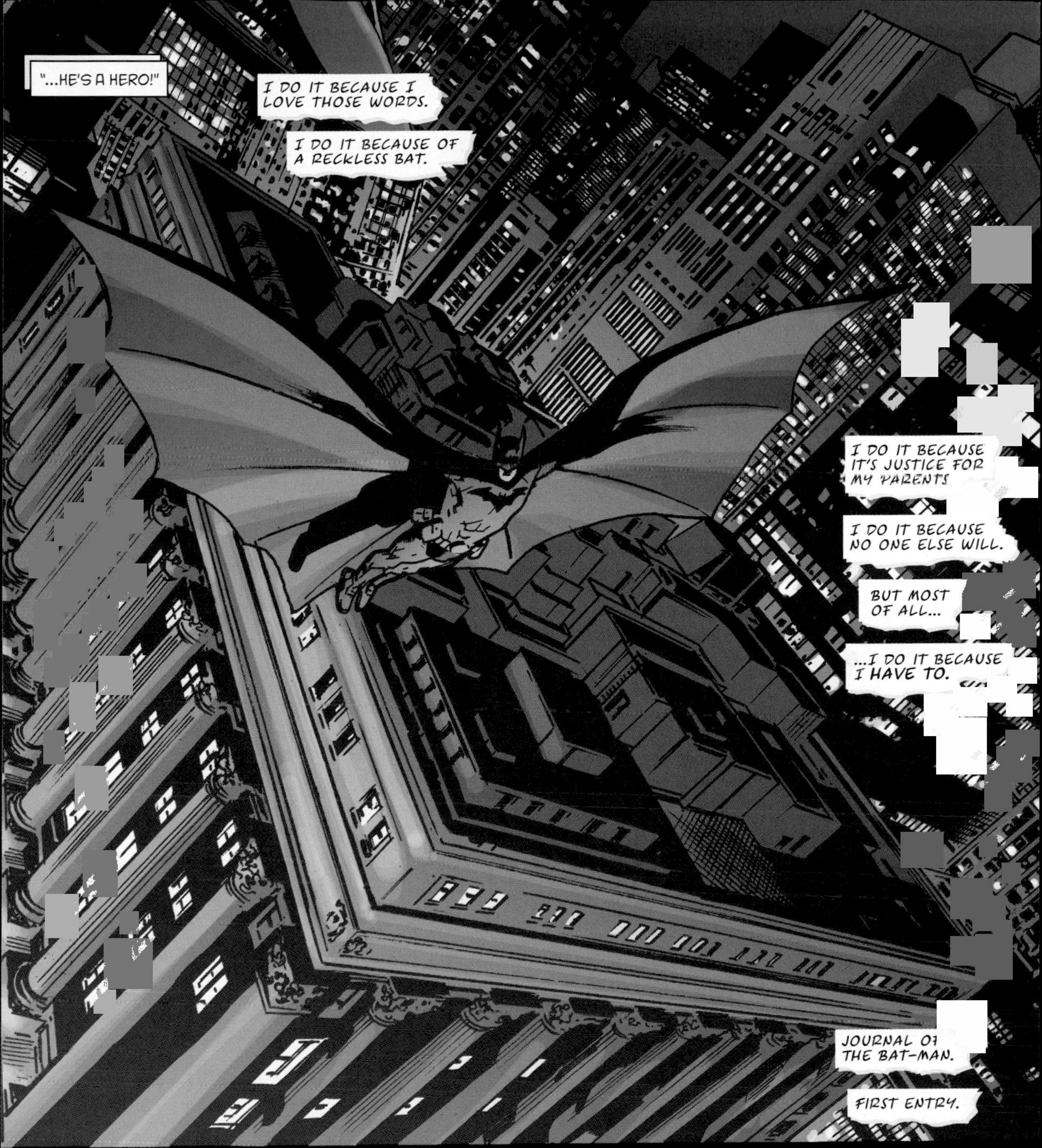
"...HE'S A HERO!"
I DO IT BECAUSE I LOVE THOSE WORDS.
I DO IT BECAUSE OF A RECKLESS BAT.
I DO IT BECAUSE IT'S JUSTICE FOR MY PARENTS
I DO IT BECAUSE NO ONE ELSE WILL.
BUT MOST OF ALL...
...I DO IT BECAUSE I HAVE TO.
JOURNAL OF THE BAT-MAN.
FIRST ENTRY.

THE CASE OF THE CHEMICAL SYNDICATE

BRAD MELTZER WRITER
BRYAN HITCH ARTIST
DAVID BARON COLORIST
CHRIS ELIOPOULOS LETTERER

BASED ON THE ORIGINAL STORY BY BOB KANE AND BILL FINGER

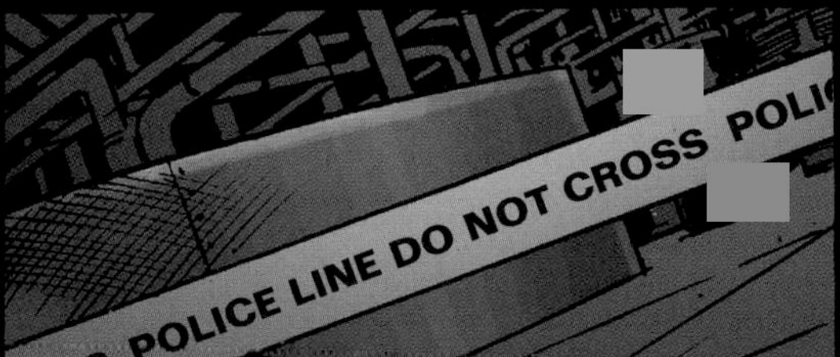
POLICE LINE DO NOT CROSS POLIC

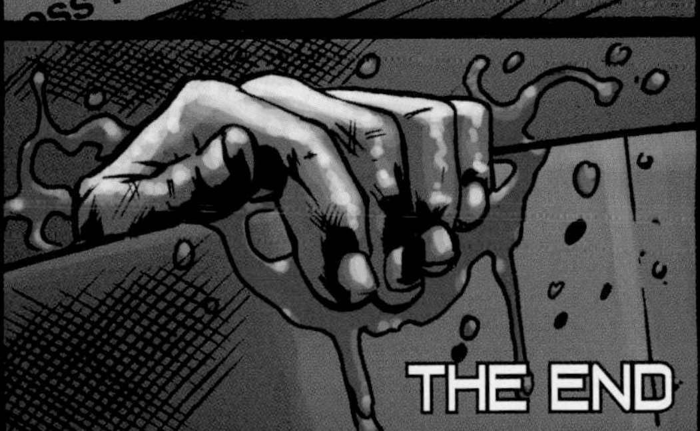
THE END

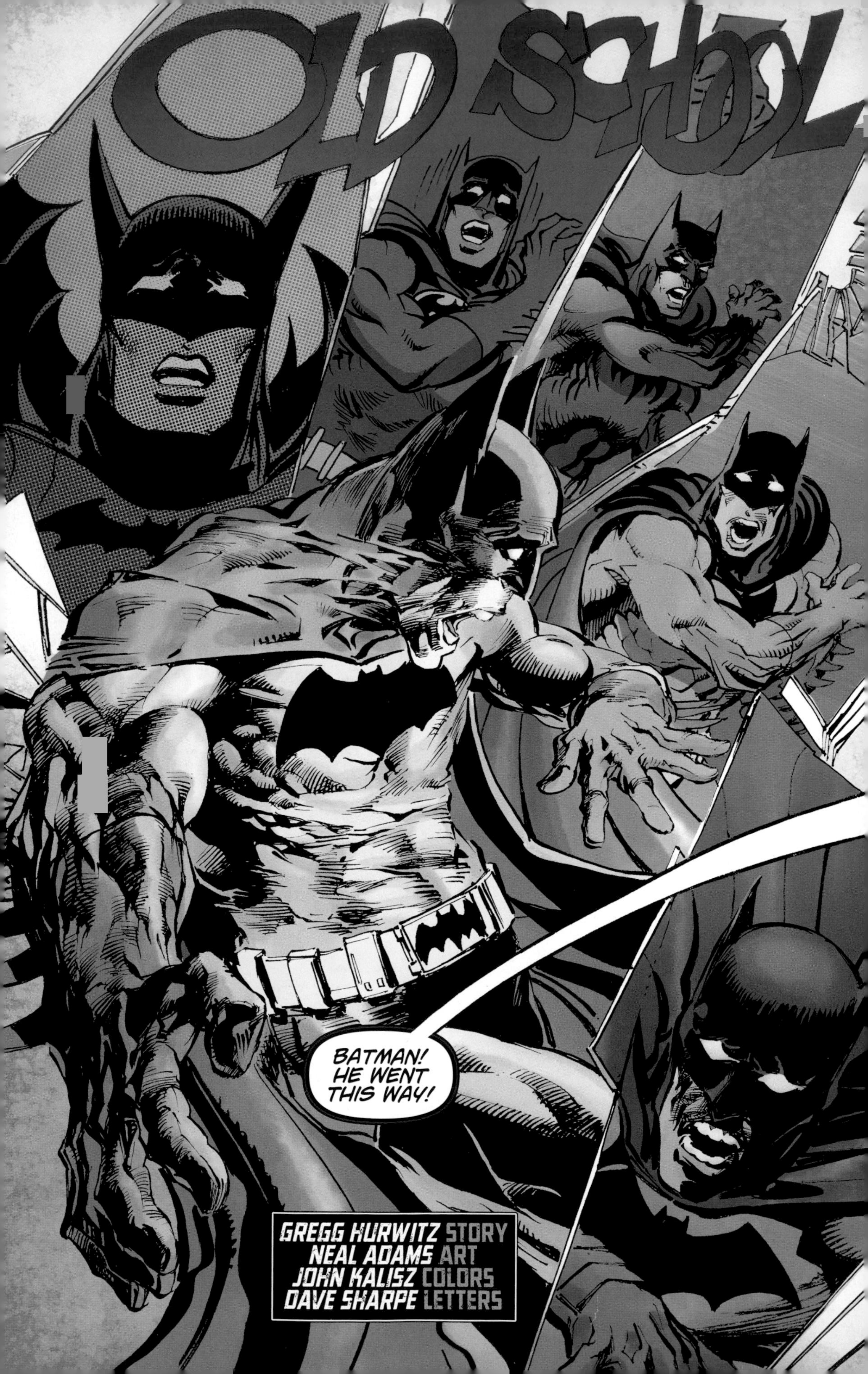
OLD SCHOOL
BATMAN! HE WENT THIS WAY!
GREGG HURWITZ STORY
NEAL ADAMS ART
JOHN KALISZ COLORS
DAVE SHARPE LETTERS

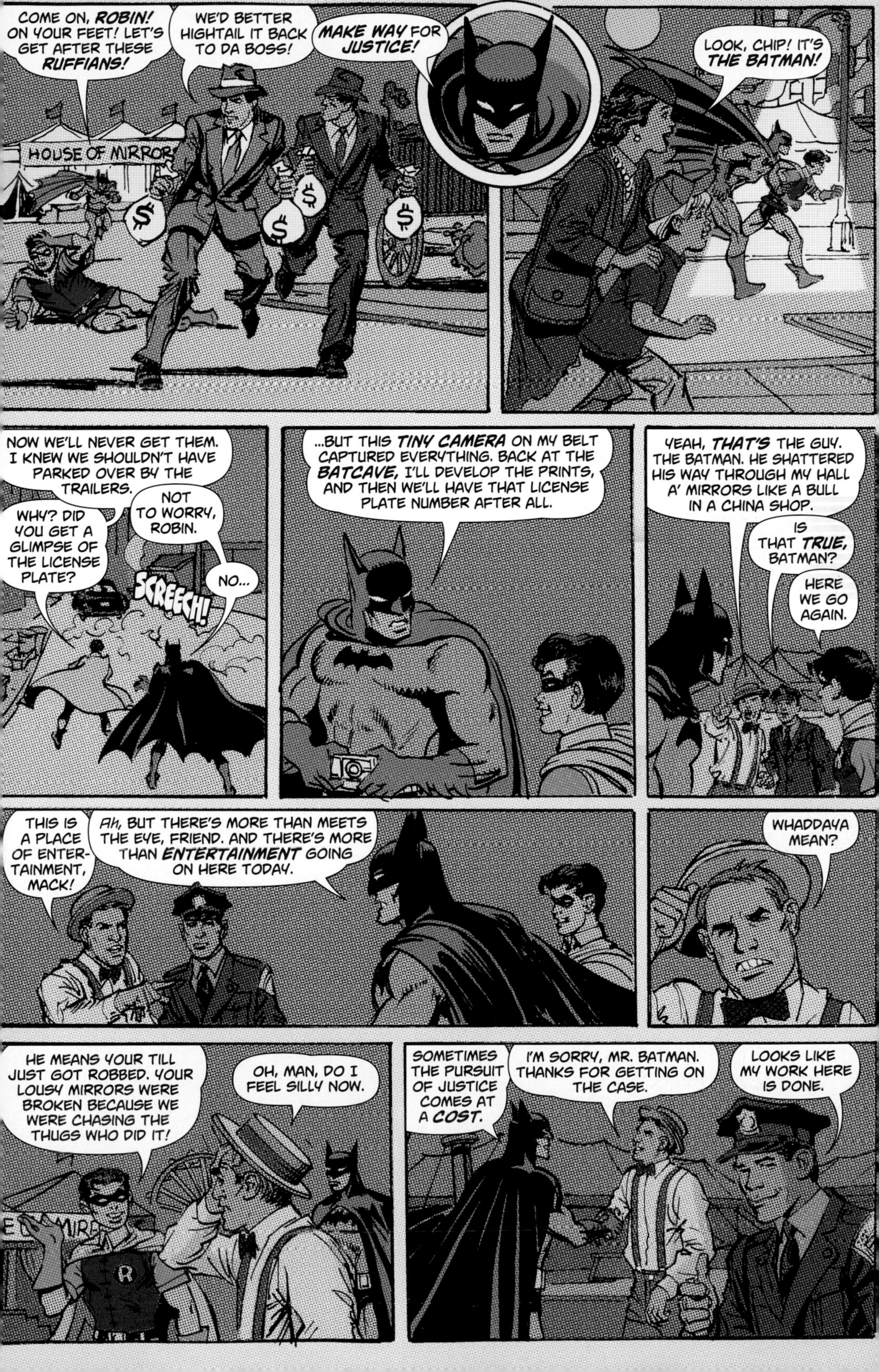
COME ON, ROBIN! ON YOUR FEET! LET'S GET AFTER THESE RUFFIANS!
WE'D BETTER HIGHTAIL IT BACK TO DA BOSS!
MAKE WAY FOR JUSTICE!
HOUSE OF MIRRORS
LOOK, CHIP! IT'S THE BATMAN!
NOW WE'LL NEVER GET THEM. I KNEW WE SHOULDN'T HAVE PARKED OVER BY THE TRAILERS.
NOT TO WORRY, ROBIN.
WHY? DID YOU GET A GLIMPSE OF THE LICENSE PLATE?
SCREECH!
NO...
...BUT THIS TINY CAMERA ON MY BELT CAPTURED EVERYTHING. BACK AT THE BATCAVE, I'LL DEVELOP THE PRINTS, AND THEN WE'LL HAVE THAT LICENSE PLATE NUMBER AFTER ALL.
YEAH, THAT'S THE GUY. THE BATMAN. HE SHATTERED HIS WAY THROUGH MY HALL A' MIRRORS LIKE A BULL IN A CHINA SHOP.
IS THAT TRUE, BATMAN?
HERE WE GO AGAIN.
THIS IS A PLACE OF ENTERTAINMENT, MACK!
AH, BUT THERE'S MORE THAN MEETS THE EYE, FRIEND. AND THERE'S MORE THAN ENTERTAINMENT GOING ON HERE TODAY.
WHADDAYA MEAN?
HE MEANS YOUR TILL JUST GOT ROBBED. YOUR LOUSY MIRRORS WERE BROKEN BECAUSE WE WERE CHASING THE THUGS WHO DID IT!
OH, MAN, DO I FEEL SILLY NOW.
SOMETIMES THE PURSUIT OF JUSTICE COMES AT A COST.
I'M SORRY, MR. BATMAN. THANKS FOR GETTING ON THE CASE.
LOOKS LIKE MY WORK HERE IS DONE.

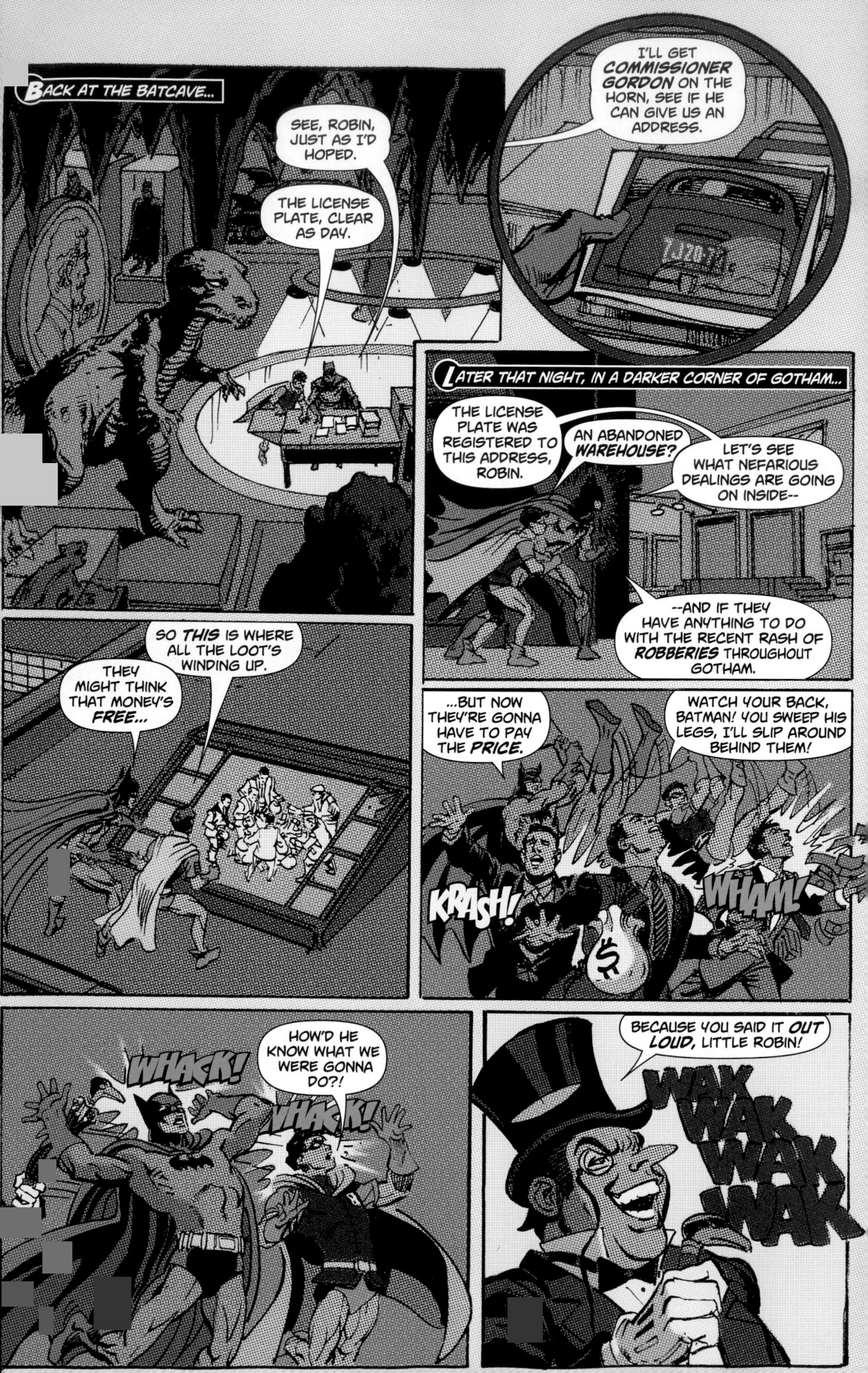
BACK AT THE BATCAVE...
SEE, ROBIN, JUST AS I'D HOPED.
THE LICENSE PLATE, CLEAR AS DAY.
I'LL GET COMMISSIONER GORDON ON THE HORN, SEE IF HE CAN GIVE US AN ADDRESS.
LATER THAT NIGHT, IN A DARKER CORNER OF GOTHAM...
THE LICENSE PLATE WAS REGISTERED TO THIS ADDRESS, ROBIN.
AN ABANDONED WAREHOUSE?
LET'S SEE WHAT NEFARIOUS DEALINGS ARE GOING ON INSIDE--
--AND IF THEY HAVE ANYTHING TO DO WITH THE RECENT RASH OF ROBBERIES THROUGHOUT GOTHAM.
SO THIS IS WHERE ALL THE LOOT'S WINDING UP.
THEY MIGHT THINK THAT MONEY'S FREE...
...BUT NOW THEY'RE GONNA HAVE TO PAY THE PRICE.
WATCH YOUR BACK, BATMAN! YOU SWEEP HIS LEGS, I'LL SLIP AROUND BEHIND THEM!
KRASH!
WHAM!
WHACK!
WHACK!
HOW'D HE KNOW WHAT WE WERE GONNA DO?!
BECAUSE YOU SAID IT OUT LOUD, LITTLE ROBIN!
WAK WAK WAK WAK

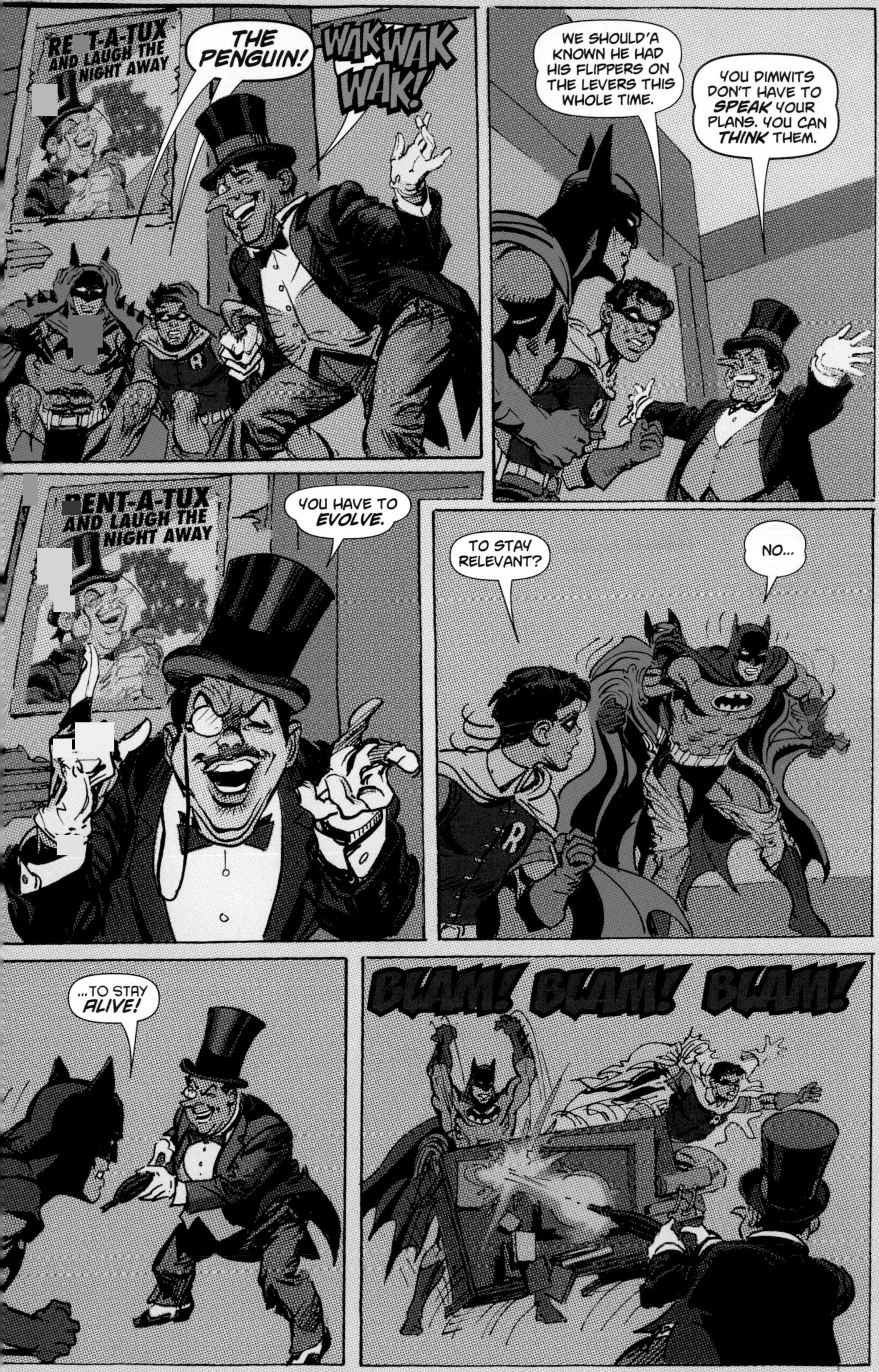
RE T-A-TUX
AND LAUGH THE
NIGHT AWAY
THE PENGUIN!
WAK WAK WAK!
WE SHOULD'A KNOWN HE HAD HIS FLIPPERS ON THE LEVERS THIS WHOLE TIME.
YOU DIMWITS DON'T HAVE TO *SPEAK* YOUR PLANS. YOU CAN *THINK* THEM.
RENT-A-TUX
AND LAUGH THE
NIGHT AWAY
YOU HAVE TO *EVOLVE.*
TO STAY RELEVANT?
NO...
...TO STAY *ALIVE!*
BLAM! BLAM! BLAM!

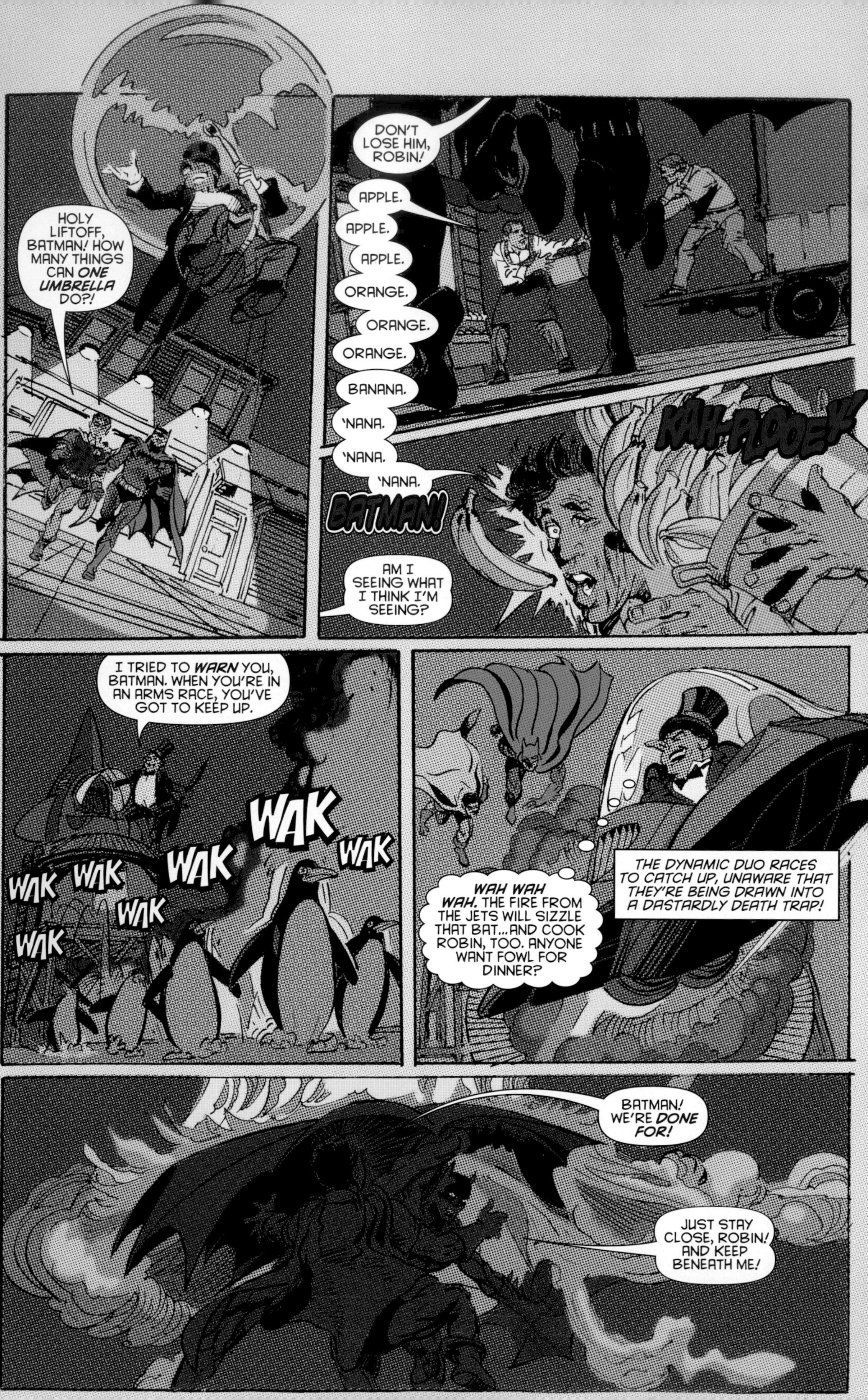
HOLY LIFTOFF, BATMAN! HOW MANY THINGS CAN *ONE UMBRELLA* DO?!
DON'T LOSE HIM, ROBIN!
APPLE.
APPLE.
APPLE.
ORANGE.
ORANGE.
ORANGE.
BANANA.
'NANA.
'NANA.
'NANA.
KAH-PLOOEY!
BATMAN!
AM I SEEING WHAT I THINK I'M SEEING?
I TRIED TO *WARN* YOU, BATMAN. WHEN YOU'RE IN AN ARMS RACE, YOU'VE GOT TO KEEP UP.
WAK WAK WAK WAK WAK WAK WAK
THE DYNAMIC DUO RACES TO CATCH UP, UNAWARE THAT THEY'RE BEING DRAWN INTO A DASTARDLY DEATH TRAP!
WAH WAH WAH. THE FIRE FROM THE JETS WILL SIZZLE THAT BAT...AND COOK ROBIN, TOO. ANYONE WANT FOWL FOR DINNER?
BATMAN! WE'RE *DONE FOR!*
JUST STAY CLOSE, ROBIN! AND KEEP BENEATH ME!

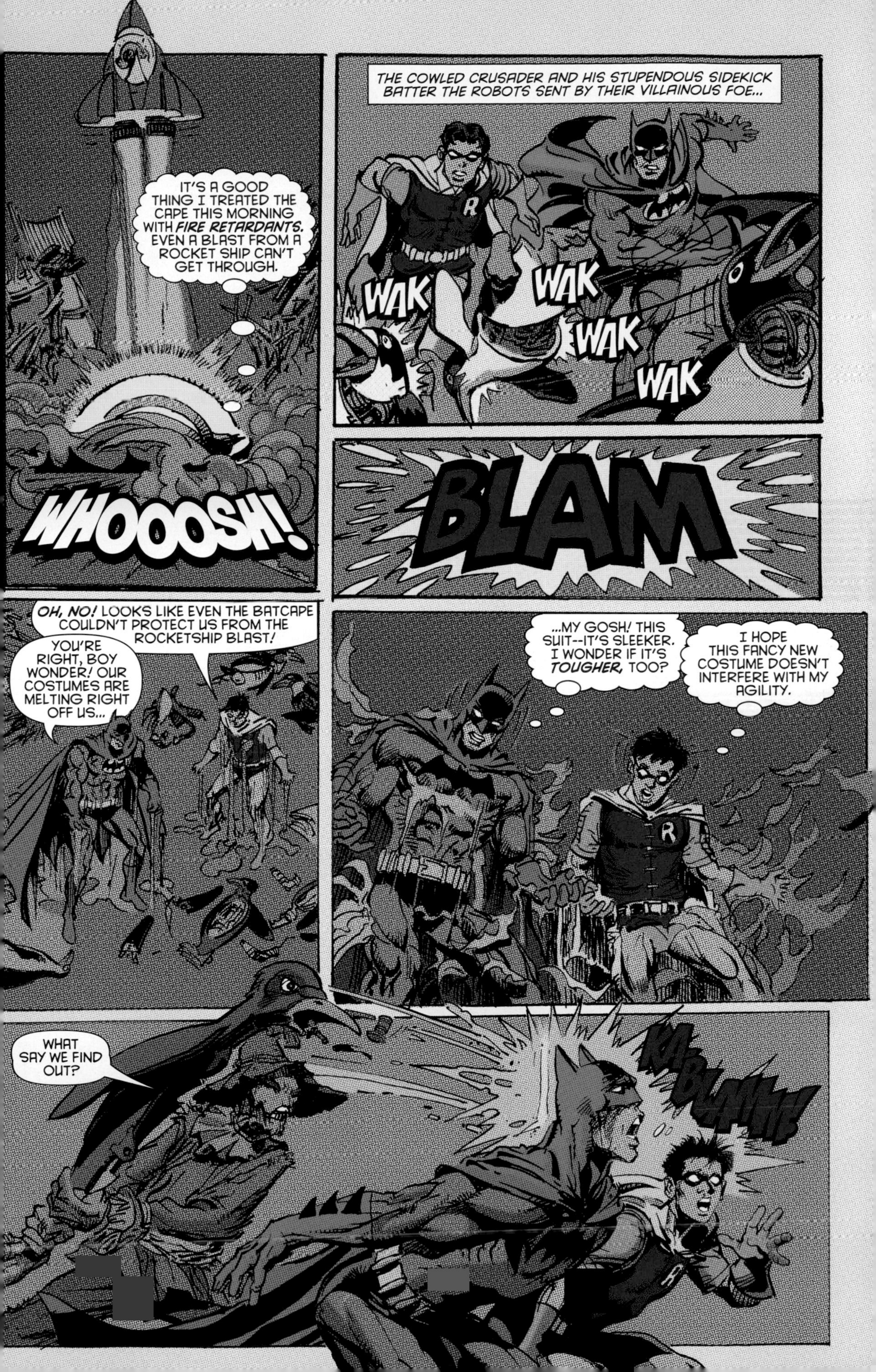
IT'S A GOOD THING I TREATED THE CAPE THIS MORNING WITH *FIRE RETARDANTS.* EVEN A BLAST FROM A ROCKET SHIP CAN'T GET THROUGH.
WHOOOSH!
THE COWLED CRUSADER AND HIS STUPENDOUS SIDEKICK BATTER THE ROBOTS SENT BY THEIR VILLAINOUS FOE...
WAK
WAK
WAK
WAK
BLAM
OH, NO! LOOKS LIKE EVEN THE BATCAPE COULDN'T PROTECT US FROM THE ROCKETSHIP BLAST!
YOU'RE RIGHT, BOY WONDER! OUR COSTUMES ARE MELTING RIGHT OFF US...
...MY GOSH! THIS SUIT--IT'S SLEEKER. I WONDER IF IT'S *TOUGHER,* TOO?
I HOPE THIS FANCY NEW COSTUME DOESN'T INTERFERE WITH MY AGILITY.
WHAT SAY WE FIND OUT?
KA-BLAMM!

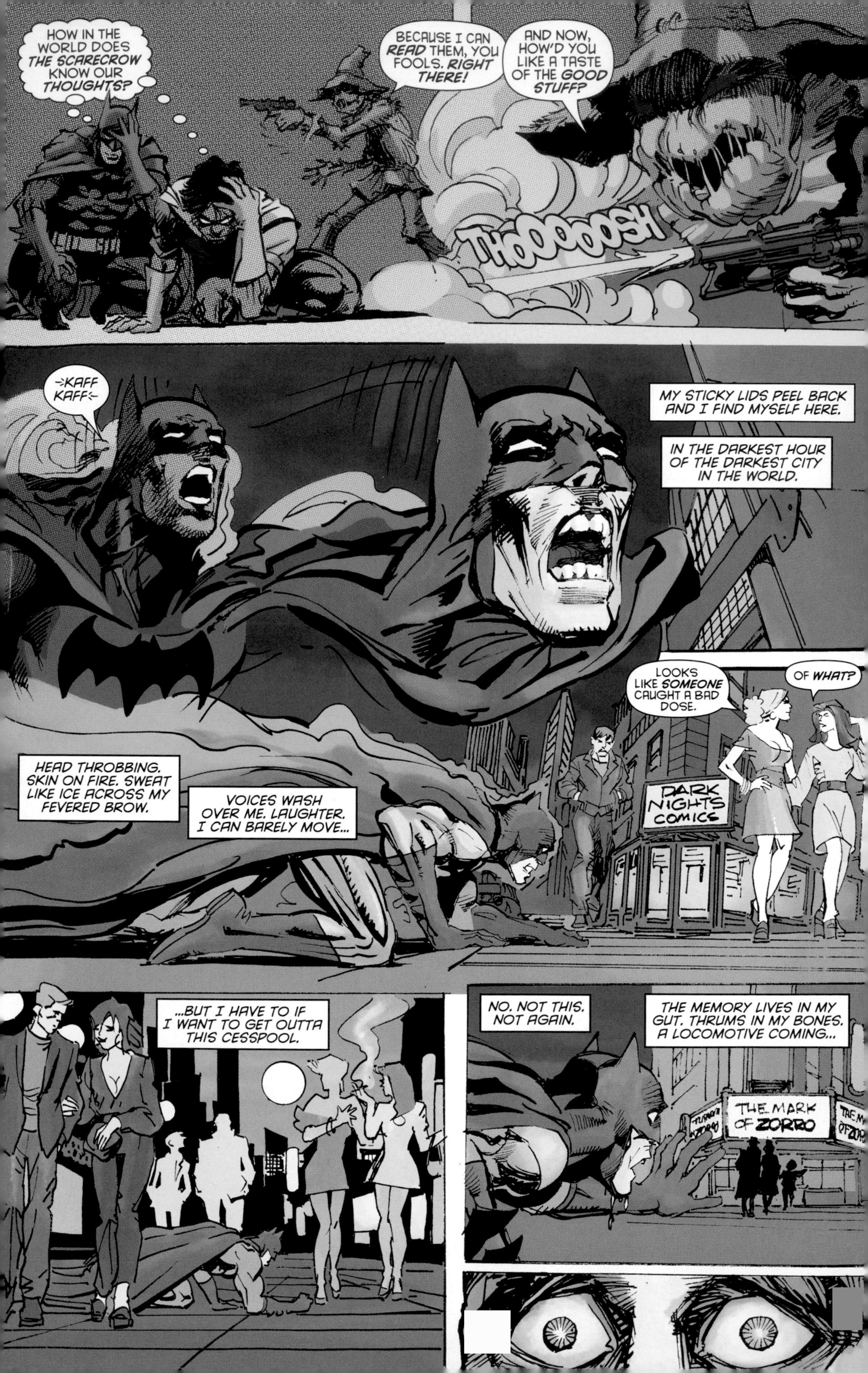
HOW IN THE WORLD DOES THE SCARECROW KNOW OUR THOUGHTS?
BECAUSE I CAN READ THEM, YOU FOOLS. RIGHT THERE!
AND NOW, HOW'D YOU LIKE A TASTE OF THE GOOD STUFF?
THOOOOOSH
KAFF KAFF
MY STICKY LIDS PEEL BACK AND I FIND MYSELF HERE.
IN THE DARKEST HOUR OF THE DARKEST CITY IN THE WORLD.
HEAD THROBBING. SKIN ON FIRE. SWEAT LIKE ICE ACROSS MY FEVERED BROW.
VOICES WASH OVER ME. LAUGHTER. I CAN BARELY MOVE...
LOOKS LIKE SOMEONE CAUGHT A BAD DOSE.
OF WHAT?
DARK NIGHTS COMICS
...BUT I HAVE TO IF I WANT TO GET OUTTA THIS CESSPOOL.
NO. NOT THIS. NOT AGAIN.
THE MEMORY LIVES IN MY GUT. THRUMS IN MY BONES. A LOCOMOTIVE COMING...
THE MARK OF ZORRO

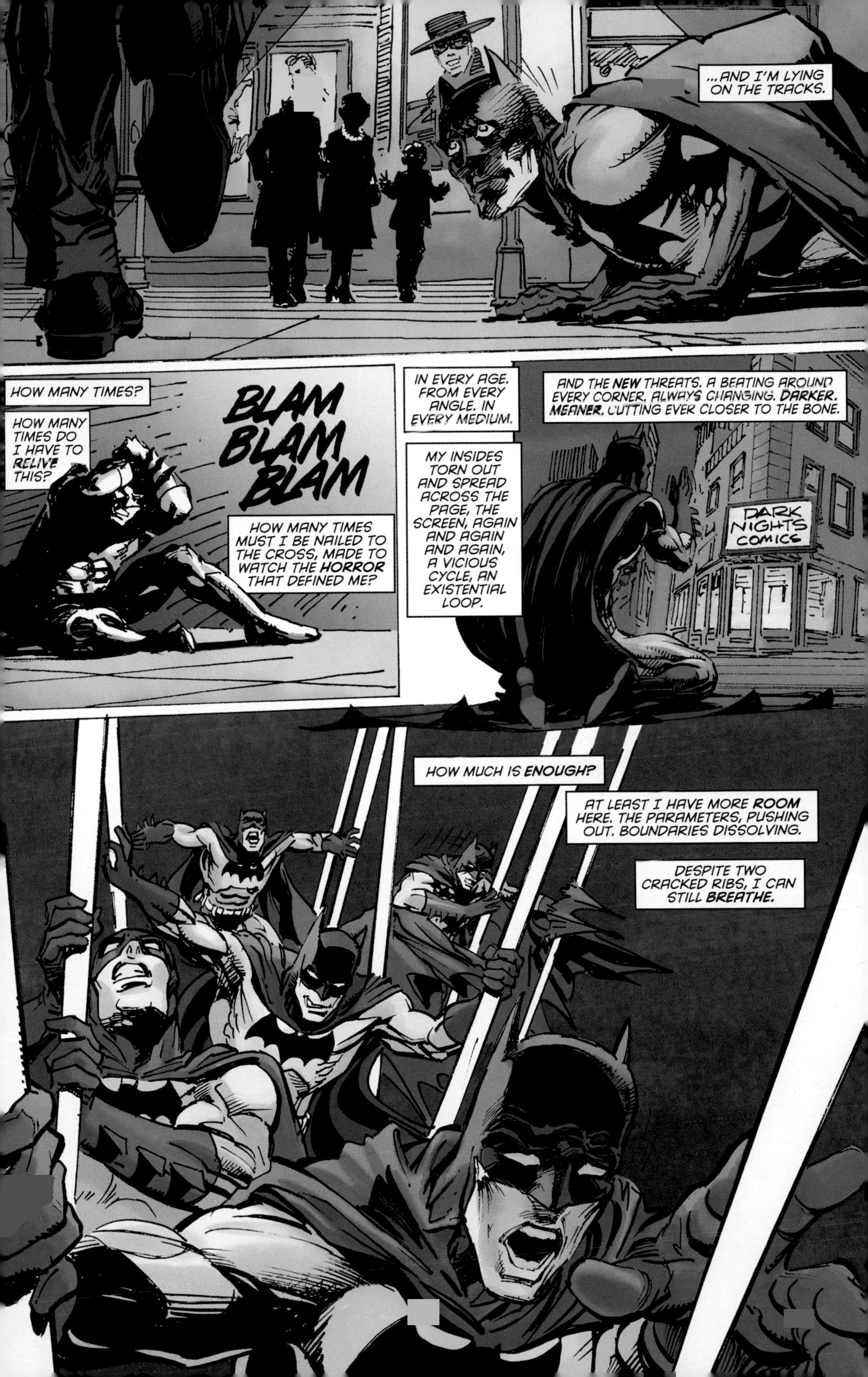
...AND I'M LYING ON THE TRACKS.
HOW MANY TIMES?
HOW MANY TIMES DO I HAVE TO RELIVE THIS?
BLAM BLAM BLAM
HOW MANY TIMES MUST I BE NAILED TO THE CROSS, MADE TO WATCH THE HORROR THAT DEFINED ME?
IN EVERY AGE. FROM EVERY ANGLE. IN EVERY MEDIUM.
MY INSIDES TORN OUT AND SPREAD ACROSS THE PAGE, THE SCREEN, AGAIN AND AGAIN AND AGAIN, A VICIOUS CYCLE, AN EXISTENTIAL LOOP.
AND THE NEW THREATS. A BEATING AROUND EVERY CORNER, ALWAYS CHANGING. DARKER. MEANER. CUTTING EVER CLOSER TO THE BONE.
DARK NIGHTS COMICS
HOW MUCH IS ENOUGH?
AT LEAST I HAVE MORE ROOM HERE. THE PARAMETERS, PUSHING OUT. BOUNDARIES DISSOLVING.
DESPITE TWO CRACKED RIBS, I CAN STILL BREATHE.

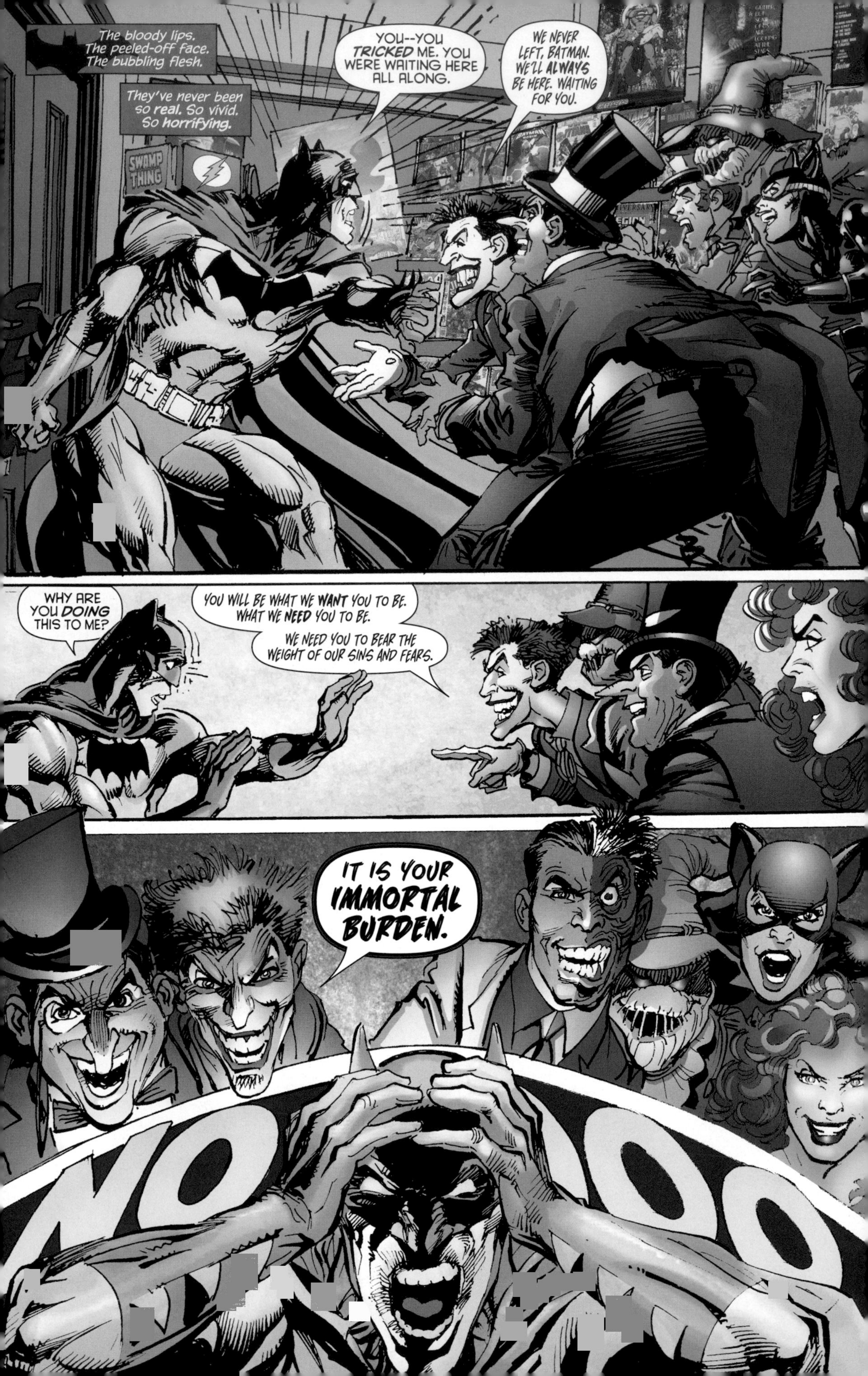
The bloody lips. The peeled-off face. The bubbling flesh.
They've never been so real. So vivid. So horrifying.
SWAMP THING
YOU--YOU TRICKED ME. YOU WERE WAITING HERE ALL ALONG.
WE NEVER LEFT, BATMAN. WE'LL ALWAYS BE HERE. WAITING FOR YOU.
WHY ARE YOU DOING THIS TO ME?
YOU WILL BE WHAT WE WANT YOU TO BE. WHAT WE NEED YOU TO BE.
WE NEED YOU TO BEAR THE WEIGHT OF OUR SINS AND FEARS.
IT IS YOUR IMMORTAL BURDEN.
NOOOO

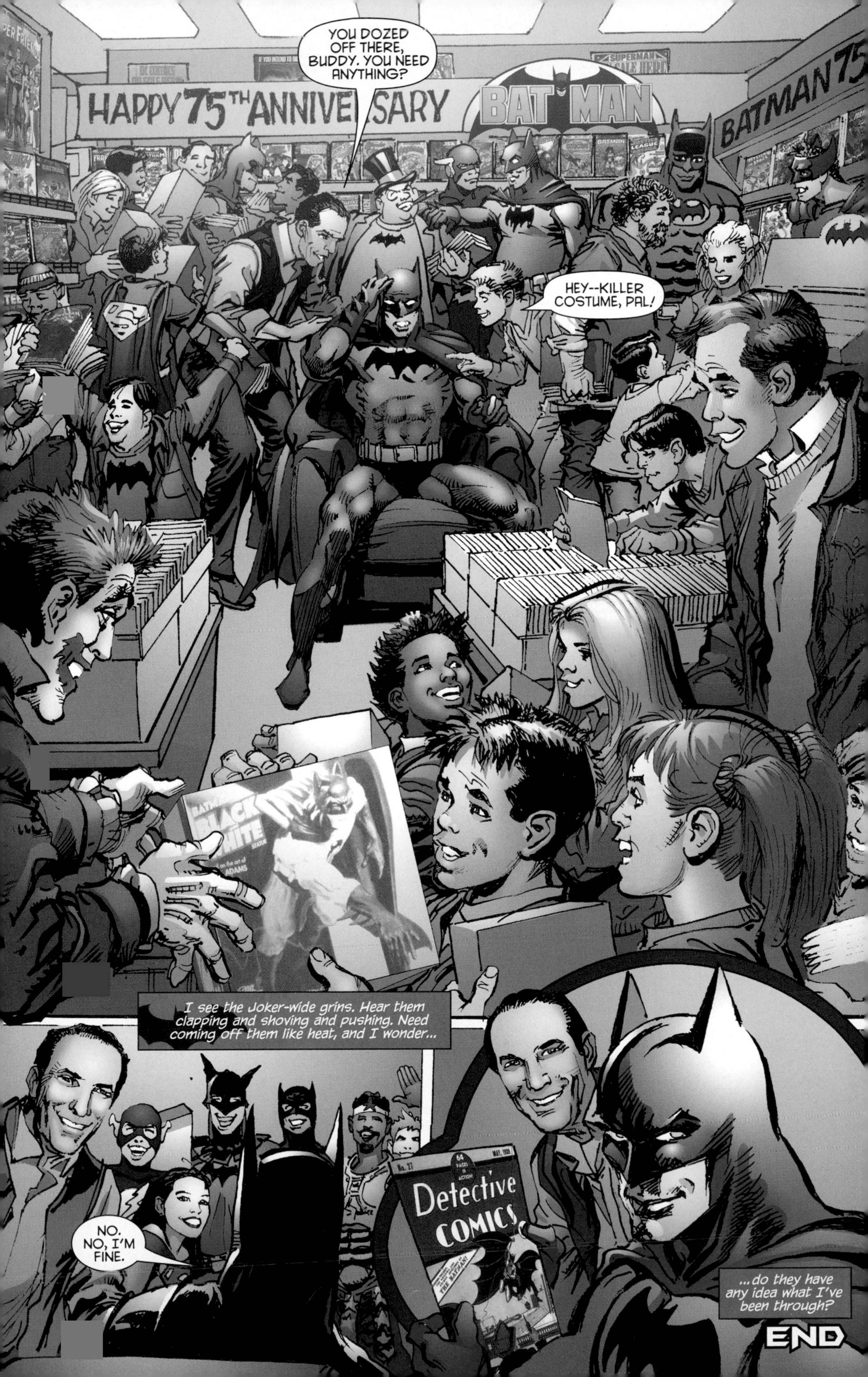
YOU DOZED OFF THERE, BUDDY. YOU NEED ANYTHING?
HEY--KILLER COSTUME, PAL!
I see the Joker-wide grins. Hear them clapping and shoving and pushing. Need coming off them like heat, and I wonder...
NO. NO, I'M FINE.
...do they have any idea what I've been through?
END

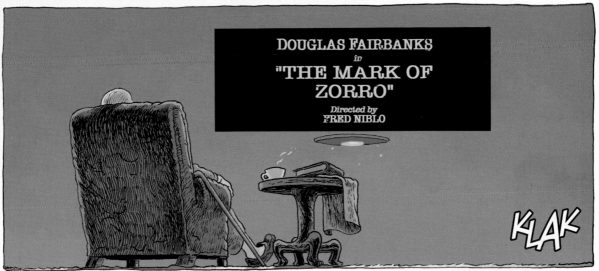

DOUGLAS FAIRBANKS
in
"THE MARK OF
ZORRO"
Directed by
FRED NIBLO

KLAK

hnn.

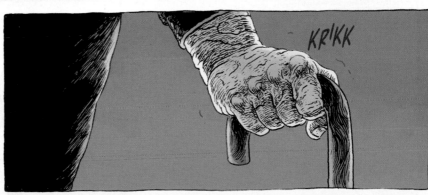

KRIKK

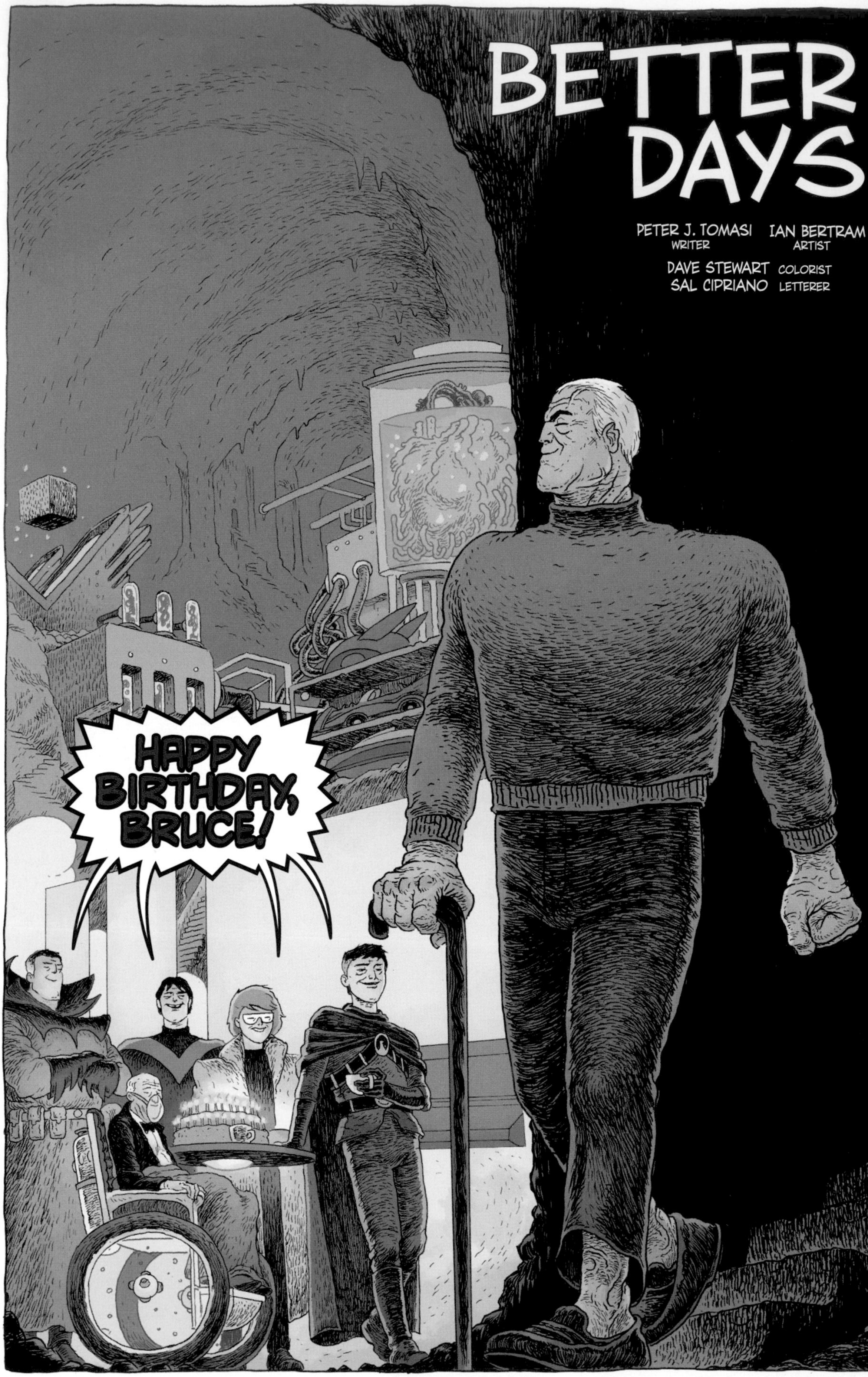
BETTER DAYS
PETER J. TOMASI WRITER
IAN BERTRAM ARTIST
DAVE STEWART COLORIST
SAL CIPRIANO LETTERER
HAPPY BIRTHDAY, BRUCE!

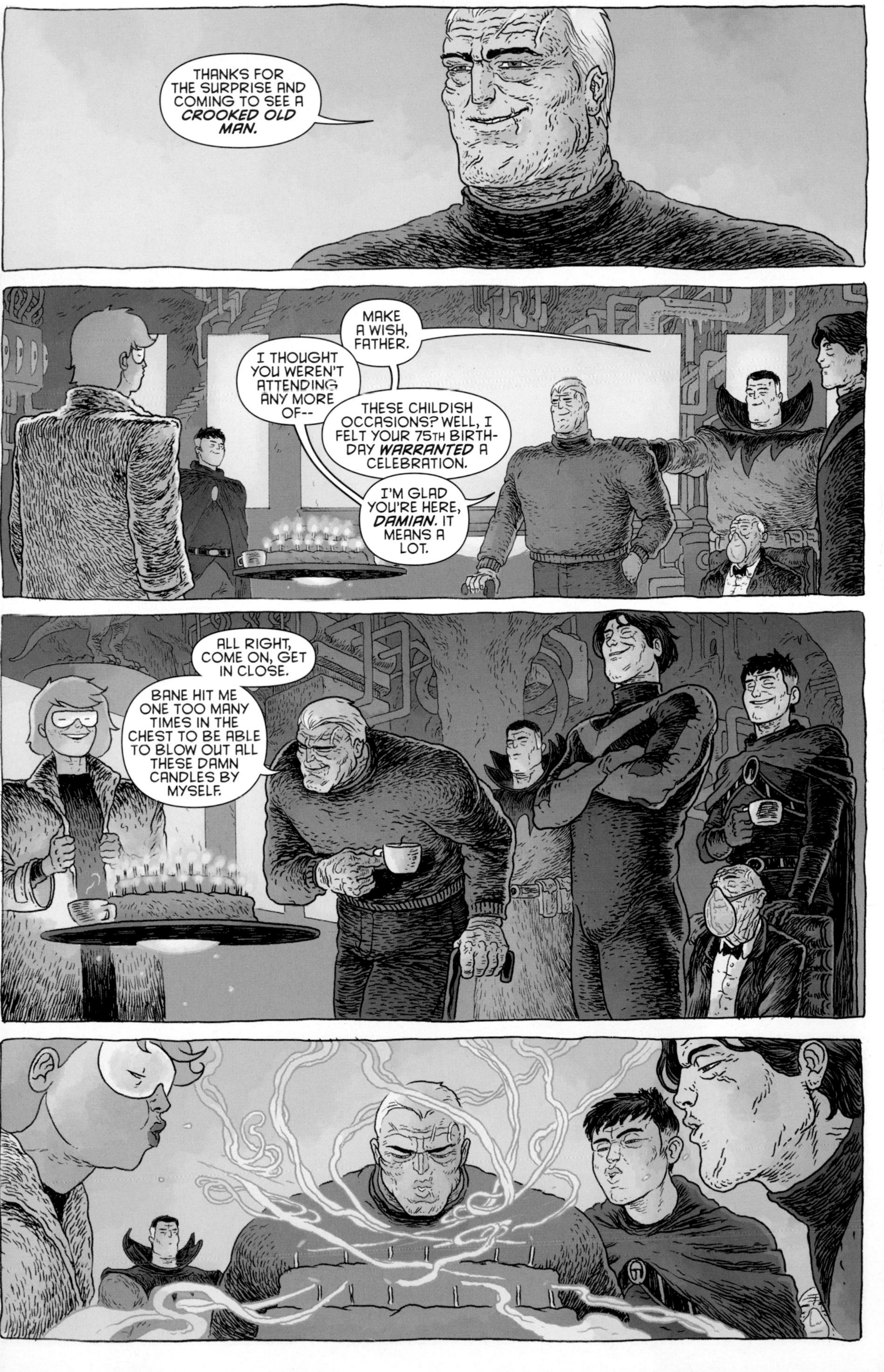

THANKS FOR THE SURPRISE AND COMING TO SEE A *CROOKED OLD MAN.*
MAKE A WISH, FATHER.
I THOUGHT YOU WEREN'T ATTENDING ANY MORE OF--
THESE CHILDISH OCCASIONS? WELL, I FELT YOUR 75TH BIRTHDAY *WARRANTED* A CELEBRATION.
I'M GLAD YOU'RE HERE, *DAMIAN*. IT MEANS A LOT.
ALL RIGHT, COME ON, GET IN CLOSE.
BANE HIT ME ONE TOO MANY TIMES IN THE CHEST TO BE ABLE TO BLOW OUT ALL THESE DAMN CANDLES BY MYSELF.

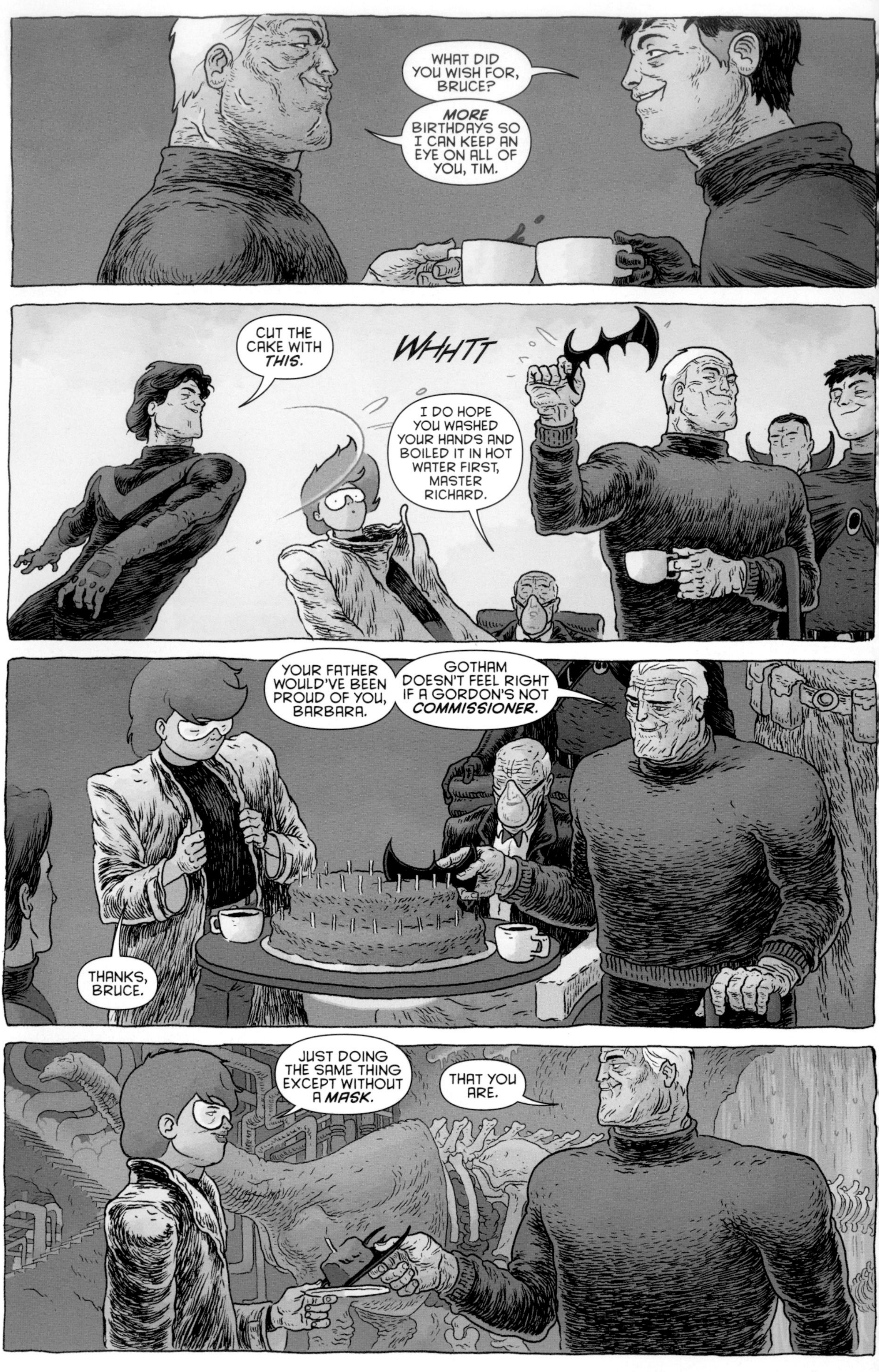
WHAT DID YOU WISH FOR, BRUCE?
MORE BIRTHDAYS SO I CAN KEEP AN EYE ON ALL OF YOU, TIM.
CUT THE CAKE WITH THIS.
WHHTT
I DO HOPE YOU WASHED YOUR HANDS AND BOILED IT IN HOT WATER FIRST, MASTER RICHARD.
YOUR FATHER WOULD'VE BEEN PROUD OF YOU, BARBARA.
GOTHAM DOESN'T FEEL RIGHT IF A GORDON'S NOT COMMISSIONER.
THANKS, BRUCE.
JUST DOING THE SAME THING EXCEPT WITHOUT A MASK.
THAT YOU ARE.

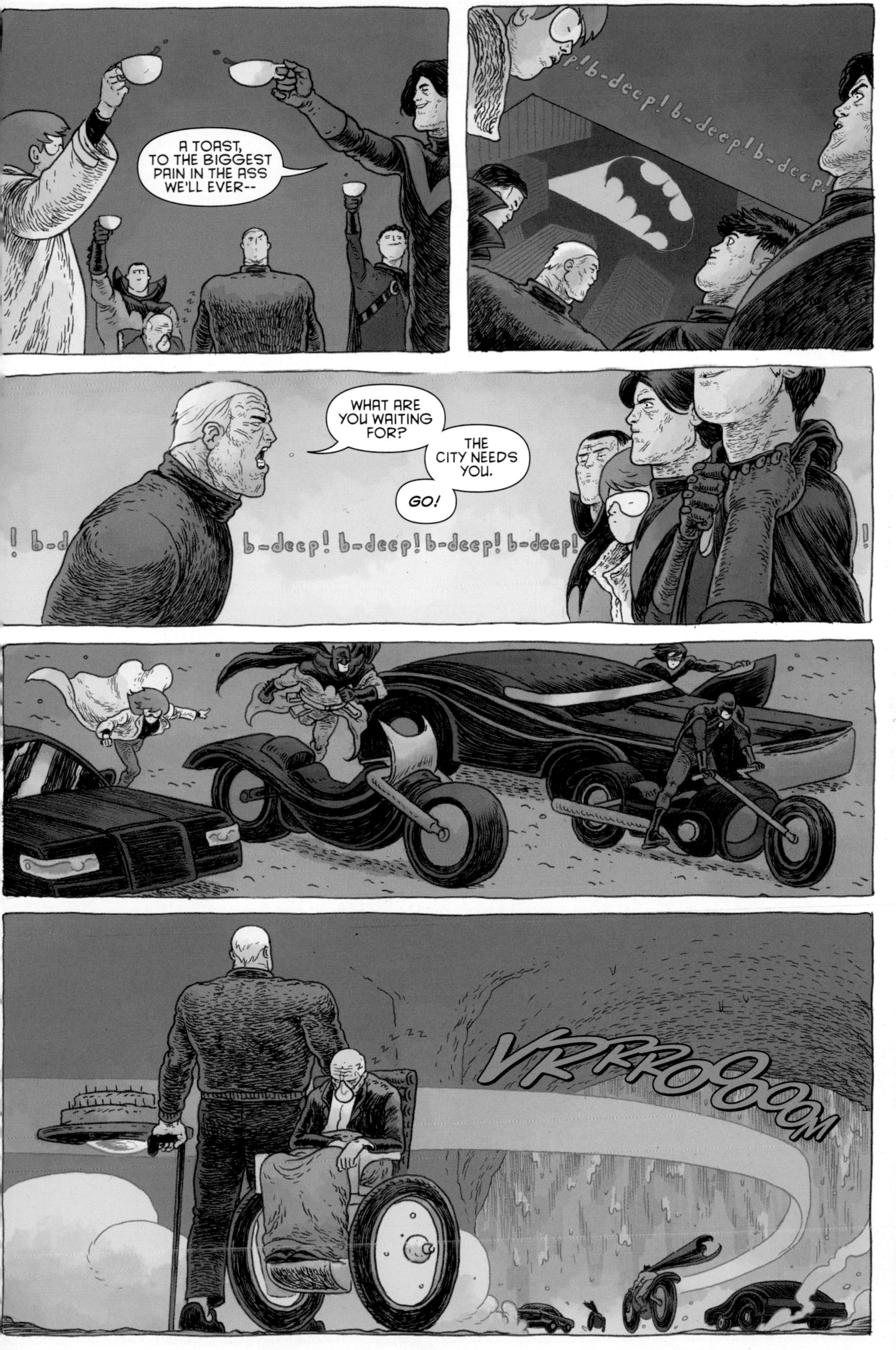
A TOAST, TO THE BIGGEST PAIN IN THE ASS WE'LL EVER--
p!b-deep! b-deep! b-deep! b-deep!
WHAT ARE YOU WAITING FOR?
THE CITY NEEDS YOU.
GO!
! b-d b-deep! b-deep! b-deep! b-deep! !
VRRROOOOOM

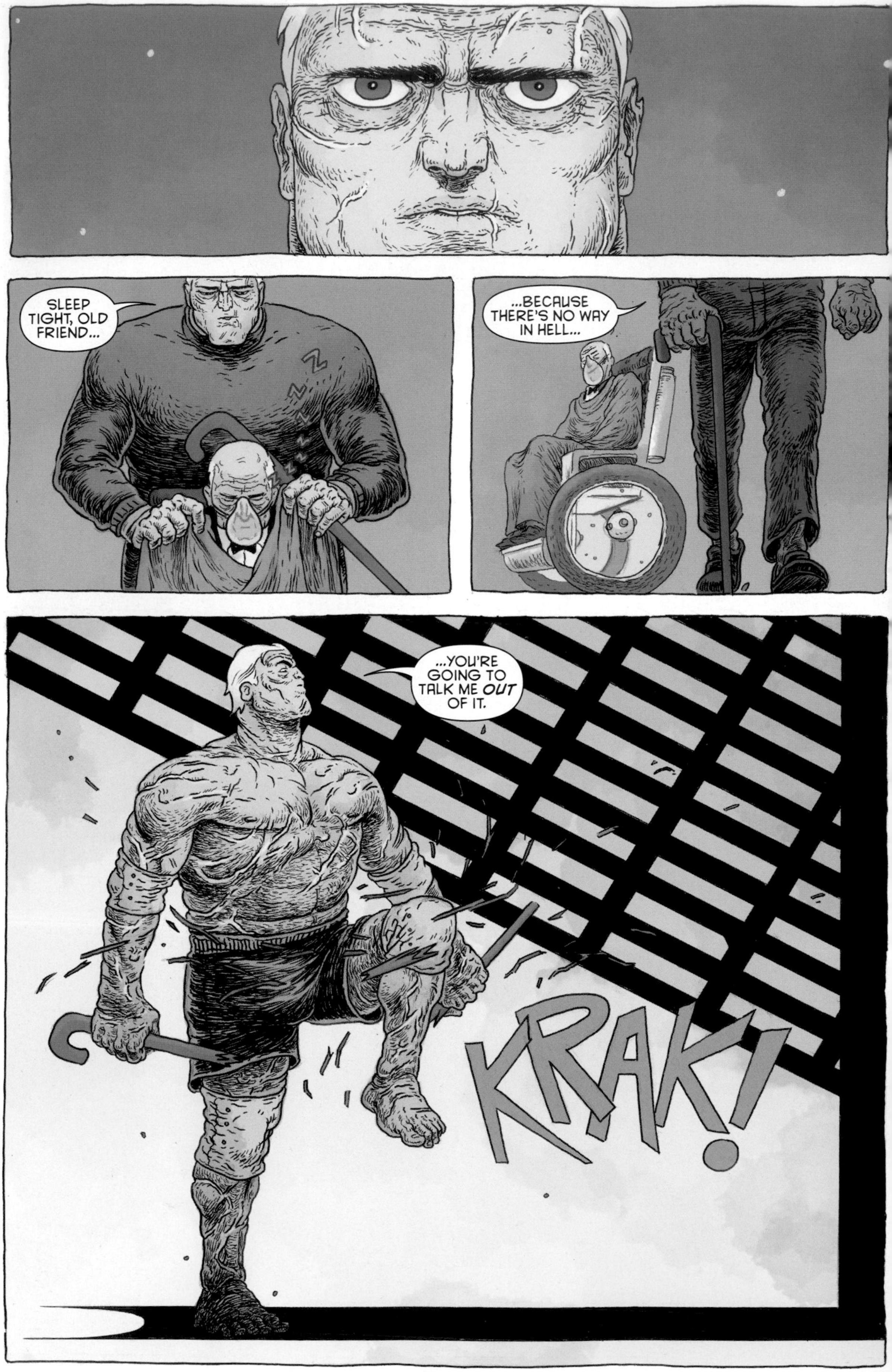
SLEEP TIGHT, OLD FRIEND...
...BECAUSE THERE'S NO WAY IN HELL...
...YOU'RE GOING TO TALK ME *OUT* OF IT.
KRAK!

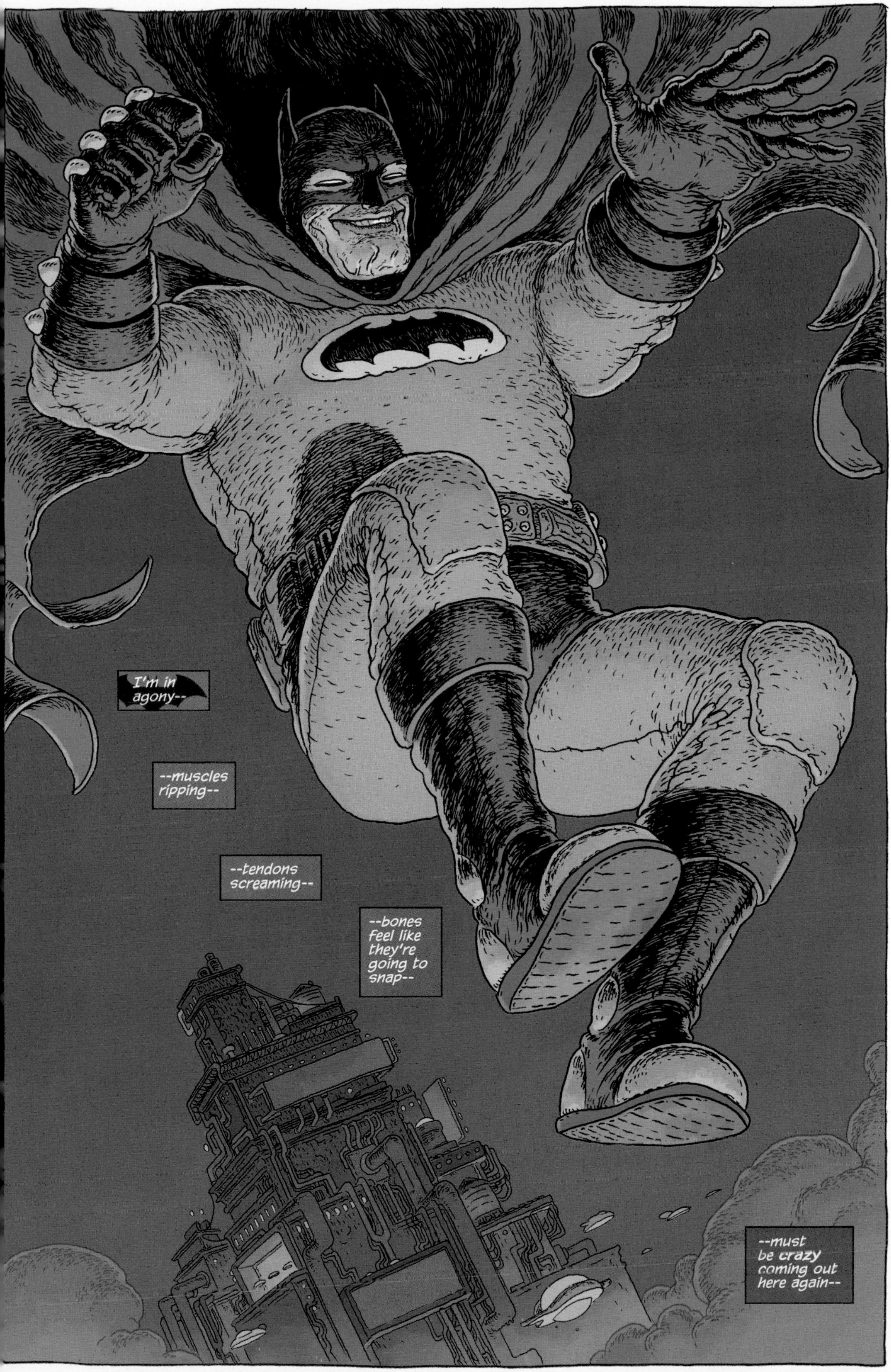
I'm in agony--
--muscles ripping--
--tendons screaming--
--bones feel like they're going to snap--
--must be **crazy** coming out here again--

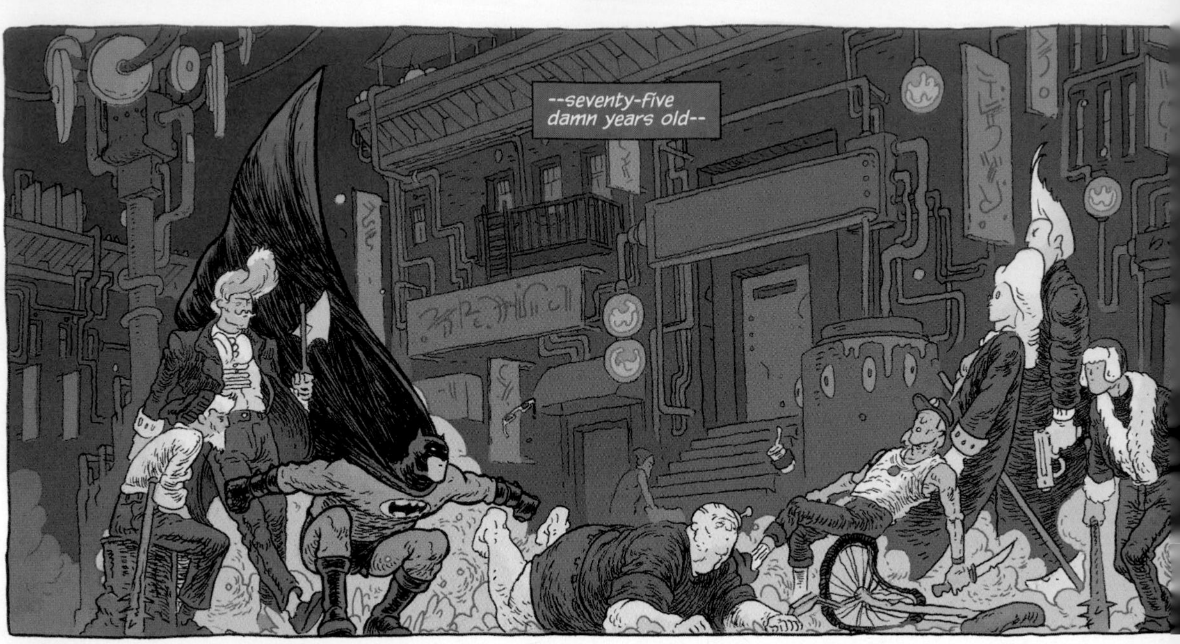
--seventy-five
damn years old--

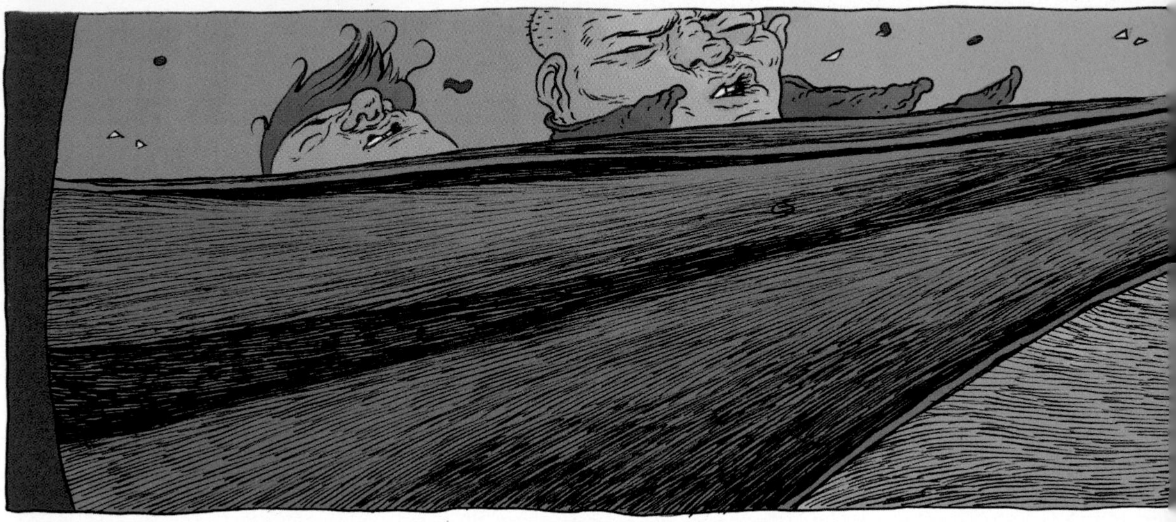

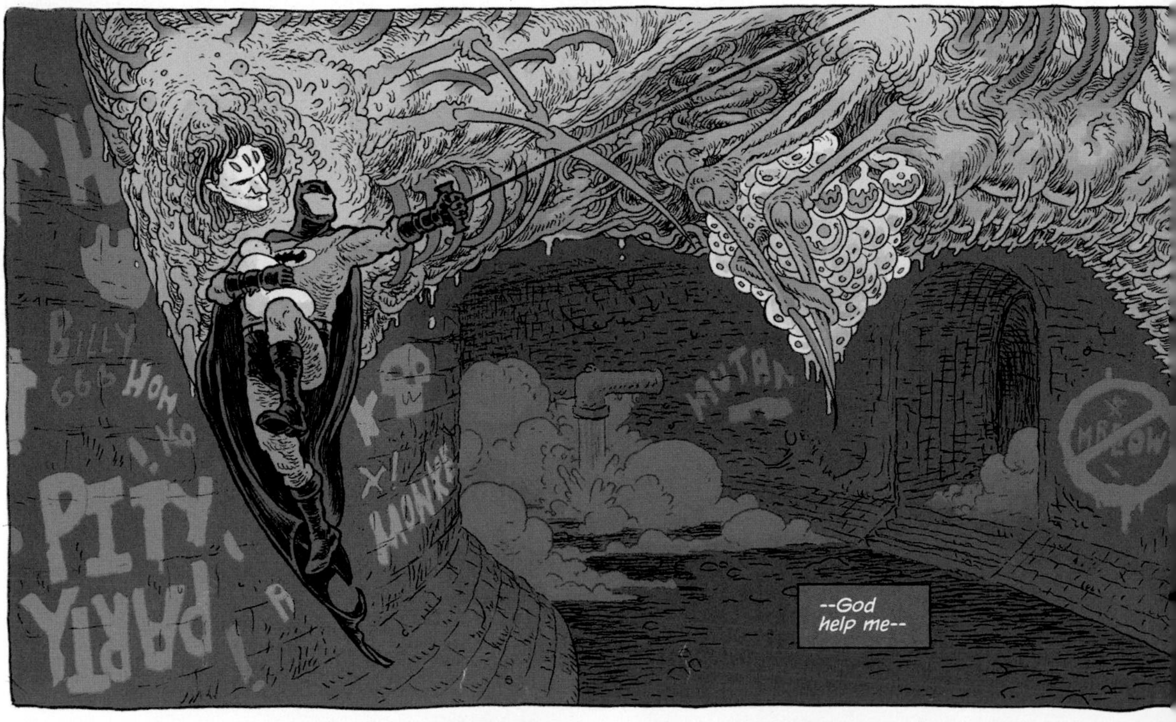
PITY
PARTY
--God
help me--

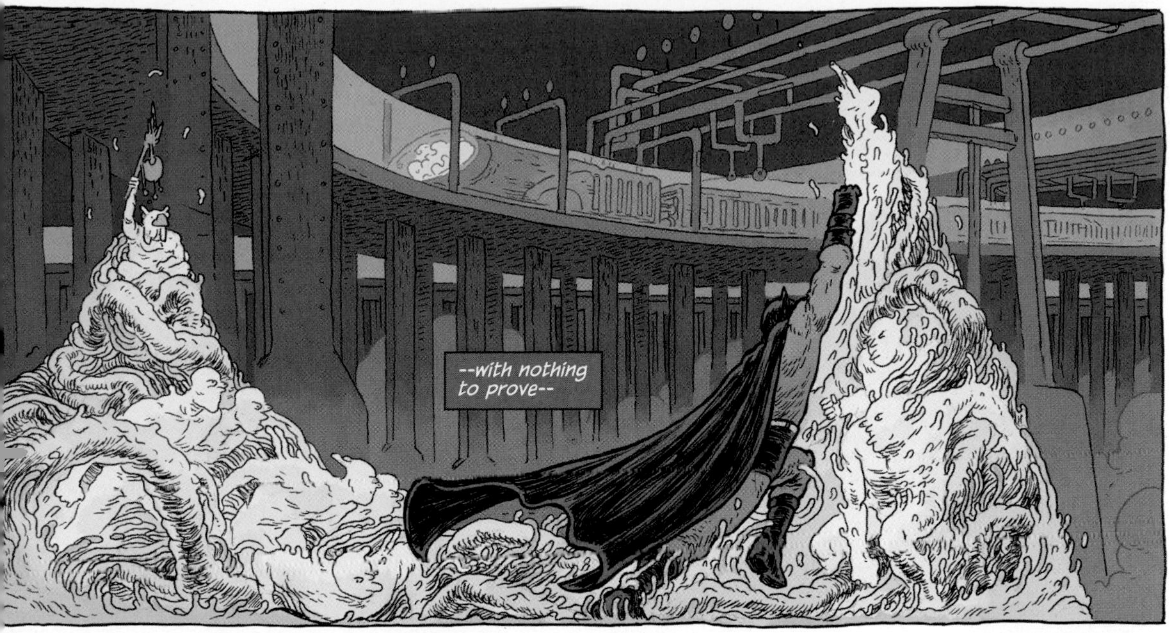
--with nothing to prove--
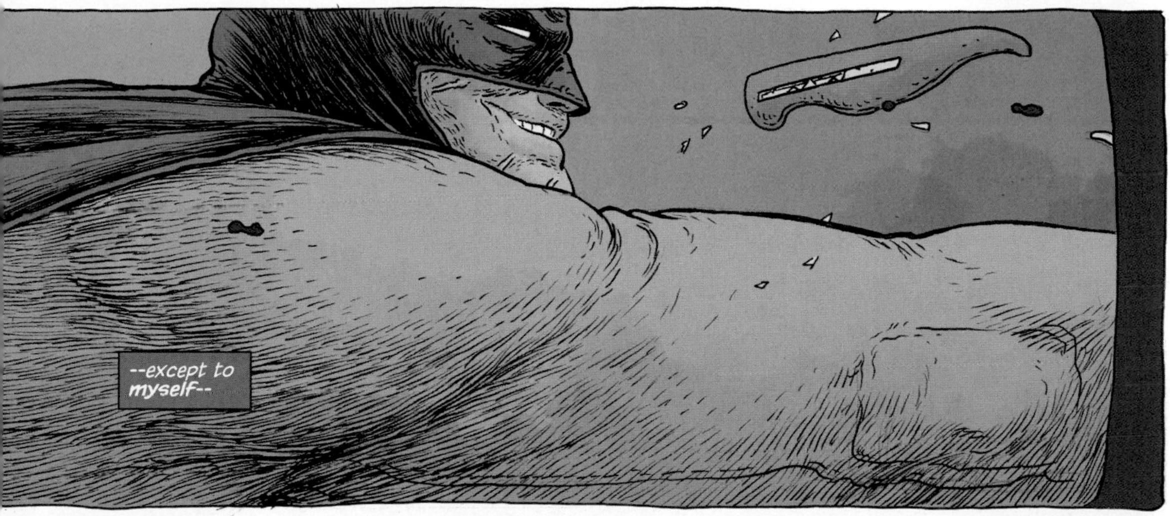
--except to myself--
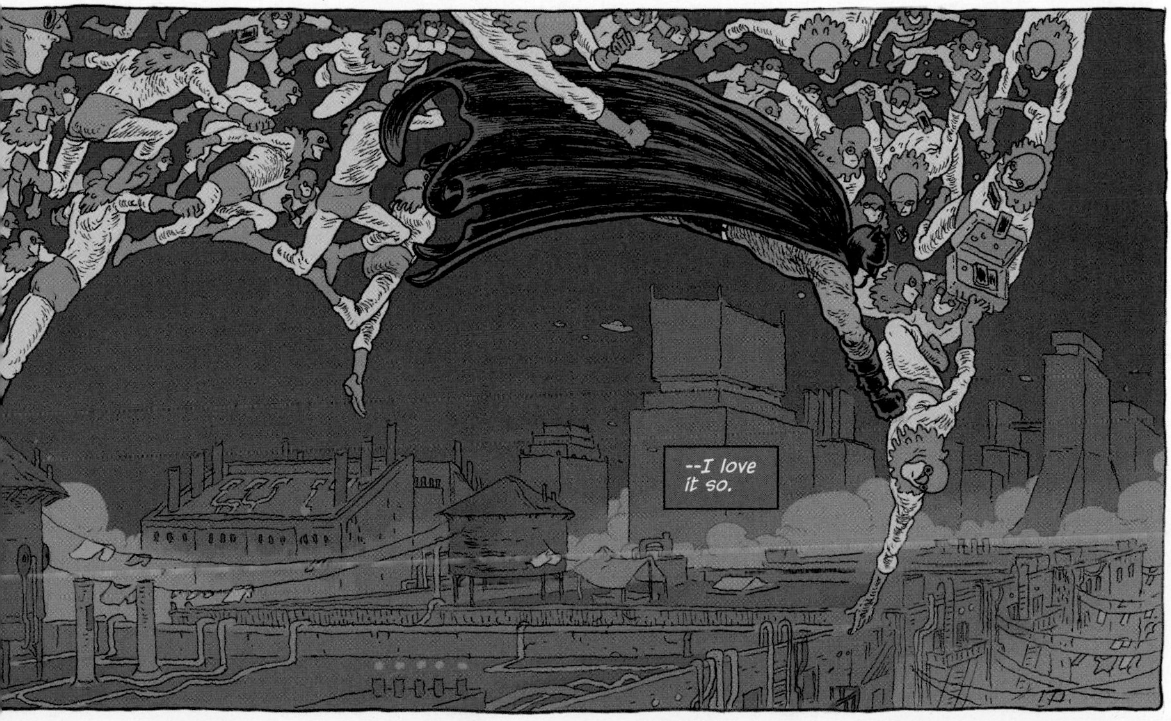
--I love it so.

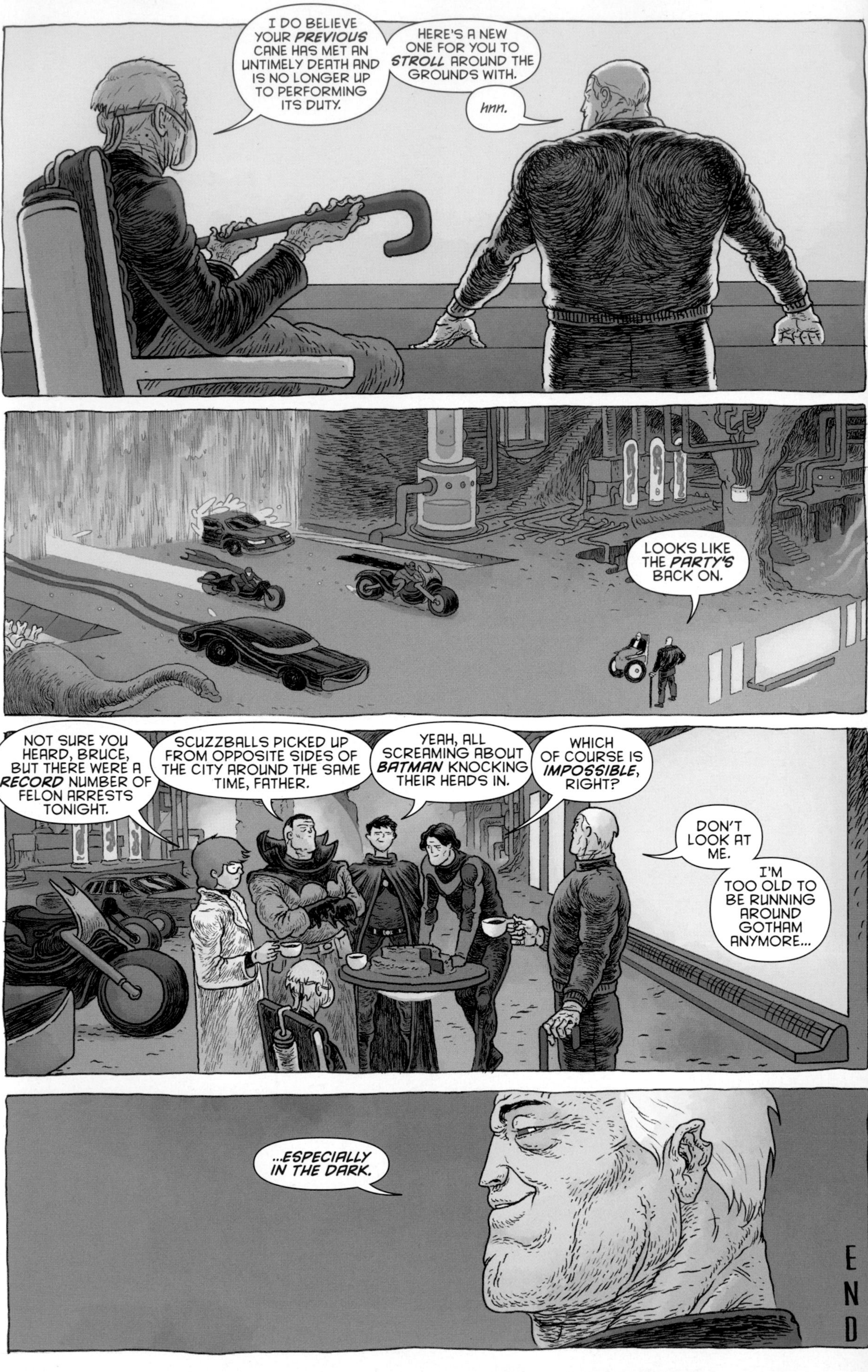
I DO BELIEVE YOUR *PREVIOUS* CANE HAS MET AN UNTIMELY DEATH AND IS NO LONGER UP TO PERFORMING ITS DUTY.
HERE'S A NEW ONE FOR YOU TO *STROLL* AROUND THE GROUNDS WITH.
hnn.
LOOKS LIKE THE *PARTY'S* BACK ON.
NOT SURE YOU HEARD, BRUCE, BUT THERE WERE A *RECORD* NUMBER OF FELON ARRESTS TONIGHT.
SCUZZBALLS PICKED UP FROM OPPOSITE SIDES OF THE CITY AROUND THE SAME TIME, FATHER.
YEAH, ALL SCREAMING ABOUT *BATMAN* KNOCKING THEIR HEADS IN.
WHICH OF COURSE IS *IMPOSSIBLE*, RIGHT?
DON'T LOOK AT ME.
I'M TOO OLD TO BE RUNNING AROUND GOTHAM ANYMORE...
...ESPECIALLY IN THE DARK.
END

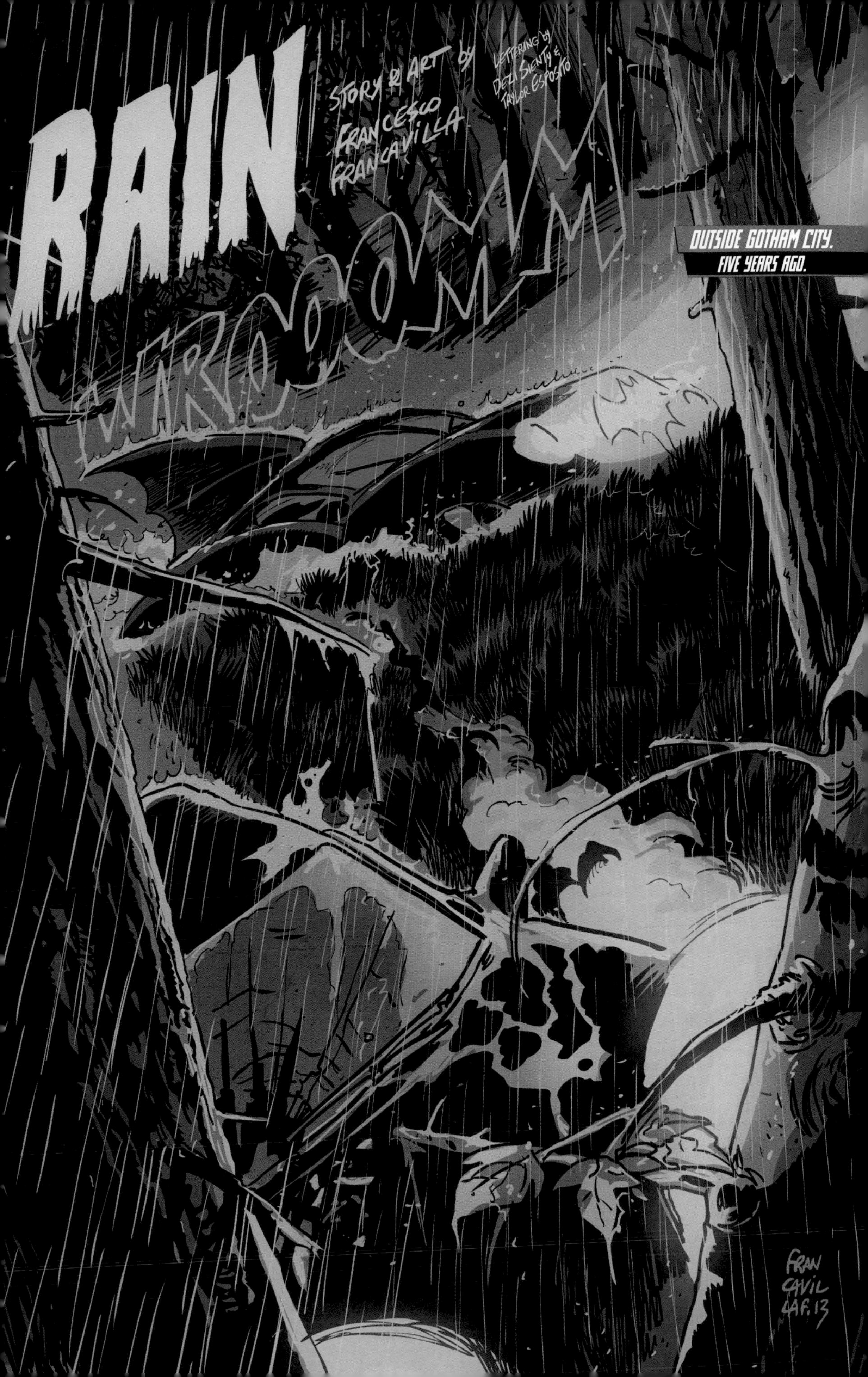

RAIN
STORY & ART BY FRANCESCO FRANCAVILLA
LETTERING BY DEZI SIENTY & TAYLOR ESPOSITO
WRROOOMM
OUTSIDE GOTHAM CITY.
FIVE YEARS AGO.
FRAN CAVIL LAF. 13

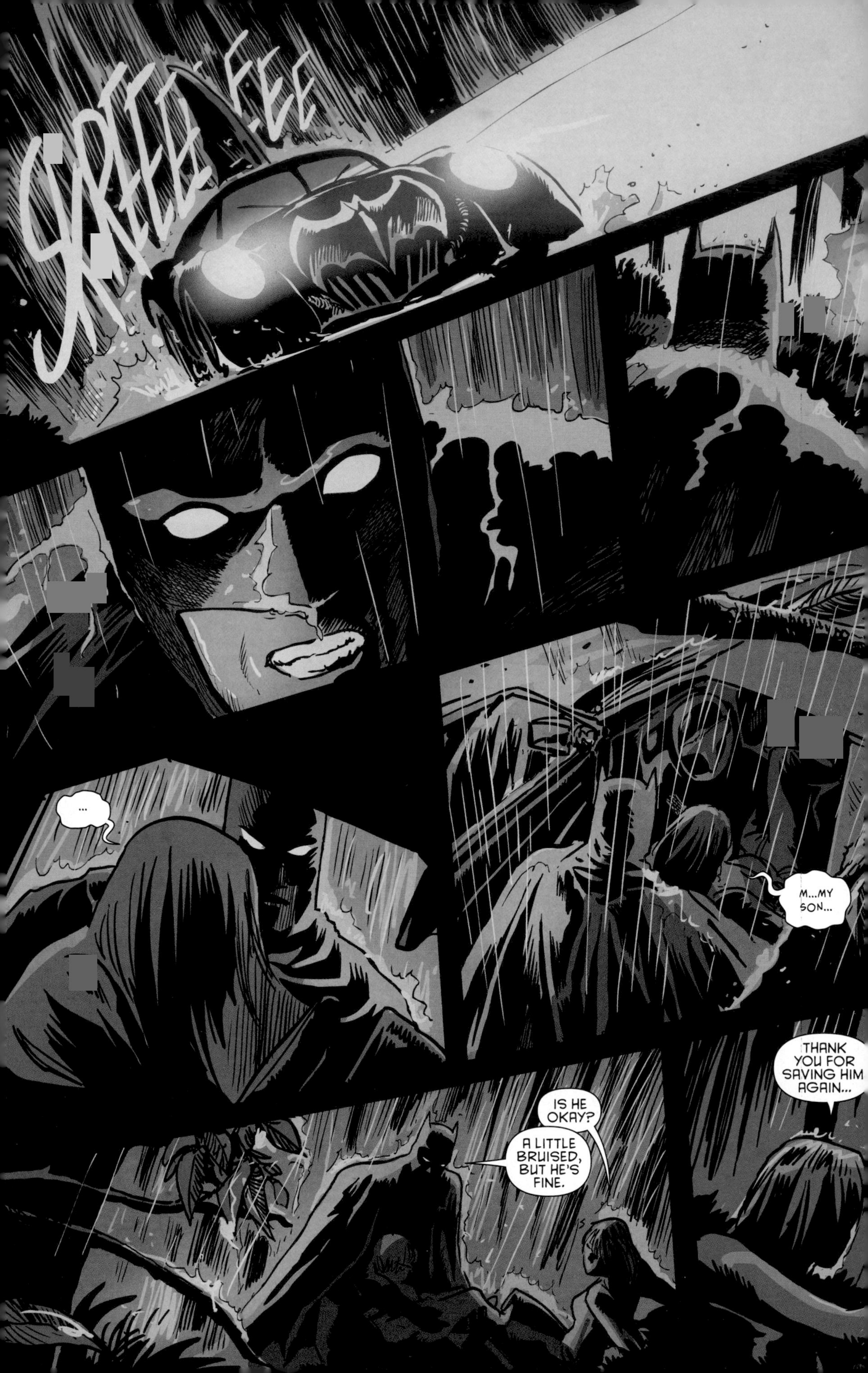
...
M...MY SON...
IS HE OKAY?
A LITTLE BRUISED, BUT HE'S FINE.
THANK YOU FOR SAVING HIM AGAIN...

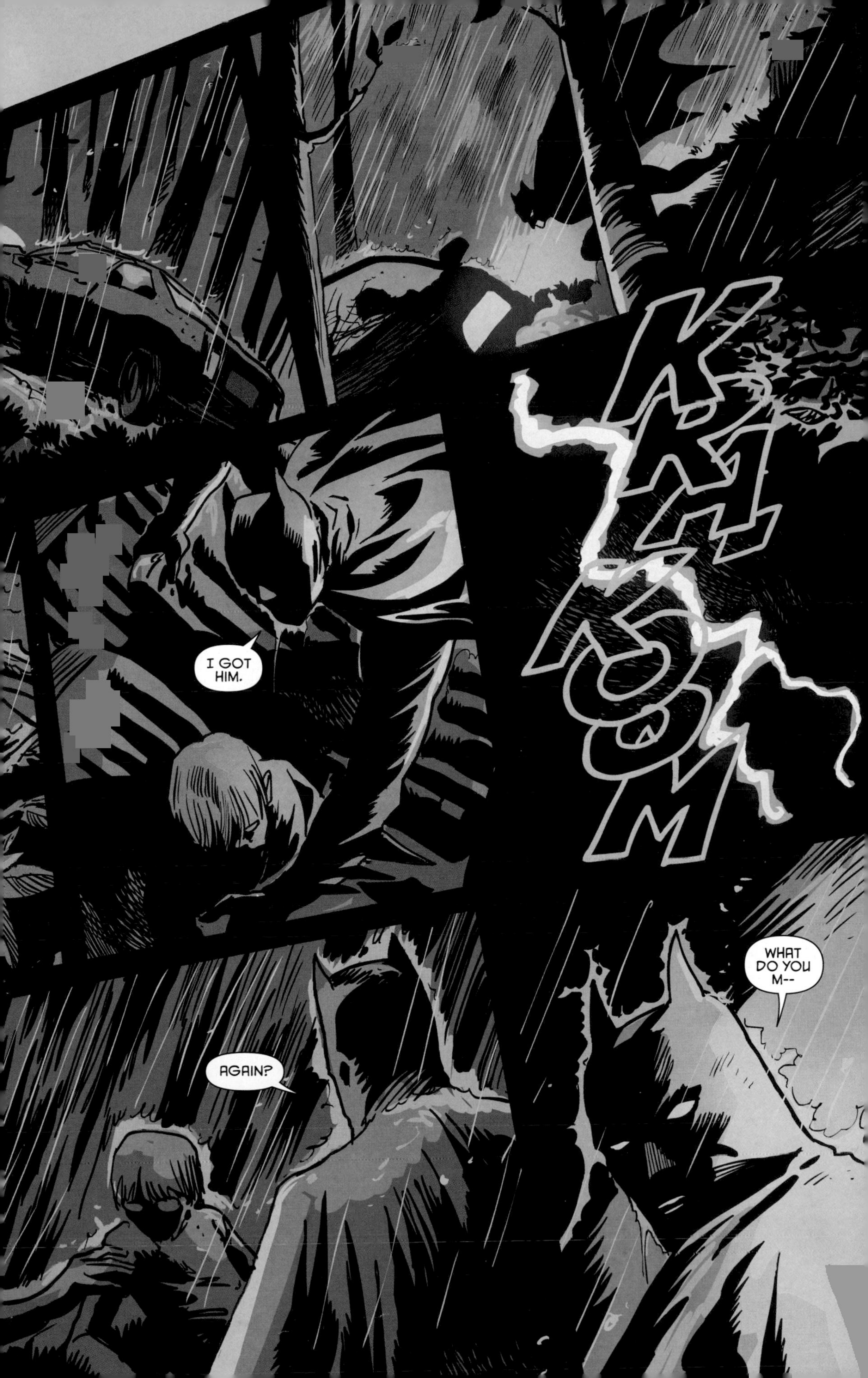
I GOT HIM.
KAHOOOM
AGAIN?
WHAT DO YOU M--

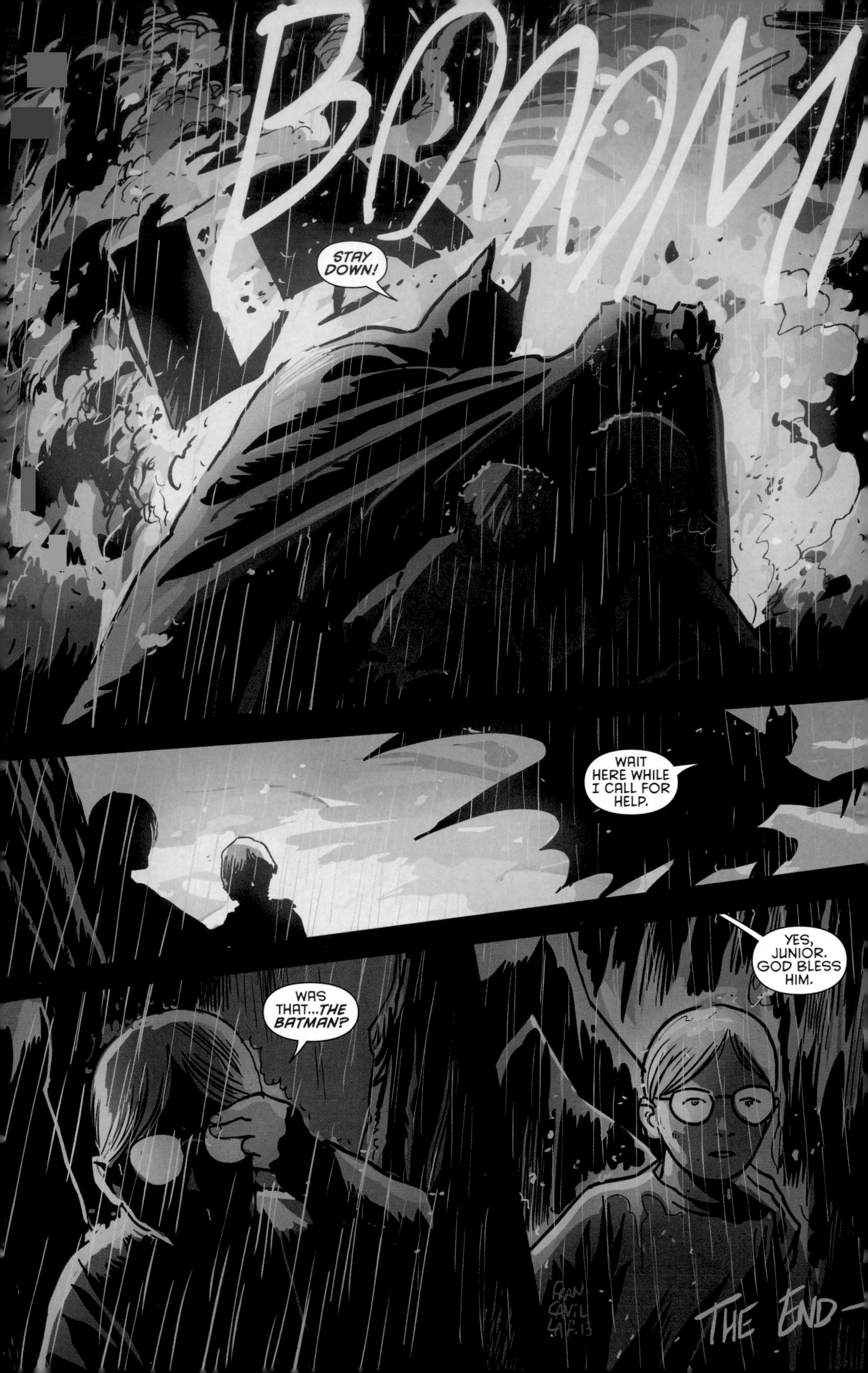
BOOM
STAY DOWN!
WAIT HERE WHILE I CALL FOR HELP.
WAS THAT...THE BATMAN?
YES, JUNIOR. GOD BLESS HIM.
THE END

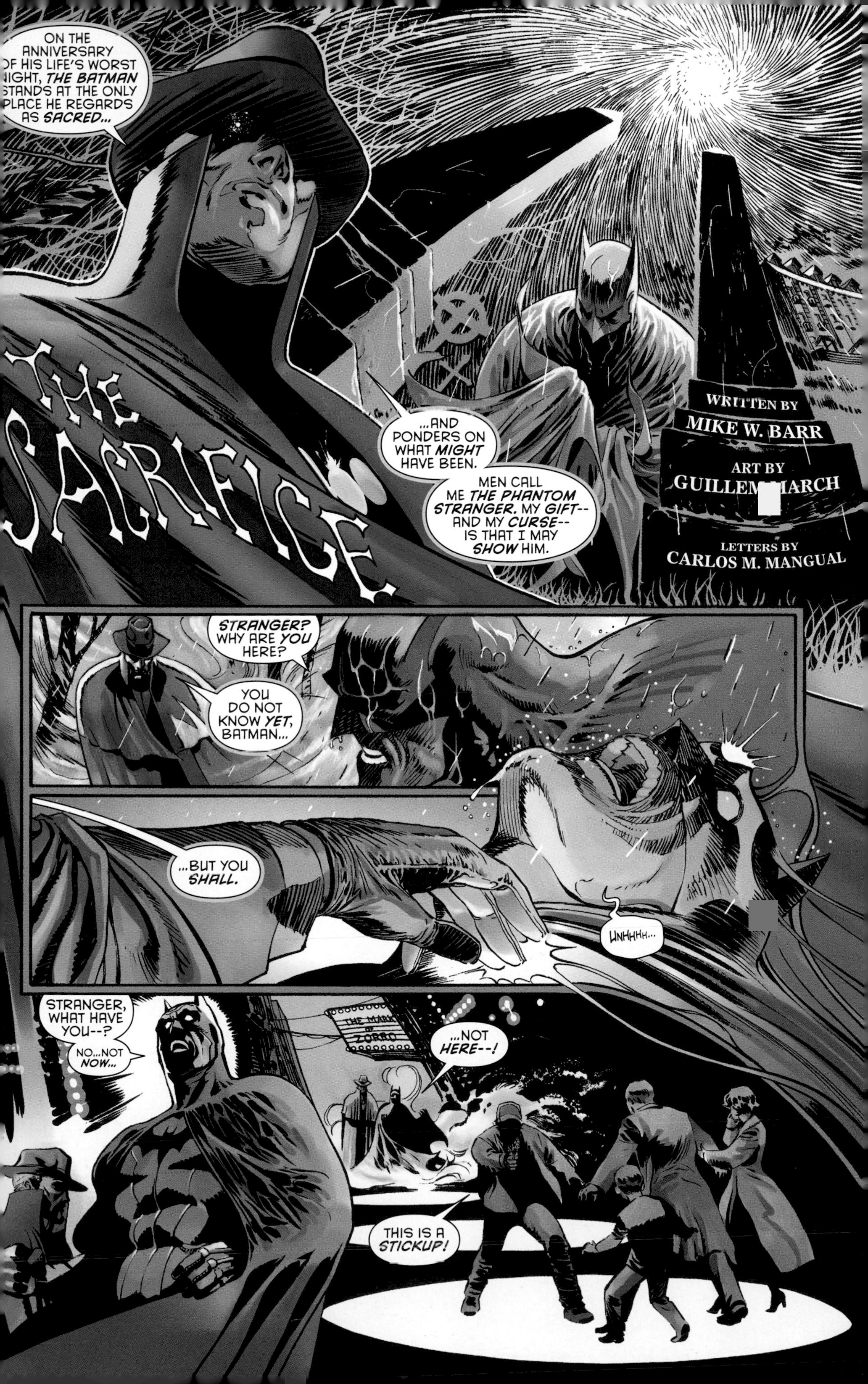
ON THE ANNIVERSARY OF HIS LIFE'S WORST NIGHT, *THE BATMAN* STANDS AT THE ONLY PLACE HE REGARDS AS *SACRED...*
THE SACRIFICE
...AND PONDERS ON WHAT *MIGHT* HAVE BEEN.
MEN CALL ME *THE PHANTOM STRANGER.* MY *GIFT*-- AND MY *CURSE*-- IS THAT I MAY *SHOW* HIM.
WRITTEN BY
MIKE W. BARR
ART BY
GUILLEM MARCH
LETTERS BY
CARLOS M. MANGUAL
STRANGER? WHY ARE *YOU* HERE?
YOU DO NOT KNOW *YET*, BATMAN...
...BUT YOU *SHALL.*
UNHHHH...
STRANGER, WHAT HAVE YOU--?
NO...NOT *NOW...*
THE MARK OF ZORRO
...NOT *HERE*--!
THIS IS A *STICKUP!*

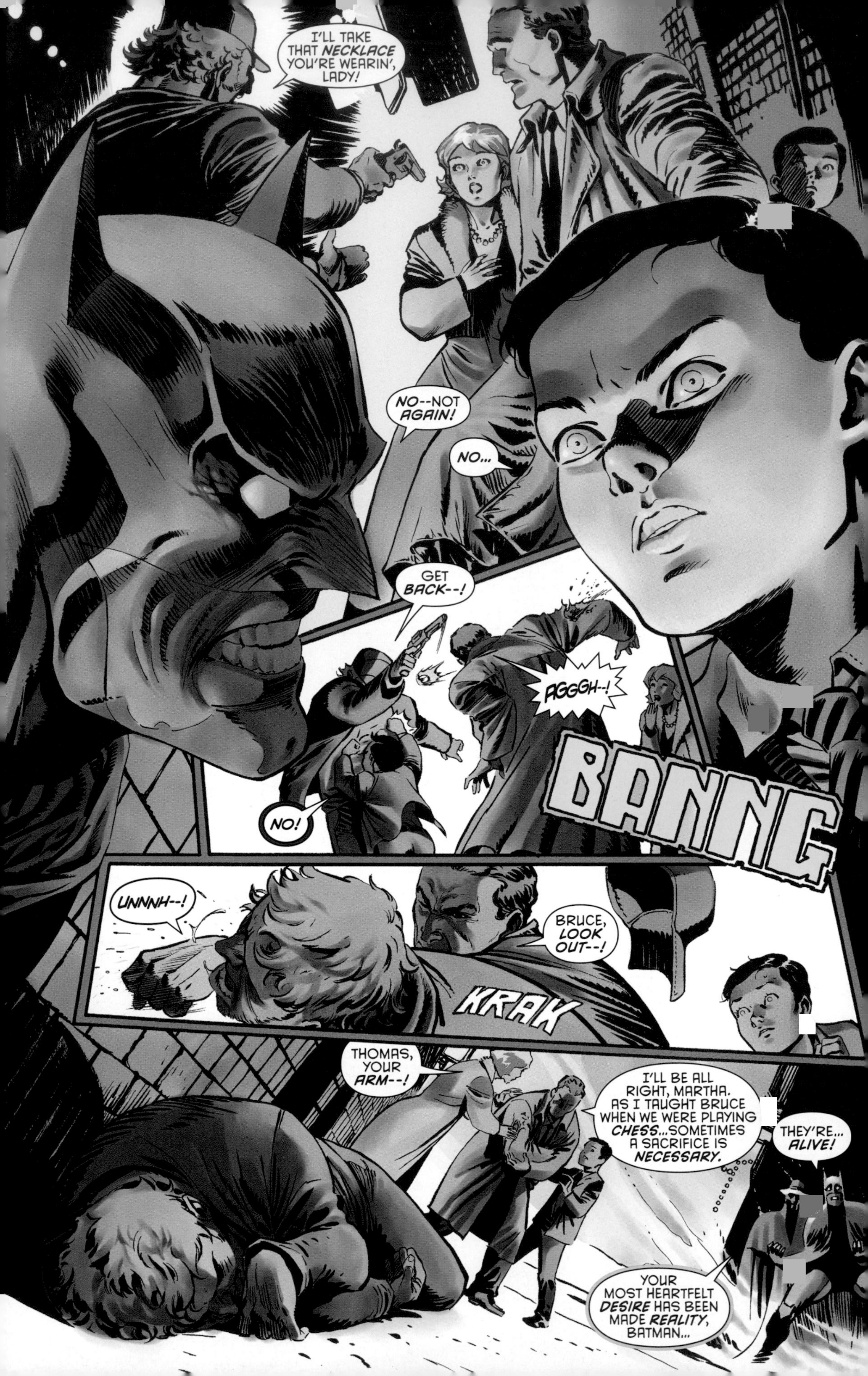
I'LL TAKE THAT NECKLACE YOU'RE WEARIN', LADY!
NO--NOT AGAIN!
NO...
GET BACK--!
AGGGH--!
BANNG
NO!
UNNNH--!
BRUCE, LOOK OUT--!
KRAK
THOMAS, YOUR ARM--!
I'LL BE ALL RIGHT, MARTHA. AS I TAUGHT BRUCE WHEN WE WERE PLAYING CHESS...SOMETIMES A SACRIFICE IS NECESSARY.
THEY'RE... ALIVE!
YOUR MOST HEARTFELT DESIRE HAS BEEN MADE REALITY, BATMAN...

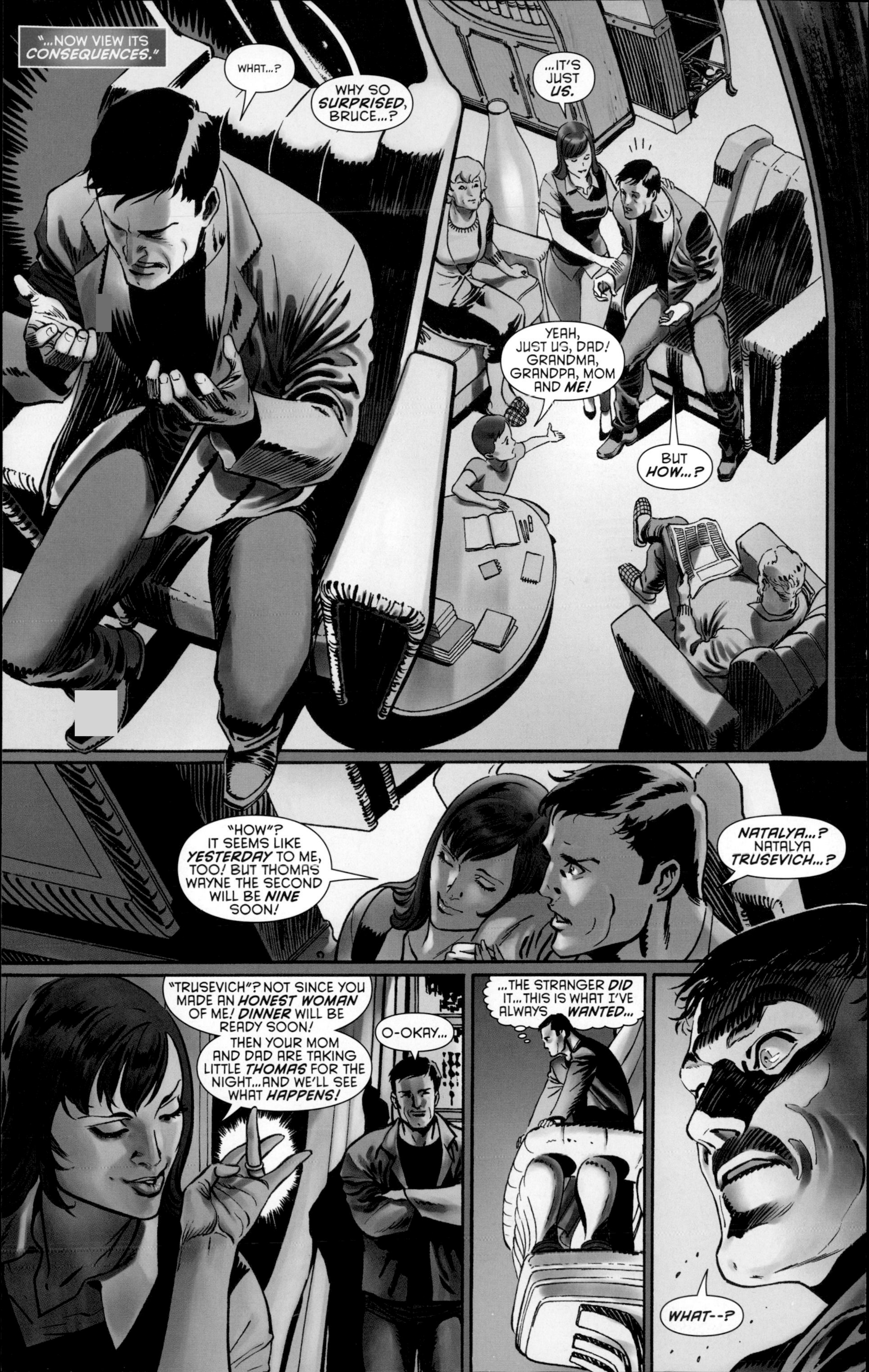
"...NOW VIEW ITS CONSEQUENCES."
WHAT...?
WHY SO SURPRISED, BRUCE...?
...IT'S JUST US.
YEAH, JUST US, DAD! GRANDMA, GRANDPA, MOM AND ME!
BUT HOW...?
"HOW"? IT SEEMS LIKE YESTERDAY TO ME, TOO! BUT THOMAS WAYNE THE SECOND WILL BE NINE SOON!
NATALYA...? NATALYA TRUSEVICH...?
"TRUSEVICH"? NOT SINCE YOU MADE AN HONEST WOMAN OF ME! DINNER WILL BE READY SOON!
THEN YOUR MOM AND DAD ARE TAKING LITTLE THOMAS FOR THE NIGHT...AND WE'LL SEE WHAT HAPPENS!
O-OKAY...
...THE STRANGER DID IT... THIS IS WHAT I'VE ALWAYS WANTED...
WHAT--?

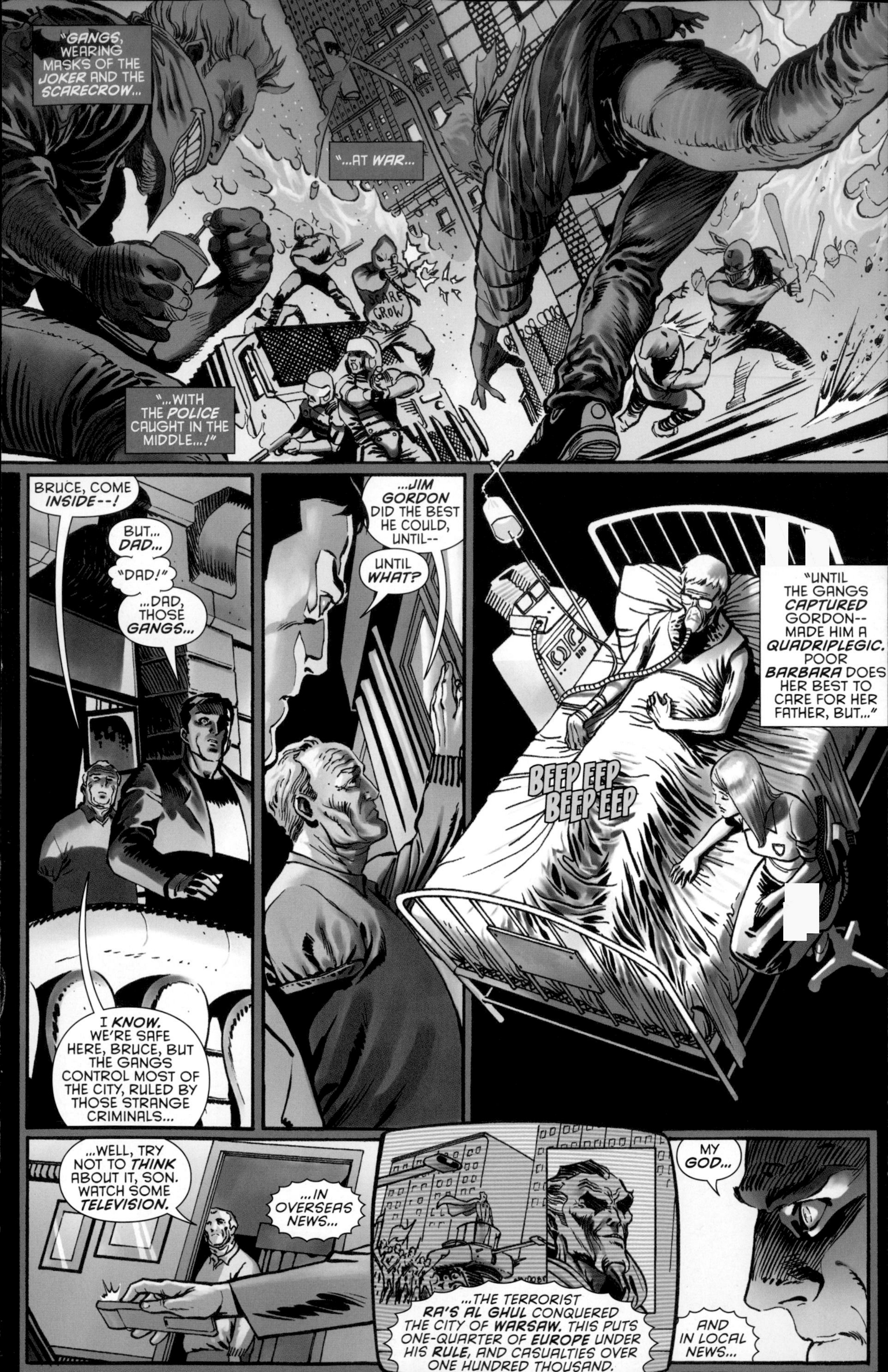
"GANGS, WEARING MASKS OF THE JOKER AND THE SCARECROW...
"...AT WAR...
SCARE CROW
"...WITH THE POLICE CAUGHT IN THE MIDDLE...!"
BRUCE, COME INSIDE--!
BUT... DAD...
"DAD!"
...DAD, THOSE GANGS...
I KNOW. WE'RE SAFE HERE, BRUCE, BUT THE GANGS CONTROL MOST OF THE CITY, RULED BY THOSE STRANGE CRIMINALS...
...JIM GORDON DID THE BEST HE COULD, UNTIL--
UNTIL WHAT?
"UNTIL THE GANGS CAPTURED GORDON-- MADE HIM A QUADRIPLEGIC. POOR BARBARA DOES HER BEST TO CARE FOR HER FATHER, BUT..."
BEEP EEP BEEP EEP
...WELL, TRY NOT TO THINK ABOUT IT, SON. WATCH SOME TELEVISION.
...IN OVERSEAS NEWS...
...THE TERRORIST RA'S AL GHUL CONQUERED THE CITY OF WARSAW. THIS PUTS ONE-QUARTER OF EUROPE UNDER HIS RULE, AND CASUALTIES OVER ONE HUNDRED THOUSAND.
MY GOD...
AND IN LOCAL NEWS...

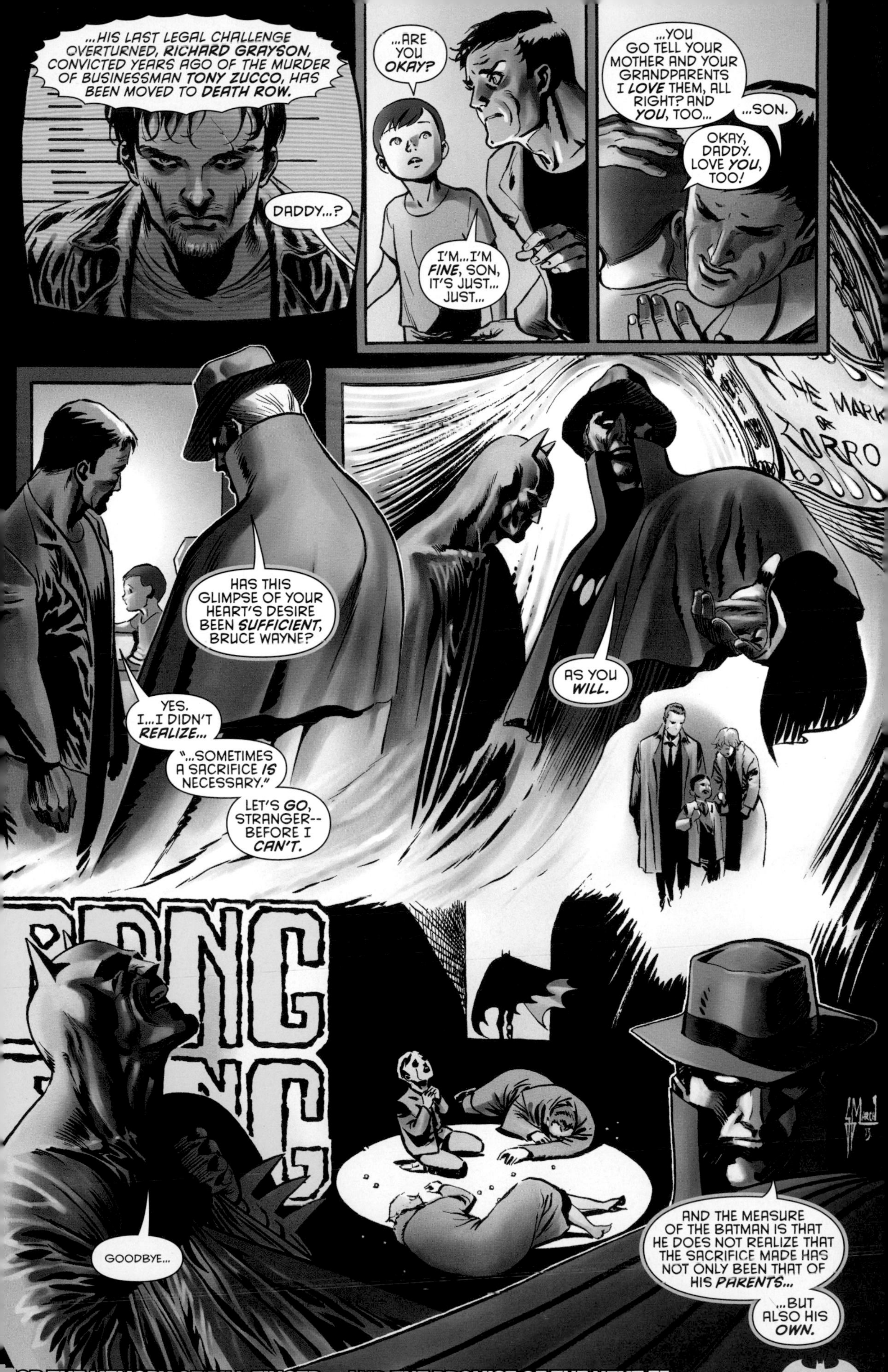
...HIS LAST LEGAL CHALLENGE OVERTURNED, RICHARD GRAYSON, CONVICTED YEARS AGO OF THE MURDER OF BUSINESSMAN TONY ZUCCO, HAS BEEN MOVED TO DEATH ROW.
DADDY...?
...ARE YOU OKAY?
I'M...I'M FINE, SON, IT'S JUST... JUST...
...YOU GO TELL YOUR MOTHER AND YOUR GRANDPARENTS I LOVE THEM, ALL RIGHT? AND YOU, TOO...
...SON.
OKAY, DADDY. LOVE YOU, TOO!
THE MARK OF ZORRO
HAS THIS GLIMPSE OF YOUR HEART'S DESIRE BEEN SUFFICIENT, BRUCE WAYNE?
YES. I...I DIDN'T REALIZE...
"...SOMETIMES A SACRIFICE IS NECESSARY."
LET'S GO, STRANGER-- BEFORE I CAN'T.
AS YOU WILL.
GOODBYE...
AND THE MEASURE OF THE BATMAN IS THAT HE DOES NOT REALIZE THAT THE SACRIFICE MADE HAS NOT ONLY BEEN THAT OF HIS PARENTS...
...BUT ALSO HIS OWN.

FOR THE MEMORY OF BILL FINGER -- AND THE PROMISE OF THE NEXT 75.

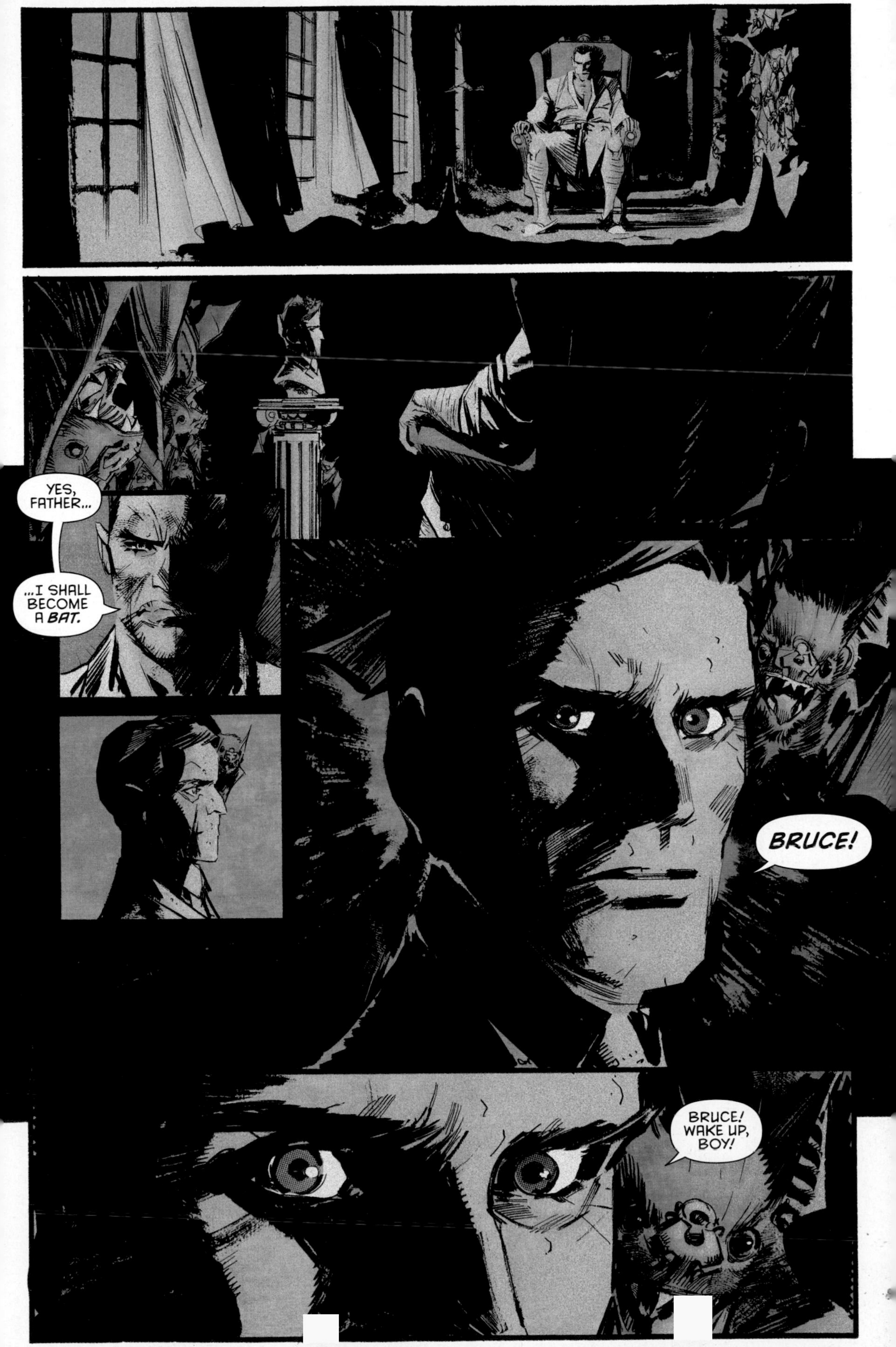
YES, FATHER...
...I SHALL BECOME A BAT.
BRUCE!
BRUCE! WAKE UP, BOY!

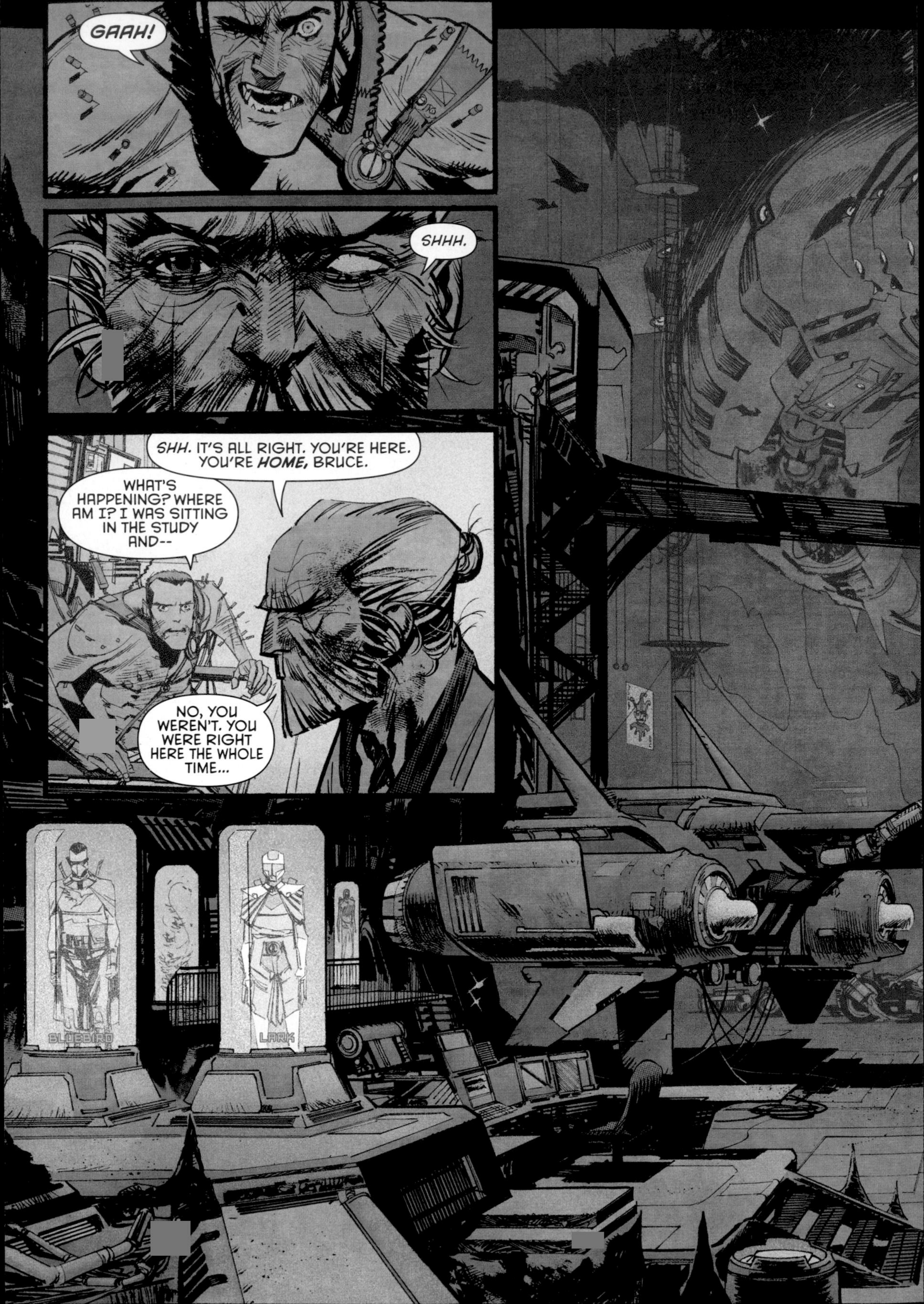
GAAH!
SHHH.
SHH. IT'S ALL RIGHT. YOU'RE HERE. YOU'RE HOME, BRUCE.
WHAT'S HAPPENING? WHERE AM I? I WAS SITTING IN THE STUDY AND--
NO, YOU WEREN'T. YOU WERE RIGHT HERE THE WHOLE TIME...
BLUEBIRD
LARK

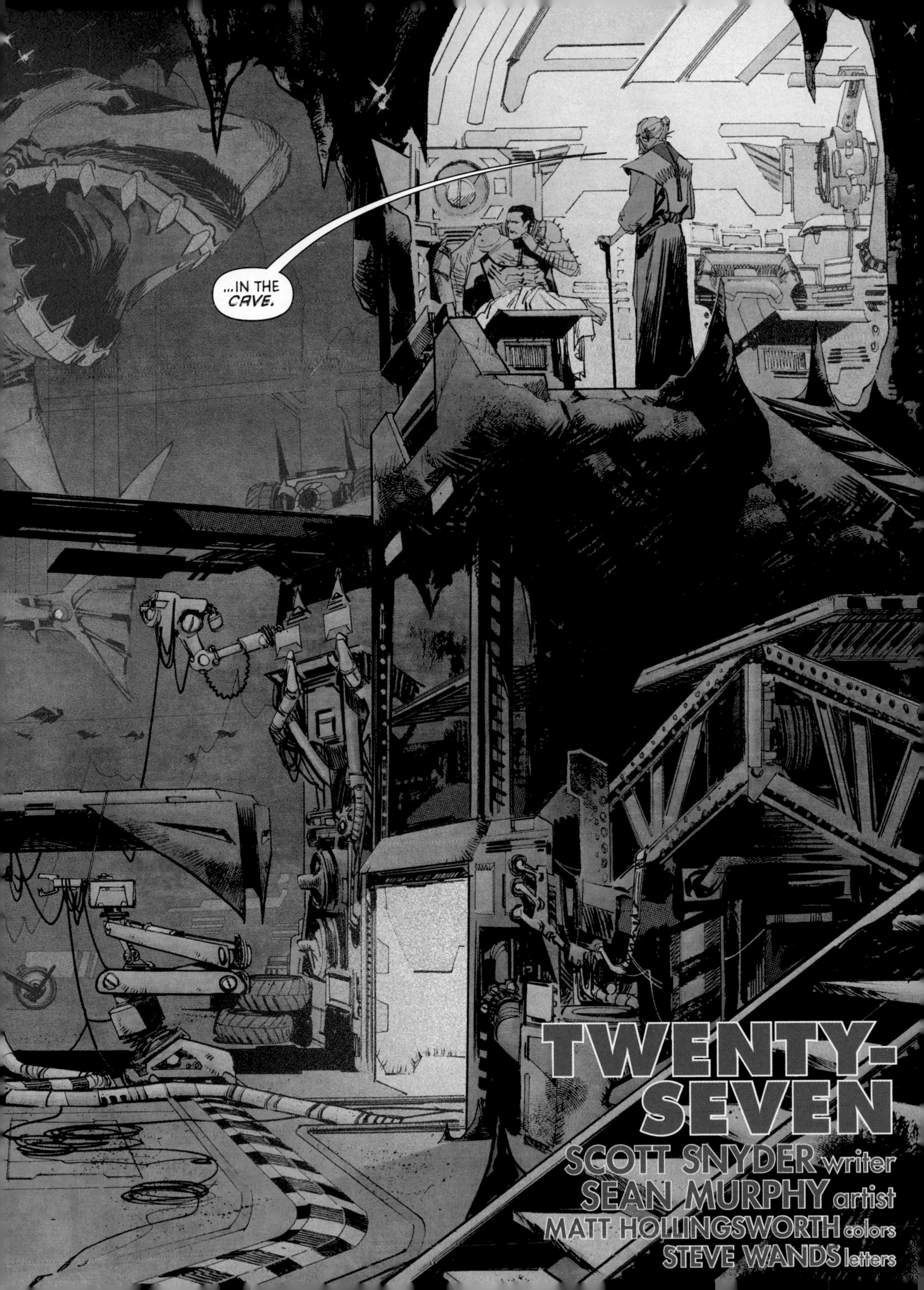
...IN THE CAVE.
TWENTY-SEVEN
SCOTT SNYDER writer
SEAN MURPHY artist
MATT HOLLINGSWORTH colors
STEVE WANDS letters

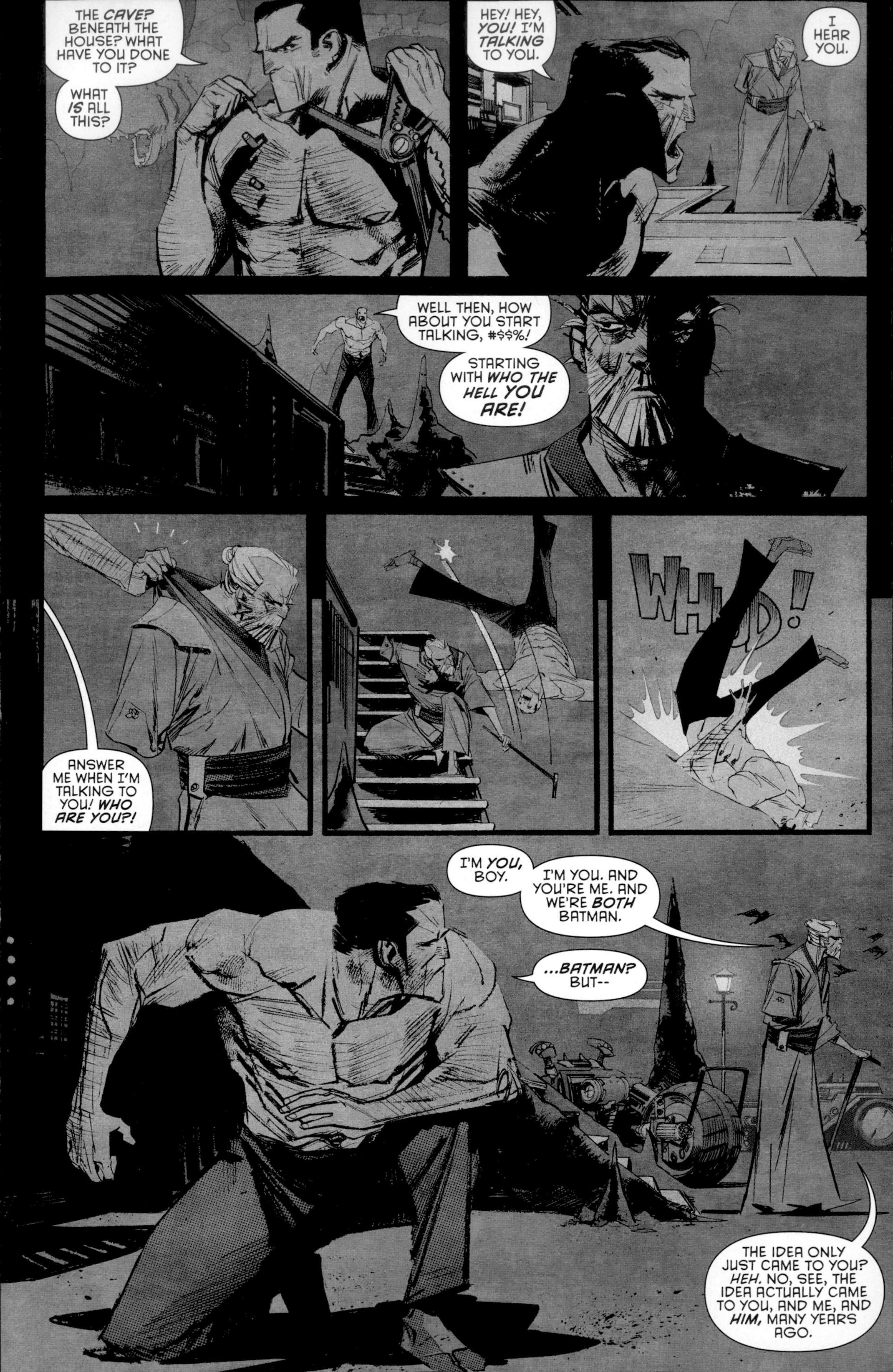
THE CAVE? BENEATH THE HOUSE? WHAT HAVE YOU DONE TO IT?
WHAT IS ALL THIS?
HEY! HEY, YOU! I'M TALKING TO YOU.
I HEAR YOU.
WELL THEN, HOW ABOUT YOU START TALKING, #$$%!
STARTING WITH WHO THE HELL YOU ARE!
ANSWER ME WHEN I'M TALKING TO YOU! WHO ARE YOU?!
WHUD!
I'M YOU, BOY.
I'M YOU. AND YOU'RE ME. AND WE'RE BOTH BATMAN.
...BATMAN? BUT--
THE IDEA ONLY JUST CAME TO YOU? HEH. NO, SEE, THE IDEA ACTUALLY CAME TO YOU, AND ME, AND HIM, MANY YEARS AGO.

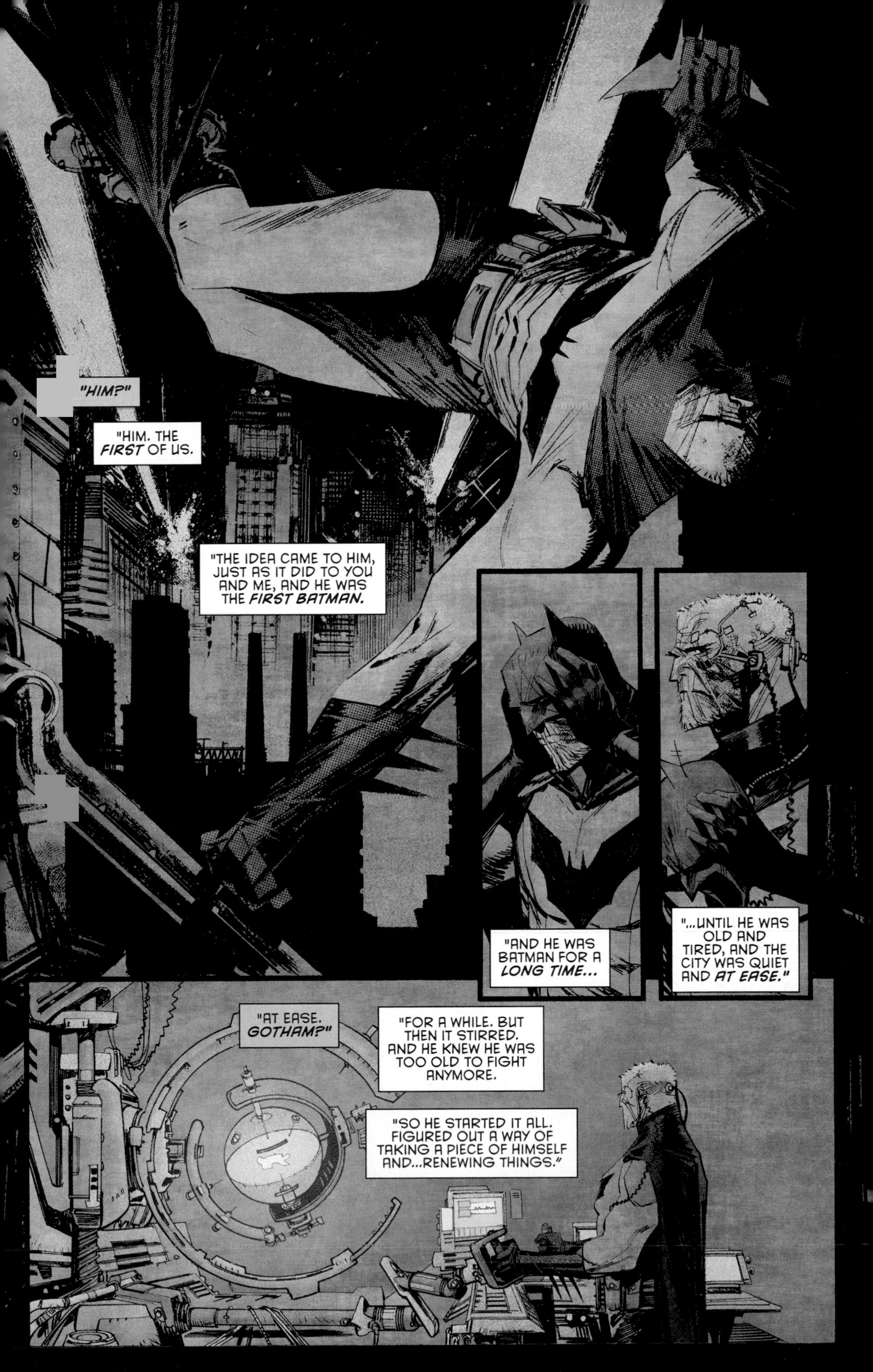
"HIM?"
"HIM. THE *FIRST* OF US.
"THE IDEA CAME TO HIM, JUST AS IT DID TO YOU AND ME, AND HE WAS THE *FIRST BATMAN.*
"AND HE WAS BATMAN FOR A *LONG TIME...*
"...UNTIL HE WAS OLD AND TIRED, AND THE CITY WAS QUIET AND *AT EASE.*"
"AT EASE. *GOTHAM?*"
"FOR A WHILE. BUT THEN IT STIRRED. AND HE KNEW HE WAS TOO OLD TO FIGHT ANYMORE.
"SO HE STARTED IT ALL. FIGURED OUT A WAY OF TAKING A PIECE OF HIMSELF AND...RENEWING THINGS."

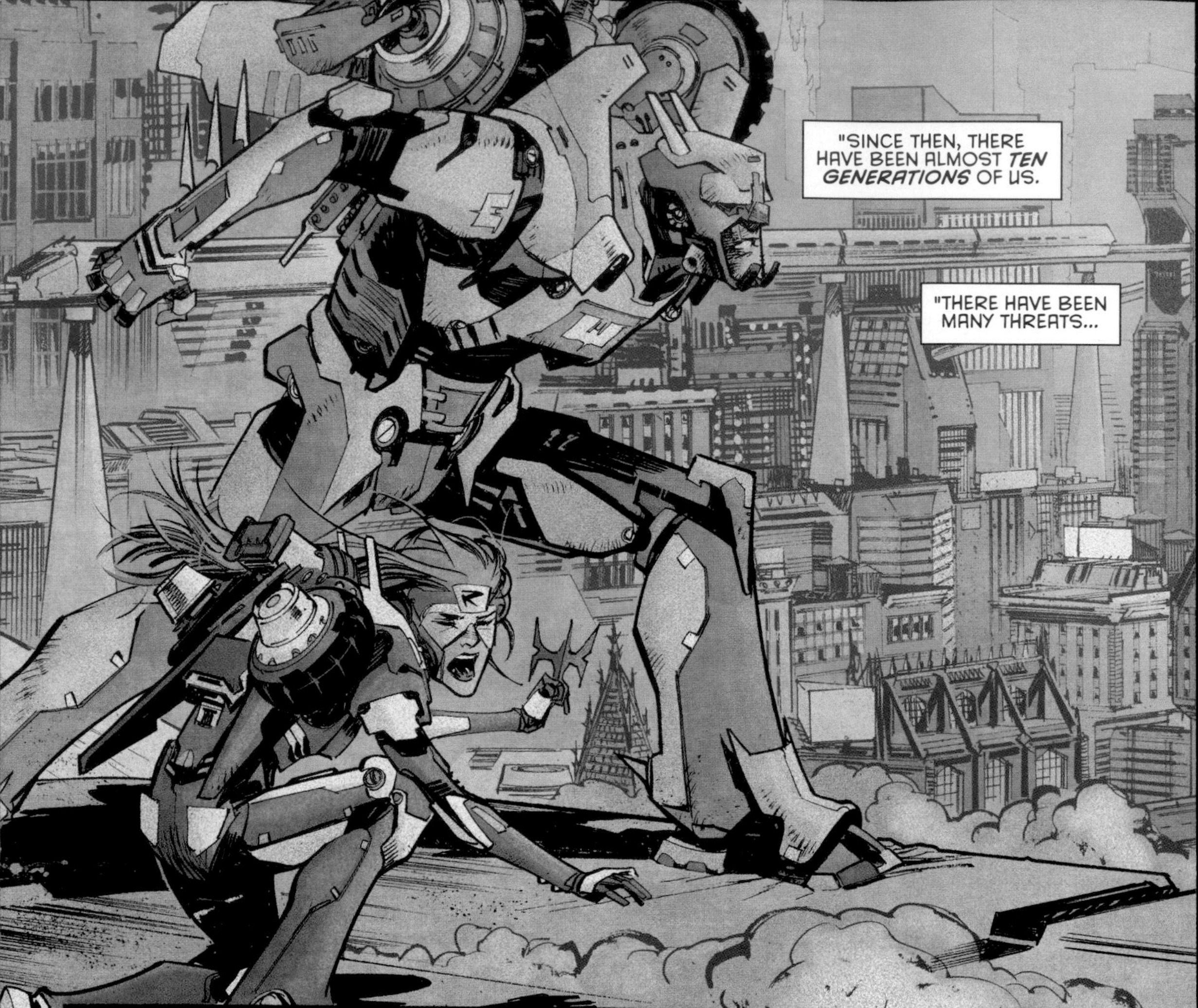
"SINCE THEN, THERE HAVE BEEN ALMOST *TEN GENERATIONS* OF US.
"THERE HAVE BEEN MANY THREATS...
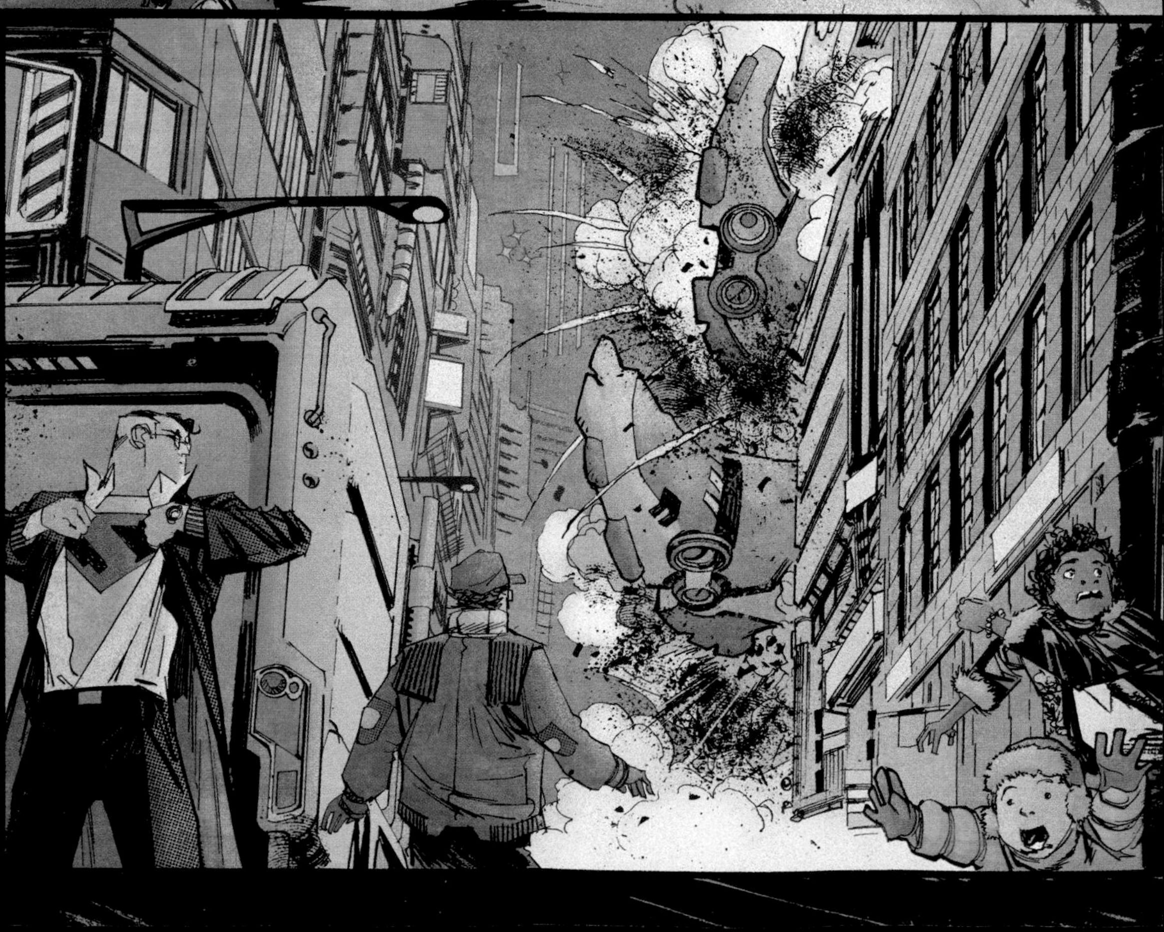

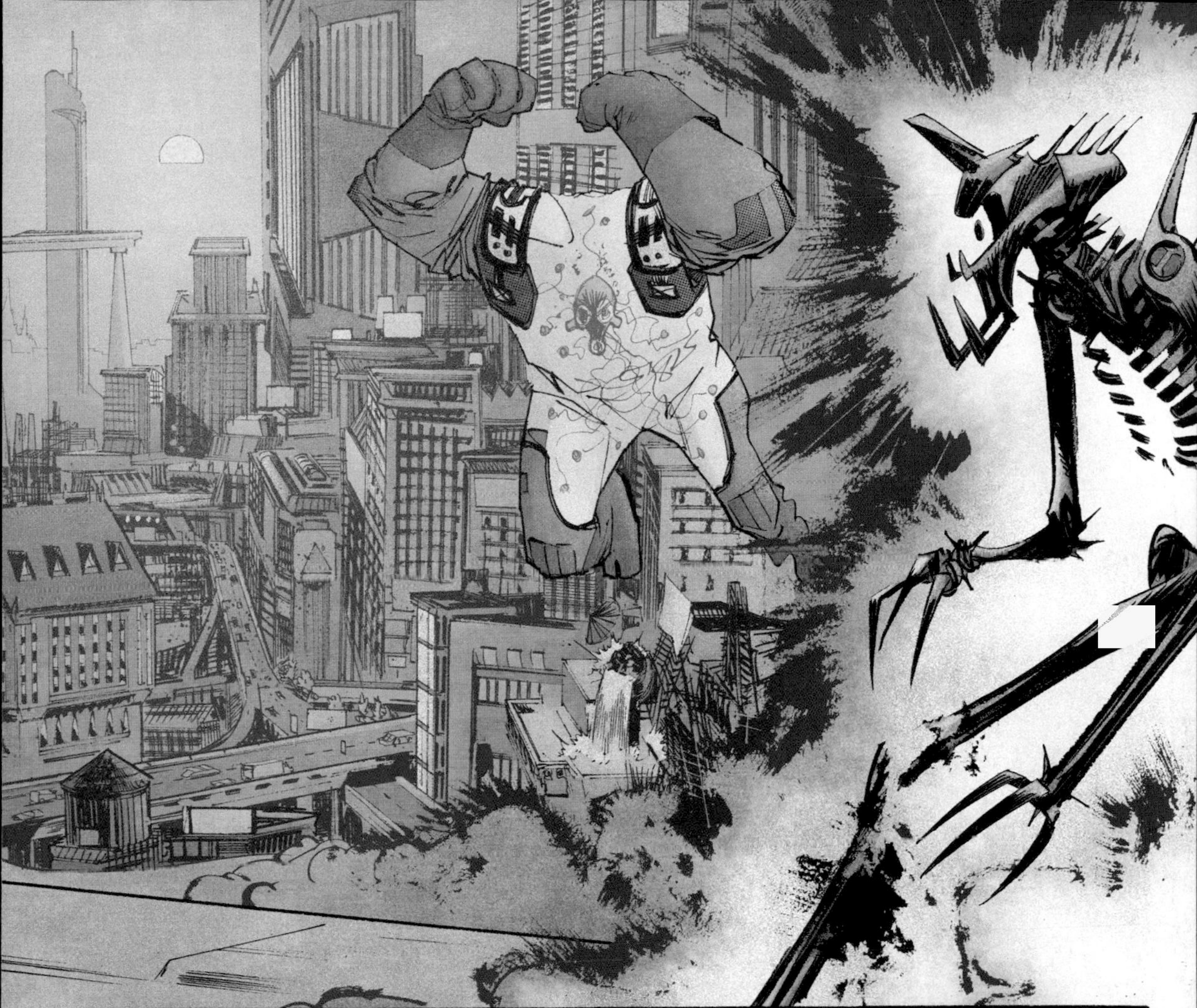

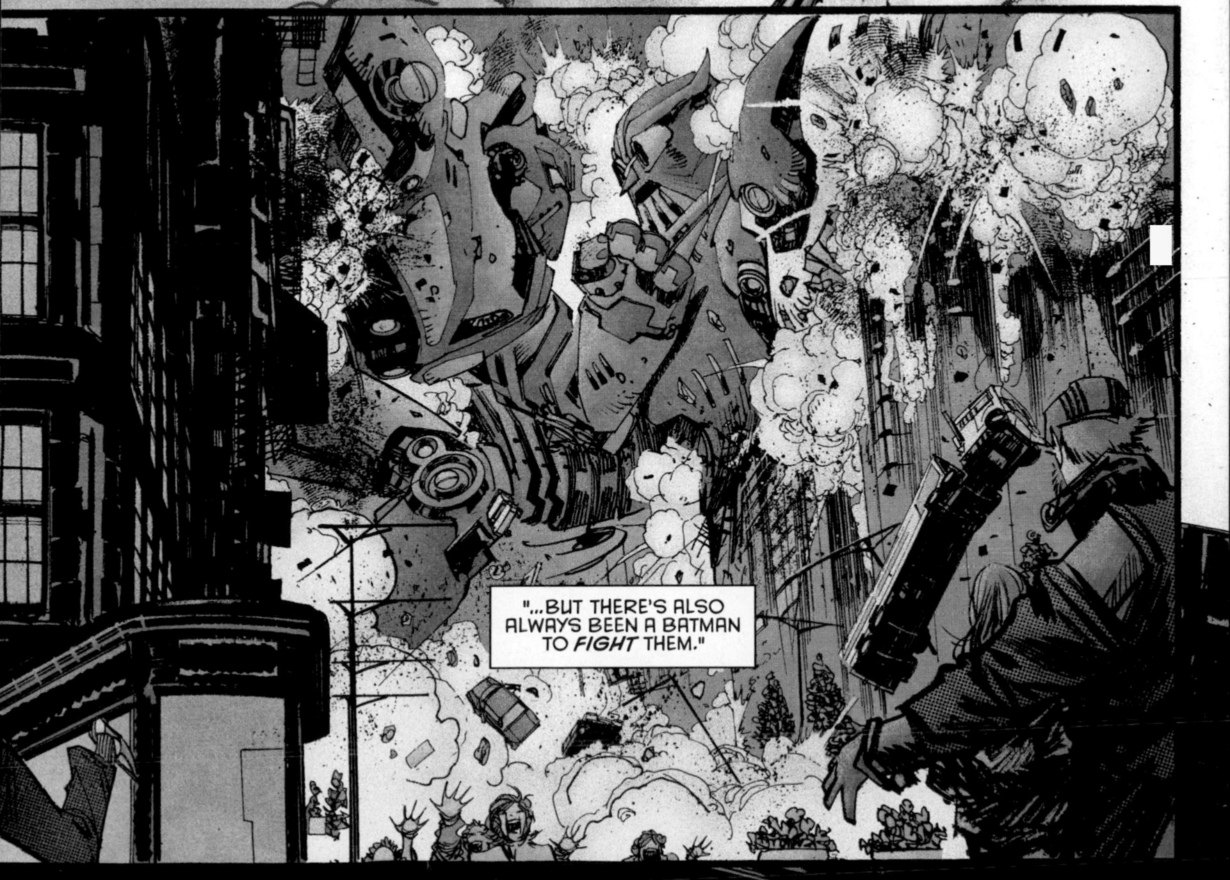
"...BUT THERE'S ALSO ALWAYS BEEN A BATMAN TO *FIGHT* THEM."

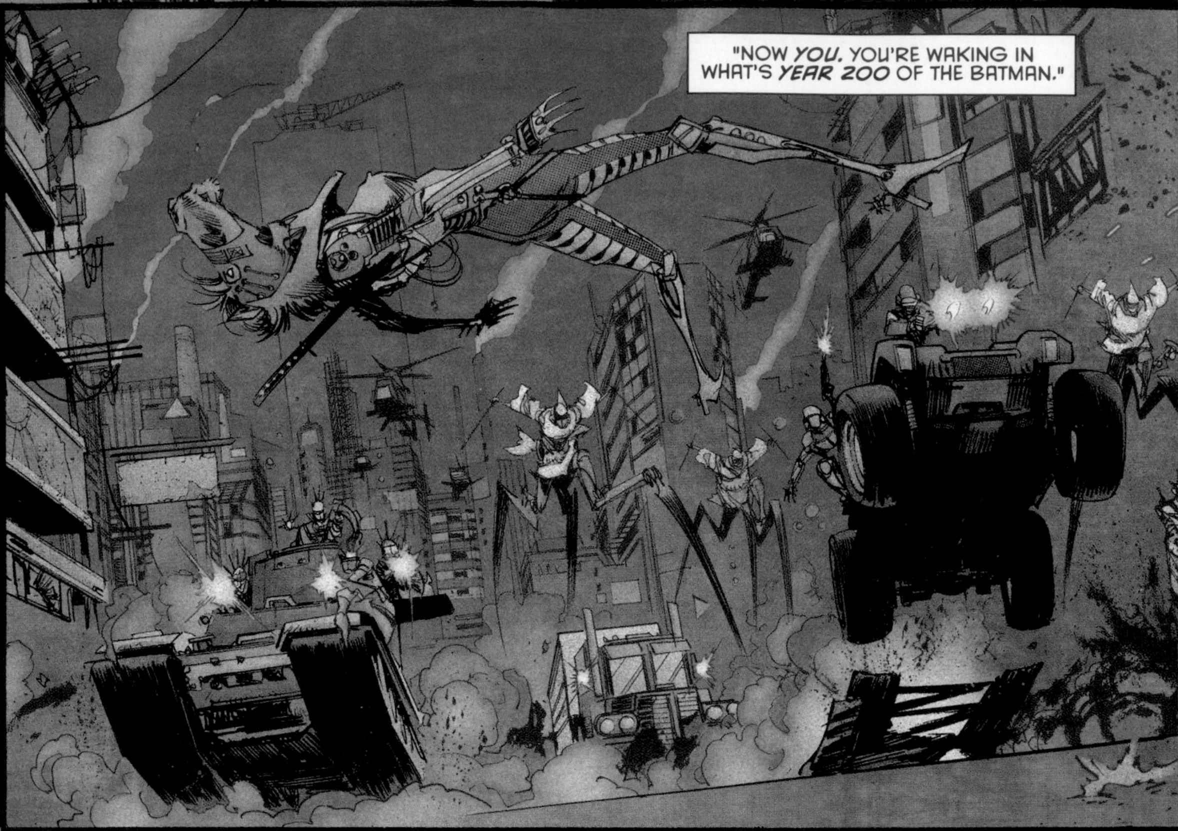
"NOW *YOU.* YOU'RE WAKING IN WHAT'S *YEAR 200* OF THE BATMAN."

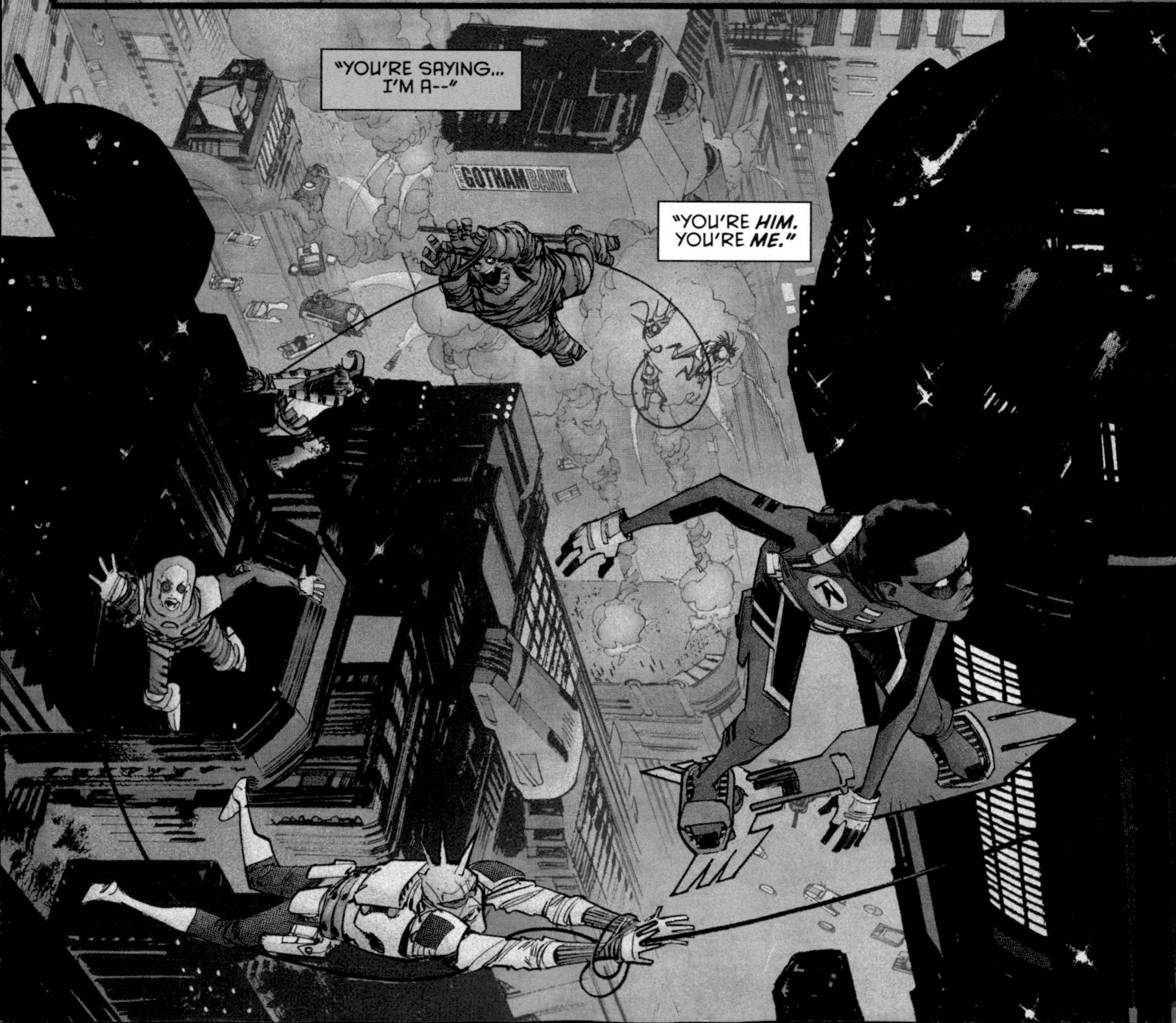
"YOU'RE SAYING... I'M A--"
GOTHAM BANK
"YOU'RE *HIM.* YOU'RE *ME.*"

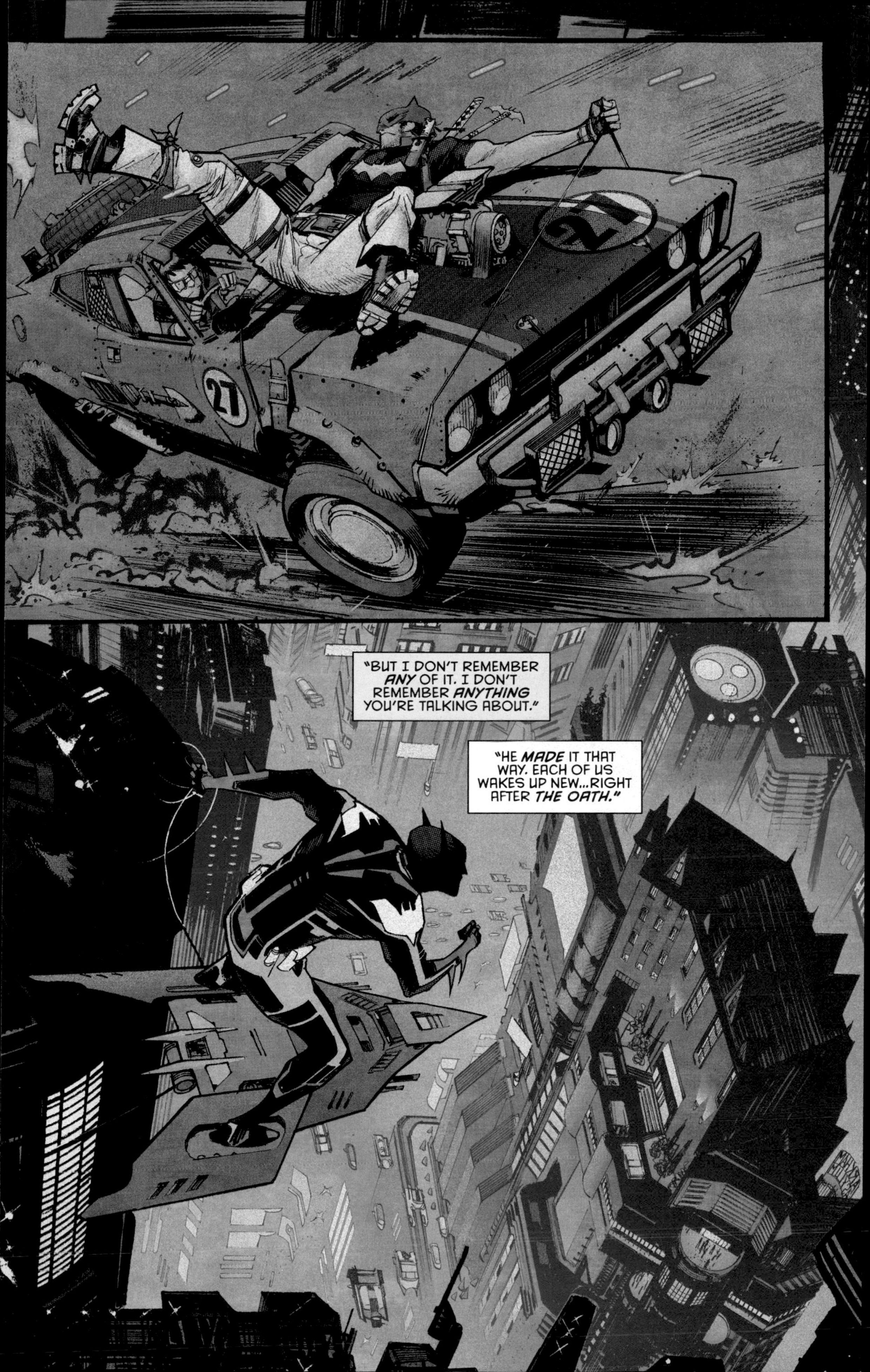
"BUT I DON'T REMEMBER *ANY* OF IT. I DON'T REMEMBER *ANYTHING* YOU'RE TALKING ABOUT."
"HE *MADE* IT THAT WAY. EACH OF US WAKES UP NEW...RIGHT AFTER *THE OATH.*"

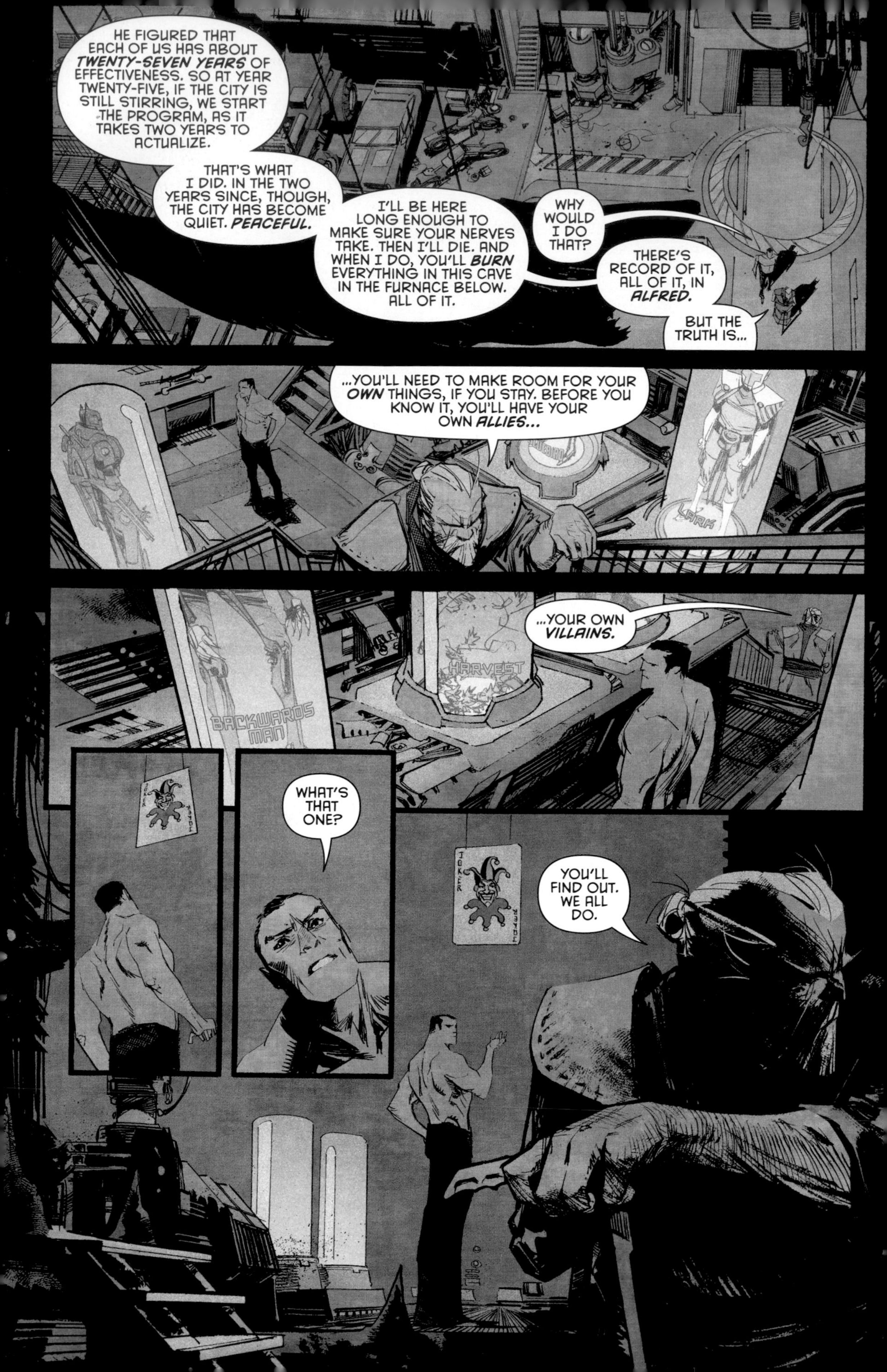
HE FIGURED THAT EACH OF US HAS ABOUT TWENTY-SEVEN YEARS OF EFFECTIVENESS. SO AT YEAR TWENTY-FIVE, IF THE CITY IS STILL STIRRING, WE START THE PROGRAM, AS IT TAKES TWO YEARS TO ACTUALIZE.
THAT'S WHAT I DID. IN THE TWO YEARS SINCE, THOUGH, THE CITY HAS BECOME QUIET. PEACEFUL.
I'LL BE HERE LONG ENOUGH TO MAKE SURE YOUR NERVES TAKE. THEN I'LL DIE. AND WHEN I DO, YOU'LL BURN EVERYTHING IN THIS CAVE IN THE FURNACE BELOW. ALL OF IT.
WHY WOULD I DO THAT?
THERE'S RECORD OF IT, ALL OF IT, IN ALFRED.
BUT THE TRUTH IS...
...YOU'LL NEED TO MAKE ROOM FOR YOUR OWN THINGS, IF YOU STAY. BEFORE YOU KNOW IT, YOU'LL HAVE YOUR OWN ALLIES...
LARK
BACKWARDS MAN
HARVEST
...YOUR OWN VILLAINS.
JOKER
WHAT'S THAT ONE?
YOU'LL FIND OUT. WE ALL DO.

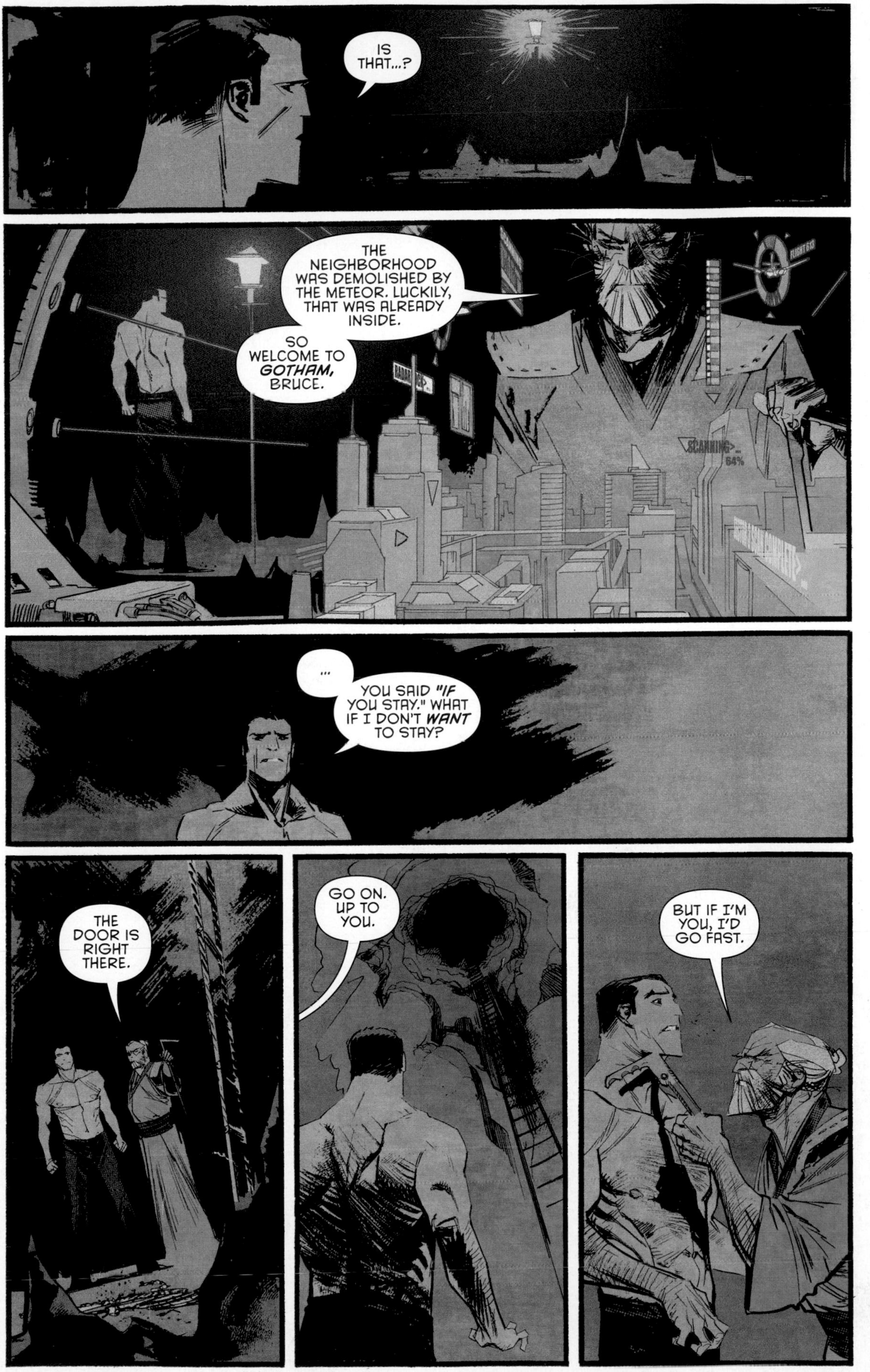
IS THAT...?
THE NEIGHBORHOOD WAS DEMOLISHED BY THE METEOR. LUCKILY, THAT WAS ALREADY INSIDE.
SO WELCOME TO ***GOTHAM,*** BRUCE.
SCANNING>..
64%
...
YOU SAID ***"IF*** YOU STAY." WHAT IF I DON'T ***WANT*** TO STAY?
THE DOOR IS RIGHT THERE.
GO ON. UP TO YOU.
BUT IF I'M YOU, I'D GO FAST.

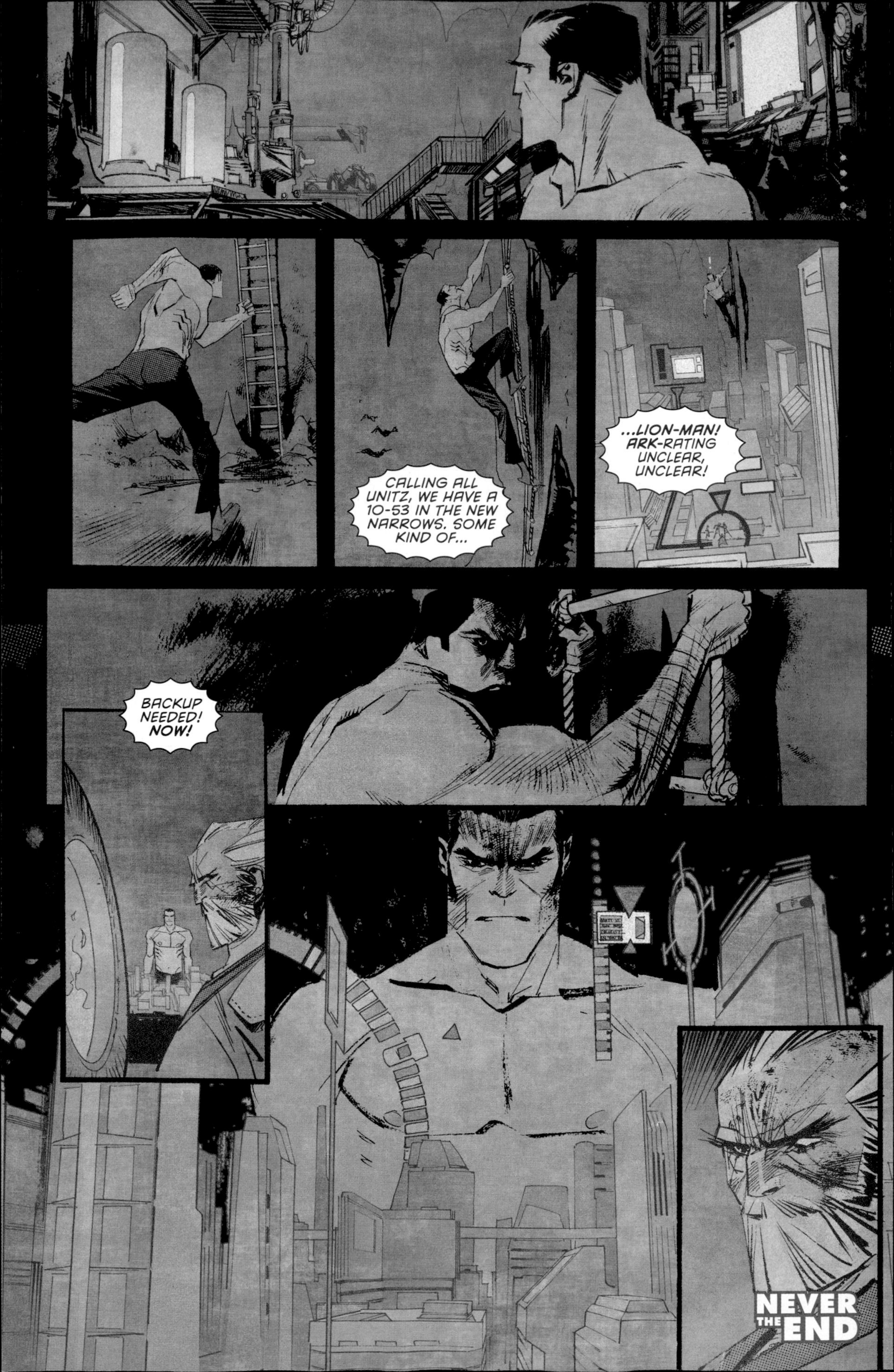
CALLING ALL UNITZ, WE HAVE A 10-53 IN THE NEW NARROWS. SOME KIND OF...
...LION-MAN! ARK-RATING UNCLEAR, UNCLEAR!
BACKUP NEEDED! NOW!
NEVER THE END

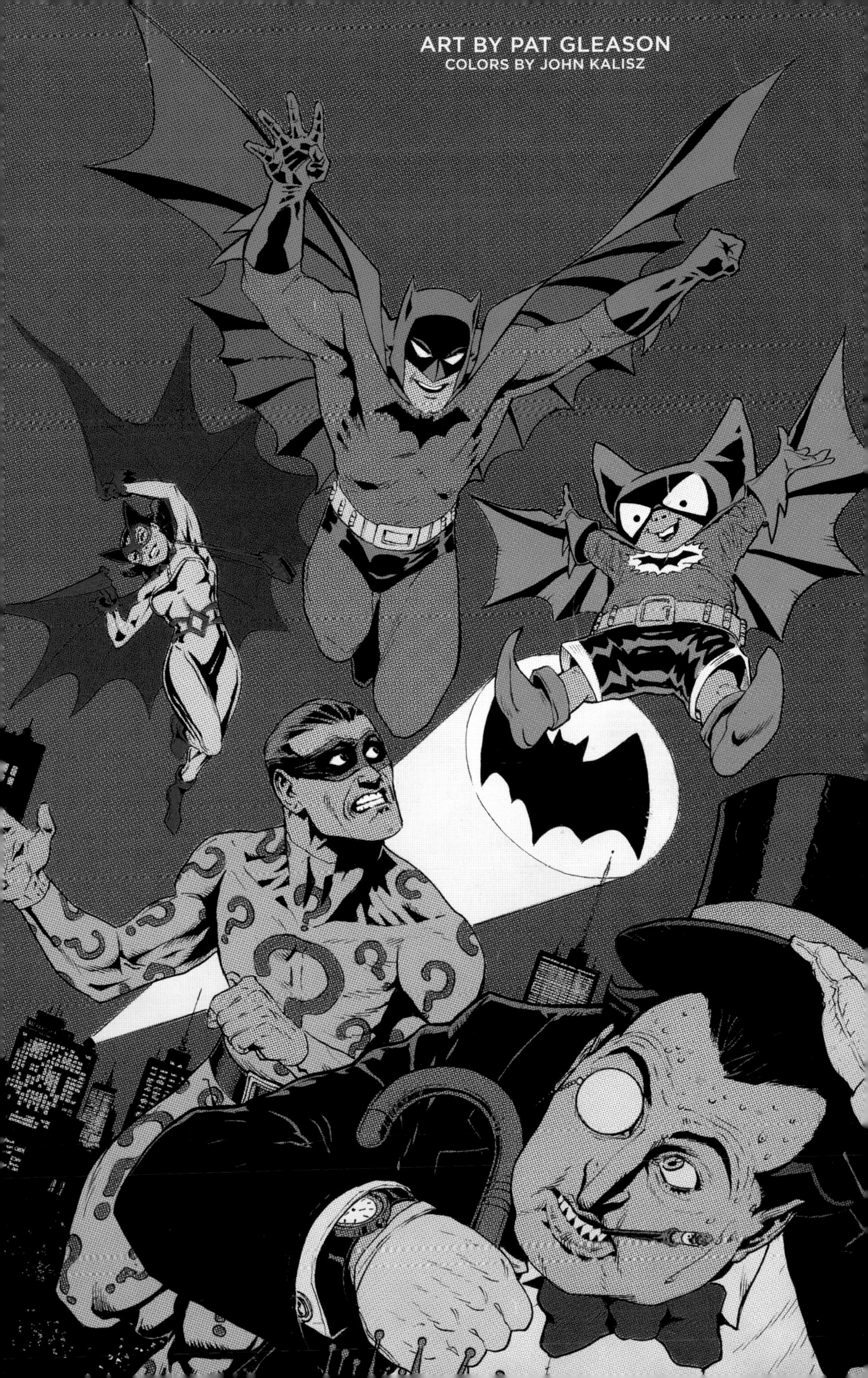

ART BY PAT GLEASON
COLORS BY JOHN KALISZ

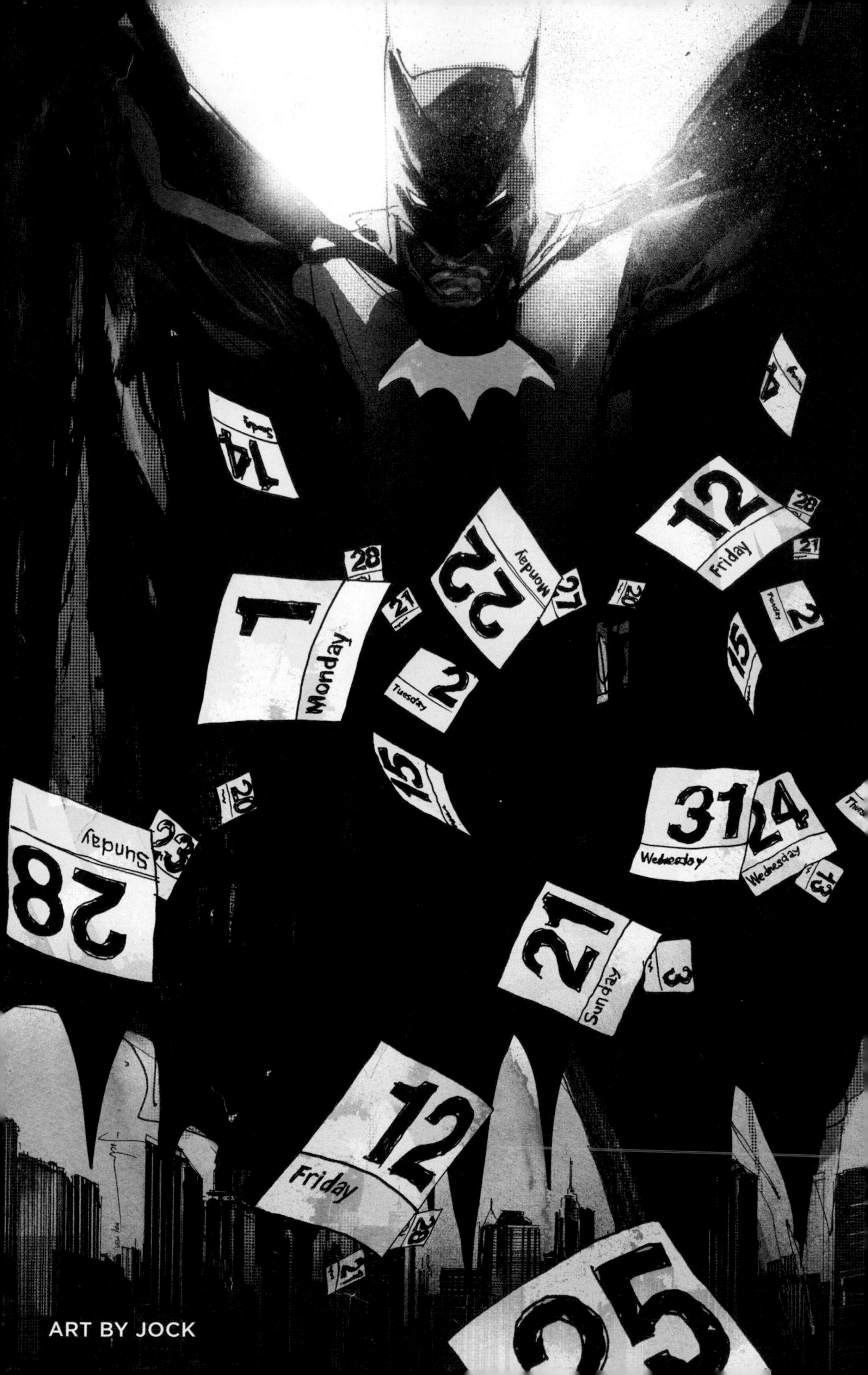

12
Friday
1
Monday
2
Tuesday
31
Wednesday
24
Wednesday
21
Sunday
12
Friday
25

ART BY JOCK

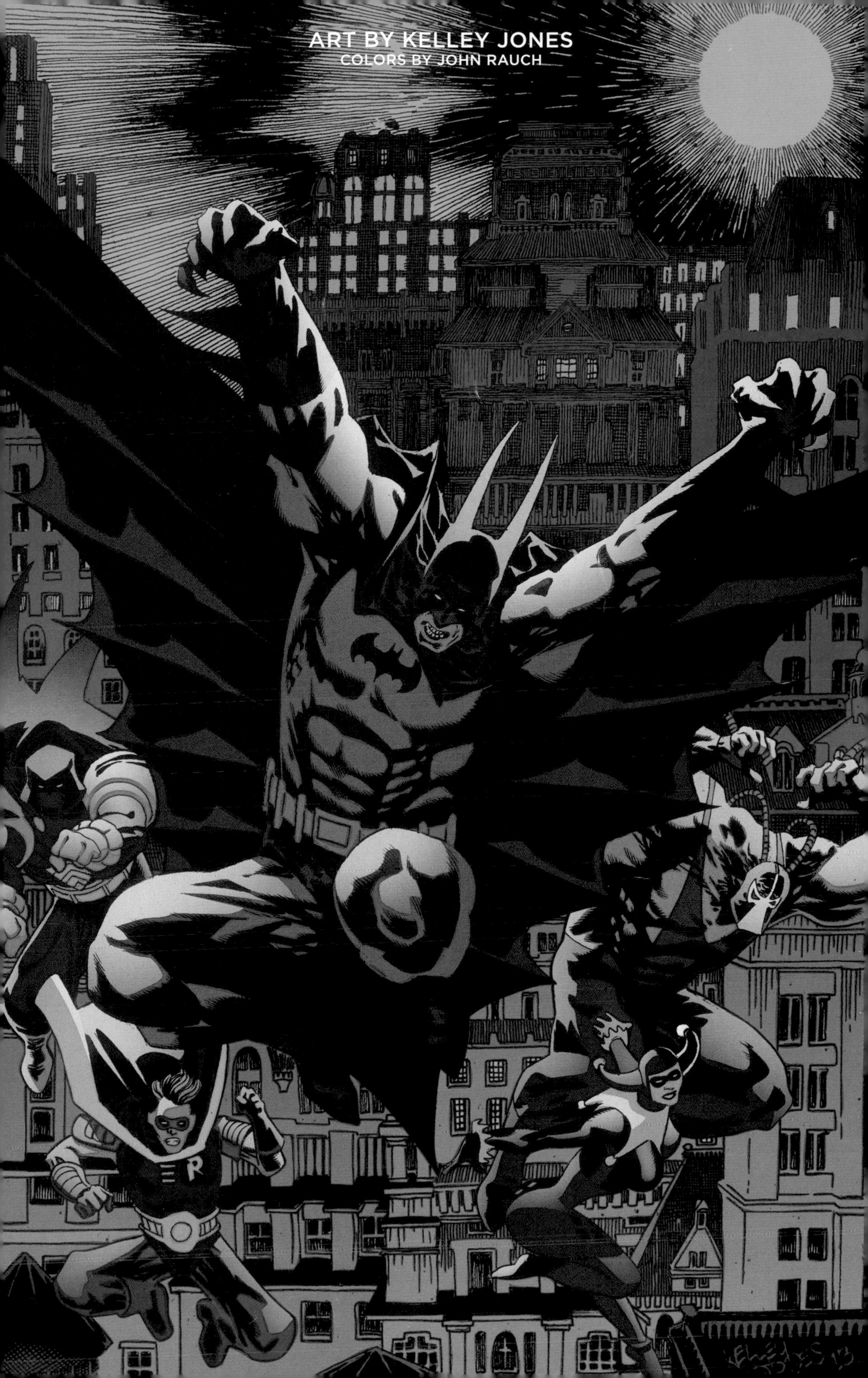

ART BY KELLEY JONES
COLORS BY JOHN RAUCH

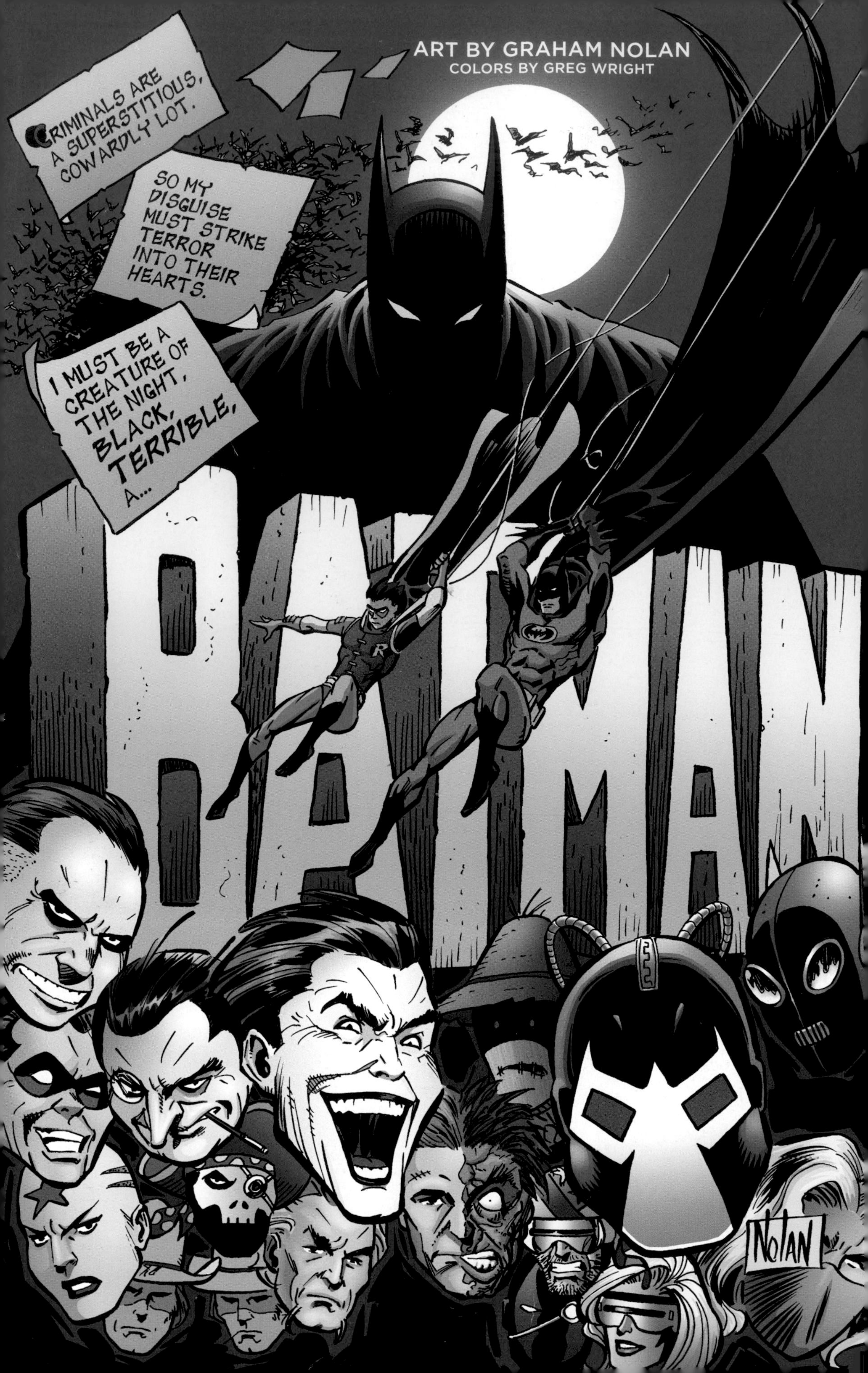
ART BY GRAHAM NOLAN
COLORS BY GREG WRIGHT
CRIMINALS ARE A SUPERSTITIOUS, COWARDLY LOT.
SO MY DISGUISE MUST STRIKE TERROR INTO THEIR HEARTS.
I MUST BE A CREATURE OF THE NIGHT, BLACK, TERRIBLE, A...
BATMAN
NOLAN

ART BY MIKE ALLRED
COLORS BY LAURA ALLRED

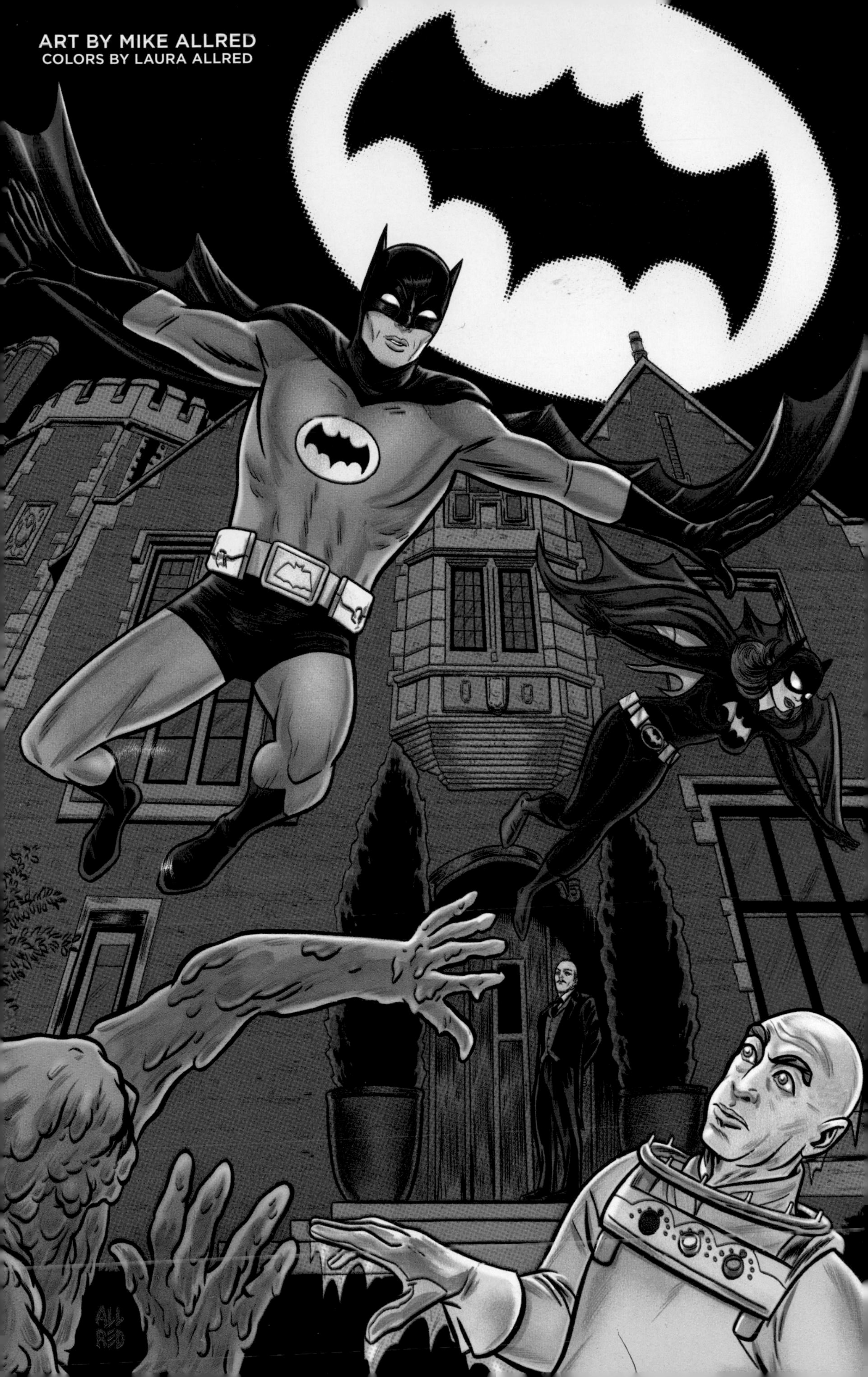
ALL
RED

Issue #27 Variant Cover by Frank Miller & Dave Stewart

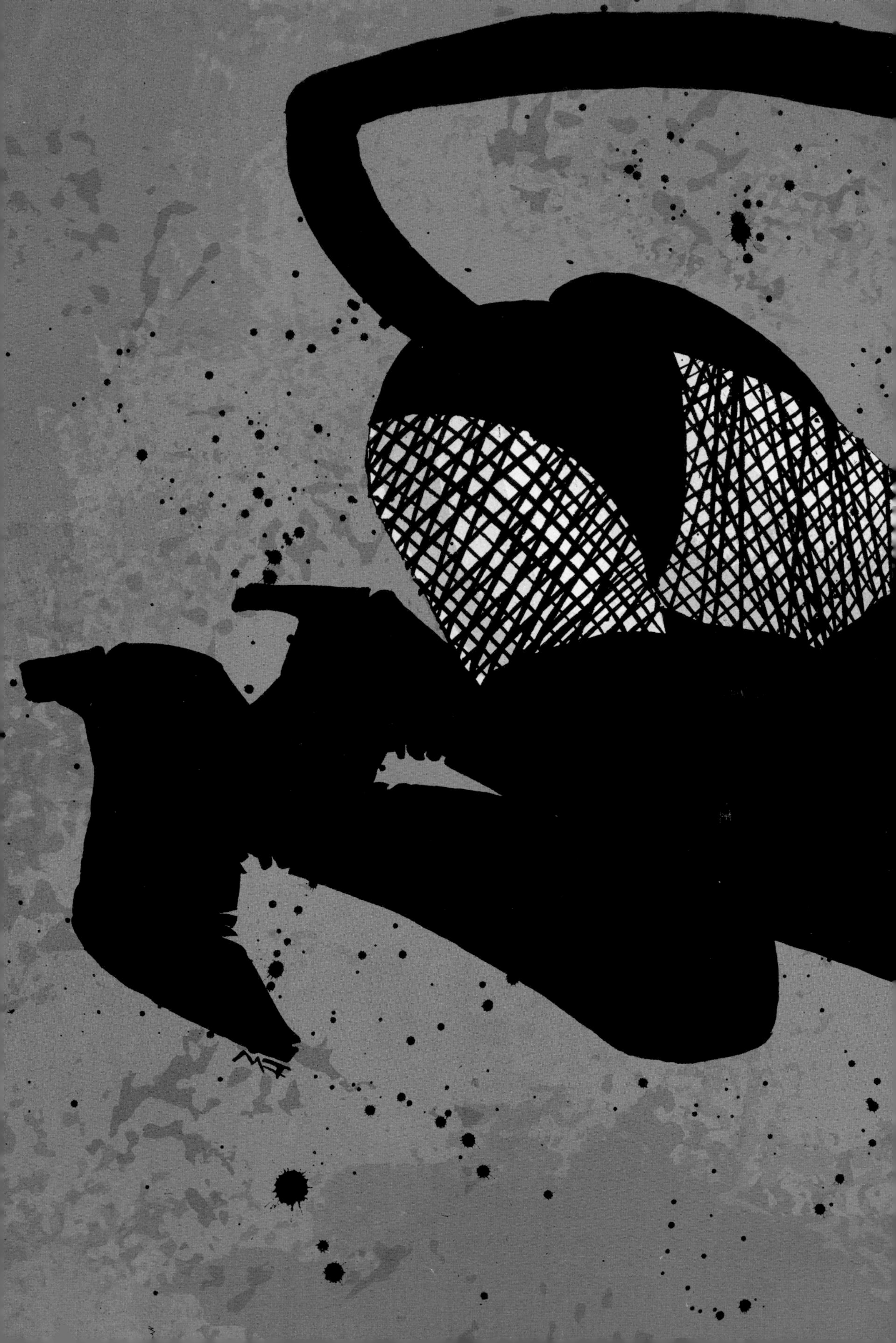

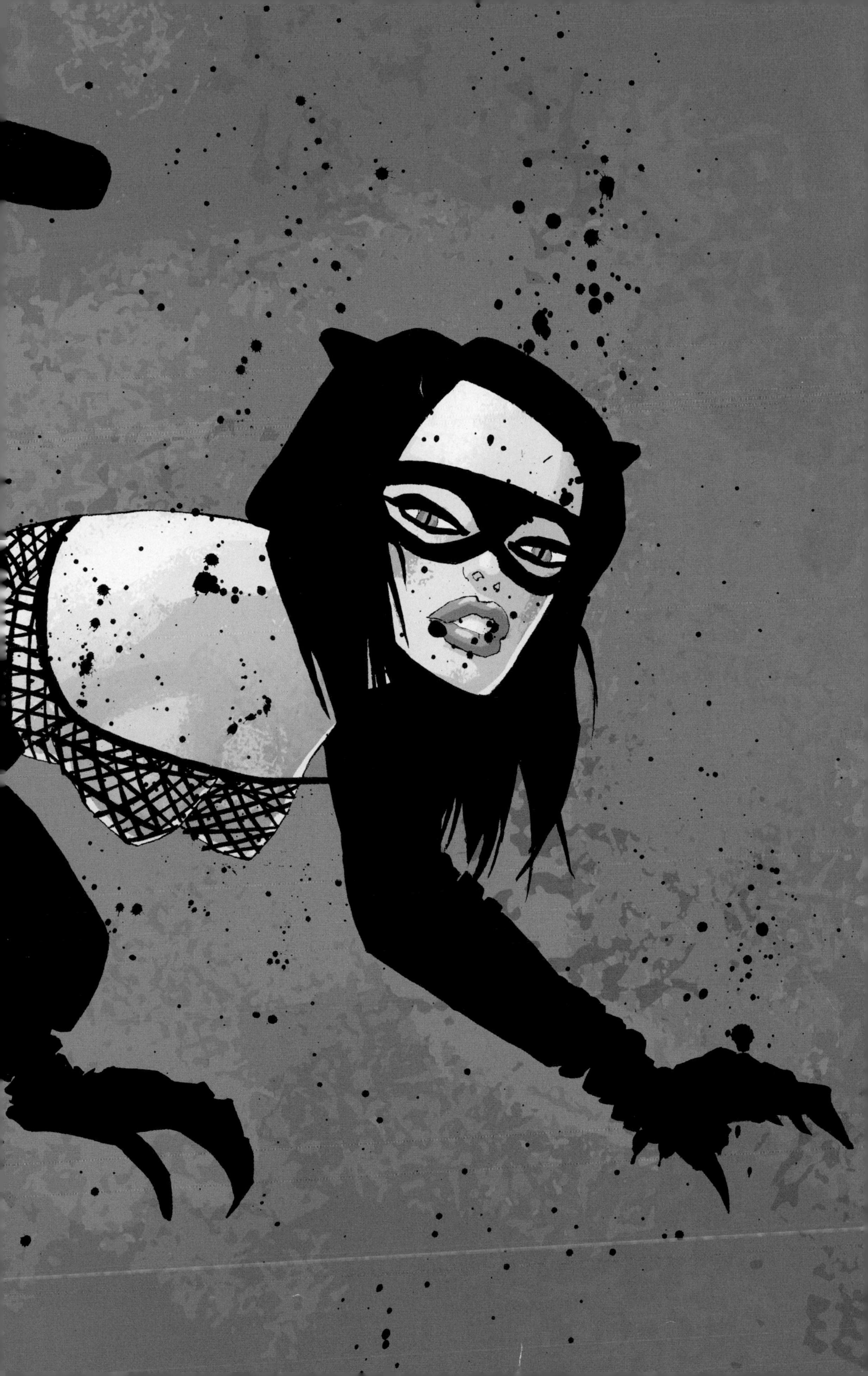

Issue #27 Variant Cover by Jim Lee & Alex Sinclair

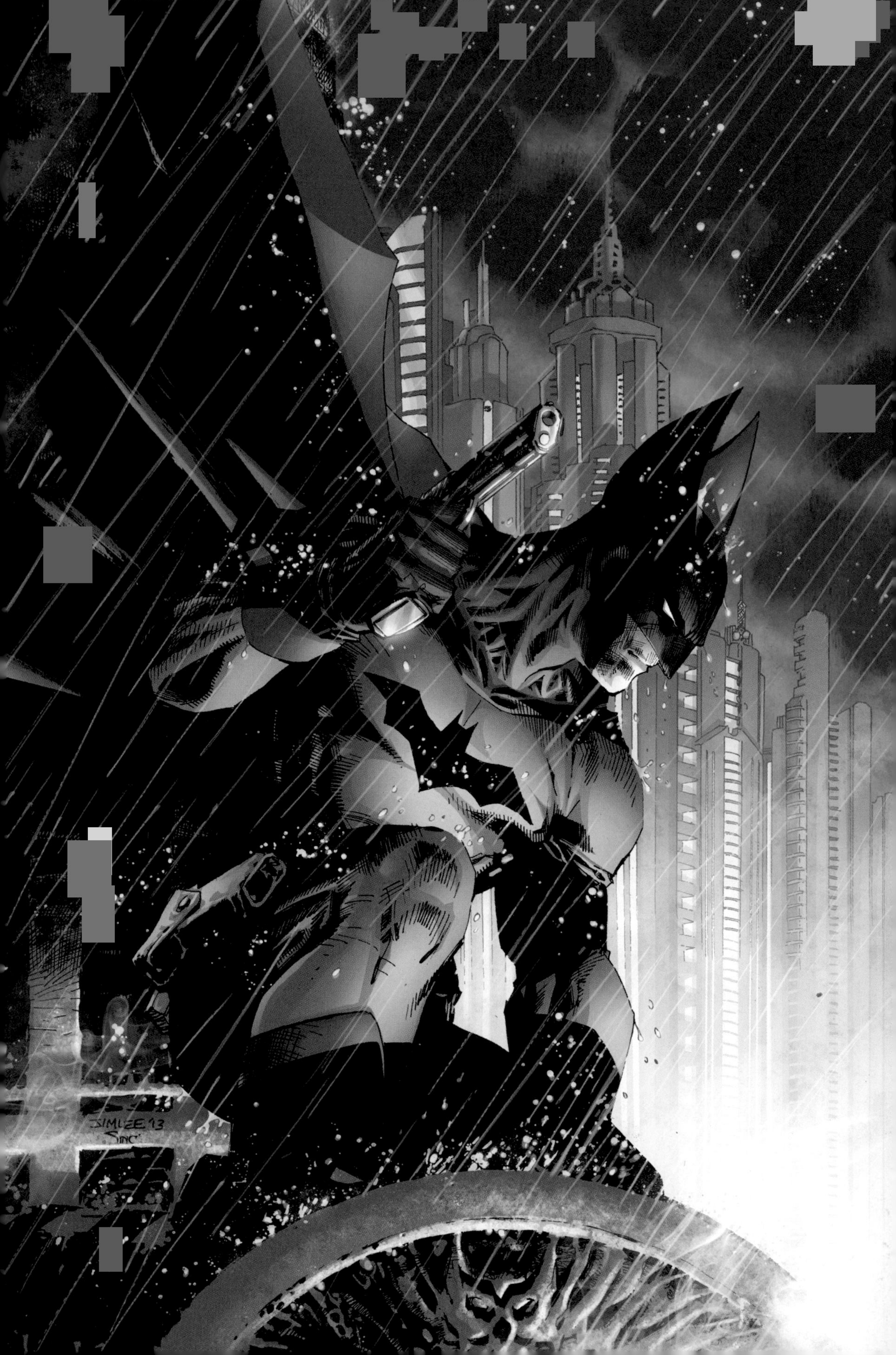

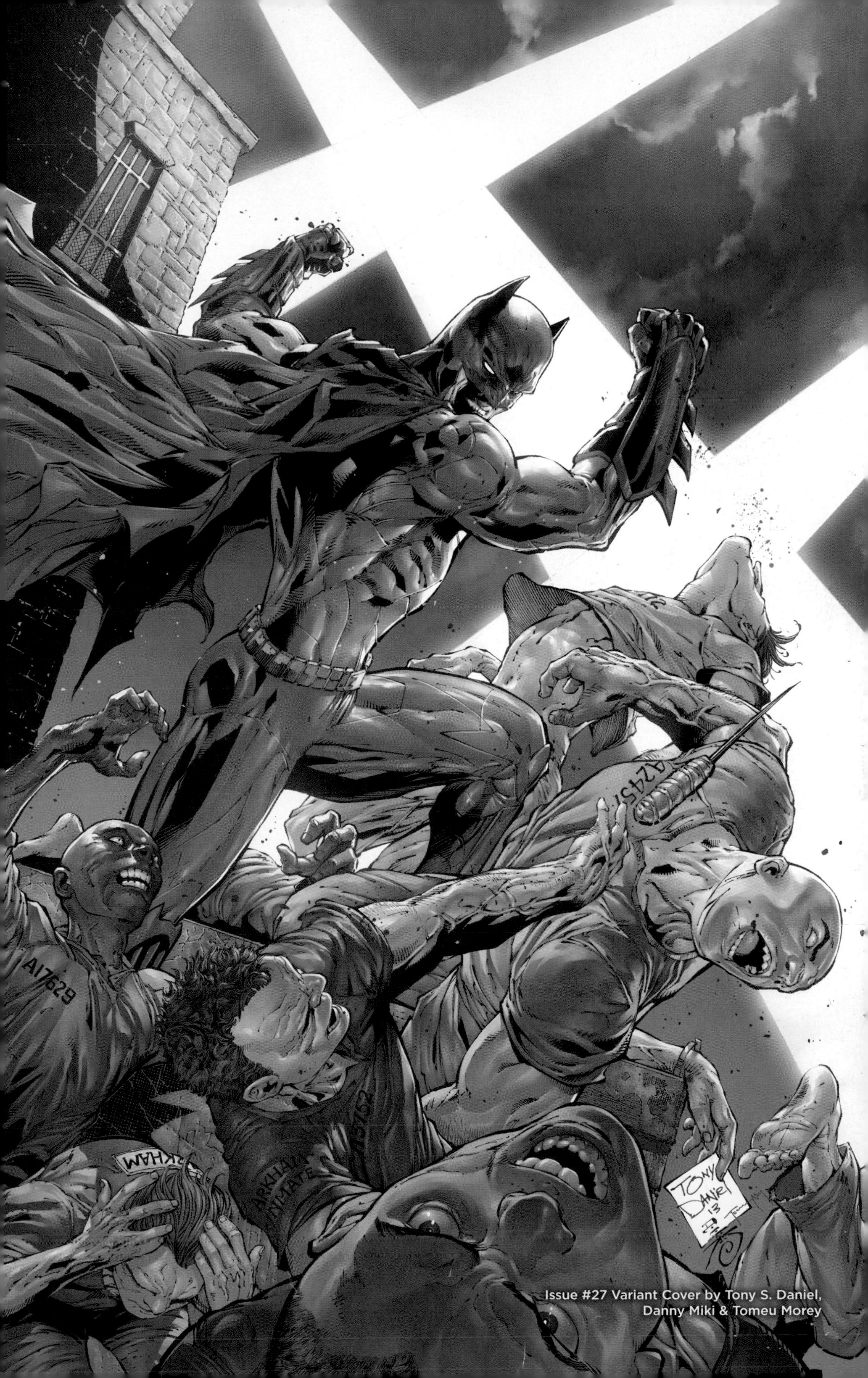
A17629

Issue #27 Variant Cover by Tony S. Daniel,
Danny Miki & Tomeu Morey

Issue #27 Variant Cover by Chris Burnham & Nathan Fairbairn

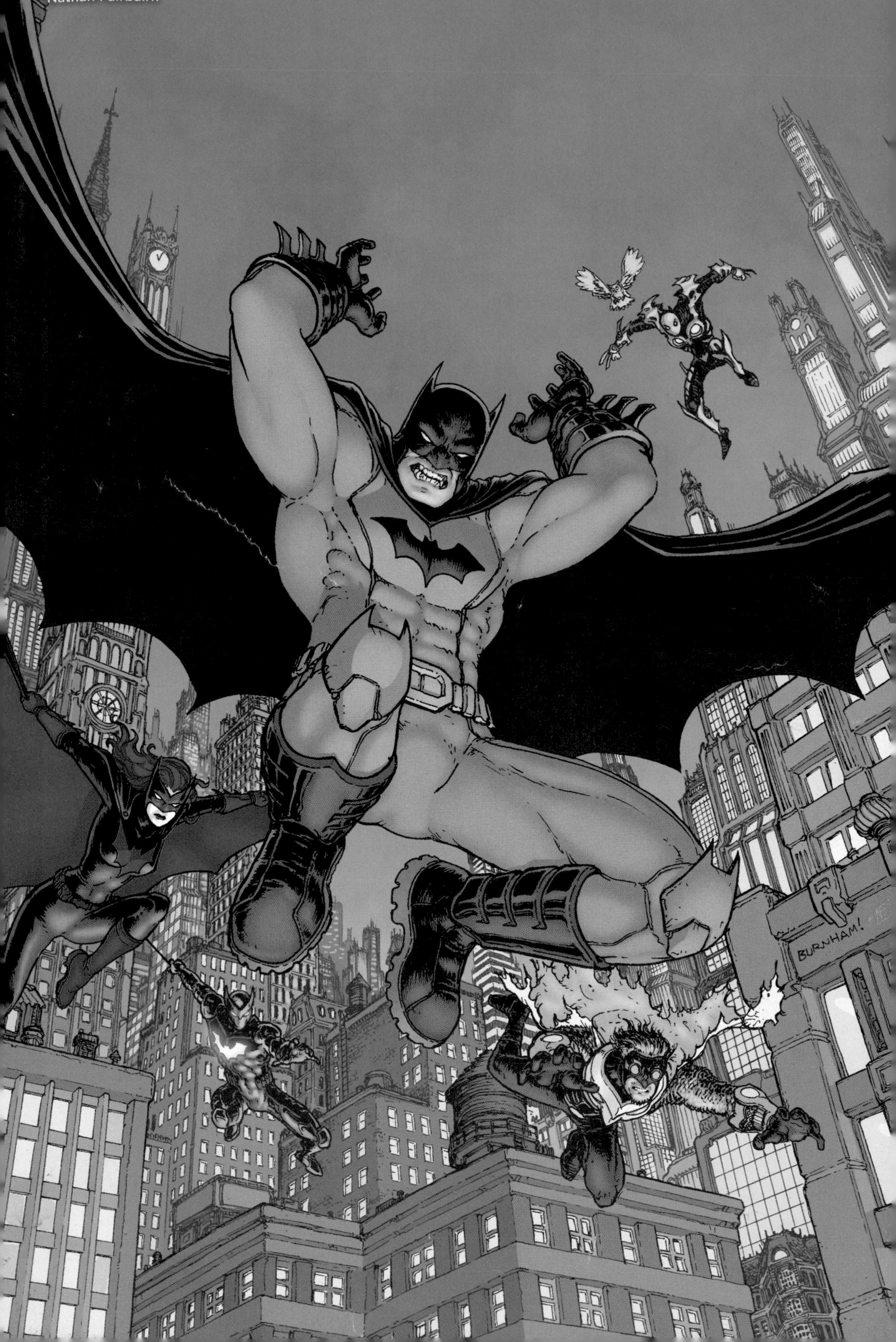
BURNHAM!

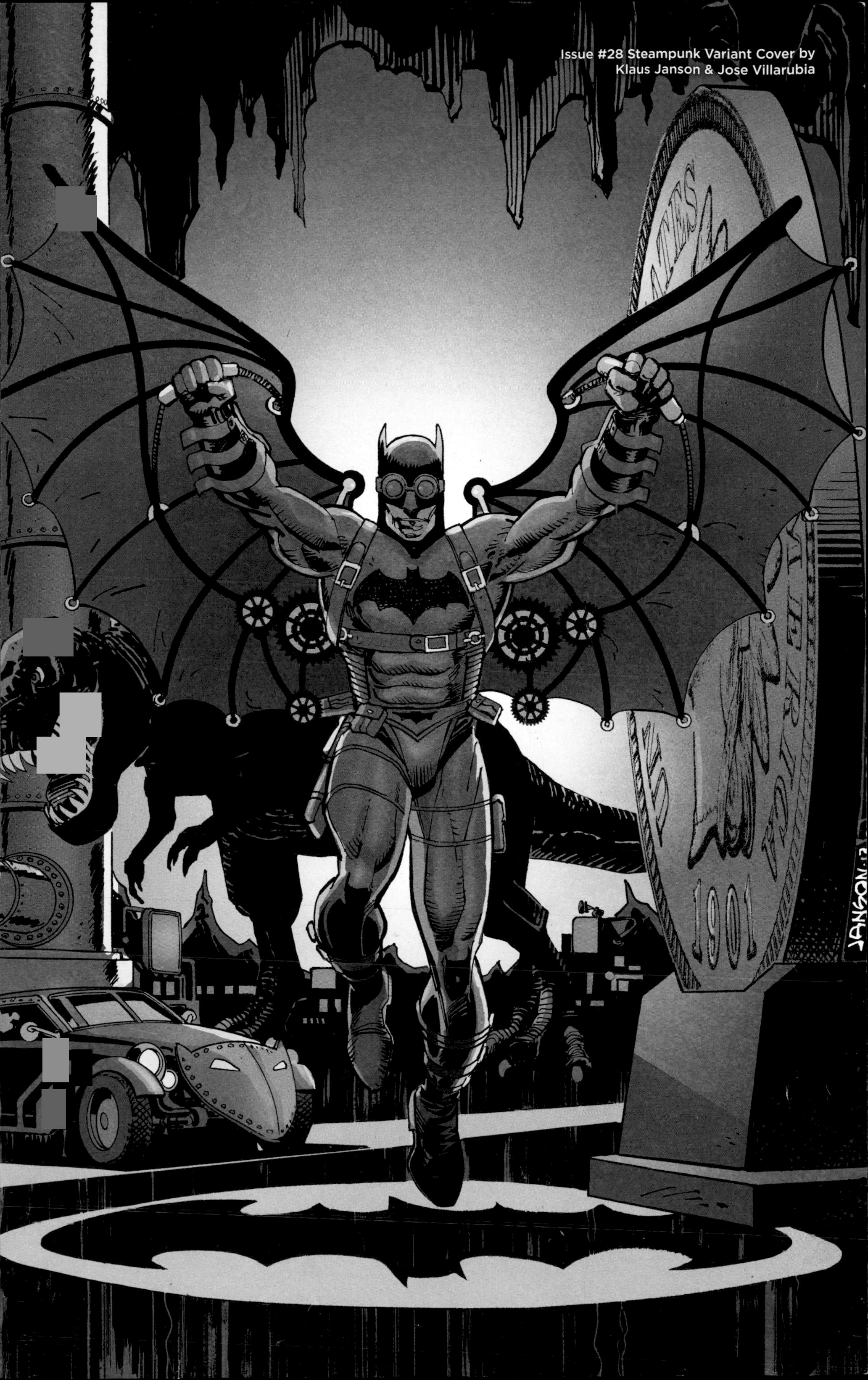
1901

Issue #28 Steampunk Variant Cover by
Klaus Janson & Jose Villarubia

Issue #29 *Robot Chicken* Variant Cover by RC Stoodios

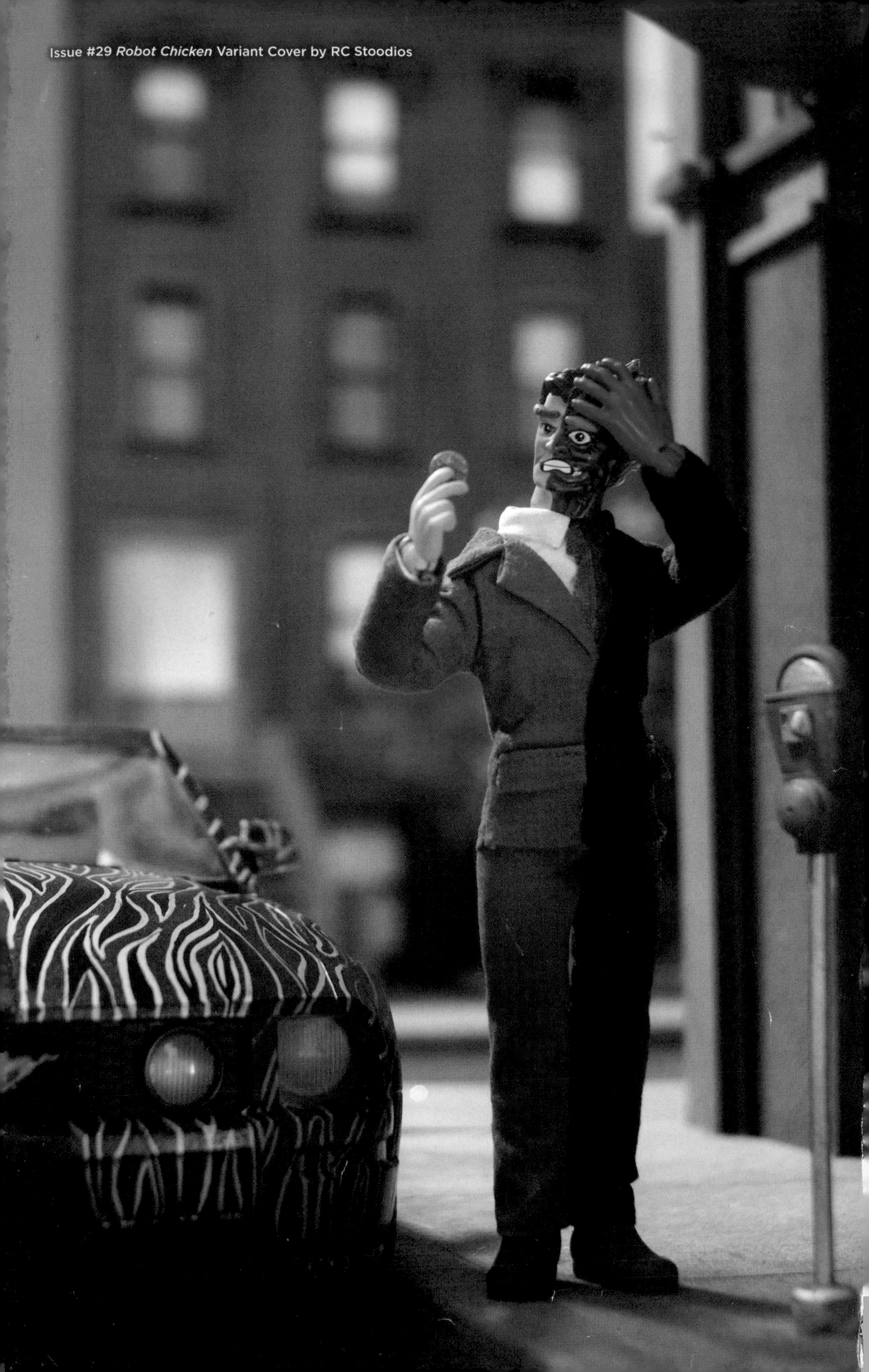